William Coutts Keppel, Earl of Albemarle

George Lacy Hillier

Cycling

WITH ILLUSTRATIONS BY

the Earl of Albemarle, Joseph Pennell, and George Moore

Elibron Classics
www.elibron.com

Elibron Classics series.

© 2005 Adamant Media Corporation.

ISBN 1-4021-7248-6 (paperback)
ISBN 1-4021-1307-2 (hardcover)

This Elibron Classics Replica Edition is an unabridged facsimile of the edition published in 1894 by Longmans, Green, and Co., London.

Elibron and Elibron Classics are trademarks of
Adamant Media Corporation. All rights reserved.

This book is an accurate reproduction of the original. Any marks, names, colophons, imprints, logos or other symbols or identifiers that appear on or in this book, except for those of Adamant Media Corporation and BookSurge, LLC, are used only for historical reference and accuracy and are not meant to designate origin or imply any sponsorship by or license from any third party.

THE BADMINTON LIBRARY.
Edited by the DUKE OF BEAUFORT, K.G. and A. E. T. WATSON.

ARCHERY. By C. J. LONGMAN and Col. H. WALROND. With Contributions by Miss LEGH, Viscount DILLON, Major C. HAWKINS FISHER, Rev. EYRE W. HUSSEY, Rev. W. K. R. BEDFORD, J. BALFOUR PAUL, &c. With 198 Illustrations. Crown 8vo. 10s. 6d.

ATHLETICS AND FOOTBALL. By MONTAGUE SHEARMAN. With 51 Illustrations. Crown 8vo. 10s. 6d.

BIG GAME SHOOTING. By CLIVE PHILLIPPS-WOLLEY. With Contributions by Sir SAMUEL W. BAKER, W. C. OSWELL, F. J. JACKSON, WARBURTON PIKE, F. C. SELOUS, &c.
  Vol. I. Africa and America. With 20 Plates and 57 Illustrations in the Text. Crown 8vo. 10s. 6d.
  Vol. II. Europe, Asia, and the Arctic Regions. With 17 Plates and 56 Illustrations in the Text. Crown 8vo. 10s. 6d.

BOATING. By W. B. WOODGATE. With an Introduction by the Rev. EDMOND WARRE, D.D. and a Chapter on 'Rowing at Eton' by R. HARVEY MASON. 49 Illustrations. Cr. 8vo. 10s. 6d.

COURSING AND FALCONRY. By HARDING COX and the Hon. GERALD LASCELLES. With 76 Illustrations. Cr. 8vo. 10s. 6d.

CRICKET. By A. G. STEEL and the Hon. R. H. LYTTELTON. With Contributions by ANDREW LANG, R. A. H. MITCHELL, W. G. GRACE, and F. GALE. 64 Illustrations. Cr. 8vo. 10s. 6d.

CYCLING. By VISCOUNT BURY, K.C.M.G. (the Earl of Albemarle), and G. LACY HILLIER. 89 Illustrations. Cr. 8vo. 10s. 6d.

DRIVING. By His Grace the DUKE OF BEAUFORT, K.G. With 65 Illustrations. Crown 8vo. 10s. 6d.

FENCING, BOXING, and WRESTLING. By WALTER H. POLLOCK, F. C. GROVE, C. PREVOST, E. B. MICHELL, and WALTER ARMSTRONG. With 42 Illustrations. Crown 8vo. 10s. 6d.

FISHING. By H. CHOLMONDELEY-PENNELL. With Contributions by the MARQUIS OF EXETER, HENRY R. FRANCIS, Major JOHN P. TRAHERNE, FREDERIC M. HALFORD, &c.
  Vol. I. Salmon and Trout. 158 Illustrations. Crown 8vo. 10s. 6d.
  Vol. II. Pike and other Coarse Fish. 133 Illustrations. Cr. 8vo. 10s. 6d.

GOLF. By HORACE G. HUTCHINSON, the Right Hon. A. J. BALFOUR, M.P. Sir WALTER G. SIMPSON, Bart. LORD WELLWOOD, H. S. C. EVERARD, ANDREW LANG, and other Writers. With 89 Illustrations. Crown 8vo. 10s. 6d. [OVER.

London: LONGMANS, GREEN, & CO.

THE BADMINTON LIBRARY.
Edited by the DUKE OF BEAUFORT, K.G. and A. E. T. WATSON.

HUNTING. By the DUKE OF BEAUFORT, K.G. and MOWBRAY MORRIS. With Contributions by the EARL OF SUFFOLK AND BERKSHIRE, Rev. E. W. L. DAVIES, DIGBY COLLINS, Sir MARTEINE LLOYD, GEORGE H. LONGMAN, J. C. GIBBONS, and ALFRED E. T. WATSON. With 60 Illustrations. Cr. 8vo. 10s. 6d.

MOUNTAINEERING. By C. T. DENT, with Contributions by W. M. CONWAY, D. W. FRESHFIELD, C. E. MATHEWS, C. PILKINGTON, Sir F. POLLOCK, H. G. WILLINK, and an Introduction by Mr. JUSTICE WILLS. 108 Illustrations. Cr. 8vo. 10s. 6d.

RACING AND STEEPLE-CHASING. *Racing:* By the EARL OF SUFFOLK AND BERKSHIRE and W. G. CRAVEN. With a Contribution by the Hon. F. LAWLEY. *Steeple-chasing:* By ARTHUR COVENTRY and ALFRED E. T. WATSON. With 58 Illustrations. Crown 8vo. 10s. 6d.

RIDING AND POLO. By Captain ROBERT WEIR, Riding Master, R.H.G. and J. MORAY BROWN. With Contributions by the DUKE OF BEAUFORT, the EARL OF SUFFOLK AND BERKSHIRE, the EARL OF ONSLOW, E. L. ANDERSON, and ALFRED E. T. WATSON. With 59 Illustrations. Crown 8vo. 10s. 6d.

SHOOTING. By LORD WALSINGHAM and Sir RALPH PAYNE-GALLWEY, Bart. With Contributions by LORD LOVAT, LORD CHARLES LENNOX KERR, A. J. STUART-WORTLEY, &c.
I. Field and Covert. With 105 Illustrations. Crown 8vo. 10s. 6d.
Vol. II. Moor and Marsh. With 65 Illustrations. Crown 8vo. 10s. 6d.

SKATING, CURLING, TOBOGGANING, and other ICE SPORTS. By J. M. HEATHCOTE, C. G. TEBBUTT, T. MAXWELL WITHAM, the Rev. JOHN KERR, ORMOND HAKE, and HENRY A. BUCK. With 284 Illustrations. Crown 8vo. 10s. 6d.

SWIMMING. By ARCHIBALD SINCLAIR and WILLIAM HENRY, Hon. Secs. of the Life-Saving Society. With 119 Illustrations. Crown 8vo. 10s. 6d.

TENNIS, LAWN TENNIS, RACKETS, and FIVES. By J. M. and C. G. HEATHCOTE, E. O. PLEYDELL-BOUVERIE, and A. C. AINGER. With Contributions by the Hon. A. LYTTELTON, W. C. MARSHALL, Miss L. DOD, H. W. W. WILBERFORCE, H. F. LAWFORD, &c. With 79 Illustrations. Crown 8vo. 10s. 6d.

YACHTING. By LORD BRASSEY, R. T. PRITCHETT, the EARL OF ONSLOW, G. L. WATSON, E. F. KNIGHT, &c.
Vol. I. Cruising, Construction, Racing Rules, &c. With 114 Illustrations. Crown 8vo. 10s. 6d.
Vol. II. Yacht Clubs, Yachting in America and the Colonies, Racing, &c. With 195 Illustrations. Crown 8vo. 10s. 6d.

London: LONGMANS, GREEN & CO.

The Badminton Library
OF
SPORTS AND PASTIMES

EDITED BY

HIS GRACE THE DUKE OF BEAUFORT, K.G.

ASSISTED BY ALFRED E. T. WATSON

CYCLING

Bibliographical Note.

First printed March 1887; Reprinted January 1889; New Edition, revised and with additions, January 1891; Reprinted, with additions to Appendix, bringing Records up to date, January and November 1894.

THE RIGHT OF WAY

CYCLING

BY THE

RIGHT HON. THE EARL OF ALBEMARLE

AND

G. LACY HILLIER

*WITH NUMEROUS ILLUSTRATIONS BY THE
EARL OF ALBEMARLE, JOSEPH PENNELL, & GEORGE MOORE*

New Edition

LONDON

LONGMANS, GREEN, AND CO.

1894

All rights reserved

DEDICATION

TO

H.R.H. THE PRINCE OF WALES.

BADMINTON: *March*, 1887.

HAVING received permission to dedicate these volumes, the BADMINTON LIBRARY of SPORTS and PASTIMES, to HIS ROYAL HIGHNESS THE PRINCE OF WALES, I do so feeling that I am dedicating them to one of the best and keenest sportsmen of our time. I can say, from personal observation, that there is no man who can extricate himself from a bustling and pushing crowd of horsemen, when a fox breaks covert, more dexterously and quickly than His Royal Highness; and that when hounds run hard over a big country, no man can take a line of his own and live with them better. Also, when the wind has been blowing hard, often have I seen His Royal Highness knocking over driven grouse and partridges and high-rocketing pheasants in first-rate workmanlike style. He is held to be a good yachtsman, and as Commodore of the Royal Yacht Squadron is looked up to by those who love that pleasant and exhilarating pastime. His encouragement of racing is well known, and his attendance at the University, Public School, and other important Matches testifies to his being, like most English gentlemen, fond of all manly sports. I consider it a great privilege to be allowed to dedicate these volumes to so eminent a sportsman as His Royal Highness the Prince of Wales, and I do so with sincere feelings of respect and esteem and loyal devotion.

BEAUFORT

BADMINTON.

PREFACE.

A FEW LINES only are necessary to explain the object with which these volumes are put forth. There is no modern encyclopædia to which the inexperienced man, who seeks guidance in the practice of the various British Sports and Pastimes, can turn for information. Some books there are on Hunting, some on Racing, some on Lawn Tennis, some on Fishing, and so on; but one Library, or succession of volumes, which treats of the Sports and Pastimes indulged in by Englishmen—and women—is wanting. The Badminton Library is offered to supply the want. Of the imperfections which must be found in the execution of such a design we are conscious. Experts often differ. But this we may say, that those who are seeking for knowledge on any of the subjects dealt with will find the results of many years' experience written by men who are in every case adepts at the Sport or Pastime of which they write. It is to point the way to success to those who are ignorant of the sciences they aspire to master, and who have no friend to help or coach them, that these volumes are written.

To those who have worked hard to place simply and clearly before the reader that which he will find within, the best thanks of the Editor are due. That it has been no slight labour to supervise all that has been written he must acknowledge; but it has been a labour of love, and very much lightened by the courtesy of the Publisher, by the unflinching, indefatigable assistance of the Sub-Editor, and by the intelligent and able arrangement of each subject by the various writers, who are so thoroughly masters of the subjects of which they treat. The reward we all hope to reap is that our work may prove useful to this and future generations.

THE EDITOR.

CONTENTS.

CHAPTER		PAGE
I.	INTRODUCTORY	1
II.	HISTORICAL	53
III.	RIDING	124
IV.	RACING	168
V.	TOURING	187
VI.	TRAINING	202
VII.	DRESS	220
VIII.	CYCLING FOR LADIES	247
IX.	RACING PATHS	258
X.	THE NATIONAL CYCLISTS' UNION	265
XI.	THE CYCLISTS' TOURING CLUB	292
XII.	CONSTRUCTION	299
	MECHANISM	299
	MODERN CYCLES	370
	APPENDIX	409
	INDEX	473

ILLUSTRATIONS.

(Executed by G. Pearson and Ford & Wall.)

PLATES.

	ARTIST	
The Right of Way	J. Pennell	Frontispiece
The Carrier in London	J. Pennell	To face p. 6
A Foolhardy Feat	Viscount Bury	,, 18
The American Star Machine	J. Pennell	,, 20
At the Mercy of his Wife	J. Pennell	,, 26
A Country Club Run	J. Pennell	,, 30
The Finish of a Race	J. Pennell	,, 40
A Road Race	J. Pennell	,, 68
'That foolish thing of modern use — the Velocipede'	G. Moore	,, 74
Last Lap!	G. Moore	,, 170
'The Anchor,' Ripley	J. Pennell	,, 188
A Club Tour	J. Pennell	,, 194
A Mid-day Halt	Viscount Bury	,, 200
Hard at Work	G. Moore	,, 214
Women's Rights	J. Pennell	,, 248
A Danger Board	J. Pennell	,, 278
A C.T.C. Hotel	J. Pennell	,, 296
Viscount Bury, K.C.M.G.	From a Photograph by Hon. A. Keppel	,, 376
Photography A-wheel	G. Moore	,, 382

WOODCUTS IN TEXT.

	ARTIST	PAGE
INTRODUCTORY	Viscount Bury	1
HOMEWARD BOUND	Hon. A. Keppel	7
REST ON A RIVER BANK	Viscount Bury	52
GOOD-BYE, SWEETHEART	Viscount Bury	53
THE CARRIER TRICYCLE		55
THE SOUTHERN CAMP	J. Pennell	94
GOING FOR A RECORD	G. Moore	116
A COUNTRY POSTMAN	J. Pennell	123
EARLY STRUGGLES	J. Pennell	125
HIS FIRST LESSON	G. Moore	131
COASTING—SAFE AND RECKLESS	J. Pennell	137
BAD AND GOOD POSITIONS OF RIDER		138, 139
CRANK AND PEDAL ACTION		146
POSITION OF FEET IN PEDALLING		148, 149
THE REAR-DRIVING SAFETY BICYCLE		156
THE 'XTRAORDINARY BICYCLE		160
ADJUSTING THE HEAD		162
THIS HILL IS DANGEROUS	Viscount Bury	167
GOING IT!	J. Pennell	168
RUSHING A RISE	J. Pennell	175
LUDGATE HILL	J. Pennell	191
A PRACTICE SPIN	J. Pennell	203
HUNTING THE WHITE HART	Viscount Bury	219
THE LADIES' TRICYCLE	G. Moore	249
LADY PREPARING TO MOUNT A SAFETY	G. Moore	252
MOUNTING, FIRST POSITION	G. Moore	253
MOUNTING, SECOND POSITION	G. Moore	254
MOUNTED!	G. Moore	255
'CAT'S CRADLE'	Viscount Bury	257
A HUMBER ROADSTER BICYCLE		300
A CONE HEAD		302
TRIGWELL'S BALL-BEARING HEAD		303
THE SOCKET HEAD		304
THE ARIEL HEAD		305

ILLUSTRATIONS.

	ARTIST	PAGE
A Common Accident		306
Adjusting the Head		307
Handle-bars		308
Whatton's Handle-bars		309
Handles		310
The Break Levers		312
The Forks		315
The Arab Cradle Spring on an Adjustable Tilt-rod		324
A Simplified Wheel		327
Methods of Fixing the Spokes		328, 329
New Rapid Tangent Wheel		330
The Hub		332
The Cheylesmore Two-chain Clutch Gear		338
Starley's Differential Driving Gear		341
The Balance Gear		346
Pulley Wheels, Gearing Level, Up, and Down		347–350
The Crypto-dynamic Two-speed Gear		358, 359
Diagrams of Safety Bicycle		368, 369
Bad Position	G. Moore	372
Good Position	G. Moore	373
The Humber Tandem		377
The Humber 'Cripper' Tricycle		379
The 'Velociman'		395
The Brighton Coach	G. Moore	459
The Start from Hatchett's Hotel	G. Moore	459
Crawley: Going Down	G. Moore	460
Turning-point at Brighton	G. Moore	461
Clayton Hill: Going Home	G. Moore	461
The 'Black Swan': Going Home—'Pacemaker coming on'	G. Moore	462

CYCLING.

CHAPTER I.

INTRODUCTORY.

CYCLING is by far the most recent of all the sports treated of in the Badminton Library, there is none which has developed more rapidly in the last few years, nor is there any which has assumed a more assured position in popular favour. Professor Huxley said in his farewell address to the Royal Society a short time ago, that since the time of Achilles no improvement had added anything to the speed or strength attainable by the unassisted powers of man. The statement is true in the sense which the Professor no doubt attached to his words, that neither the stature nor the speed of man had improved since Homer's day;[1] but it is no less true that a man by his unassisted powers can propel one of the machines with which we are now familiar at a pace which would have put Achilles to shame, and over distances which would have utterly amazed the heroes of the Homeric world. The circumstances attending this revolution—for such indeed it is—cannot be considered unworthy of record, and the following pages are an attempt to perform the task.

England may be looked upon as the home of cycling; the national habit of organisation which our countrymen possess in an eminent degree, and the national love for every form of strong personal exertion, combine to make it a pursuit in every way adapted to the taste of our people. The shady lanes of the south country, and the hilly roads of the north, appear to offer equal attraction; and now, though scarcely ten years have elapsed since the first bicycle made its appearance, there are few districts in which some form of cycle is not a familiar object

In the streets of our great cities and in highways and byways throughout the land, carriages, swift and serviceable, propelled by the power of human muscles alone, have become common. The sight of a traveller of either sex, seated on a light machine, and proceeding with considerable rapidity and apparently but little exertion, is so usual that the wayfarer hardly turns his head to look at the accustomed sight. Yet it is but a very short time ago that the passage of a cyclist was wont to produce an exhibition of considerable excitement, and sometimes even demonstrations of hostility.

It is however not only as a means of locomotion that the cycle has produced a change in this and many foreign countries. The manufacture of these carriages has caused a considerable trade to come into existence, and a new and very exciting

[1] In recent times, however, the records have improved year by year both in walking and running.—ED.

mode of racing has been added to the sports of the world. The historian of cycling has therefore something to say of it as a trade, as a sport, and as a pastime : beyond this, again, there is something to be said as to the social organisation to which it has given rise, and the not inconsiderable industry to which the requirements of the cycling public give employment outside the limits of the cycle-builder's factory. It is difficult to say, with any approach to accuracy, what number of persons come within the designation of cyclists. In the year 1885 I set on foot some inquiries which led to the conclusion that they then numbered not far from 400,000. The estimate is a rough one, but it must still not be considered quite in the light of a random guess; for it is founded on the reports of an organisation of which the reader who will accompany me through the following pages will hear a good deal—viz. the Cyclists' Touring Club, a body which has chief officers in every large town, and minor officials in every considerable village in England, and is therefore quite able to make an approximate estimate sufficiently accurate for our purpose.

The volume now in the reader's hand is designed not only to interest the general reader, but to form a useful handbook for all who are interested in any of the various ramifications of cycling. The intending purchaser may consult it as to the points about which he should satisfy himself before concluding his bargain. The racing man will find his prowess recorded, and be able to fight his battles over again; the tourist will discover all that can help him to prepare for his intended outing, the advice given being founded on the accumulated experience of many predecessors. The young amateur who possesses a turn of speed, and proposes to become a candidate for the honours of the 'cinder-path,' will find minute directions as to his training and general preparations. The mechanic, and the rider who is interested in the details of the construction of his machine, will read descriptions of all the processes by which iron, steel and silver are made to assume the shape of the graceful piece of mechanism which adds so largely to the power of locomotion possessed by unaided muscles.

Though there are many fancy varieties which do not come under either category, cycles fall generally into two divisions, those with three wheels and those with two. Riders also arrange themselves into two sharply-defined classes: the speedy bicycle rider and the more staid possessor of the tricycle. The racing man comes in as a connecting link between the two; for almost as many races are ridden on one class of machine as on the other. The enormous improvements introduced within the last year or two in the tricycle have made the tricycle as available, if not quite so speedy, as the bicycle for racing purposes. As regards speed, there is a considerable, though not an overwhelming, difference between the two. A really first-class bicycle rider—anyone, that is, who is sufficiently prominent in the pursuit to hold his own in a long-distance championship race—can travel, when at his best, considerably over twenty miles within the hour; only one tricycle rider has yet accomplished twenty miles in the hour. But it has been done several times by tandems. It is evident that machines which can maintain such a rate of progression must be sufficiently fast to make a race between well-matched competitors amusing: and those who have been fortunate enough to witness a well-contested race will be the first to testify that it lacks none of the elements of excitement and of sport.

One of the questions most frequently asked by those who intend to purchase a machine is, What pace can a reasonable person expect to get out of it? and what distance can conveniently be covered in a day? The answer naturally varies very much according to the strength and skill of the person interrogated; but it is a fair question and deserves a candid answer. The Records Committee of the National Cyclists' Union can show duly authenticated performances which the average rider can only look at with respectful astonishment; 300 miles have been ridden on an ordinary high road by a wonderful young athlete on a bicycle, within twenty-four consecutive hours, and 264 miles have been covered on a tricycle within the same time. A hundred miles have been travelled by a bicyclist on a cinder racing path in 5 hrs. 50 mins. 5⅔ secs. Fifty miles were ridden by Messrs. A. J. Wilson and G. P. Mills, on a tandem, in 2 hrs. 46 mins. 3 secs., along the Great North Road. The 'best on record' for a single mile at the moment these lines are penned is, for a bicycle 2 mins. 31⅘ secs., and for a tricycle 2 mins. 41⅗ secs. Before this book is in the hands of the reader these times will very likely have been surpassed; for every day sees new and important, though minute, improvements in the construction of machines, and though riders may not be better than their predecessors, they are good enough to take advantage of all improvements that are offered to them. But the foregoing of course are extraordinary performances. The question is what an ordinary mortal can do.

One of the writers jointly responsible for the present work —need it be concealed that it was the author of this introductory chapter?—lately asked his colleague, in a careless manner, the following question: 'How far ought an ordinary man, in fair condition, to be able to ride easily in a day?' And the other made answer and said, with the air of a man who was absolutely giving himself away: 'If he intends to keep it up, say, for a week, he ought only to do a moderate day's work on the first day—say a hundred, or a hundred and twenty miles; of course, you know, he can increase his distance as he gets into condition.' The present writer agreed with the speaker. 'Yes,' he said, 'a man ought to restrain his ardour at first; he ought not to attempt to do more than a hundred and twenty miles on the first day.' He refrained from confessing, though perhaps it was disingenuous to do so,—that he himself looked back with some exultation to his own 'best on record,' which amounts to thirty-six miles in one day, and he takes this opportunity of copying from his private journal a few lines which have unconsciously assumed the form of an affidavit or vow. They run as follows:

And the said deponent further maketh oath and saith, that if he, the said deponent, *suadente diabolo*, shall at any time hereafter attempt to cut, break, surpass, or otherwise defeat, the said record of thirty-six miles in one solar day, he hereby giveth to any witness of such attempt, be the said witness credible or otherwise, free leave to mention the fact. And the said deponent doth further declare, that he is credibly informed, and doth sincerely believe, that many persons who make a great fuss about cycling have never done so much.

But this is a digression: there is no use in saying that sort of thing to a man who has ridden a hundred and forty-six miles in ten hours, and who holds half a dozen championships besides. A moderate rider, not being an athlete or a flier on the one hand, nor exceptionally weak on the other, can, when he is in practice, get over in an hour seven or eight miles of ground on a tricycle and from nine to ten on a bicycle without much exertion, and can keep it up about as long as he could comfortably walk with the same amount of exertion, say four or five hours. But there are many who cannot do so much as that, and who still manage to get a good deal of amusement out of their pursuit. Persevering riders cover enormous distances in the course of a year; and as most of them keep some sort of riding journal, we hear from time to time what their performances have been. A letter now before us from Mr. Whatton, a well-known member of the Cambridge University Club, contains the following paragraph:

The year has been memorable to me as an individual in one or two respects. The early part of it saw the completion of twenty thousand miles of cycling, the work of eight years' pleasure—pleasures such as no other bodily exercise, unless it be racquets, can, in my opinion, approach; and, of course, that lacks the great glory of cycling, the multitudinous opportunities it adds for an intellectual and may one add—a spiritual appreciation of life.

This is the proper spirit in which to look at the pastime of cycling as it may be followed by ordinary individuals, though it is not everyone who can ride twenty thousand miles. It is, however, not only for amusement that cycling is avail-

THE CARRIER IN LONDON

INTRODUCTORY.

able; both in the pursuit of health and of business it is of great value. In many parts of the country labourers are able to live at a considerable distance from their work, and mechanics are to be seen in considerable numbers with their tool-bags slung at their backs riding home at the end of their day's labour. Not only does this imply a saving of rent—for it is cheaper to live in the country than in the crowded town—but it is a distinct gain both in health and, in many instances, in sobriety as well. The wife and children of a mechanic are sure to be more healthy if they live in the pure air of the country than in the crowded streets of a town. Rates and taxes are less; and, as regards sobriety, a man who has to make his way home over ten or a dozen miles of road will be pretty sure not to handicap his chance of a safe arrival by lingering too long at the public-house. In Coventry, which may be looked upon as the peculiar home of cycling, it is fast becoming the custom for workmen to go home on their bicycles during the dinner-hour.

HOMEWARD BOUND.

As a vehicle for business purposes the tricycle has even a larger future before it than the bicycle. It will carry a considerable quantity of luggage, and can be drawn up to the side of the street and left unprotected until the owner returns.

The number of shopkeepers who employ the carrier tricycle for the purpose of distributing their parcels, or circulating daily supplies to their customers, is steadily increasing. The milkman, the newsvendor, the butcher, send an active lad on their daily rounds. For light parcels it is especially adapted, and there has even been lately a talk of establishing in London a service of tricycle cabs—machines something like Bath chairs with a rider behind.

One is tempted to say with Horace :

> Illi robur et aes triplex
> Circa pectus erat, qui fragilem truci
> Commisit——

But hold : 'pelago ratem' will not convey my meaning ; and I fear 'Pall-Mallo Bath-chairum' would neither scan nor construe. Harrogate, well known to cyclists as the scene of the Annual Cycling Camp, has already shown the way in this respect. There the terrors of the streets are disregarded; even the steep pitches of the hills appear to have no deterrent effect. There among the long row of Bath chairs drawn up for hire may always be found three or four Coventry chairs. They appear very popular, and may be seen on fine afternoons in all the walks and drives round the fashionable wateringplace, with their freight of invalids. If smiling faces and rosy cheeks may be trusted as an indication, the use of them is not confined to those who have the excuse of ill-health for adopting them. It is, no doubt, much more amusing even to an invalid to travel at a decent speed of six or seven miles an hour, and to get over a considerable stretch of road, than to crawl, at the pace of a walking funeral, backwards and forwards along the length of a parade. At Harrogate one sees parties of three or four of these machines going along in company ; the occupants of the chairs are able to converse in comfort, and the drivers encourage each other up the hills, which, as cyclists acquainted with Harrogate know, are not to be despised. They go long distances too. A lady, next to whom the present writer found himself at the table-d'hôte dinner one day, mentioned that she had just returned from an expedition in one of the chairs to Fountains Abbey, nine miles away ; and her driver told her that he often took his customers similar or even longer distances without thinking anything of it. I asked whether the man had dismounted at the hills, which are on that road long and steep ; the lady had not observed whether he had done so. I could not help thinking, though I did not give audible expression to the remark, that if the fair customer had changed places with the driver for half a mile, the hills would have occupied a somewhat different place in her memory.

In our opinion, after seeing the practical working of these chairs at Harrogate, at any rate in health resorts where there is a large Bath-chair population, the ordinary form of that vehicle must die out. A thoughtful mind may not unreasonably wonder what, in that event, will become of the very old and decrepit persons who now man Bath chairs. The sole qualification for the post seems to be great feebleness and very restricted powers of locomotion; and it must be confessed that a Coventry-chair rider must be in possession of at least average physical strength.

But, after all, great as are the advantages of tricycles for business purposes, their principal claim on the gratitude of mankind is the large amount that is added by their means to the sum of human happiness. No one can fail to observe that such is the case who will take the trouble to station himself on some summer afternoon at one of the chief arterial outlets of any great city, and watch the stream of people going away into the country for their Saturday to Monday holiday. He who will take his stand on the bridge at Kew, or at Highgate Archway, will see a perfect stream of cycles speeding away into the country. Not only is there a light brigade of young men, bent on some favourite country resort forty miles away or more; but steady middle-aged citizens on sober tricycles, some of them on sociables, with wife or daughter at their side, are bound on less distant expeditions. As regards the younger men, it is more than probable that the light and swift machines upon which they are mounted make all the difference to them whether they pass the brief holiday at the week's end in the stifling city or among the free breezes and shady lanes of the country; and the advantage both to morals and health can hardly be overestimated. Among young ladies, too, the tricycle is a source of enjoyment. It is better for any young creature with sound limbs and healthy spirits to speed away over heaths and downs than to pore over a novel under the trees, or even to play lawn tennis on one eternal acre of grass-plot. It may be said that there are few country houses where some form of cycle is not to be found. The young ladies have their light machines, the boys have their bicycles; and in the stables there is sure to be found a bicycle belonging to some active young footman who will be delighted to get the chance to carry a note and bring back the answer in shorter time than it would take the groom to saddle a horse. No one who thinks of the confined indoor life led habitually by domestic servants would grudge him the outing.

If royal and imperial example count for anything, the practice will soon be universal ; for there is not a crowned head in Europe who has not a stud of these useful iron steeds. Whether the grandees of Middle Europe personally career about the well-trimmed allées of their royal castles I do not know ; but we may at least, from custom and precedent, infer the existence in dignified leisure of many a Kaiserliche-Königliche Hochoberhoffvelocipedenkurator.

The Khedive of Egypt has several tricycles ; one in particular, which I have had the honour of inspecting, is so covered with silver plating, that one can hardly see the black enamel it is supposed to adorn. It will doubtless come in handy should His Highness take it into his head to ride across the Bayuda Desert. He would there 'scorch' after a fashion not contemplated by the North Road Club. The officials of that body should look to this seriously and without delay. No one knows more accurately than Mr. A. J. Wilson the perversity, to call it by no harsher name, of the N. C. U. executive ; and if any claim were founded on His Highness's performance, backed as it might easily be by French or Russian intrigue, and such claim were disallowed by the Records Committee, no one can foretell the political complications that might arise. 'Faed' should at once communicate with the official time-keeper, and arrange that at least His Highness's watch shall be properly compared at the Kew Observatory, under N. C. U. rules. Among gorgeous tricycles some of the Indian princes possess vehicles which will hold their own, though after seeing the Khedivial state tricycle, I cannot affirm that they are pre-eminent. I have seen a picture in which the Maharajah of an Indian state, together with the British resident at his court (an enthusiastic cyclist whose predilections perhaps somewhat influenced the royal taste), and all the great officers of the durbar, are seated on tricycles at the gate of the palace, and gaze at the lens of the camera with the breathless attention usual on such occasions. They present an odd effect of costume. Wearers of shawls and jewelled turbans sit on some of the tricycles, British shooting jackets and knickerbockers figure on others. I understood from the possessor of the picture that the whole party were going out for a 'club run,' and that His Highness is the president of that institution.

One of the great advantages of the tricycle over its two-wheeled rival is that it permits the rider to stop at will. A bicycle, on the contrary, only retains its stable equilibrium on the condition of being kept in constant motion. An attempt at a halt is instantly rewarded by an upset. An active rider can dismount very quickly; but an elderly gentleman, however skilful he might be, would feel the impossibility of performing the necessary gymnastics if he should be so ill-advised as to ride a bicycle through crowded streets. The construction of the bicycle, too, makes it an impossible mount for ladies, to whom the tricycle offers no sort of difficulty. For town work and for the use of the gentler sex the tricycle is decidedly the more convenient machine. On country roads, and for young and active riders, it is a matter of taste which should have the preference.

Although the advantages and pleasures of cycling are open to all able-bodied persons, the choice of a machine is a matter of individual preference. Practically no one would ever hesitate to decide under which category, bicyclist or tricyclist, he himself ought properly to come. A lady, a middle-aged man, or a heavy father, will naturally go in for a tricycle. An active lad, especially if he lives in the country, would probably give his voice for the bicycle, unless, indeed, he had reached the age or attained to the condition of mind which might prompt him to invest in a 'sociable,' on the chance of inducing some adorable being of the gentler sex to share his pilgrimage on wheels.

There is another form of double tricycle which has lately come into fashion, principally as yet among racing men, in which two performers sit one behind the other on the backbone of the machine, and pedal in unison. This is known as a tandem. The pace to be got out of this sort of vehicle is very great, and it will no doubt be still further improved; but it can hardly be said that to an outsider it looks very comfortable. There is also a horrible engine in existence known as a bicycle tandem. It is formed by joining the large wheels of two full-sized bicycles one behind the other with a stout bar of iron between them, on which two saddles are fitted. It is said to be capable of being driven at a speed exceeding anything else on wheels. 'Il faut respecter tous les goûts,' as the French proverb teaches us, but Providence will surely so far intervene as to prevent the general public from succumbing to its attractions. I am bound to add that, with 'the owner (and inventor) up' in company with some efficient coadjutor, this machine is capable of being so handled as almost to convince the spectator that to ride it is neither dangerous nor difficult; but then Mr. Rucker is not only a very clever and a very persuasive gentleman, but a first-rate rider as well. Full descriptions of every kind of cycle will be found in the following pages, and it is not now necessary to dwell upon them at length. Almost all the machines that now compete for public favour partake of the wonderful qualities of lightness combined with strength which is the distinguishing characteristic of modern workmanship.

It is remarkable how quickly both the bicycle and the tricycle after their first inception assumed the form which they have since retained. It is hardly too much to say that no material change has been made in the type of either kind of machine, though the new 'dwarf' and 'safety' bicycles may not improbably be found to herald a new departure. But it is yet too soon to speak positively on this point. As regards the ordinary bicycle and tricycle, improvements in detail have been numerous and important; subsequent makers still adhere very closely to the broad lines laid down by the first designers. This is the more remarkable, because it can hardly be supposed that the original form was reasoned out on strict mathematical principles. It would almost seem that the proportions of the original design were hit upon by intuitive perception rather than by close adherence to rule. But it is a curious fact that the more the question is subjected to scientific investigation, the more patent does it become that the first attempts embodied correct mechanical ideas. Of course I speak only of the type of machine now so common, and not of the various 'velocipedes,' as they were called, which enjoyed a short-lived popularity before the present class of cycles came into existence. In our account of what may be called the history of cycling, we shall show what the precursors of modern cycles were like. The Draisnene, the hobby horse, the dandy horse, and the four-wheeled velocipedes, resembled the modern cycle principally in this, that they all alike utilise the power of human muscles as a motive agent; in the principles of their construction they differed entirely from the cycle of to-day. But when the first bicycle was made it came complete and perfect from the maker's hand, even as Minerva fully armed sprang from the brain of Jupiter. The new type differed from any mechanical adaptation that had ever been thought of before; and the idea, once embodied in a machine, has since been improved constructively only; the principle, so far as anything mundane can be so, is perfect of its kind.

The theory embodied in the two kinds of machine is this: the bicycle consists of a large front wheel, with pedals attached to its hub, over which the rider sits and works upright; his saddle is arranged on a bar of iron, which droops like a tail from the head to the ground, the end of it supported by a small trailing wheel, which bears a part of the rider's weight and prevents him from falling backwards.

In the case of the tricycle all this is changed. The rider sits on a saddle suspended above the axle, between two wheels of moderate size ; a third point of contact with the ground is afforded by a smaller wheel, which, like the bicycle trailing wheel, bears a portion of the weight ; the third wheel sometimes follows, but more often precedes the other two. The rider's seat is arranged either slightly in front of, or behind, the axle, according to the position of the third wheel, which serves the purpose of a rudder, and gives to the machine the name of front or rear steerer, as the case may be. In the case of the tricycle, as the rider rests on three points, he need not trouble himself about his balance, which is secure whether the carriage is in motion or not. This is the main point which makes the tricycle easier to ride than the bicycle ; the rider need not dismount when it is necessary for any reason to come to a halt. He sits still and 'waits till the clouds roll by.' Nor is he compelled to maintain his balance by the sway of his body ; he sits quiet and guides the machine by the movement of his wrists on the steering gear.

Falling forwards from a bicycle is by no means a difficult exploit—indeed, the difficulty is to avoid performing it. The manœuvre is so common that the peculiar form of tumble that ensues is known by the distinctive name of 'the cropper,' or 'Imperial crowner.' The habitual recurrence of the Imperial crowner is prevented by placing the rider's saddle a trifle behind the centre of gravity of the machine : his balance is secured, when the machine is in motion, by guiding the driving wheel slightly in the direction to which his weight inclines, in exactly the same manner as a skater executes his long and graceful curves on the outside edge. After a certain amount of practice, the skilful bicyclist ceases to think of his steering handles any more than a skater does of his skates. In both cases the steering is regulated by subtle action of the muscles, but in the case of the cyclist, as in that of the skater, so far as conscious action is concerned, his course is determined by the poise and sway of his body.

INTRODUCTORY.

Endless are the stories told by bicyclists of the curious and complicated falls which are thus executed 'over the handles' Of them, as of Cleopatra's charms, we may say—

> . . . Age cannot wither them nor custom stale
> Their infinite variety.

A few, but fortunately very few, have terminated fatally. More frequently the active lads who form the main body of bicycle riders escape with bruises only, and learn caution from their escapes. The Hon. Arnold Keppel, late of the Scots Guards, had when a lad two most remarkable tumbles, concerning which, in reply to an inquiry for particulars, he writes as follows :—

In the year 1876 I was returning by night from Worthing with two friends to Storrington, in Sussex, where we were reading for the Army examinations. We were each riding a fifty-four inch Coventry Machinist bicycle. There was only one lamp among the party, and the owner of this was told off to ride in front. There is a long hill on this road, down which we had to come, and the night was very dark. Our friend with the lamp was fifty yards ahead, going at a great pace, when on nearing the bottom of the hill he saw a horse and fish-cart coming in the opposite direction. He had just time to go between the hedge and the cart. The horse was scared and turned suddenly right across the road. I was next, and, less fortunate than our leader, I struck the shaft of the cart fair and square. Before I had time to realise the situation I found myself lying in the road on the other side, the machine and I having fallen clear over the horse. The marvel was that not a bolt was sprung in the machine, and the only evidence it bore of a collision was a dent and scratches on the top nut of the head. I did not break my neck, but I broke my nose, and sustained other cuts and bruises which it is needless to particularise. I must confess that, if I have to tumble, I prefer to take my chance of the vicissitudes of the hunting-field.

The other tumble about which you ask sounds too like 'a yarn' for me to risk my reputation by narrating it. G. H. (naming a friend and relation, then a fellow-student at Storrington, and now an officer in the Life Guards) says positively that he saw it happen.

I cannot myself be considered an eye-witness; for I remember nothing till I found myself in a cottage, being 'brought to' with restoratives.

The header in question came about in the following fashion :—The Storrington Army students were holding a race meeting among themselves, and the competitors were taking a preliminary canter before the start. Mr. Keppel, going best pace through a lane of spectators, ran over a piece of coal which had fallen from a passing cart The machine turned a somersault—so complete a somersault that the rider came uppermost again, and the wheel went on several yards before it finally fell. Mr. Keppel, though still in the saddle, was unconscious of anything, as he says in his letter, from the moment his head and shoulders touched the earth. The handles of the machine were bent upwards in a very extraordinary manner.

The 'Imperial crowner' is of comparatively frequent occurrence. Dogs, pigs, fowls, and children share with sheep the honour of causing it. A course of bricks or a string across a road placed in the course of an approaching cyclist by playful youth has not unfrequently produced it; and the British rough has discovered that a stick inserted into the moving wheel frequently inflicts sufficient damage to give the assailant time to escape bodily chastisement by flight.

There seems to be hardly any limit to the skill that can be acquired by assiduous practice on the bicycle, and the exhibitions of address and daring which sometimes take place fairly take one's breath away. The following appeared in the English 'Bicycling News' of October 10, 1886. I reproduce it in a slightly curtailed form, and before doing so have had the curiosity to inquire whether the event referred to really happened. I was informed that it actually occurred as described, and that the machine ridden on the occasion was a Star bicycle; the peculiarity of which is that the small wheel is in advance and steers the machine, while the weight of the rider rests mainly on the large driving-wheel, which is of the

INTRODUCTORY.

same dimensions as an ordinary full-sized bicycle—viz. fifty or tifty-two inches. This make of bicycle has enthusiastic admirers in America, and it may be noted that the extraordinary trick-riders Kauffman and McAnney, who exhibited in 1886 at the Westminster Aquarium, performed their wonders upon it:—

A daring and foolhardy feat was performed by a bicyclist the other afternoon at Cabin John Bridge, near the city, says a Washington telegram to the 'Pittsburg Dispatch.' The place is a general pleasure resort about twelve miles from town, over the military road built by Jefferson Davis while Secretary of War. The bridge is said to be the largest single span of masonry in the world. It is 125 feet high, and about 200 feet long, a single magnificent arch spanning a deep and rocky gorge. A good many people go out there to see the bridge, and the man who keeps the little hotel known as Cabin John, just at the end and across the bridge, does a good business, especially on Sunday. Every nice Sunday the sheds about the place are crowded with vehicles of every description, and sporting men, family parties, wheelmen, and gentlemen of leisure, are loafing about the house, getting country dinners or picnicking in the wild gorge below the bridge. As at all such places, there are always a few wheelmen lounging in and out, and a number of machines were stacked about the yard that afternoon, and a lively party within could be heard telling stories and boasting of their personal skill on the road. In the midst of the hilarity one young man suddenly came out alone, and, singling out his machine, mounted, and without a word rode towards the bridge. There is a brownstone coping on the three-foot wall on either side of the roadway. This coping is about a foot broad, and is bevelled on the two upper edges for an inch or two. On the inside of these walls is the solid roadway above the duct. On the outside is a perpendicular descent of about 125 feet in the centre of the bridge, and no less than 75 feet at either abutment. The young man stopped and dismounted at the end of the bridge and lifted his machine upon the coping. The act was noticed by a couple of gentlemen smoking under the trees, but it was looked upon as a freak, and no particular attention was paid to it. The next moment there was an exclamation of horror, for the young man was seen mounted upon his bicycle deliberately riding along the narrow coping. The sight froze the blood of the ladies and children picnicking in the gorge below, and was enough to appal the stoutest heart. The gentlemen in front of the hotel started to their feet and called to the other wheelmen within. It was too late. The young man was already in the centre of the bridge. He never swerved a hair's breadth from his seat. From the end of the bridge he seemed a toy machine running by mechanism, so erect and motionless he sat, and so evenly he rode. 'Let him alone,' cried one of his companions, 'he could ride it if it was a rope!' Nevertheless, the fear that interference might hasten the horror that all wished to prevent left the party rooted to the spot. In two places the coping makes a zigzag by the widening of the roadway, and at these places the rider must steer his wheel through a very narrow space at nearly right angles with his course. The daring fellow had passed the first of these ticklish spots, and, when he carefully wore round the second, not a single one of the horrified spectators could draw a breath for fear. From thence to the end was a short and straight run, and in another moment the young man had completed his dangerous ride, dismounted, and was waving his hand laughingly at the frightened men and women and children who had witnessed it. The young fellow calmly remounted his wheel and rode on towards the city as if he had done a very common thing not worth mentioning. He was induced to undertake the feat because someone had doubted whether he had the requisite ability and nerve to perform it.

Kauffman and his companion McAnney mentioned above executed wonders almost beyond belief. One of their feats, though I witnessed it several times, still appears to me when I think of it almost incredible. Kauffman brought into the arena a common strongly built kitchen table; upon it he placed two chairs, one to receive the front wheel of his bicycle and the other the hind wheel. He then mounted on the table, climbed on to the chairs, and from thence slowly and carefully, with almost imperceptible motions, balancing his unstable mount the while, crept up the spokes of his machine and finally stood upright on the saddle, at a height of twelve or fourteen feet from the ground. The newspapers tell us from time to time that he is still performing to large and enthusiastic audiences in various parts of Europe, so that it may be supposed that he has not yet broken his neck. I asked the performer at the close of one of his performances whether in his learning stage

A FOOLHARDY FEAT

INTRODUCTORY.

he had fallen or hurt himself much—his reply was somewhat characteristic. 'No, sir,' he said, 'I perceived at a very early stage of my training that I should have "to quit falling," so before I went any farther I trained myself to that.' 'What do you mean?' said I; 'you cannot prevent an accident.' 'No,' said he with a smile, 'but I have trained myself so to keep my balance at every stage of the performance that a slip, even though it should take place at apparently the most critical point of the performance, would almost infallibly land me on my feet.' Several times he did fall—though not in the most dangerous feats, which were executed with extreme slowness of movement and care—and on each occasion he lighted, as he declared he would, on his feet.

It is needless to say that for people who are not in the enjoyment of that activity and elasticity which belongs mainly to youth, the tricycle presents many advantages. It has drawbacks; the machine is necessarily heavier in itself; having three wheels instead of two, it offers more resistance to obstacles on the road; and this is increased by the circumstance that in the case of the bicycle the two wheels follow each other, and so practically make only one track, whereas the three wheels of the tricycle make each a track of its own.

On the other hand, the tricycle can be made to carry a considerable amount of luggage; enough may be packed about the body of the carriage to supply the wants of a moderate-minded person for a tour of two or three days or even more. It is quite easy to stow away a bag weighing ten or twelve pounds. After all, a complete suit of flannels is all that a tourist absolutely requires, and the weight of such a kit is hardly felt on a tricycle. Many enthusiastic artists carry about a whole photographic outfit; and it is darkly rumoured that the members of the Tricycle Union, a select body who are the objects of a good deal of harmless 'chaff' among the main body of cyclists, and who love to combine various branches of science with their favourite pastime, secrete about the frame of their iron steeds all the paraphernalia of their several mysteries.

The late Sir Charles Napier used to declare that he considered a soldier amply provided if he started on a campaign with a piece of soap and a toothbrush. A bicyclist on a tour, unless he agrees with the hero of Scinde in his estimate of what are necessaries in life, can only provide for his requirements by elaborate prevision in the way of forwarding luggage to points ahead on the line of march. Bags christened by their inventors by the suggestive names of Saturday-to-Monday, or Multum-in-parvo, can be obtained in great variety from the stores of cycling outfitters. These little valises are said (by the makers) to be amply sufficient for the wants of a travelling cyclist; but a kit, when packed in a multum-in-parvo bag, and strapped on the backbone of a bicycle, presents a very attenuated appearance, and a man's desires must be very strictly subordinated to the force of circumstances if he looks on such an outfit as sufficient.

One of the most remarkable characteristics of modern machines is the extreme lightness, it might almost be said the attenuation, of the parts of which they are composed. Every portion of the frame is made as strong and as light as possible; and the greatest mechanical ingenuity is shown in adjusting the shape of the various parts so as to produce the maximum of stability with the least possible weight. It is an established axiom in mechanical construction that, weight for weight, a hollow bar of proper form is stronger than solid metal. Advantage has been taken of this circumstance by cycle constructors; every part that can be made hollow is made so, and the resources of applied mechanics are exhausted to discover the form which most efficiently utilises the allotted material. The rims or felloes, for instance, which are the steel peripheries of the wheels, and which serve to form the stiff and perfect outside of the circle, are hollow, and though the exact form varies according to the taste of different manufacturers, they are all made by passing a tube of round steel between rollers of such construction that the tube is brought into a section of crescent form, the outer semilune serving for a bed to

THE AMERICAN STAR MACHINE

contain the thick rubber tires, which are also invariably employed.

It is worth the while even of the most careless rider of cycles to pause for a moment over the construction of the suspension wheel. It is not too much to say that the ingenious invention designated by that name alone made it possible to construct the modern cycle. Before the invention of the suspension system, wheels were made of light and strong hickory or other wood, like the wheels of the ordinary carriages intended to be drawn by horses, which are still in use on the roads. In wooden wheels, the weight of the whole carriage rests on the particular spoke which happens to point perpendicularly downwards, and the stability of the wheel depends on the rigidity of that particular spoke. Exactly the reverse of this occurs in the case of the suspension wheel; in it the weight of rider and carriage rests on the centre of the wheel and is suspended from that part of the felloe which happens to be uppermost, by means of the spoke then most perpendicular. The weight is thus constantly shifted from spoke to spoke as the wheel revolves, and the lateral spokes, being all braced tight, prevent the wheel from buckling, or getting out of shape. The result of this most ingenious arrangement is, that comparatively fine steel wire is substituted for a stiff wooden spoke, and the cycle wheel presents the beautiful and graceful, though apparently fragile, appearance which everyone no doubt has admired. In order to realise the magnitude of the revolution which this invention has brought about, it is only necessary to fancy what the appearance of a bicycle would be if it had wheels like even those of the lightest Victoria. Some enthusiasts have seen and ridden upon machines made after that fashion, but if it had not been reformed, cycling would never have attained its present popularity. Mr. S. Maddison is said to have described, and Mr. Edward Cooper to have been the first practically to use, the suspension wheel.

From the moment that the cycling Columbus broke the egg —from the moment, that is, that the inventors of the suspension wheel showed how a practical carriage could be made light enough to be worked easily by human muscles—manufacturers began to vie with each other in diminishing the weight of each minute part. This has been done with such assiduity, that at length, in the opinion of competent observers, the limits of attenuation have been pushed almost up to the border line which divides safety from instability. It is now no longer necessary, as it was even a couple of years ago, to enjoin upon the maker from whom a purchaser orders a machine, to make it as light as possible. He is sure to do that. The necessity is rather that the rider should make sure that his mount is up to his weight. A hundred, or even a hundred and twenty, pounds was recently thought a not unreasonable weight for a tricycle: but nowadays even these small weights are reduced by twenty or thirty pounds. The reader will of course understand that, whether the higher or the lower scale of weights is taken, the same type of machine will be made by a good builder considerably stronger and consequently heavier for a large man than for a small one. Indeed, to enjoy anything like the full amount of enjoyment that can be got out of the pastime of cycle riding, a man's machine should be built to his measure with the same solicitude that his tailor displays in producing his coat. It sounds, perhaps, like attributing selfishness to a very estimable class of persons to mention with approbation the fact that a practised cyclist is very unwilling to lend his machine to anybody else: but such is the case; and though the non-cyclist may perhaps have tried a friend's machine without observing the look of agony with which the loan was unquestionably conceded, he may rest assured that, like the celebrated parrot, his friend, if he said little, thought a good deal.

A beginner who takes up cycling and does not at first find it as pleasant as he expected, should not give it up in despair until he has satisfied himself that he has fulfilled all the requirements which make success possible. He exercises a new set of muscles, so that after his first essays, even though he be a practised athlete, he will certainly be stiff and uncomfortable. He will be certain to ride badly; he will turn out his toes, probably graze his ankles against the pedals, wriggle on his seat, twist his knees, or perform other cycling enormities; but even if he did not, there are obstacles which must be removed before success is possible. Even the winner of last year's championship could not ride twenty miles on a saddle that did not fit him, and that Great Being himself would stop from sheer agony, exhausted and leg weary, if his seat were at an inconvenient distance from his pedals; or, as he would probably himself phrase it, if he were not placed properly over his work. Let not the novice, therefore, whether of the gentle or of the sterner sex, be too easily discouraged. Let him ascertain, as may be done from a book as well as in any other way, what the essentials of the situation really are, and see that they are complied with, before giving way to the idea, erroneous in the great majority of cases, that in his case cycling is a forbidden luxury.

Actual demonstration and personal assistance of friends are useful. But almost as much is to be learned from books as from oral instruction. A book, unlike a friend, is always at hand with a complete account of the matter in all its bearings. Minute particulars assume a very different relative importance when the subject begins to be familiar than they did at first, and a matter at first dismissed or disregarded as unimportant can be referred to at leisure and reconsidered. Besides, in a book the accumulated and carefully noted experience of many beginners has been noted. A beginner, knowing nothing of details, does not know what information to ask for should a difficulty arise; the printed friend can always be summoned, which may possibly not be the case with the oral adviser.

But we are digressing from the subject of cycle building. The first point, as we said above, to ensure success and save a surgeon's bill, is to order a machine fully up to your weight, otherwise there will certainly be a breakdown, and probably an accident. Next take care that your machine fits you. If these points have been attended to, and the small amount of practice be taken which is necessary to accustom the muscles to the new labours they are called upon to undergo, there will be no inclination to drop the practice in disgust.

Though we are not now going to enter into a disquisition on the mechanical theory of progression as exemplified in cycle riding, it would be well that every rider and purchaser of a machine should keep the first principles of that theory in his mind.

Those who wish to pursue it in detail cannot do better than consult the work of Mr. Warner Jones, a writer who very ably unites practical cycling and theory; to his scientific little treatise we refer readers interested in the mathematical bearings of the subject.

It will be sufficient for our present purpose to note that the science of progression as regards cycling, as in all applications of mechanics, consists in a due apportionment of quantities in an equation, which deals with the three factors, weight, force, and time. A machine with a rider upon it offers a certain weight or resistance to be moved. If the strength that the rider can put forth be measured, and his weight and that of his machine be ascertained, it only remains to calculate to what distance the force at disposal can move the weight in a given time.

If, when a carriage is in motion, it is desired to quicken the pace, the force employed must be increased: because, from the conditions of the problem, the weight is a fixed quantity and the time within which it is to be moved is diminished. But in the case of a rider who is already putting forth all his strength, the force cannot be increased; therefore, as he cannot increase the driving power, the rider must have a lighter machine, or be content to go more slowly. Every alteration of one factor is obtained only at the expense of another; increased resistance from hills, for instance, requires more power or less speed, probably both; and when, in cycling phrase, the rider has 'put in all he knows,' he comes to a standstill.

INTRODUCTORY.

Hills are not the only obstacles that have to be overcome in cycling; and when the mud, ruts, stones, and the general surface of the road have to be taken into account, all these may be classed under the general name of resistance to the performance of the work required. The best solution of the equation is to reduce the weight of the cycle to the lowest point consistent with safety; to build the machine so as most effectually to minimise the friction of the road; and to utilise in the best possible manner the strength exercised by the rider.

The first point in designing a machine is to make it of such form that it shall offer the minimum of friction, and support the weight of the rider in an attitude which will enable him with the least effort to put forth all his strength.

A man's natural means of progression are designed by nature in such a manner as to afford him a power of advancing under all the circumstances under which he is likely to be placed. This is a roundabout way of saying that the human leg is, so to speak, a compromise that fulfils varying and sometimes opposite requirements. It, or rather we must say they, are not constructed especially for speed: a pair of them will carry their possessor, though with varying rapidity, along a level road, across rough ground such as a swamp or a Scotch moor, or up an Alpine mountain. The bicycle or tricycle is designed to help him along under one condition only; that is, over a moderately even road. An athletic man, putting forth all his strength, could perhaps walk five miles along a level road or three miles across a stretch of grouse ground, within the hour. Mounted on a bicycle, he could go fifteen or even twenty miles in the same space of time; but if, still mounted on his bicycle, he transferred the scene of his operations to the moor or the mountain side, he would not advance a mile in a week. Yet the amount of force expended, supposing that he puts forth his utmost strength, must in each instance be the same; and the motion of his legs, whether in walking or in cycling, is substantially the same. The human limbs practically act like the spokes of a wheel, the thigh joint representing the hub, the leg on which the walker stands is the spoke perpendicularly beneath the centre; when he advances, the hindmost leg comes forward, and as the centre of gravity is shifted the human wheel rolls forward through a certain portion of its periphery. The same action takes place when the man travels on a tricycle, only in that case with the same amount of exertion he goes faster, because he has employed mechanical devices to overcome friction. Instead of taking a succession of springs and shifting his balance at every forward step, he has interposed between himself and the ground a continuous bearing surface, namely the tire of his cycle wheels; he has substituted a steady mechanical pressure for a forward jump, and his weight, steadily supported over the centre of gravity of the carriage, leaves his legs free to exert their strength to the greatest advantage, and adds momentum to his course in the exact direction of motion of the machine.

It hardly needs proof that if mechanical means are to be adopted to reduce friction, a wheel of some sort is the best device. It therefore only remains to consider what the size of the wheel is to be. The exact dimensions depend on the size of the obstructions that have to be overcome. A large wheel overcomes an obstacle more easily than a small one, as may be easily seen by moving the wheel of a child's toy cart against a brick, and then moving a carriage-wheel against the same object. The small wheel will stop dead short, and the larger wheel will mount over it, because in the first instance the whole or the greater part of the circle is behind the point of impact, and in the other a sufficient part of the circle is in front of the point of impact. This is not a scientific statement, because it does not take into consideration all the conditions stated, but it is sufficiently accurate for our purpose.

In practice, obstacles likely to be encountered on the road will probably not exceed two, or at the most three, inches in height. It is to be hoped that few stones of that size are ever found on a road: at any rate, if any are so placed the road

AT THE MERCY OF HIS WIFE

INTRODUCTORY.

surveyor of the district ought to be summarily hanged. If ruts, mud, or anything else is encountered which exceeds three inches, the best plan for the cyclist who is condemned to meet such obstacles is to get off and walk till he reaches a part of the road that is under the management of a surveyor with some Christian feeling. But while the wheel must be made sufficiently large to surmount ordinary stones with ease, it must not be larger than is absolutely necessary; for not only is a large wheel unduly heavy, but it offers more surface to the wind—and wind is almost harder for a cyclist to encounter than a rough or hilly road. The limit of size as regards bicycles is affected by another consideration—the length of the rider's leg, and the limit of size in bicycle wheels is practically governed by that consideration. The same condition is also present in the case of tricycles, though in this case other circumstances must also be taken into account. The tricycle rider should when sitting on the saddle, with his leg extended to the full extent, have the pedal on which his foot rests three or more inches from the ground, in order to clear the inequalities of the road. Mathematical considerations, with which we need not trouble the reader, show that the centre of a wheel which will support the weight of the rider in such a position as to enable him to put forth his utmost strength should be about 24 inches from the ground. The saddle on which the rider sits is raised a few inches above the axle of the wheels; and as a matter of practice a 48-inch wheel has been found a convenient size. Recent experiments seem to indicate that a wheel of 40 inches in diameter is even better than 48. The decision will no doubt be made in the case of each rider on considerations which vary with individual tastes and requirements. There are some among the exponents of cycling who are hotly in favour of wheels greatly larger or smaller than this standard, just as there were, in the country discovered by Captain Gulliver, Bigendian convicts who were undergoing punishment for obstinately cracking the large ends of their eggs. But of their opinions we need take no note. Mathematical reasoning has also determined the theoretical best position for the smaller wheel of the tricycle, as may be seen at large in Mr. Warner Jones's volume.

Up to a very recent period it was not possible to adopt the mechanical device called 'gearing up' to the bicycle; consequently it was necessary to have the driving wheel as large as possible consistently with the pedal being within easy reach of the rider's foot, in order that a single revolution of the wheel might cover as large a space of ground as possible. Any diminution of size of wheel necessitated faster pedalling or slower speed. Now that a means has been found to gear up bicycle wheels to any required pitch, the large wheel is no longer found essential, and a change has apparently set in in favour of small wheels. Numerous forms of dwarf bicycle have lately appeared, and the marvellous performances that have been made by their aid on the road shows the value of the change.

We shall describe farther on the construction of 'dwarf' or 'safety' bicycles, as they are sometimes indiscriminately called. But the two terms are by no means convertible. Many of the dwarf bicycles now offered for sale, though they have merits of their own, are anything but 'safeties.' It is true that if you tumble you do not fall so far as from a high bicycle. Still one class alone, that known as the 'Rover' type, offers immunity from the dreaded 'header.' And a machine of that type is now offered by a great many of the leading manufacturers. It is very desirable that the two terms 'dwarf' and 'safety' should not be confounded.

The term 'gearing up' occurred a few lines back; as it is a phrase which will often meet the eye of a reader of this book, it may be as well to explain the meaning of the term. It is a well-known principle of mechanics that by the use of large and small toothed wheels acting upon each other, power may be obtained at the expense of speed or speed at the expense of power. This principle has been adapted recently both to bicycles and tricycles. The revolutions of the driving wheels can be increased as compared with the pedals, or diminished, at the will of the rider, who by the turn of a handle or the movement of a lever can throw either speed or power gear into action. Many machines are now furnished with apparatus by which the rider may drive his wheels 'level,' that is one revolution of the wheel for one of the pedal; 'up,' by which one revolution of the pedal produces more than one revolution of the driving wheel, resulting of course in increased speed; or 'down,' by which a revolution of the pedal produces only a part of a revolution of the driving wheel, and power for hill climbing and the like is obtained, at the expense of speed. This is a practical exemplification of the truth stated above, that when one factor of the equation, viz. the strength of the rider, is a fixed quantity, either speed or power must be sacrificed when the other conditions of the problem are varied. But this part of the subject will be more fully treated in future chapters; it is only necessary here to say that the proportions and general form of the tricycle rest, not on caprice nor on mere guesswork, but on defined and well-understood rules.

When cycles began to increase and multiply in the land, it was natural that the riders of them should organise themselves and assume a corporate existence for mutual support and defence. This was no doubt a matter of more urgent necessity in the early days of cycling than it is now. Cyclists were at first looked upon with distrust, if not with positive dislike. It is possible that bicyclists, who were the earliest exponents of the art, were more aggressive and made their presence felt more acutely than is now the case. It was some time before horses got accustomed to them, and at first it was the fashion among some of the younger men to cover their coats with braid and blow bugles in the streets. The dislike with which they were regarded, if not deserved by the great majority, was in some instances sufficiently well merited. But these customs have long been things of the past. Cyclists now behave with the decorum of judges on the bench; the equine race seems to have made up its mind that there is nothing in it; and even in the wildest districts of the country the half-brick of welcome is now seldom heaved at the cycling stranger.

Though the number of wandering cyclists increases year by year, it is probable that none of them will ever again undergo the experience of an early martyr in the cause, who roused the wrath of the driver and guard of the St. Albans coach; the latter worthy provided himself with a lasso, and when the cyclist tried as aforetime to race the coach, he found himself dexterously lassoed and dragged in the mud. That guard is reported to have discovered by practical experience that a cyclist is a being not outside the protection of the law, and the incident is generally supposed to have contributed considerably to the development of the institution, then, and for a short time afterwards, known as the Bicycle Union, now merged in the larger and more important body called the National Cyclists' Union.

The organisation which was at first necessary for defence was continued for convenience; and side by side with it there grew up another institution called the Cyclists' Touring Club. They are independent of each other, but work together very harmoniously. The N. C. U. (for convenience' sake, the two ruling bodies are always spoken and written of by their initial letters) undertakes the legislation and legal defence as well as what may be called the police of cycling, while the C. T. C., as its name implies, attends to everything that conduces to the comfort of cycling tourists.

The cycling public, constantly moving along the roads and streets, finds itself in contact with all bye-laws and regulations which affect locomotion. The N. C. U. have been able to establish the fact that it is for the public convenience that they should be consulted whenever Parliamentary or local legislation deals with the question of street traffic. The relations between cyclists and the railway companies present another subject of attention; and the organisation of racing, race meetings, and championships, together with the legal business just mentioned, affords constant employment to the Executive of the Union.

The work of the Union is divided into two main sections:

A COUNTRY CLUB RUN

first, the representation of cycling in its relation to Parliament, to other sports, or to the general public ; and, secondly, the internal regulation of cycling itself. The first embraces all legal matters concerning the cycle and its use on public roads and highways ; including questions relating to rights-of-way, legal obstruction, gate tolls, assaults, and other things affecting wheel riding throughout the country ; the second embraces the promulgation of rules and regulations for racing, the establishment and management of the amateur bicycle and tricycle championships, and the general supervision of the innumerable complaints and appeals which incessantly arise.

A very successful system of local self-government has been adopted, by the formation throughout the country of Local Centres, by means of which the Union maintains its central control without losing the practical usefulness which can only be acquired by detailed local knowledge of men and things. Several of these centres have been formed in the great centres of population throughout the country, and have worked well in practice. The Union is governed by a council, composed of members of affiliated clubs, together with the honorary secretaries and chairmen of the Local Centres. The operation of the Union being intended for the benefit of cycling as a whole, no direct personal benefit is obtained by membership : it differs in this respect considerably from the other great cycling organisation, the C. T. C., in which membership certainly does secure considerable advantages.

We have mentioned that the unit of formation from which the National Union has been formed is the Cycling Club. Almost every town and large village has one of these institutions, which are formed according to the exigencies of local society, and flourish in proportion to the energy of the elected captain and honorary secretary. Each club, provided its rules are in accord with the model rules formulated by the National Society, has the right to send, in proportion to its numbers, one or more members to the Council of the Union.

The Council meets at stated intervals and forms a very real

and workable Parliament for the discussion of cycling affairs. The national love for discussion, and the considerable aptitude for speechifying shown by many of the members, find full opportunity of exercise at the monthly meetings, and the temptation to a somewhat florid and lengthy style of oratory is found by many ardent spirits too great to be resisted. Time fortunately will not permit questions of mere detail to be discussed, and only matters in which some principle is involved are put on the agenda paper; details are left to the consideration of an executive elected from among the members, which meets weekly at headquarters. Before this body are brought in the first instance all complaints, appeals, and projects of cycling legislation. The system, order, and expedition with which a large amount of detail is examined and disposed of offers an example which might without any disadvantage be followed by more pretentious assemblies. The National Union rests on the widest basis of publicity, and commands general allegiance and support. There was a time, it is true, when it was threatened with dissensions from within. This danger was, perhaps, almost inseparable from the constitution of the society. The original organisation belonged to bicyclists, who were first in the field, and who, in fact, began to organise themselves before tricycling was invented. But the development of tricycling brought another and, as a rule, an older set of men to the front, who were not quite ready to acquiesce in the leadership which priority of possession had placed in the hands of their juniors in years. *Beati possidentes* was not unnaturally the motto of the bicyclists, and the situation was one which at first presented some obstacles to harmonious working. It seemed possible, at one time, that tricyclists would break off and form an organisation of their own. But wiser counsels prevailed, and the united association has now for some years past offered a solid front to the world. A large, and perhaps in the eyes of some persons an undue, amount of the attention of the executive is taken up with racing; but this is not to be regretted. Even those who do not care for racing in itself

INTRODUCTORY.

may agree that the racing path is the place where a new invention is sure to be tested to the utmost ; and if the invention be really an advantage it will be adopted. The opinions of the best riders and the keenest wits are concentrated upon it, and if it successfully undergoes the severe tests to which it is sure to be subjected by racing experts, it will certainly be adopted by manufacturers, to the manifest advantage of the general body of riders, who, if not so assisted, would have had to wait long ere the natural conservatism of the workshop was overcome ; for new patterns mean fresh outlay of capital, and the remodelling of existing traditions.

While the National Union takes under its cognisance the police, the legal defence, and the legislation of cycling, there devolves upon a kindred, but at the same time quite a separate, institution, the care of individual comfort. The C. T. C. exists for the mutual aid and protection of those among its members who travel along the Queen's highway, and sojourn temporarily in the towns and villages along its course. Although the rules of the Club contain the usual provisions for the election of President, Vice-Presidents, and other officers of a large organisation, all these dignified posts are vacant, and the club flourishes under the control of an energetic and most efficient secretary, assisted, rather than controlled, by a somewhat shadowy council. It is true that at long intervals, once or twice a year, the secretary is called upon to meet the council of the club. He often passes through several—perhaps eight or nine consecutive—*mauvais quarts d'heure de Rabelais*, during which he listens, not unmoved, to the bottled-up grievances of 20,000 members, detailed by their choicest grumblers. But, like the lead-keeled racing yachts that one sees in the Thames, he lies down on his beam-ends and lets the storm blow over him. When the council adjourns, the Secretary resumes his sway, and continues to rule despotically—till next meeting.

The Touring Club, like the National Union, was in the first instance founded by bicyclists. It was formed in the provinces in the year 1878, and was enlarged to include tricyclists in

1882. The defined objects of the club are to promote touring by bicycles and cycles amongst amateurs (a term which has supplied an endless source of dispute both to the N. C. U. and the C. T. C.), and arrange for mutual defence, assistance and support. The plan of operation is as follows : a map of the British Isles is divided into districts, twelve of which are in England, four in Ireland, and seven in Scotland, and each is placed under the charge of an officer called a Chief Consul. This consular system is quite original. The Chief Consul, chosen always for his special knowledge of the requirements of cycling, selects assistants, known as Consuls, from among the local members of the club, in the towns and villages of the district. He also appoints hotel headquarters, conducts correspondence with members asking information, attends the meetings of the Council, and generally is responsible for the interests and working of the club in his immediate district. Consuls acting under the direction of their chief give information as to the state of the roads, and the places of interest within the district, to any member applying for it. They are expected to assist the Chief Consuls in filling up any vacancies that may occur in the list of hotels or repairing smiths, to look up subscriptions in arrear, and to secure new adherents for the club. All this organisation having been achieved, the chief consuls, consuls, hotel headquarters, recommended houses and repairing smiths appointed, the result is embodied in a handbook, convenient for carrying in the pocket, which, after being carefully revised every year, is supplied to members at a nominal charge. In any strange place, if a member's machine breaks down, or he is assaulted, or in any way wronged, even if he is only benighted, he sees by a glance at his handbook who is the nearest friend to whom he can apply, where he can sleep and eat, and where he can get his damages repaired. The cases are few within the British Isles where a member of the C. T. C. cannot get all his wants supplied by his own club, within four or five miles distance from the place where any misadventure occurs to him. A member wishing to travel in any direction through the country, applies to the Chief Consul of the district through which his intended journey lies, and obtains every information necessary respecting roads, hotels, best route to pursue, &c., besides being speeded on his way by the Consuls of the chief towns through which he passes: for part of a Consul's duty is to keep a watchful eye to the comfort and interest of any touring members who may be temporarily sojourning in the hotel headquarters. These last are by no means the least important part of the organisation; the club has either headquarters or recommended houses in all the chief towns and large villages of the kingdom. Recommended houses, as opposed to hotel headquarters, are houses which can in many cases hardly be designated hotels. Sometimes they are snug roadside inns in remote country villages. In such places it is often of great importance to the wet or belated traveller to find rest, refreshment, and recognition, even though a sanded parlour may be the only sitting-room, and a smiling maid may represent boots and waiter. The proprietor of a C. T. C. house enters into a contract with the club, specifying that he will at all times 'receive and entertain any members of the club, whether ladies or gentlemen, who produce a valid ticket of membership for the then current year, and that he will charge them a tariff of prices,' which the contract then proceeds to set forth.

These agreements are mutually beneficial. They suit the innkeeper, because to him it means practically the monopoly of the trade to be done with cyclists, the number of whom would hardly be believed. Many hotels fell into sleepiness and decay when railroads took the place of coaches, and have now through the medium of cycling tourists revived, and do a profitable business, though teams of galloping posters have disappeared for ever. But the arrangement is by no means one-sided. The cyclist also profits by it. He is a new creation; his wants are novel and strange, and a specimen of the class descending on an hotel not specially prepared for his reception would probably cause more consternation than delight. The cyclist's hours are uncertain; he is as likely as not to arrive in the middle of the night, or long before breakfast. Whatever the hour of his arrival, he is quite certain to be very tired, very hungry, and very hot. He will have very little luggage; and though he should arrive at midday, he will certainly want to go to bed; not necessarily to sleep, but for the practical reason that bed is the best place for him to wait in while his clothes are being dried. To the good people at a cycling inn, these vagaries are the merest matters of routine; equally a matter of course is the request of the guest to be called and have breakfast ready at an unearthly hour of the morning; for the favourite plan of the younger spirits, who go careering over the country at the rate of eighty or a hundred miles a day, is to get over thirty or forty of them before breakfast. Great is the convenience to these young athletes of finding houses all over the country at which their requirements are studied, and their arrival hailed not only with cheerfulness but with welcome, and many are the travellers who have found the little silver badge of the club a passport to cheery kindness, which no agreement for special tariffs would alone suffice to secure.

Nor is it only the young athletes of rapid journeys and abnormally early hours who may benefit by the C. T. C. agreement. It is not necessary for a member to avail himself of all his privileges. Older and more steady-going persons, as well as those of a higher social grade, may wish for more accommodation and a more diversified table, and so may not choose to avail themselves of the special tariff; yet if the cyclist be journeying for health or pleasure, which I take to be the true definition of touring, he will not carry any considerable quantity of luggage, and the demands on the resources of his hostelry will not differ much from those of his more rapid brother of the wheel. Every one in fact who uses bicycles or tricycles and who takes pleasure in wandering by road and lane may at some time or other find himself glad to take advantage of the C. T. C. arrangements, which place at his disposal skilled assistance and intelligent comprehension of his wants. Half-a-crown a year can hardly be considered an exorbitant sum to pay for these advantages. The Club last year numbered over 20,000 members.

The only obstacle that I know of to the use of the cycle becoming universal in this country, is that year by year the roads seem in many parts of England to be getting worse and worse. But, as we shall have occasion to point out further on, even in that respect there is likely to be improvement. A revolt against the present system of road repair and road surveying is being organised, and is likely to have a considerable success.

In fact, among the best of the works that have been accomplished by the two cycling organisations is the change which they are attempting in the direction of road reform. Their efforts are young as yet, and there has not been time for more than an attempt to rouse public opinion. But it has been a move in the right direction, and it is to be hoped will bear fruit ere long. No one who knows what our highways were in the coaching days can deny that road-making has greatly deteriorated since then. In many districts it seems to be almost a lost art. Any local busybody is considered good enough to act as road surveyor, and apparently the very last thing that occurs to those who appoint the road surveyor is the necessity of inquiring whether the candidate knows anything of road-making or not. Yet every one must admit that it is an art; and an art that requires a considerable amount of study to acquire. Everybody is interested in having good roads, yet our highways are allowed to go from bad to worse. What is everybody's business is nobody's business; wasteful, futile, and ridiculous methods of road repair are allowed to continue, till even the tradition of good road-making is well nigh lost. McAdam, the great father of our road-making system, used to say that no stone ought ever to be cast upon a road, for the purpose of repairing it, which could not be put in a man's mouth. The reason is obvious; small stones under the pressure of the traffic fit each other's angles, and in a short time form a mass nearly as hard as solid granite. Large stones, on the contrary, leave great gaps between their angles which hold the wet and break up the roadway, and, finally grinding upon each other, force the upper layer out above the surface. Carriage wheels are thus alternately lifted up into the air and brought down with a jerk, till the whole surface of the road is roughened. Not only is the present plan inefficacious, it is expensive as well. Twice as much material is used as would make a good roadway, and repairs have to be done very much more frequently than would be necessary if a proper system were adopted from the first.

Though the whole community are interested in the goodness of the roads, it is easy to see that the man who is dragged through ruts and over stones by the labour of his horse is not quite so keen in his appreciation of a bad road as the man who feels its effects in an aching spine and twisted muscles. So cycling roadsters, after a considerable amount of preliminary growling, have girded up their loins for action. At the beginning of 1885, or the end of 1884, a meeting was called by the Birmingham Local Centre of the N.C.U. to discuss the question, and, if possible, devise a remedy. Somewhat to the surprise of those who called the meeting, it was attended not only by cyclists, but by horse-owners and horse-users in considerable numbers; and it was generally agreed, after lengthened deliberation, that the law was not so much at fault as the administration of it. The great difficulty was, and will no doubt continue to be, to get public opinion to bear upon a matter of rather dry detail. I venture to suggest the formation of a National Society for road reform, and I am sure that we can promise the hearty co-operation of a large body of cyclists to anyone sufficiently patriotic to set the scheme on foot. The Birmingham meeting made a small, but only a small, beginning. Eight road surveyors were summoned for neglecting to keep their roads in proper repair. The magistrates, who were informed that the prosecution was undertaken in no spirit of vindictiveness, but only to test the state of the law, eventually gave the defendants time till the second week of February in the following year, 1886, to put their roads in order. I have not learnt what the result of the proceeding has been, or whether the Birmingham roads are any better than they were. In any case a national movement is necessary if anything is to be done on an effective scale. Since these lines were in type the N. C. U. have appointed a special Committee to act jointly with a similar Committee of the C.T.C., and the joint Committee have commenced active operations under the title of the 'Roads Improvement Association,' which earnestly requests advice and co-operation from influential members of the two cycling institutions.[1]

Several meetings have been held in various parts of the country, pamphlets on road repair have been circulated by the N. C. U. and C. T. C., and the work is being pushed steadily ahead. With the Halesowen precedents to quote, the road surveyors in many districts are listening to the N. C.U. requests for the improvement of the highways.

That something worth doing could be achieved if proper action were taken is proved by the following instance. In the Donington Trust road, at about the time when the old road trusts came to an end, it was found that on the highways which for the last six years of the trust had been in the skilled hands of a civil engineer instead of a non-professional road surveyor, an annual saving had been accomplished of over 267*l*. per annum over twenty-six miles of road ; while at the same time the roads were so much improved that a horse could draw twice as great a load as before.

It is now about four-and-twenty years since the old Turnpike Trust Acts began to expire. Sir George Grey was then at the Home Office : about the same time the formation of highway districts became permissive. Owing to that permissive character, and to the fact that the rating in unions and parishes is very unequal, only about one-third of the parishes in England are included in highway districts. From the year 1864 annual Turnpike Trust Continuance Acts have been passed. In the Bill of 1870, a clause threw the maintenance of the

---

[1] The result has been the formation of an Association for Roads improvement, under powerful auspices.

disturnpiked roads, of which there were at that time about 1,800 miles, not upon the parishes through which they ran, but upon the highway districts, wherever such existed. The entire cost thrown upon the county rate by the Disturnpiking Act has been computed at 200,000*l*. annually, and in many districts the highway rate has been increased threefold.

It will thus be seen that there are plenty of anomalies to be dealt with and many hardships to be redressed by the action of such a society as we have suggested.

That part of the cycling sport which relates to racing no doubt appears to assume, from its public character, a degree of importance disproportionate to the numbers of those who engage in it. Yet it is well worthy of attention, being both amusing in itself and productive of great good to the general body of cyclists who care nothing about racing. It is on the racing path where new inventions are tried, and improvements accepted.

If a new machine or a new detail for adding to the efficiency of an old one passes the fiery ordeal of the cycling experts, it is sure to come into favour with the outside cycling public within a short time. A cycling race meeting is in itself a spectacle well worth seeing. We cannot help thinking that many who know and care nothing about such meetings would, if once they attended a good one, think well of the sport they afford. The pace is good, indeed considering the distances run it may fairly be called unequalled. The best horse ever foaled would be beaten to a hopeless standstill not only by the winner, but by the last man who passes the post in a fifty miles championship race. Still more would this be the case if the race were for a distance of a hundred miles ; in fact, recorded times of horses and cyclists show that after about twenty miles the horse slowly but surely falls behind.

The racing path is usually a cinder track, about a quarter of a mile in length, and square, or rather oval, in form. Owing to the high speed maintained the corners must be rounded off, even though the general shape of the ground should be square.

THE FINISH OF A RACE

INTRODUCTORY.

The cinder track is carefully prepared, and on the morning of a considerable race meeting presents a beautifully firm and even surface. The distances are scrupulously measured at a distance of one foot from the inside of the track, and a small block of wood, let into the turf at the side, records the number of yards from the starting-post. These permanent marks are necessary, because at all race meetings, excepting only the annual championships, each competitor is allowed by the official handicapper of the N. C. U. a certain number of yards start, according to the nature of his public performances. In championships all start level, and if, as is generally the case, the competitors are sufficiently numerous, the races are run in heats with seldom more than three competitors in each. The result is that in races of five or ten miles the best men left in, who perhaps have to compete in two heats and a final, have to cover a great distance at top-speed before their evening's work is over. The tricycle 25 miles championship of 1885 was one of the prettiest contests ever seen. It was fought out between G. Gatehouse, of the Cambridge University Bicycle Club, and R. H. English, of the North Shields B. C.

The scene of the contest was the ground of the Crystal Palace, where the track lies round the ornamental water known as the Intermediate Lake. The ground slopes sharply up from the track in all directions, making a large amphitheatre of somewhat more than a quarter of a mile in diameter. On the north side nearest to the Palace are situated the grand stand and various other buildings which are used by the spectators or the competitors. A little on one side are the stands allotted to the press and the public, and further on again are the dressing-rooms in which the competitors arrange the shower-baths, rubbing-rooms, and other toilet requisites dear to the athletic mind. This description will stand with few variations for that of most of the tracks where cycling races are decided; but it is rare on this or any other path to see a contest such as that of which we are now speaking. It is not unusual for one or other of the competitors to decide on riding a waiting race. The leader not finding himself pressed, does not hurry himself—a comparative term, not inconsistent with the keeping up of a good steady pace of eighteen or nineteen miles an hour. The result is, or so say the public (who could not themselves go ten miles an hour to save their lives), a slow race. But in this particular instance nothing of the kind took place. Both men started at a pace which was simply astonishing. In a few minutes, competitors, noted for their powers of speed and endurance, were left hopelessly behind by the two riders who alone, as was seen from the first, were 'in it.' Mile after mile was passed in the fastest time on record, and still the speed of these marvellous young athletes kept on undiminished. Twenty-four miles and three-quarters were thus covered, and the leaders never at any time were more than three yards apart. They occasionally passed each other, and in the intervals the leading man had his opponent close to his hind wheel. The spurt which the winner put on at the end of the last quarter-mile, which landed him the winner by a few yards, was a sight to be seen once in a lifetime. Mr. Gatehouse has since ridden twenty miles and more—the details will be found farther on—within the hour on a tricycle; the first who has ever performed the feat, though it has been done many times on the bicycle.

I never can understand why cycle racing has not yet become more in vogue than it is among fashionable people, who are always on the look-out for some new excitement. The scene is generally a pretty one, the grounds on which the meeting is held are usually picturesquely situated, the racing is first-rate, and, unlike some other competitions of which we occasionally hear, one may be perfectly certain that the best man will win.

It is greatly to the credit of cycling that nothing in the nature of a 'ring' has ever been allowed to be established. There is little or no betting, and there are none of the sights which make many racecourses, especially racecourses in the vicinity of towns, unfitted for the presence of ladies. They are meetings purely for sport, and if once their attractiveness was discovered, I do not doubt that they would take a very prominent place among the sports which people crowd to see.

So jealous have cyclists been as to the purity of their favourite sport, that a battle royal has been waged in recent times on the subject which no doubt has occasionally attracted the reader's attention in the newspapers, and caused him to wonder what all the disturbance was about. It is that which is known among cyclists as the 'maker's amateur' question. One of the fundamental canons of cycling law is, that no man, calling himself an amateur, may compete for a money prize, or in any way make a money profit, out of his cycling prowess. If he does, he forfeits his amateur status, and can thenceforth only race as a professional. Makers of cycling machines naturally look upon it as of great importance to have their machines ridden by the best performers, and to see them win as often as possible. To build a machine good enough to win a championship race is the best form of advertisement that could possibly occur to a maker, and he would adopt any honourable means of achieving that distinction. This is only reasonable, and indeed praiseworthy; but it came to pass in process of time that a line of conduct was adopted which, though not discreditable to the makers, who might naturally be supposed to do the best they could for their own interests, was not quite so worthy of praise when practised by racing cyclists. A class of men calling themselves amateurs and competing in amateur races, were known, or at least shrewdly suspected, to accept money from manufacturers for riding their machines. If anything of the kind was really done, it was obviously a matter very difficult to detect, and also one that was very unfair to the real amateurs who raced for a love of the sport, and for honour and glory only. The latter were at a great disadvantage; occupied during the day in business pursuits of various kinds, they were unable to give the same exclusive attention to training as those who devoted their time to it professionally. Besides, amateurs naturally wished to keep amateur races to themselves, not merely for social reasons, but because it might reasonably be supposed that persons who would race under false colours would not improbably carry their inaccuracies even farther. The result was a series of protests, an examination by a committee of the N. C. U., and the disqualification of a considerable number of the racing men whose names had been prominently mentioned.

Besides the amateur performers, there is, especially in the Northern and Midland counties, a considerable professional body, to whom, as to professionals in other sports, the rules about money prizes and gate-money do not apply. It is, however, remarkable that the best performances of the professionals do not, except in a very few distances, exceed that of the amateurs. Cycling is not like billiards, in which professional performers are far and away in advance of all competitors. The performances of amateurs surpass at most distances those of their professional rivals, and, as a rule, at distances over twenty-five miles up to a hundred the record is held by amateurs.

I do not know whether any other opportunity will present itself of discussing a subject on which a considerable amount of nonsense is occasionally talked. I mean the possibility of applying electricity to tricycles. We often read that such a machine is on the point of being perfected, and there follows incontinently a great deal of quite unwarranted speculation in the newspapers as to the way in which the new adaptation of motive power will revolutionise locomotion. Fancy runs away with enthusiastic scribes, who declare that a man will be able to run from the Land's End to John o' Groat's, surmounting the most difficult hills that are encountered on the way, with an ease greater than the most accomplished cyclist can now attain to. This assumption is altogether beside the mark. The truth is that it would be quite easy to construct such a carriage, but that, as far as the ordinary cyclist is concerned, it would be absolutely useless when made. As a toy to run over a track, fitted beforehand with the necessary appliances, or between two points at which ample engine and electrical-power was available, the design of such a carriage would present no difficulty. I will produce a dozen members of the 'Dynamicable Society' who will be happy to construct one at the shortest notice. There is only one objection. It would be utterly useless when made. It would not pay. That is, for the same expense that the cost and maintenance of it would require, greatly superior modes of locomotion could be provided, whether horse or steam power, that would be available for general use, instead of the extremely limited service which could be obtained from the electric machine. The limitations of which I speak depend on electrical considerations which may in future be somewhat modified but can never be entirely removed. It must be clearly understood that I am not speaking of electrical traction generally, in which I am a firm believer, and which I think is destined at no distant time to revolutionise our known modes of locomotion. I speak only of electrical traction as applied to tricycles such as are now in ordinary use.

The reasons on which these remarks are founded will be better understood if we examine the conditions on which electrical traction is possible. To make an electrical carriage travel you must have two things—(1) a motor to communicate motion to the wheels, and (2) either a dynamo or a battery of electrical storage cells popularly known as accumulators, to communicate energy to the motor, and (3) a steam engine or gas engine, to drive the dynamo, and charge the accumulators. It would be impossible in practice to carry on the tricycle itself a dynamo to impart mechanical energy to your motor, because the dynamo must itself be driven by a gas or steam engine, and if you employed either the one or the other, it would be easier, cheaper, and more economical from a mechanical point of view, to drive by steam or gas power direct, without any dynamo at all. Besides, the weight would put an engine and dynamo out of the question for a tricycle. Accumulators only need be taken into consideration.

The electrical energy to be obtained from a given accumulator is proportionate to the weight of the metal plates forming the cell. At present one of the best known and trusted forms of storage cell in the market is that known as E.P.S. : the cell made by the Electric Power and Storage Company. I do not say it is the best. Who shall decide when doctors disagree? I am myself inclined to believe, and indeed have reason experimentally to feel convinced, that we can get a greater power in proportion to weight than is given by this cell ; but in our present state of electrical knowledge the E.P.S. is a fair cell to take as a standard. A single E.P.S. cell is known when fully charged to give one electrical horse-power of energy for one hour, with a weight of between 70 and 80 lbs. If used at full power for an hour this cell will run down, and will have to be re-charged from a steam-engine and a dynamo before it is again used. If used at half-power the cell would last without re-charging for two hours ; and so on in proportion.

Suppose the weight of your tricycle to be 90 lbs., and a single cell, or a lot of small cells, to be 70 lbs. ; your motor and machinery could not possibly be less than 50 lbs., which makes up 210 lbs. Taking the rider at ten stone, the total weight to be driven would be at least 350 lbs. ; and as an ordinary cyclist finds it as much as he can conveniently do to propel his own weight and a machine of 80 lbs., we may fairly assume that the electrical tricycle would require half a horse-power to drive it efficiently. The one horse-power of electrical energy at the rider's disposal would therefore last about two hours, and would then be exhausted.

For electrical reasons, it would be requisite to have more than one cell, because you could not get the full amount of efficiency out of your motor unless it was wound in such a manner as to take a current of higher tension than would be given by a single cell. But it is not necessary to go into that. I assume that one horse-power for one hour can be got with a weight of 70 lbs. If at any time the electrical energy fails, the rider will be obliged to drive by his unassisted exertion a machine of 210 lbs.; which, as any cyclist knows, would be too much for the strength of any ordinary person. The ordinary machine weighs no more than between 80 and 90 lbs.

But the contingency of the electric energy failing would occur as a matter of course at the end of a couple of hours, for by that time the stored electricty would be exhausted. Unless at the end of that time the traveller was fortunate enough to find himself in the immediate neighbourhood of some person possessed of (1) a steam-engine, (2) a dynamo, and last, but not least, the accommodating disposition which would prompt him to place these advantages at the disposal of the passing cyclist, he would have to stop, or else trust to his muscles. Even if a good Samaritan with an engine and dynamo were available, the traveller's troubles would by no means be at an end; for he would have to wait while his accumulators were being re-charged. This is a long process taking eight or nine hours. If his two hours' run had taken him twenty miles from home, by the time he started on his journey for another stage, he would have been ten hours on the road, and would have travelled at the average speed of two miles an hour. At this rate he would take nineteen days, travelling day and night, to go from the Land's End to John o' Groat's; and as the distance has already been performed in five days and some hours on a tricycle, and in even less time on a bicycle, the existing record time would not be broken by such a performance; and to do the journey even in nineteen or twenty days he would have to provide an engine and dynamo ready to his hand at the end of every twenty miles; which is absurd, as the great mathematician Euclid learnedly remarks in his celebrated thesis 'De ponte asinorum.'

Doubtless it would be open to the owner of the electric tricycle to disregard electric horse-power, and proceed on his journey by the aid of such man-power as nature has gifted him withal; but in that case he had better discard his electric carriage, and get a lighter one. It is possible, no doubt, that in the distant future, the use of electricity may be so generally diffused that accumulators may be found everywhere available and ready charged; as a glass of beer and a crust of bread and cheese are now. It is, however, hardly worth while to speculate about possibilities which depend for their fulfilment on a total reversal of the present habits of the people.

As regards *the construction* of an electric carriage, there is really no insurmountable difficulty whatever. It is quite possible that along given lines of road electric carriages, whose arrivals and departures are carefully arranged for beforehand, may travel expeditiously and economically, but that has nothing to do with what men usually mean when they talk of electric tricycles.

It is also quite possible that even now a proprietor or manager of works where steam and electric energy are always available and constantly in use, and who has a round of twenty miles or so to make every day, might conveniently adopt an electric tricycle as a means of locomotion. In that case all the conditions of success would be at hand. After the daily round the accumulators could be re-charged; but even here there is a good deal to be said in favour of a horse and a comfortable carriage behind it. The insoluble problem of an electric tricycle may be stated in a few words as follows: *How to have electric energy always at hand, and always available.*

Among other institutions which have been called into existence by the requirements of the cycling world, are a number of newspapers, magazines and annuals which deal almost entirely with the events and gossip of cycling life. With the exception of one or two which have a more stable existence, the newspapers die, amalgamate, and reappear in new dresses so often, that it is difficult to say with any certainty how many of them there are. In the early days, when everybody was learning to ride, and all who had taken to the wheel were busily engaged in designing new dresses, and inventing new dodges to add to the comfort of the rider, letters, editorial comments, and leaders appeared from week to week which were amusing and readable. But the best way of doing everything was at length fairly

INTRODUCTORY.

established, and it became more and more difficult from week to week to write anything new. It was a critical time for the Cycling press, and it has not as yet finally discovered a way out of the difficulty. The imperative demand for 'copy' is sometimes satisfied by personalities, which are inexpressibly dreary to outsiders. Even more dreary are the jokes, which refer to persons and events not generally intelligible, and are worse than the personalities. There is evidence that the leading cycling papers have been induced, by the good sense of their editors, and the opinions of the majority of their subscribers, to turn away from these defects, and revert to the healthy condition which distinguished cycling journalism when it was in the hands of a small knot of clever pioneers. As the sport spreads and cycling events of various kinds take place in all parts of the kingdom, it is increasingly difficult to supervise the lucubrations of an extended staff: but if cycling journalism is to become all that its well-wishers hope and anticipate for it, the effort must be resolutely made.

The thoughtful observer may draw for himself, from the pages of these weekly papers, a tolerably vivid picture of the social organisation which has sprung up through the intervention of cycling. The first point that suggests itself is the extent to which club life has taken possession of the younger members. Almost every village now has its cycling club, and in the towns, the accidental camaraderie afforded by a common pursuit seems to have afforded just that degree of impulse which was necessary to induce the formation and preserve the cohesion of such associations. Apart from politics as cycling necessarily is, and apart too from mere sociality, though it lends itself easily to the encouragement of social meetings of the youth of both sexes, it is difficult to find outside of cycling any inducement, operative all the year round, for the formation of clubs such as are now so common. A cricket club in January would be an absurdity, and, besides, cricket, good game as it is, does not include the gentler sex among its votaries. The reverse is the case with cycling; and anyone who will take the trouble to study the cycling papers in the winter time will see that not only do the ladies of the cycling world join in the club life to which they are by this means almost for the first time admitted, but they make their presence and influence felt in a variety of ways. In a number of a cycling paper now before me, dated on a certain winter day, there are descriptions of not one, but of half a dozen, dances given under the auspices of one or other of the well-known cycling clubs. The ladies' column, edited generally by a lady, does not omit to chronicle amongst other and less weighty matters the pretty toilettes which have figured at these entertainments, or to discuss with an authority to which male writers could never pretend, details of feminine cycling outfit.

Besides these dances every club has its dinners and social meetings of various kinds, and the speeches at these entertainments figure often at a considerable length in the cycling papers. It may be noted as a matter of satisfaction that, although all shades of politics must almost necessarily be represented at gatherings like these, the toasts and speeches are, without any exception that has ever come under my observation, enthusiastically loyal. The speeches naturally refer for the most part to local matters, the merits of the energetic Captain of the club, the perfect amiability under provocation of the long-suffering Honorary Secretary, or perchance the health is proposed of some local flier who has carried off an important contest on road or path. These and trade advertisements, descriptions of mechanical improvements, or of patented nicknacks related to cycling machines, and in some instances a well-written series of papers on mechanics, photography, or some branch of physics which might prove valuable to the cycling public, form the staple of the weekly sheets. In the number which chances to be before us the festivity fixtures occupy a whole closely printed column. There are three or four columns of editorial gossip about cycling matters, not only in this country, but also on the continent and in America. Then follow half a dozen columns of paragraphs twenty lines long giving an account of the proceedings of the more important clubs, their dinners, elections, and preparations for the next season, a balance sheet of the N. C. U. Reserve Fund, with a stirring appeal from Major-General Christopher, a veteran who with almost boyish enthusiasm has devoted a large amount of his leisure, and his experience gained in the larger field of Indian administration, to the advancement of the interests of cycling. Then come columns devoted to the reports of 'own correspondents' in the various local centres of the N. C. U. There is a column devoted to inventions and inventors, and a goodly array of illustrated advertisements which shows that the circulation of the paper must suggest satisfactory reflections to the proprietors.

There is one reflection which can hardly fail to suggest itself to a recent arrival in Cyclonia, and that is the strange but undeniable fact that every third cyclist is a photographer. Perhaps photographer is too harsh a term to apply to these well-meaning persons; the justice of the case would be met in most instances by describing them as dabblers in photography. They are for the most part harmless, and operate chiefly on each other, and on their friends and relations. It is to be hoped, by those who are interested in such matters, that future generations may not be reduced to the necessity of taking their impressions of the personal appearance of the greater lights of cycling from these libellous productions. The advertising columns of the cycling papers are full of announcements of photographic materials fitted for conveyance on tricycles. The way in which cameras fold up into impossible dimensions, and so to speak almost annihilate space, is among the things no fellow can understand. I have never myself encountered one of these artists at work, but I have been told that the camera is designed to screw on to the wheel, the machine itself forming a tripod stand, and that a number of sensitive plates can be stowed away inside the backbone, or at least quite out of sight: but that perhaps is an exaggeration.

It should not be omitted while discussing the subject of cycling journalism that some of the periodicals are adorned with excellent illustrations. It is not so easy as it might seem—or if it be easy it is not often done—to draw a tricycle correctly; it need not be said that any carelessness in that respect would not be tolerated by a society of experts like those to whom the artist referred to appeals, and so his tricycles, and other cycles too, are models of correct design, and what is more, the riders of them satisfy by their correct positions on their iron steeds the strictest requirements of the most classical masters of the art. The Christmas number of 'The Cyclist' for 1885, written by Messrs. A. J. Wilson and Morrison, and illustrated by Mr. George Moore, illustrated in verse and prose, and with pen and pencil, a journey through the imaginary kingdom of Cyclonia. It was a clever squib on things and persons best known among the world of cyclists. Among notable cycling productions there should also be mentioned one which has gone through several editions, and is indeed almost, as its title indicates, indispensable to those who wish to understand the mechanism of tricycles, or to know the history of the trade—I mean Mr. Henry Sturmey's 'Indispensable Handbook both for the Bicycle and the Tricycle.' But the bibliography of the sport will be found elsewhere in these pages, so here I will say no more.

REST ON A RIVER BANK.

CHAPTER II.

HISTORICAL.

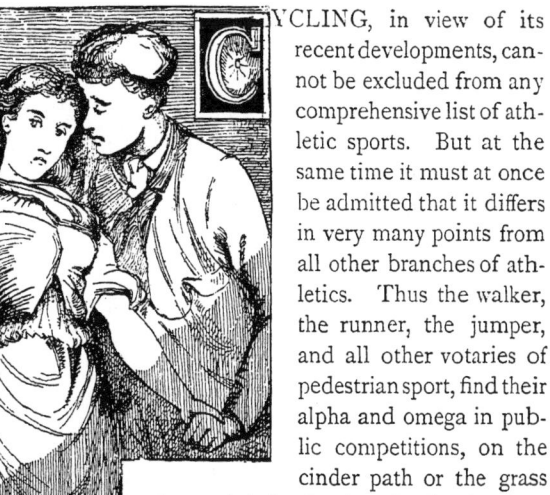

CYCLING, in view of its recent developments, cannot be excluded from any comprehensive list of athletic sports. But at the same time it must at once be admitted that it differs in very many points from all other branches of athletics. Thus the walker, the runner, the jumper, and all other votaries of pedestrian sport, find their alpha and omega in public competitions, on the cinder path or the grass plot, and their exercises for the development of their powers, in one direction or another, are engaged in solely with a view to complete their preparation for some forthcoming contest. Although these exercises undoubtedly conduce to a healthy habit of body, sound wind, and strong, muscular limbs, yet beyond this very great gain, athletics, as such, fulfil no purpose of value to the community at large, and least of all an economic one. The cycling sport, on the other hand, has an economic side, which in real value, in its relations to everyday life, far exceeds the merely competitive developments of the pursuit; and were cycle racing, in all its branches, utterly abolished to-morrow, the interest in, and more particularly the practical value of, the sport would still continue unabated, owing to the fact that it possesses certain solid advantages which really constitute the life and soul of its particularly vigorous and healthy existence. The economic side of the sport so much insisted on may be found in the practical use of the wheel in daily life; its hygienic value as a means primarily of healthy exercise is recognised and proved by the personal and practical experiences of thousands of people throughout the world, to whom a little exercise, combined as it is with a little pleasurable and stimulating excitement, is of the very greatest value from a medical point of view. Last, but by no means least, must be considered its great convenience in the stern business of life, whether as a means of economy in time or in money. The number of clergymen who use the tricycle in the discharge of their parish duties, and find in the silent carriage, always ready at a moment's notice, the most useful and convenient of vehicles for their work, is very large; but no more need be added to what has been already said as to the economic side of the sport, as the most casual investigation will at once demonstrate clearly the growing value of the machine.

It is intended to chronicle in the following pages the past of the sport which promises to have so remarkable a future, and we may begin by remarking that the bicycle of the present day is a descendant in the right line of the 'dandy,' or 'hobby horse' of 1819, so successfully and unmercifully caricatured in the facetious prints of about that date. The 'hobby horse' was a foreign introduction, having been brought from France, where its use had been almost stopped by the bitter satire and the fierce ridicule which met its users. The machine was introduced under the name of the 'Draisnene,' or 'célérifère,' the first name being derived from the alleged inventor, but probably only the first introducer of the hobby horse into England, who is in contemporary records called impartially Baron von Draise, Baron de Drais, M. Draise, and is said to have come from Mannheim, or from Frankfort-on-the-Main. He at any rate introduced into England from France the 'hobby horse.' This machine consisted of two stout equal-sized wooden wheels

CARRIER TRICYCLE.

held in iron forks, the rear fork being securely bolted to a stout bar of wood, 'the perch'; whilst the front fork passed through the perch, and was so arranged that it could be turned by a handle, so as to steer the machine after the manner of a modern bicycle, though of course the construction was much more clumsy and complicated. In the middle of the perch or longitudinal bar was placed a cushion, on which the rider sat; and just in front of this was another and smaller cushion raised on a bracket, on which he leaned his chest. The feet, when the rider was seated astride this contrivance, just touched the ground comfortably, and he propelled the machine by running with long and forcible strides, the machine of course progressing between the strokes and of its own accord down hill. If the contemporary sketches are any guide, this was always done at a breakneck pace; in fact, none of the earlier dandy horses had any breaks fitted to them, and, owing to their great weight, there is little doubt that they must have rushed down the hills in a somewhat startling manner. The exercise was, as may easily be imagined, by no means graceful, and those who indulged in it got unmercifully laughed at, one wit defining hobby-horse users as riding in their own carriages and walking in the mud at the same time. A glance at the caricatures of the period, of which there is a good collection in the British Museum, will show to what an extent the novel exercise must have been taken up. In one graphic sketch the blacksmiths of a posting village are seen pursuing the hobby riders, upsetting them and smashing their machines to pieces with hammers, the inscription showing that this was done because the hobby never required shoeing, whilst a glance at a genuine hobby, several good specimens of which exist, demonstrates the fact that, unlike their successors of 1885, the blacksmiths of 1819 could hardly have earned anything for the repair of break-downs, the sturdy proportions of the machine looking as if they would defy all attempts to injure it; albeit the spectator naturally wonders what would have been the fate of an unfortunate rider who got mixed up with the clumsy and heavy vehicle in the case of a fall. Unmercifully lampooned and ridiculed, the beaux and dandies of the day soon dropped this somewhat laborious exercise, and the hobby disappeared almost entirely from public view. A few yet remained, and were ridden by a small body of enthusiasts who still hoped to popularise the sport. But the jar of the iron-tired wheels, and the peculiarly awkward position (which tended to produce hernia), soon obtained for the machine a very bad name, and its use gradually lapsed. Still, eleven years after the great hobby year of 1819, namely in 1830, it is recorded that certain 'improved dandy horses' were issued to the postmen in a rural district, where, doubtless, they were used for many years, but they were not replaced as they wore out, and the postmen had once again to trudge on foot.

It was not until two or three years prior to the Great Exhibition of 1862 that the first real advance is recorded towards the production of the bicycle of to-day. 'Velocipedes' or 'carriages to go without horses,' 'manivelociters,' 'bivectors' 'trivectors,' 'accelerators,' 'allepodes,' had one after another been brought before the public, as the latest and most valuable invention in this direction. Some of the designs were marvellous in their impracticability. One, for example, was a full-sized coach with accommodation for six persons, one of whom steered from the box, four passengers sat inside, and the whole was to be driven by means of two foot levers *by one footman*, who was to stand in full uniform at the back of the coach as footmen usually do. This unfortunate is represented in a three-cornered hat and a laced coat, and cyclists of to-day will doubtless be ready to sympathise with the unfortunate persons who were called upon to attempt this light and easy task. A glance at some of the scientific journals of the time will show that in the early days of velocipedes inventors were as enthusiastic, in their belief in their designs, as the most impracticable of modern geniuses. Our manufacturers claim for the machines they make the highest qualities of lightness, strength and speed, ignoring the fact that the last named qualification depends upon the man, and not on the machine he rides. Inventors nowadays invariably pooh-pooh opposition, and assert the great advantages possessed by their last invention; and so, we find, did their anti-types before the bicycle was invented. Thus the following appears in No. 57 of the 'Mechanics' Magazine, Museum, Register, Journal, and Gazette,' published on Saturday, September 25, 1824:—

Self-Moving Carriage.

Mr. D. McDonald, of Sunderland, informs us that he has invented a 'Self-moving Machine' for travelling on roads, which has carried seven persons. It is propelled by means of treadles. A man sits behind working the same, and there is a fly-wheel operating upon two cog-wheels, which operate on a square axle. You will, perhaps, think the man behind has hard labour—not so. From the velocity of the fly-wheel, together with the aid of a lever, which is in the hand of a person in front steering, he has not often to put his feet to the treadles. Mr. McDonald intends, when he shall have improved the friction of the body of the carriage, to present the same to the Society of Arts; and as he desires to receive no emolument for the same, he hopes it will come into general use.

How charming was the confidence, how great the magnanimity, of Mr. McDonald! Perchance he 'improved the friction of the body of the carriage' too much; for, strange to say, it never seems to have come into the general use anticipated by its inventor. 'You will perhaps think the man behind has hard labour?' Perhaps! With seven persons in the 'self-moving' carriage it would have been doubly interesting to have heard the sentiments of 'the man behind.' In the same magazine, in its issue for September 6 of the same year, there is a record of another of these facetiously named 'self-moving carriages,' invented by a carpenter of Buckland, near Chard, which is said to have been of 'very light construction,' whilst 'K. W.,' a Welshman,' describes a lever-action machine, which accommodated two persons besides 'the one who conducted it,' and it is further stated by its inventor that it 'went with ease eight miles per hour.' This must have been under favourable circumstances, say down a very steep hill, for a steep hill only would have sufficed to overcome the friction of the numerous cogs and chains introduced into the Welshman's design. All the 'self-moving carriages' of this early date were to be propelled by levers, but there seems every probability that the credit of first applying the crank action to velocipedes belongs to an English firm, as Messrs. Mehew of Chelsea showed in the Exhibition of 1862 a three-wheeled velocipede, the front wheel

HISTORICAL.

steering as in a modern bicycle or the old dandy horse, the other two wheels, which were of course somewhat smaller, being placed side by side behind. This type is to be seen to-day in children's toy tricycles, and also at the Crystal Palace and other places where velocipedes are let out on hire by the hour. This English-made machine was fitted with a pair of cranks to the front wheel.

The hobby horse of forty years before was not forgotten, and it is more than probable that several of the visitors conceived the idea of fitting the cranks to the dandy horse from seeing the Chelsea firm's velocipede at the Exhibition, albeit there is pretty good evidence forthcoming to prove that the crank had been so adapted previously to 1862. The most generally conceded claim is that of Gavin Dalzell, a cooper of Lesmahagow, Lanarkshire, who is said to have constructed and ridden a practical bicycle in 1836. Be this as it may, the crank-fitted velocipede gave a hint to the ingenious mechanicians of this country as well as of France, and very soon crank-driven dandy horses began to make their appearance on the highways. These machines, however, were only dandy horses, and it was not till about 1866 that English athletes began to have any idea of the claims and possibilities of the new sport. About this date, a Parisian firm, Messrs. Michaux & Co., sent over to England a perfected bicycle, which was considered at that time the acme of ingenuity and lightness—it is scarcely necessary to add that the same machine would nowadays excite amusement and derision by its weight and clumsiness. It was natural that the first machines imported should find their way to the gymnasiums, and one of the earliest arrived, in January 1869, at a gymnasium conducted by Mr. Charles Spencer, who was destined to do much towards the introduction of a sport which has now taken so great a hold upon the public favour. The account which is given in an old magazine [1] of the arrival of this machine may be briefly epitomised as follows:

[1] *Ixion.*

In the early part of January, 1869 (writes 'John M., Junr.,' who may now be identified with Mr. John Mayall, Junr., the photographer of Regent Street), I was at Spencer's Gymnasium in Old Street, St. Luke's . . . when a foreign-looking packing-case was brought in. . . . As the case was opened I recognised a piece of apparatus consisting mainly of two wheels, similar to one I had seen not long before in Paris, but the one I saw in Paris was much smaller, and a lad being mounted upon it who drove the machine by putting his feet easily to the ground, I looked upon it as a mere *jouet-d'enfant* such as the Parisians are so clever in designing. It produced but little impression on me, and certainly did not strike me as being a new means of locomotion. A slender young man, whom I soon came to know as Mr. Turner of Paris, followed the packing-case and superintended its opening; the gymnasium was cleared, Mr. Turner took off his coat, grasped the handles of the machine, and with a short run, to my intense surprise, vaulted on to it, and, putting his feet on the treadles, made the circuit of the room. We were some half-dozen spectators, and I shall never forget our astonishment at the sight of Mr. Turner whirling himself round the room, sitting on a bar above a pair of wheels in a line that ought, as we innocently supposed, to fall down immediately he jumped off the ground. Judge then of our greater surprise when' instead of stopping by tilting over on one foot, he slowly halted, and turning the front wheel diagonally, remained quite still, balancing on the wheels.

'John M., Junr.'s' experiences are curious as illustrating the fact which so few can realise nowadays, that at that time the possibility of remaining on two wheels arranged bicycle-wise was not recognised. This writer's ideas of riding at this early stage were confined to a conviction that he must hold the handle straight, in a most unyielding manner; but he soon mastered the machine sufficiently to ride from London to Red Hill, in an attempt to get to Brighton, and he returned from Red Hill by train, exhausted and covered with dust and glory.

Such, then, was the advent of the bicycle. These earlier machines were of great weight and very strong, calculated to carry the heaviest of mortals with safety, a radical fault which speedily began to be corrected, the riders of the machine, even at this early period, having a very clear appreciation of the value of lightness in the vehicles they had to propel. English manufacturers very soon began to take up the business, and, with characteristic thoroughness, went in for improvements from the first. Capital was invested, plant laid down, and a rapid change took place. The French vehicles, light as they were by comparison with the old velocipedes and dandy horses, were soon surpassed by the English-made goods. The French machines were indeed regarded merely as toys, and the manufacturers, with the experiences of the dandy horse before them, thought that the new fancy would die out as rapidly as did the earlier one; but their English *confrères* with greater perspicuity saw that the new machine had a great future before it, and made their arrangements accordingly.

The earliest enterprises of note in connection with the manufacture of cycles were started in Coventry. The trade in woollen and worsted stuffs of this city and of the county of Warwickshire was at one time very extensive, but it gradually decreased owing to the establishment of an important branch of the ribbon trade, employing at one time 17,000 or 18,000 looms. This latter branch of industry had been much depressed, partly through foreign competition, and other branches of business were similarly affected. The city was therefore eager to welcome a new enterprise, and, the bicycle having attracted a good deal of attention, it was taken up by the late James Starley and other ingenious inventors, and Coventry soon became noted for the excellent machines which were despatched from its workshops, as they were a great improvement upon the imported specimens. 'The city of spires,' as Coventry is called (from the three spires which stand close together; two of them belonging to the two parish churches which stand side by side in one churchyard, and the third to a church long since demolished, the three forming a conspicuous landmark from whichever direction Coventry is approached) thus became the metropolis of the cycling trade, and the centre from which thousands of the best machines are distributed annually throughout the civilised world, and, as a natural sequence, the headquarters of the largest and most widely circulated of the many papers devoted to the interests of the sport, 'The Cyclist.' The influence of intelligent manufacture, combined with the resources of capital, was soon recognised in the English-made machines, and the bicycle daily became more widely popular. In a very short time it may be said to have fully established itself in England. The three- and four-wheeled velocipedes of a former day fell rapidly into disuse, and the light and speedy two-wheeler grew as quickly in public favour. The bicycle was soon encountered in every part of the kingdom. Many a good story is told of its first appearances in out of the way places. *Punch's* benighted countryman, bolting from an apparition which 'looked like a man a-ridin upon nawthin,' illustrated but one phase of the astonishment with which people regarded the novelty. Another amusing circumstance marked the introduction to the bicycle of one who has since proved an ardent votary of the machine. The gentleman in question, having encountered a bicycle in the city for the first time, described, and eventually drew it, for the edification of a party of friends who were dining at his father's house. He was immediately and emphatically snubbed by a rude, if learned, philosopher, who clearly demonstrated to the entire satisfaction of every one present the utter impossibility of the thing described being accomplished. The youth, naturally irritated at the doubt cast upon his assertions, or the accuracy of his powers of observation, sought for and eventually found a rider of the new machine. He rapidly learned to master it, and his first lengthy trip was a round of calls at the houses of the guests at the eventful dinner party, the learned philosopher being of course the first visited and favoured with a practical illustration of the fallacy of his theories. The growth of the sport in public favour was very rapid, and cautious observers again began to remind manufacturers and cyclists of the fate of the hobby horse, and to prognosticate the early fall of the bicycle from its mushroom elevation in the minds of the public; but, just at this time, when a slight lull in the interest occurred, the records of several feats of long-distance road-riding found their way into the papers, and at once opened the eyes of the public to the fact that the toy of the hour possessed solid advantages which would ensure for it a permanent place amongst the pastimes of the age. A machine, of whatever type, which would enable a man to ride forty, fifty, or even sixty miles in a day, with comparative ease and comfort, must, the observers argued, be of some service, and accordingly every day brought fresh recruits to the cycling teachers to acquire a practical acquaintance with, and take an active part in, the new sport.

In the meantime the makers were by no means idle, and various modifications of the original machine were rapidly introduced. The large back wheel was one of the first points altered, the heavy solid backbone was soon replaced by a tube, whilst hickory wheels and iron tires scarcely survived the first three months; and all these vast improvements upon the old machine were but embryos of the novelties of to-day. The heavy piece of gaspipe has developed into the scientifically constructed tapered backbone. The lightening of this part of the machine soon led to the lightening of the wheels, which began to be constructed of wire on the suspension principle, and known as 'spider wheels.' These soon superseded the dished hickory wheels, so much admired by the early riders of the bone-shaker. The iron tire was necessarily incompatible with the light iron wheel; rubber tires were introduced, and thus improvement after improvement was devised, until the invention of the step made it possible to mount still higher wheels.

The pioneer makers deserve the gratitude of the cyclists of to-day. In very many cases it would have paid them best to stand still, but instead of so doing they went on improving, although each improvement possibly converted into waste iron sets of castings and elaborate machines used in construction. Competition was not by any means so severe in those days, and in most cases the makers laboured *con amore*, spending their time and money in carrying out experiments and inventing methods of perfecting the machine.

Many ingenious mechanicians laboured at this time in the field of cycling invention, prominent amongst them being Mr. James Starley. Keen of apprehension, fertile in expedients, Mr. Starley had been for a long while mixed up with business in Coventry, principally directing his attention to the development of sewing machines, in which he had introduced considerable improvements. He had, in addition, invented a host of useful and ingenious appliances for one purpose and another. After a time Starley settled down in the employ of the Coventry Machinist Company, then devoted to the manufacture of several classes of sewing machines, the trade having been encouraged in Coventry to find employment for a number of persons hitherto engaged in the watch trade, which was then at a very low ebb. As far back as 1865 Starley had made a velocipede with suspension wheels. It was not so marked a success as to encourage him to persevere in that direction, but in 1868 he saw a bicycle for the first time, a French-made machine having been brought to Coventry by a nephew of Mr. J. Turner, the manager of the Coventry Machinist Company. This gentleman, Mr. Rowley Turner, is probably identical with the 'Mr. Turner, of Paris,' who took a velocipede to Spencer's gymnasium. Mr. Turner was anxious to place an order for a number of these machines, and the manager of the company happily accepted it. The result was the foundation of the vast cycle trade now carried on by the company in question.

A visit to the works of Messrs. George Singer & Co., of Coventry, will at once give a stranger an idea of the extent of the cycling trade. Established in 1875, Messrs. Singer & Co. did not make any speciality of racing machines until the season of 1885, having devoted their attention almost entirely to turning out all classes of road machines, bicycles, tricycles, manumotive velocipedes, children's velocipedes, and in short every description, the number of patterns made being remarkable. The works in Alma Street are excellently arranged. Entering through a large hall, partly occupied by a clerks' office through want of more accommodation, the visitor passes into the large shop, on either side of which are to be seen storerooms containing an apparently inexhaustible supply of parts and fittings, piles of castings, bundles of steel tubing, coils of wire, lengths of iron material, indiarubber tires, all stacked ready for use ; whilst in every room not otherwise used may be seen, in the spring of the year, hundreds of completed machines packed as closely as they will go, ready to be dispatched from the great packing-room across the road—which is the old Coventry Rink—now converted into a cycle shop, where machines of all classes are daily being packed and dispatched to every part of the globe. In the main shop all the operations for the production of the various machines are to be seen going on with steady activity. Here is a workman drilling holes in a hub with the aid of a machine which not only drills them at the proper angle, but spaces them as well. Another is running the thread of the screw on to the spoke. Yet another is heading them. And all these varied operations go on continuously and without intermission throughout the year. For during the dead season Messrs. Singer work hard to lay up the stock which is to be seen in the store-rooms early in the spring. The Premier Works are also extensive and very interesting, Mr. Hillman being responsible for a number of valuable designs. At Beeston, near Nottingham, Mr. Thos. Humber carries on the manufacture of the well-known 'Beeston Humber,' with which his name has been identified from the earliest days of cycling ; and under the eye of the original inventor, the works, a model of neatness, turn out the machines which have secured so high a reputation on both road and path. The widow of Mr. D. Rudge disposed of her late husband's business to a Coventry capitalist, who carried it on under the title of D. Rudge & Co. until the end of 1885, when the business, under the same title, was transferred to a company. The sons

F

of Mr. Starley still carry on the cycle trade in Coventry at the St. John's Works.

There are a large number of other firms engaged in the production of specialities, and so extensive is the industry that the production of minor parts and castings for the trade finds employment for large firms and much capital. Messrs. Thomas Smith & Sons, of Saltley Mill, Birmingham, supply the trade with castings and finished parts to almost any extent; Mr. W. Bown's ball-bearings have won an excellent name for themselves, and are largely adopted by the manufacturers; Messrs. Lamplugh & Brown, of Birmingham, the cyclists' saddlers, supply the trade with saddle-bags and other leather goods, requisites which have done a great deal to make riding comfortable; and a number of other instances could be given to show how great is the general demand in connexion with the cycling trade. Competition is very keen, and the result is that each maker tries to excel the others in some way. One firm makes a speciality of one class of machine, another of another, and in all cases the result is of direct benefit to the active cyclist, for any point which requires attention is instantly looked into by ingenious and clever mechanicians, and a remedy or improvement suggested. To those who have not deeply investigated the matter the price paid for machines seems high, but it must be remembered that before the cycle can be brought to the necessary pitch of excellence a vast amount of money has to be spent in experiments, and every small item of alteration or improvement may throw out of use machines or parts which lie ready to hand: thus the manufacturer is constantly finding himself burdened with obsolete patterns in castings and machines which, but a few weeks before, represented the 'latest improvements.' Moreover, the skill employed in the construction of a trustworthy machine has to be paid for, and paid for highly. Skill has much to do with it. It is perfectly well known that two workmen may be working side by side with the same materials, and that one will make a wheel which may last ten years, whilst the other may make one which will

HISTORICAL.

not stay true for ten days. The exact reason is difficult to discover, but the fact remains; and, as no test but a practical one is of any service in these cases, it will be easily understood that the services of a good workman are not to be obtained for nothing, whilst a visit to one or other of the manufacturers mentioned above will demonstrate the circumstance that many machines and much skill and ingenuity have to be exercised before the modern cycle can be placed satisfactorily on the market.

A trade thus rapidly developing necessarily implied a steady and increasing demand for its productions, and that demand could only be legitimately fostered and encouraged by the performance of some noteworthy feats upon the newly-introduced machine. In the earlier days of the sport these took the form of long rides upon the roads. One of the first of such performances was a trip undertaken by certain members of the Middlesex B.C. from London to John o' Groat's House, the most northern point of the British Isles. The four tourists were Messrs. C. Spencer, Hunt, Leaver, and Wood, and the ride was begun on June 2, 1873. The machines were of the most approved type, although of course very unlike the vehicles of to-day. The four adventurous riders were accompanied for a few miles of their way by friends, but they soon distanced their escort, and, pressing on, reached Buckden in the evening, having rather injudiciously ridden sixty-five miles in the first day, this being a very notable performance at this period. On the 3rd the party rode on, and, after encountering a rustic who upset one of their number, they eventually reached Newark, the second day's journey being forty-three miles. On the 4th, Wentbridge was reached, the distance covered being forty-seven miles. June 5 proved wet and windy, and the wayfarers suffered accordingly, only accomplishing twenty-three miles, and reaching Wetherby very much exhausted. The 6th of June was more favourable, and the party covered forty-seven miles ere resting for the night at Darlington. On the 7th Newcastle was reached, distance for the day thirty-two miles;

8th, Alnwick, thirty-four miles ; 9th, Dunbar : the roads and weather being very favourable, the riders went fifty-five miles ; 10th, Edinburgh only, in very bad weather, twenty-eight miles ; 11th, Birnam, a journey of seventy miles, some part of it however being represented by the Ferry across the Firth of Forth ; 12th, Kingussie, a good ride of sixty miles ; 13th, Moy Inn, forty miles ; 14th, Dingwall, a distance of twenty-three miles ; 15th, Helmsdale, seventeen miles ; and on the 16th, fifteen days from the start, the party reached John o' Groat's House, and thus brought to a conclusion the first long-distance road ride on record. This of course attracted a great deal of attention at the time, and did much to bring home to the observant public the real value and capabilities of the bicycle.

In 1869 Mr. Mayall, junior, after his early experiences with the bicycle, determined to ride to Brighton, and this he did on February 17 of that year. He started in company with some friends, but was the only one of the party who accomplished the feat. He reached the popular watering-place in about twelve hours ; and it may be noted, as an illustration of the improved pace now achieved, that Mr. S. F. Edge, of the Surrey B.C., has recently performed the distance in 3 hrs. 18 mins. 25 secs.

The peregrinations of the members of the Canonbury Cycling Club, Messrs. H. Blackwell, junior, C. A. Harman, and others, over the London to Land's End route, the fine performances of the Hon. Ion Keith-Falconer and Mr. Lennox on bicycles, from Land's End to John o' Groat's, and the remarkable journeys over the same route of Alfred Nixon, Lawrence Fletcher, and T. R. Marriott, have constantly kept up the interest, and served to demonstrate clearly the possibilities of cycling. Mr. T. R. Marriott's ride, on a tricycle, from Land's End to John o' Groat's, a distance but little short of 900 miles, in 6 days $15\frac{1}{2}$ hours, is a marvellous exhibition of endurance, and shows what can be done on the tricycle by a good man ; and in 1886 George P. Mills, of the Anfield B.C., of Liverpool, eclipsed this grand performance by two others still more mar-

A ROAD RACE

vellous, riding on a Beeston Humber bicycle from Land's End to John o' Groat's in 5 days 1¾ hour, taking only *six hours* sleep in all *en route*, and within two or three weeks accomplishing the same journey on an Automatic tricycle under very disadvantageous circumstances as to wind and weather in 5 days 11 hours, a performance which can only be regarded as wonderful in every way.

The interest excited by the road rides was soon diverted into parallel channels, and bicycle racing became a popular branch of the sport, the public evincing great interest in the new form of athletic exercise. Early in 1869 some cycling races were held at the Crystal Palace on the top terrace (the paved one), on which the Sphinxes stand, the races being straight away, without a turn; whilst inside the Palace a velocipede show was held, in which were exhibited some wonderful manumotive carriages, notable amongst them being an eight-oared boat, mounted on wheels, and propelled by levers arranged to represent oars, the coxswain sitting at the stern of the boat and steering with straps which passed to the bow, so anxious were its inventors to maintain the aquatic parallel. On the same occasion some sports took place, riders in fancy costumes tilting at the ring and the quintain in front of the Handel Orchestra.

This description of entertainment, however, soon gave way to the more legitimate forms of racing, and meetings were held in the Agricultural Hall at Islington, and also at Nottingham, Wolverhampton, and elsewhere. It is noticeable that the above race at the Crystal Palace was one of the first meetings ever held anywhere, and that the Crystal Palace now possesses one of the best paths devoted entirely to cycle racing, on which many of the finest records of cycling have been made.

From 1869 until to-day the sport of cycle racing has continued to increase in popular favour with only one slight check in 1883, when interest somewhat waned, only to become all the stronger in 1884. The inclusion of cycling races in the programmes of athletic sports has increased the popularity of those gatherings to a marked extent, and the rapid spread of cycling has of course been much encouraged by the public performances of the racing men.

Thousands of followers of the sport first had their interest aroused by the performances of our leading path riders, noticeably by the deeds accomplished by John Keen during the time he held championship honours or shared them with F. Cooper, and also by the fine riding of the late H. L. Cortis. When that splendid cyclist first accomplished the feat, on which he had so long set his heart, of riding twenty miles in the hour, the fact was widely commented on in the public press, and of necessity drew the attention of many an outsider to the sport, whilst, as has been pointed out, the long rides of Messrs. Keith-Falconer, W. F. Sutton, and others, attracted the notice of those who took little or no interest in path work.

In the earlier days the doctors were very much opposed to cycling, a prejudice having arisen against it owing to the fact that the jerks and jars of the original boneshaker induced headache and sometimes hernia, which latter result was very common amongst constant users of the original hobby horse; but ere long many of them saw reason to modify their prejudices against the bicycle. It was not, however, until the advent of the perfected tricycle that the faculty gave their support with anything like unanimity to cycling; but when the tricycle was sufficiently perfected, a large number of medical men adopted it for their own use, and very soon saw that the sport possessed special advantages from a merely health-giving point of view. Many a business man has found in the use of the tricycle an exercise which combines healthy exertion with a certain amount of excitement and novelty, an amusement which affords the necessary exercise without being monotonous, and many instances could be quoted of its value in this connexion. One will perhaps suffice. A medical man through ill health occasioned by a carriage accident suffered from headache and nervousness, could no bear to sit in either a carriage or a railway train, and often walked long distances to avoid the dreaded methods of conveyance. One day at a friend's house he saw a tricycle, and becoming interested he ventured to try it. The exercise pleased him. He investigated the details of the machine and occasionally rode it, and one day awoke to the fact that he had covered ten miles without suffering, although his common sense told him that there was more jar about it than there would be in either a railway train or a carriage. Confidence thus established, he purchased a machine and rode continuously; his nervous affection was quite overcome, his own remark being that he was so concerned to know whether he was going to run over a chance half-brick in the road that he quite forgot that his head ought to be aching; and he eventually was able to overcome the trouble which threatened seriously to interfere with his comfort in life. This is but one of the many instances which might be quoted of the special value which the tricycle more particularly possesses in such cases. The novelty, mild excitement, and gentle exercise, all combine to make the pursuit so fascinating that the rider becomes expert while interest in the new pastime is fresh, and then, being expert, finds new pleasures in the pursuit. These advantages are daily being augmented by the improvement in the machines used. Springs are devised which will all the more effectually break the shock of the road, and every other point is a matter of constant study.

The popularity of bicycling in time led to the introduction of bicycling races, and as sketched above these events assumed considerable importance at athletic meetings, till eventually the Amateur Athletic Club decided to establish a championship, and to it belongs the credit of first recognising the claims of bicycling by establishing a four miles 'amateur championship,' which for some years, until the formation of the 'Bicycle Union,' now known as 'The National Cyclists' Union,' held its position in the world of athletics.

The popularity of the new vehicle continued to increase, whilst its economic capabilities were also fully recognised by the press. In the issue of the *Daily News* for August 23, 1876, there was a leader upon the bicycle, pointing out its various advantages, and emphatically endorsing its claim to notice. It contained *inter alia* the assertion that the bicycle 'ought to be regarded not as a mere plaything of the hour, but as a substantial addition to the conveniences of life.' A considerable advance this upon the 'Jouet d'Enfant,' from Paris!

On September 2, 1876, Messrs. Frank Smythe and W. E. N. Coston (the latter afterwards became a celebrated amateur walker) rode 205 miles in 22 hours on the road, the actual time in the saddle being 17 hours 17 minutes. This feat eclipsed Mr. H. S. Thorp's ride from London to York in $22\frac{1}{2}$ hours, the distance being $195\frac{1}{2}$ miles, which may be amusingly compared with the following announcement, a copy of which is still preserved at the 'Black Swan' at York:

YORK FOUR DAYS COACH BEGINS THE 18TH OF APRIL, 1703.

All that are desirous to pass from London to York, or from York to London, or any other place on that road, let them repair to the Black Swan in Holbourne, in London, and to the Black Swan in Coney Street, York, at each which places they may be received in a stage coach every Monday, Wednesday, and Friday, which performs the whole journey in four days, if God permits.

Rides like these naturally attracted much attention, but unhappily, then as now, there existed a number of evil-disposed persons who seemed to imagine that the bicycle had no right upon the roads, and who constantly seized every opportunity of hampering and interfering with any cyclists they chanced to meet. One very flagrant case occurred on Saturday, August 26, 1876, when the driver of the St. Albans coach lashed, with his whip, a bicyclist who was passing, whilst the guard, who had provided himself beforehand with an iron ball on the end of a rope, threw it between the spokes of the machine and dragged it and the rider to the ground. The driver was fined 2*l.* for the assault, and also paid the rider 10*l.* towards the damage to his machine, while the guard was fined 5*l*. As an outcome of this case 'a protection society for cyclists,' the embryo N.C.U., was discussed at some length in the contemporary press, but without producing any immediate result. The popularity which the little Surrey village of Ripley and its neighbourhood now enjoys (some hundreds of cyclists being accustomed to visit the place on holidays and such-like occasions) renders the following extract from a journal published in October 1876 very amusing : 'As some proof of the hold bicycling is taking as an exercise,' writes the editor, ' despite the fearful state of the roads and sky overhead, no less than thirteen men rode to Ripley and dined there on Sunday last, including two of the racers at the Oval on the previous day.'

On October 9 John Keen, the then almost invincible professional champion, rode 50 miles in 3 hrs. 6 mins. 45 secs., which was at that time a best on record, and welcomed with enthusiasm by those who followed with interest the spread of bicycling. No less than 102 race meetings were held in 1876, which demonstrates clearly the advance made, amounting to an increase of just 50 per cent. beyond the previous year, and the season closed with a marked advance in the number of cyclists and the interest taken by the general public in the new branch of athletic sport. The winter of this year was devoted by the wheelmen to discussion and debates, a style of amusement which, when confined entirely to one subject, soon palls upon the appetite, and these entertainments have long been dropped in club life in favour of more lively methods of passing the evening.

The year 1877 was destined to see a still more notable advance in the sport. In February the London B.C., an association which has always held a foremost position amongst the cycling clubs of the Metropolis, decided to promote the now celebrated 100 miles road trial from Bath to London. Although this is ostensibly a private, and altogether a club affair, the position held by the racing members of the L.B.C. has long made it one of the features of the earlier part of the season.

The rivalry between John Keen and Fred Cooper at this time ran high. The pair contested frequent races for the One Mile Professional Championship, and one athletic paper grumbled because 'twelve thousand people attended a Wolverhampton meeting to see two men ride a mile'—a somewhat amusing commentary on the rapid spread of the sport which had but a few months back been somewhat patronised by the athletic section. W. Tomes of the Portsmouth Club succeeded, in April 1877, in beating the one-mile bicycle record by no less than five seconds, his record, which was, however, soon eclipsed, standing at 3 mins. 5 secs.

The 'West Sussex Gazette,' one of the largest provincial newspapers, was much taken to task for its assertion that 60,000 machines were in use at this time in the United Kingdom, and the calculation does appear somewhat excessive for 1877. On September 7 of this year the 'Daily Telegraph,' in the course of a leader, said: 'Bicycling is a healthy and manly pursuit with much to recommend it, and, unlike many foolish crazes, it has not died out;' and during the following week the West Kent B.C., a leading organisation of which the late Prince Imperial was a member, held a race meeting on the terrace of the Crystal Palace, Sydenham, at which Mr. Robert Lowe, now Lord Sherbrooke, presented the prizes to the successful competitors. In the course of his remarks he praised the bicycle as a pleasing and healthful method of recreation, and claimed to have ridden a dandy horse in the reign of George IV. Lord Sherbrooke differed, as will be gathered, from the editor of the 'Percy Anecdotes,' who speaks of the Marquess of Worcester, who lived in the sixteenth century, as having suggested 'that foolish thing of modern—though now almost obsolete—use, the velocipede.' In this year a bicycle with hollow spokes was ridden in a race at Wolverhampton, and on the August Bank Holiday the first meet at Harrogate was held; the Cyclists' Camp Scheme, which has since become so popular, being still *in nubibus*. The Amateur Championship of the year fell to Mr. Wadham

'THAT FOOLISH THING OF MODERN USE—THE VELOCIPEDE'

Wyndham, one of the most popular of cyclists, and a member of the London B.C.

Even at this early date the cyclists were complaining of the position assumed towards the sport by the athletic associations and clubs; energetic protests were made, and cyclists were urged to combine to promote their own championship contests in place of the A.A.C. competition 'with its half-guinea entrance fee and half-guinea medal.'

Mr. Wyndham's was the last contested A.A C. Championship, as, after two walks over, the race was finally dropped in favour of the championships then started and since carried on by the N.C.U., first established as the Bicycle Union in 1878, a complete return of which will be found in the appendix to this volume. Meets which have now become widely popular with cyclists also assisted in drawing public notice to the sport. A great gathering of riders was annually organised at Hampton Court. Mustering in Sandy Lane or on the Green, the riders started in a procession in pairs, each club being headed by its captain, and rode round a course previously set forth, some four to five miles in extent, ending at the top of the Chestnut Avenue, Bushey Park; this the riders passed down, and, going to right and left of the Diana Fountain, rode out through the double gates and dismounted. The press and the public took much interest in the demonstration, which, at its best, attracted some two thousand riders, and the sport and trade received a valuable fillip just at the right time of the year.

Judged by the light of subsequent events, June 16 was a red-letter day in the history of cycling, as on that date the late Mr. H. L. Cortis, of the Wanderers B.C., made his *début* at a private meeting of his own club, held in the grounds of the Caterham Asylum, where the future champion at all distances ran second in a one mile handicap, with 100 yards start, and first in a five mile handicap with 350 yards start, the scratch man being Mr. A. P. C. Percival.

The 'cycling press' was now crowded with letters suggesting the formation of unions, associations, or leagues, for the furtherance and development of bicycling, and letters appeared weekly in support of various plans for the consolidation and organisation of the cycling interests, with results which will be found duly set forth in the chapters devoted to the N.C.U. and the C.T.C., those great associations of which cycling is so justly proud. In this year the proprietors of 'The Sporting Life' placed in the hands of the proprietor of Lillie Bridge Grounds, as representing the Amateur Athletic Club, which was at that time promoting the Four Miles Amateur Championship of Cycling, a fifty-guinea cup, to be run for over a distance of fifty miles, under the title of 'The Sporting Life' Cup. This gift was duly announced to the cycling world, and was first competed for on October 27, when it was won by Mr. Harry Osborne of the Surrey B.C. after a very fine race. The cup was put up annually for a time after this first contest, but the assumption by the A.A.C. of the Four Miles Championship as *the* championship, and the subsequent claim that this cup represented the Fifty Miles Championship, clashed unsuccessfully with the claims of the fifty miles championship established by the Bicycle Union, and caused loyal supporters of the latter body to oppose the event. It eventually collapsed, and nothing has been heard of the cup since 1883.

1877 had shown a steady advance in the position of the sport. New clubs had been formed, more races run, and generally more interest awakened. The makers were reaping the natural results of increased demand, and everything presaged a good cycling season in 1878. Early in that year a good deal of fun was made out of the fact that, at the annual meeting of the Society for Promoting the Employment of Additional Curates, the Bishop of Manchester stated that he understood a brother bishop had suggested the use of the bicycle to curates in his diocese; the Bishop of Carlisle, following in the same strain, regretting the hilliness of the country in his diocese, and facetiously remarking that if there was one thing a bicycle objected to, it was going up hill. The bishops only anticipated by a very few months the practical use of the cycle in its three-wheeled form by hundreds of the clergy throughout the length and breadth of the land.

On June 10, 1878, Mr. F. E. Appleyard made his magnificent record between Bath and London in the London B.C. 100 Miles Road Race, his time (see appendix) being 7 hrs. 18 mins. 55 secs., and his actual time in the saddle but 6 hrs. 38 mins. 55 secs., a splendid performance, more especially as for many miles towards the end of the journey the rider suffered severely from cramp, and on one or two occasions had to dismount, so great was the pain. Appleyard scarcely did anything afterwards to show his powers of cycling, and has long dropped out of the sport; but his record was left undisturbed until 1884, when it fell, and has since been beaten several times in open road races. On the day on which Mr. Appleyard performed this feat another very well-known rider, who still takes an active interest in cycling, Mr. G. Pembroke Coleman, the official timekeeper and handicapper to the N.C.U., traversed the 100 miles in 7 hrs. 25 mins. 20 secs., finishing third, Mr. W. T. Thorn, the well-known racing man, being second. Mr. Coleman's performance stamps him as a sound and practical exponent of a sport in which he holds so important a post. Later in the same year this gentleman rode from Hayling Island to Norbiton, very little short of 60 miles, over some of the hilliest of Hampshire and Surrey roads, without leaving the saddle once during the journey.

In this year the tricycle was first really advertised as a practical vehicle. Messrs. Haynes & Jeffries, of the Ariel Works, announced the 'New Patent Coventry Tricycle,' which had been invented for the firm by James Starley. The 'Coventry Tricycle' was the Coventry rotary tricycle of to-day, but in place of the rotary action it was driven by levers and steered with a Bath-chair handle from the front wheel. Still it found much favour: one or two ladies were stated to be riding it, whilst several tricyclists can remember their first essays on this, one of the earliest and best machines obtainable before the practical introduction of the balance gear. Long rides again marked the close of an important season. W. Britten, of the Clarence B.C., rode from the Marble Arch to Bath and back, 212 miles, within 24 hours on September 12, and in the same month Mr. Smythe, who rode with Mr. W. E. N. Coston in a similar attempt some time before, again essayed the 24 hours road record on the Wisbech Road, and covered 218 miles; but as he picked his ground, and simply traversed it over and over again, the performance cannot compare with that accomplished by the captain of the Clarence. On the 13th, the day after Mr. Britten's feat, Mr. W. T. Thorn, the London B.C. racing man, made a bold and nearly successful attempt to ride from London to York in the 24 hours. He succeeded in reaching Doncaster, 162 miles, in 17 hrs. 10 mins. from the start, having thus 6 hrs. 50 mins. in hand in which to cover the remaining 35 miles, and he felt both well and confident of accomplishing the feat with nearly two hours to spare, when the felloe of his wheel unfortunately broke under him, thus destroying his chance of putting on a record which would have stood nearly as long as Appleyard's 100 miles.

On September 5 an event occurred which drew a vast amount of attention to the bicycle. 'The Times' on that date published a lengthy and appreciative leader upon the new vehicle, containing the following remarks upon the steel steed:

> The bicycle has come to the front, and is fighting for existence. Dimly prefigured in the mythical centaur, and then in the hobby horse of mediæval games, and attempted in the velocipede, now half a century old; long prejudiced by the evident superiority of wings to wheels, the bicycle has now surmounted the difficulties of construction, and adapted itself to human capabilities—it augments at least threefold the locomotive power of an ordinary man. A bicyclist can perform a journey of a hundred miles in one day with less fatigue than he could walk thirty; fifty miles—that is, from London to Brighton—as easy as he could walk ten; and a daily journey to and fro between London and the distant suburbs with just the usual results of moderate exercise.

After alluding to possible ills which might arise from indulgence in the sport, the writer says:

Bicyclists are aware they run dangers, and suffer a percentage of casualties; but they have counted the cost and found it worth while running the risk. From other points of view the objections are loud and numerous, but have upon the whole a striking family resemblance to many former objections, such, for example, as those made at the introduction of railways. The chief objection reappears in great force. Horses, it must be admitted, do not like bicycles, but neither do they like railways, and they will probably like street locomotives still less.

Going at length into the question of the dangers to the public arising from the use of the bicycle in the public streets, the writer winds up a lengthy and essentially favourable article by saying:

The legislature would be very unfaithful to the courageous principles which have hitherto guided it in the treatment of discoveries and improvements if it showed any prejudice in this matter. That would be a great injustice to the men, most of them still young, who have won for themselves a great convenience, and no less pleasure, at no cost whatever, it may be said, and without drawing upon the common fund of the food of man. Society used to be divided into the equestrian and the pedestrian orders: these people have found a third rank. Their success proves, as Johnson says, what man can do.

The closing event of 1878 was the practical retirement from the Presidency of the Bicycle Union of Mr. G. F. Cobb, who had undoubtedly been the means of establishing that body upon a firm basis, and of arranging the conditions under which it has since become so marked a success. Fuller details will be found in the chapter on the National Cyclists' Union.

1879 was destined to see a still further spread in the popularity of the sport and the initiation of many new votaries into its mysteries. Early in the year the now celebrated Surbiton path, upon which the late Mr. H. L. Cortis did several of his finest performances, was thrown open to the public, and found much favour. Its fastest rival, the Cambridge track, was the scene of some further alterations of the record table, as on May 21 Mr. Fred T. East of the Surrey B.C. won the University Ten Miles Invitation Race in 30 mins. 45 secs., then a best on record, and on the same occasion by special permission a mixed contest between amateurs and professionals was held, the distance being two miles. The selected riders were John Keen and Fred Cooper for the professionals, and the Hon. Ion Keith-Falconer and Mr. H. L. Cortis for the amateurs. The race was a very remarkable one. Cortis dashed off from the start at a rapid pace, closely followed by Keen, Keith-Falconer, and Cooper, in the order named, and these positions were maintained up to the three-quarter mile post. Cooper, who was essentially a sprinter, waited until two hundred yards from the completion of the half distance, and then dashed away, leading the quartette by some yards at the mile, reached in 2 mins. $47\frac{2}{5}$ secs.; best on record. Keith-Falconer dashed after Cooper, with Keen on his hind wheel, and Cortis was left a yard or two in the rear. In this order they covered one and a half mile. Still keeping in front, Falconer stalled off a tremendous spurt on Keen's part, and won by about three inches in the marvellous time of 5 mins. $36\frac{3}{5}$ secs. The merit of this performance is best gauged by the fact that only a day or two before Cortis had been credited with the amateur mile record, he having covered that distance in 2 mins. $52\frac{1}{2}$ secs. at the Surbiton track; this shows what speed rates were at that time, and Keith-Falconer's performance as a natural consequence must have been marvellous, very much on a par with a man doing two miles in about 4 mins. 30 secs. in 1890. If any further evidence was wanted of the extraordinary nature of the feat, it is to be found in the length of time it stood in the record books, as it was not till the autumn of 1884, more than five years after it had been accomplished, that the flying Tynesider, R. H. English of the North Shields Club, beat these figures by covering two miles in the race for the Fifteen Miles Crystal Palace Challenge Cup in 5 mins. $33\frac{2}{5}$ secs., which was the first beating Falconer's

HISTORICAL.

record received, although Cortis had several times attempted to take it down, and had got very near it on more than one occasion. English's record was in its turn defeated after but a short existence by M. Webber, who on the Cambridge track, in the Two Miles Invitation Race, in which he defeated W. A. Illston, covered the distance in 5 mins. 30⅔ secs.

With so satisfactory a commencement the season was bound to be successful. Mr. W. B. Tanner, of the West Kent B.C., initiated an agitation for a path in the south-east of London, and after a good deal of quiet work the representations of the committee charged with the task were successful, and the Crystal Palace Company agreed to lay out a track in their grounds at Sydenham. This popular path is three and a half laps to the mile, dead level and singularly fast. Since its establishment a number of grand performances have been accomplished upon it by Cortis, English, Osmond, and other well-known men.

On June 28, at a race meeting promoted by the Druids B.C., G. Lacy Hillier made his first appearance on a London cinder path (his *début* having been made on the gravel track at the Alexandra Palace). At Lillie Bridge, in the One Mile Handicap, receiving 155 yards start from Cortis, after winning his heat he ran into the fence at the grand stand end of the track and fell. He was unplaced in the final.

In August yet another record was established between London and John o' Groat's, H. Blackwell, junr., of the Canonbury C.C. (then B.C.) having covered the distance in 11 days 4 hours, arriving at John o' Groat's house on Aug. 27. Mr. Blackwell was at this time an active tourist, and his experiences as one of the earliest long-distance riders would be very interesting. In September the Surrey B.C. offered for the first time a fifty-guinea cup, to be won three times in all, for competition in their scratch race, distance ten miles, and H. L. Cortis placed his name upon it for the first time, accomplishing also a best on record for ten miles on grass, his time being 34 mins. 31½ secs.; Walter Popplewell, the

G

Ipswich cyclist, was second, and A. S. Brown third. The tricycle had now begun to make its way steadily in public opinion, and as a result a well-known agent at Kensington decided to promote a fifty miles road race, the course being from Kew Bridge to Blackwater and back. The winner turned up in A. E. Derkinderin, who covered the distance in 4 hrs. 55 mins., on a machine constructed by Messrs. Hillman, Herbert & Cooper, and named by them, after the rider on this occasion, the Flying Dutchman. This race was carried on from year to year by a committee, until it was stopped by the police, near Caterham Junction, as a nuisance.[1]

In October of this year the name of Frederick Wood, of Leicester, who has held the professional championship several times, appears in an amateur handicap in which the embryo champion is given the liberal start of 190 yds. In this month Cortis did the Alexandra Palace managers a good turn, as on the old path, which was by no means in good condition, the 'Long Wanderer,' as Cortis was called, made a three mile record, covering that distance in the final of the Three Mile Open Handicap in 8 mins. $55\frac{2}{3}$ secs. All who saw the race must remember how the white-vested athlete flew down and up the hill and dashed at top speed round the, then unbanked, lower corner, whilst the last lap was a magnificent effort, and the victor well deserved the cheers which welcomed his return to the dressing-room. 'Bobby' Woolnough (320 yards) was second, and A. S. Brown from the same mark third.

The celebrated Over Turnpike case, in which the gate-keepers were fined for demanding an exorbitant toll, five shillings, from a bicyclist, upsetting him and detaining his lamp because he would not pay it, was decided about this time in favour of the rider, and the decision encouraged the cycling fraternity considerably.

The Cortis-Keen matches, which created such a sensation

---

[1] For details of the contests till prohibited see appendix.

at the time, were run off in 1879. Much discussion had taken place in cycling circles as to the relative merits of the acknowledged champions of professional and amateur cycling. Keen possessed fine speed, and his judgment was far more matured than that of Cortis, who the next year lost the mile championship through want of 'head.' The Union showed its real strength by granting a permit for a series of contests at one, five, and twenty miles, and as Keen's old friends in Wolverhampton of course wished to see him ride, the twenty mile race was run there. The idea that the amateur had a ghost of a chance with the professional was scouted by the *habitués* of the Molyneux Grounds. Messrs. M. D. Rucker and Jameson judged; both men rode Eclipse bicycles made by John Keen. The professional adopted waiting tactics, and Cortis made all the running at a good pace. Three hundred yards from home Keen made a tremendous effort, but the amateur won handsomely by three yards. Times: five miles, 16 mins. $10\frac{4}{5}$ secs.; ten miles, 32 mins. $11\frac{2}{5}$ secs.; fifteen miles, 48 mins. 19 secs.; twenty miles, 64 mins. $43\frac{1}{5}$ secs. Keen rode a 56-inch and Cortis a 60-inch 'Keen's Eclipse' bicycle.

The one and five mile races were run off at Stamford Bridge. Keen had been taking much care of himself after his Wolverhampton experiences, whilst Cortis had without doubt been made anxious by the over-solicitous attentions of his friends, and he was conspicuously nervous on coming to the mark. Keen, inured by a larger experience, was by far the cooler of the two, and as usual was content to wait. Cortis cut out the running in the mile at a fair pace, and no change occurred until rounding the corner into the straight for home, when Keen drew up and going wide spurted in marvellous form. Cortis, probably from over-anxiety, seemed to go to pieces, and though he struggled gamely was very erratic in his steering, and suffered defeat by a foot. Time, 2 mins. $52\frac{1}{5}$ secs. This result upset Cortis altogether, and in the five miles (in which his only chance lay in forcing the pace) he sat up to make Keen lead at 1½ mile. Keen being forced in front only crawled round, and Cortis in disgust did what he should have done at first and spurted marvellously. When the bell rang Cortis went for the last lap, but Keen timing his effort to a nicety won by a yard, Cortis swerving all over the track at the finish.

Time.

	min.	sec.
One mile	2	$56\frac{4}{5}$
Two miles	6	$14\frac{3}{5}$
Three miles	9	$14\frac{3}{5}$
Four miles	12	$27\frac{1}{5}$
Five miles	15	30
Last lap, 440 yards		$39\frac{4}{5}$

Cortis was dreadfully upset at his defeat, but it was, without doubt, a lucky thing for his cycling reputation that he was defeated, as had he proved victorious he would probably have finally retired from the path, and the grand performances which he subsequently accomplished would not have been placed to his credit. The attendance at Stamford Bridge was perhaps the largest ever known, and this was, it is believed, the only occasion on which a declared professional athlete has raced upon the London A.C. path.

It was about this time that a course of action regarding highway by-laws was adopted, and this has since been steadily followed out by the N.C.U., to the great advantage of the cycling public. A memorial, opposing certain by-laws, was presented to the justices of the county of Cambridge, signed by upwards of seventy persons, of whom sixty were fellows or late fellows of colleges, including *inter alia* four fellows of the Royal Society, three professors of the University, eight past or present proctors, six deans of colleges, and several holders of the highest legal honours, chancellor's medallists, Whewell scholars, &c. &c.

In the course of an article on cycling Mr. Charles Spencer, at whose gymnasium Mr. Turner of Paris first rode the bicycle in England, claimed to have taught the late Charles Dickens to ride a bicycle.

In February 1880 the season was duly opened according to precedent by the holding of the Stanley Show at the Holborn Town Hall; this locale replaced the Foresters' Hall by reason of its greater accommodation – soon, however, to be found in its turn too small. The show was an immense success, though the machines then exhibited would now be considered sadly heavy and old-fashioned.

In March the Union finally decided to appoint an official handicapper, and the choice fell upon Mr. M. D. Rucker, who was admittedly the best man for the place then before the public. At the end of the month the Surrey B.C. by resolution decided to accept no protest against any rider who had not broken the rules of the Union. This action was taken in consequence of a threat on the part of some of the anti-Union party to protest against Cortis because he had competed with Keen under Union sanction.

On April 24, a most important athletic gathering was held at Oxford, whereat the Amateur Athletic Association was formed. The cyclists of the two Universities desired to be represented at this meeting, but the athletes decided not to admit them, having in view the fact that the cyclists already possessed a ruling body, and it was pretty generally understood amongst wheelmen at that time that cycling was to be left alone. Yet the only sport specifically mentioned in the first small leaflet circulated, containing a report of the proceedings, was cycling, a fact which raised a vast amount of feeling, which was only subdued when the Treaty of Fleet Street, as the arrangement now well known among cyclists was called, put things on a clear and indisputable footing between the N.C.U. and the A.A.A.

Coventry at this time mounted its police officers upon the Silent Steed, and the fact was duly commented upon at some length in the 'Daily News,' the author facetiously suggesting that 'a defaulting debtor pursued by a constable mounted on a tricycle, and armed with a summons, sounds more like a horrible dream than a probable reality,' and quoted the Laureate's

> New men who, in the flying of a wheel,
> Cry down the past,

as appropriate to the occasion.

The Hampton Court Meet was a great success, a large number being present, and distant towns—Tynemouth, Hull, Portsmouth and others—were represented by a contingent of riders. Over 2,000 cyclists took part in the parade. In June Mr. Frank W. Weston, an Englishman domiciled in the United States, and the pioneer of American cycling, brought over a party of four Americans, the most prominent amongst them being Mr. J. S. Dean of Boston. The visitors made a somewhat lengthy tour through the Midland and Southern districts, and were entertained at dinner in Coventry and London.

A mysterious association, known to fame as the Connaught Rangers B.C., which appeared to consist of but one member, who subsequently pleaded infancy when called upon to pay for the prizes, held a race meeting late in August on the Surbiton track, and in the Ten Miles Scratch Race, H. L. Cortis rode in magnificent form, establishing a record for ten miles inside 30 mins. for the first time in cycling history, his time being 29 mins. $54\frac{1}{5}$ secs.

In the summer of this year Messrs. H. Blackwell, junr., and C. A. Harman, of the Canonbury C.C., rode from Land's End to John o' Groat's, nearly 900 miles, in 13 days, establishing in an easy-going manner a record which has since been beaten, but which is still a record, inasmuch as the riders were not attempting to make an uncomfortable labour of their holiday trip. In August the North of England meet was held under the auspices of the Bradford B.C. at Harrogate, in Yorkshire, and led to the establishment of the Harrogate Camp, which under the energetic management of the same club has each year been a great success, a large number of wheelmen from all parts of the United Kingdom mustering under canvas for four days, at the beginning of August. In connexion with this notable meet, a general meeting of the then Bicycle Touring Club took place in the concert-room of the Spa Grounds, Low Harrogate, at which an agenda of considerable length was submitted to the assembled members, some of whom had come long distances for the purpose of taking part in the deliberations. After a comparatively short session, it was suddenly announced that the room must be vacated for the evening concert, and the meeting was asked to adopt the rules submitted without consideration. A very heated discussion ensued, and was continued in a smaller room to which the meeting adjourned ; a party dubbed the 'Malcontents' was formed, and they eventually brought about the very necessary reforms in the organisation of the great athletic club which without doubt have led up to its present success.

In riding southward from this meet, Mr. Henry Sturmey, of 'The Cyclist,' took particular note of the 26-inch handle-bars which Mr. Hillier had had fitted to his bicycle, and on August 10 his journal contained an able leader on the value of long handle-bars. The fashion thus set withstood the test of time and experience, and has proved of value to young riders, a long handle-bar, as will be seen in the following chapters of this work, being particularly serviceable in assisting the novice to acquire a good style.

On September 2 Cortis made his first attempt to cover 20 miles in the hour, encouraged by his success at 10 miles above recorded. The Surbiton path was chosen for the attempt, and every effort was made to get it into good condition. This track was—in common with most London paths—then ridden with the right hand inside. A number of well-known cyclists were asked to assist as pace-makers. At 6.10 P.M., when the start took place, a very slight breeze was blowing which went down with the sun. The weather was warm, and singularly suitable to the occasion. C. E. Liles started with Cortis and covered two miles in 6 mins. 5$\frac{2}{5}$ secs., when the record-breaker not being satisfied with the rate of progression went in front and covered the third mile in 2 mins. 59$\frac{2}{5}$ secs. Liles made a dash at the end of four miles, when he gave way to J. F. Griffith, who with a flying start rode the next four miles in 11 mins. 54$\frac{4}{5}$ secs., and thus knocked off the odd seconds for Cortis, whose time for eight miles was 24 mins. 0$\frac{3}{5}$ sec. Sidney Kemp then came on, but he, like Liles, could not make pace, and at twelve miles Cortis was 14$\frac{3}{5}$ secs. outside even time. G. Lacy Hillier took up the running, and forcing the pace for two miles he assisted the record-breaker to knock two seconds off his loss. Hillier then gave way to Griffith, who took Cortis along in excellent style, so that at sixteen miles he was but eight seconds outside. Liles joining in, he and Griffith raced hard against one another, and the seventeenth mile was a very good one, being covered in 2 mins. 52$\frac{3}{5}$ secs., Cortis being only $\frac{1}{5}$ second outside even time; Kemp joined the trio, and the eighteenth mile was completed in 53 mins. 56$\frac{3}{5}$ secs., or 3$\frac{2}{5}$ secs. *inside* evens. In the third lap of the nineteenth mile, Liles on the inside swerved from exhaustion and came into collision with Griffith, the pair falling heavily right in front of Cortis, who came down on them, Kemp escaping in the most marvellous manner, just getting clear of Cortis' machine as it fell down. Cortis was not very much hurt beyond flesh wounds, but J. F. Griffith broke his ankle, and the shock of the fall severely injured his heart; although this was not discovered till much later. The mile times from eleven to eighteen were then best on record. The 'Daily Telegraph' based a lengthy and amusing article upon Cortis' feat, in which, amongst other remarks emphasising the value of the new sport, the writer said, 'Not the worst thing that they have done, these knights of the road, has been to rehabilitate and set on their legs again many of our old posting-houses and decayed hostelries all over the country. Bicycles have to a certain extent taken the place of coaches; they frequent all our great main roads, and gladden the hearts of innkeepers, who look out for the tinkling bells which herald the advent of a "club" of wandering velocipedists, just as they anticipated of yore the gladsome tootling of the horn that bespoke the approach of the Enterprize, the Highflyer, or some other well-known conveyance of the old coaching days.' A fortnight later Cortis made another attempt to ride twenty miles in the hour, but he had in the interval had another fall whilst racing at Lincoln, and was decidedly unfit; under these circumstances he failed to approach his former times, falling very weak in the fourteenth mile, and being 38⅔ secs. outside the hour when twenty miles had been covered. The rider was awfully disgusted when Coleman told him that he was outside the limit, but doubling testily to his work he dashed on for five miles more, covering twenty-five miles in 1 hour 16 mins. 41¾ secs., which stood as a best on record until 1886, when the time was beaten in the presence of a few spectators on a modern path, by J. E. Fenlon. Cortis won the Surrey Cup for the third time at the autumn meeting, and thus became its absolute possessor.

On October 9 the now celebrated Crystal Palace track was opened by a grand race meeting, the programme including a club challenge cup for a team race, an idea which has since been dropped, and a one mile handicap. The day was a dreadful one, and the new track very heavy in consequence. G. Lacy Hillier won both events from scratch in very slow time. On November 6 the second Fifty Miles Road Tricycle Championship was promoted by the Finchley and London T. C.'s jointly, the course being from Tally Ho Corner, Finchley, N., to a point just this side of Hitchin and back. Fifteen men in all started. The morning was very foggy, and consequently the trains were late. Hillier, who had been training for the event, and who practically introduced the double-steering Humber tricycle to London riders in this contest, arrived late, and J. R. Hamilton had actually started upon Hillier's machine when the latter rushed up in hot haste from the station. A change of pedals was an absolute necessity, whilst Hillier did not find out until he had started that the saddle had been moved forward, with the result that he struck his shins continually against the axle. He eventually started thirteen minutes late, but at twelve miles from the start he had passed every one except Vesey, who was only one minute in front of him at this point. Vesey was riding a 'bicycle' fitted with two small hind wheels, which public opinion universally decided was an unfair machine, and eventually won somewhat easily, Hillier finishing second, C. Crute third, R. C. Baker fourth, G. D. Godbolt fifth, and H. L. Cortis sixth. The Tricycle Association, then recently formed, established a remarkable and utterly impracticable 'amateur definition,' providing for a neuter class of riders neither amateur nor professional, and generally complicating matters by attempting to decide 'what is a tricycle.' The result of the attempt to cobble the amateur law was the eventual absorption of the Tricycle Association into the Bicycle, or as it is now termed the National Cyclists' Union, as the only way out of the difficulty in which one of its members had placed it.

Yet another great advance is that recorded in 1880. The Union began the publication of the executive reports, a course which brought it considerable advantage, whilst the energy and enthusiasm of the votaries of cycling were controlled and concentrated so as to produce the best results. 'The Cyclist,' started in the last month of 1879, came very strongly to the front, and, supporting the governing body of cycling in contradistinction to the attitude assumed by some of the other journals, secured a world-wide circulation, and took a leading place in that section of journalism.

In February 1881 the season was opened in the orthodox manner by the holding of the fifth Stanley Show—for the second time at the Holborn Town Hall. A very excellent show was arranged, and a large number of persons visited it during its continuance. A steam tricycle, the invention of Sir Thomas Parkyns, was shown on this occasion, but the requirements of the law as regards steam-driven vehicles put a complete check upon the development of the invention, of which nothing has since been heard.

News from Cairo about this time recorded the fact that a Mr. E. F. Rogers had ridden from that city to the pyramid of Cheops, thus bringing two vastly distant cycles into close approximation, whilst within a week or two it was announced that Prince Yeo, son of the King of Siam, Lord of the Thousand White Elephants, &c., had purchased a bicycle for his own use

The Union accepted the principle of moveable championships for the first time, and ran two of its four contests in the Midlands. The principle then adopted has proved of inestimable value to the ruling body of cycling, as it has brought the leading men of the various sections and districts into actual contact, and extended and developed in a most valuable manner the resources of the Union. Much of the accord which now exists between the various local centres and the Central Executive is due entirely to the meetings and intercourse of the men in the promotion of the championship contests.

On May 21, 2,050 riders attended the Hampton Court meet, and the weather being fine the sight was an exceedingly picturesque one, whilst later on 136 tricyclists met on Ealing Common and paraded with great effect, the tricycle lending itself much more easily to that sort of work than the unstable bicycle.

On June 25 the third Fifty Miles Road Race for the tricycle championship was run under singularly unpleasant conditions, and over muddy and stony roads, from Hounslow *viâ* Maidenhead and Cookham to a point twenty-five miles out and back. The race fell to G. Lacy Hillier in 4 hrs. 53 mins., 33 minutes in front of P. G. Hebblethwaite second, H. A. Venables third, W. B. Parker fourth.

On July 6 the N.C.U. held at Surbiton its first championship for 1881, which fell to G. Lacy Hillier by eighty yards, after a good race with Liles, Palmer, and Milner, this being the first occasion on which a really representative Midlander had visited London to compete for championship honours. C. A. Palmer, waited on by Liles, stuck closely to Hillier's hind wheel during the first four miles, Milner making all the running. $2\frac{3}{4}$ laps from home Hillier dashed to the front, and sustaining his spurt, Palmer cracked three-quarters of a lap from home, and Hillier drew away and won easily in 15 mins. $39\frac{2}{5}$ secs.

On the 16th Hillier won the One and Twenty-five Miles Championships at Belgrave Road Grounds, Leicester, the final of the Mile being a match between Hillier and Liles. A very slow pace was set by the former till the bell rang, when he sprang off at top speed and won by six yards, making a best on record for a flying ¼ mile, viz. $36\tfrac{1}{5}$ secs. In the Twenty-five Miles he also won easily by forty yards; C. Crute second, C. E. Liles third. On July 21 Hillier established a mile grass record, covering that distance, at Priory Park, Chichester, in 2 mins. 51 secs. On July 27 Hillier won the last championship of the year, the 50 miles, by 30 yds. from C. Crute, J. F. Griffith third; time, 2 hrs. 50 mins. $50\tfrac{2}{5}$ secs., best on record by nearly 4 minutes. He thus won the five open championships of 1881.

The first Harrogate Camp was held in August. Although rain fell heavily most of the time, the campers so far managed to enjoy themselves that the camp has become one of the best and most enjoyable holidays a cyclist has to look forward to.

On June 3, 1882, H. L. Cortis, who had been doing a good deal of riding, competed at the Crystal Palace in the West Kent B.C.'s Open Mile Handicap, of course from scratch, and in the sixth heat beat the mile record, covering that distance in 2 mins. $43\tfrac{1}{5}$ secs., the last lap being a marvellous one. The previous records were: amateur, Keith-Falconer's 2 mins. $46\tfrac{3}{5}$ secs.; professional, Fred Cooper's 2 mins. 46 secs.; whilst on the 7th Cortis again reduced the time on the Surbiton path in the One Mile Invitation Handicap of the Wanderers B.C., covering the mile in 2 mins. $41\tfrac{3}{5}$ secs. On the same evening Cortis had a try at Keith-Falconer's two-mile time, but failed to beat it by $2\tfrac{4}{5}$ secs. The Hon. Ion Keith-Falconer, who is practically the father of Land's End to John o' Groat's rides, went over the celebrated route in 12 days 23 hours 15 mins., a very grand performance at the time, though it looks very small alongside 1886's developments. About this time an Oxford man, H. R. Reynolds, went over the 'Turpin route,' from London to York, a distance of $196\tfrac{3}{4}$

miles, in 21 hours 43 mins. His predecessor was W. T. Thorn of the L. B. C., whose machine broke down some few miles out of York as previously related.

The first Union championships ever held in Birmingham came off on July 8, when Frank Moore won both the One Mile and the Twenty-five Miles, being followed home in the short distance race by M. Whish and M. J. Lowndes, and in the longer contest by F. R. Fry and C. Crute. On the 9th W. F. Sutton, of the London Scottish, on an ordinary bicycle covered 222 miles on the Great North Road in 23 hrs. 55 mins., riding time 21½ hours, which it is needless to say was the best on record. On July 22, J. S. Whatton, the flying Cantab, of whose strange bicycle some account will be found in a subsequent chapter, won the Five Miles Amateur Championship on the Crystal Palace track in 15 mins. 12⅘ secs., Keith-Falconer being second, and C. Crute third; whilst on the 29th Keith-Falconer handsomely won the Fifty Miles Amateur Championship from C. D. Vesey and W. K. Adams in 2 hrs. 43 mins. 58¾ secs., a best on record by nearly seven minutes. Vesey broke a spoke two miles from the finish. This was indeed a busy week at the Crystal Palace track, as W. K. Adams covered 3 miles in 8 mins. 41⅕ secs., a best on record; and H. L. Cortis at last accomplished the feat he had so often attempted, and covered twenty miles in the hour. It was a model evening, with not a breath of wind. The flags hung motionless against the posts. Cortis was assisted by Woolnough, Hunter, Vesey, Tacagni, Adams, and last but by no means least Alfred Thompson. Well coached, led, and clocked, Cortis covered the 20 miles in 59 mins. 31⅘ secs., and 20 miles 300 yards in the hour. He rode a 60-inch Invincible. Not satisfied with this grand performance, Cortis desired to make yet another attempt, and at last, to the delight of all sportsmen, it was announced that Cortis and Keith-Falconer would ride twenty miles together. There had long been a desire to see these two great riders meet, and a crowd visited Surbiton on August 2. Pace-makers, including Messrs. Adams, Woolnough, Tacagni, McKinlay and others, assisted. Up to six miles Falconer retained the post he had taken up, dead on Cortis' hind wheel. But he was palpably labouring, though the fact was not within Cortis' ken. Peter McKinlay taking the post of pace-maker at this juncture, set a hot pace, and in the second lap, along the top of the ground, Falconer was beaten ; Cortis looking under his arm, took in the situation at a glance, and shouting excitedly 'Go on, Peter,' he doubled to his work in a moment, and left the Cantab, who shortly afterwards gave up. From 7 miles every record was beaten up to 20 miles in 59 mins. $20\frac{1}{8}$ secs., and 20 miles 325 yds. were covered in an hour.

This year Harrogate Camp was favoured with fine weather and was a pronounced success in every way. In the latter part of the month the Wanderers gave a farewell dinner to H. L. Cortis, who shortly afterwards departed with his newly married wife to Australia. It was with the deepest regret that the wheel world heard of his early death at Carcoar, New South Wales, on December 28, 1885,

HISTORICAL.

of a complication resulting from low fever caused by the climate. After his arrival in the colonies Cortis did little or no cycling, but rode several horses in steeplechases, in the course of which the ex-champion broke his arm, though he had never broken a bone from his bicycle. He named one of his steeplechasers 'Lacy Hillier' because it could stay, in kindly remembrance of an old friend. The private and personal friends of Cortis have erected in the church of Ripley, in Surrey—a spot much frequented by cyclists—a window and brass to his memory, which will long be honoured wherever cyclists most do congregate.

On October 14 the Union promoted its first Tricycle championship, distance five miles. There was an excellent entry, and after a fine struggle the race fell to C. E. Liles, H. W. Gaskell second; the much fancied Midlander, M. J. Lowndes, was disposed of by the winner in the second round.

In November the members of the Tricyclist Conference met at supper to signalise the success of the road race they had promoted, and the establishment of a 'new T.A.' was first mooted. This was soon attempted, but a majority of practical tricyclists were opposed to the movement, and 'The Tricycle Union' at last ceased to exist shortly after an unsuccessful attempt to promote an 'Amateur Championship.' On the day fixed no one put in an appearance at the Crystal Palace track, either as official or competitor, and the T.U. eventually metamorphosed itself into 'The Society of Cyclists,' who proclaim themselves followers of what they call the 'higher aims' of cycling, read papers on botany and geology at their meetings, and are the objects of much good-humoured chaff on the part of cyclists, who do not take the 'cycling' part of the Society's title very much *au sérieux*, and are inclined to resent the ridiculous light in which the so-called Society of Cyclists occasionally presents to the public the sport to which they are attached.

On December 14, at a council meeting of the Union, certain suspended riders appealed to the council for reinstatement. Mr. W. B. Tanner took the lead on behalf of the executive, Mr T. E. Scrutton occupying the chair. The appellants requiring some assistance, the chairman asked if any gentleman—preferably a legal man—among the delegates present would undertake to assist them. Then, in the words of an amusing skit written at the time, 'Someone with legal bent, deep voice, and twinkling eyes, rises to the occasion.' This was Mr. Robert Todd, of the Stanley B.C., a newly elected councillor, who soon after became honorary secretary to the Union, to its immense advantage; and so this year closed with much promise for the future.

The Stanley Show, held at the Albert Hall in January, was the first notable event of 1883; but the big rambling building, with its many square yards of unavailable space, its tortuous passages and poor light, was by no means suitable for the purposes of the show, which nevertheless attracted a numerous crowd of visitors, including a strong contingent of West End people, whom the associations of the hall, and curiosity, brought to view the exhibits.

It is recorded that a cyclist in the spring of this year rode his bicycle for half an hour on the Goodwin Sands. Why he went there is a mystery, but the fact remains, a bicycle has been ridden on the Goodwins.

The Hampton Court meet was duly held, though scarcely so well supported as before, an increasing number of leading clubs standing out. Eastern and Western civilisation was brought into pretty close contact, as a Japanese '*jinricksha*' was taken alongside the procession for some distance by two well-built Japs.

Early in this year the Bicycle Touring Club, after lengthy consideration, changed its name to that under which it now exists, viz. the Cyclists' Touring Club, or C.T.C., these letters replacing the then more favoured formula 'B.T.C.'

About this time C. H. R. Gosset covered just over 200 miles in the twenty-four hours on a tricycle, the first time this feat was accomplished on the road.

Early in July Alfred Thompson of the Sutton B.C. cut two of Cortis' records at the Brixton Ramblers' meeting at the Crystal Palace, covering the starting quarter in $40\tfrac{3}{8}$ secs. and the half mile in 1 min. $19\tfrac{4}{5}$ secs. The Hon. Ion Keith-Falconer's Land's

End to John o' Groat's record was beaten by James Lennox of Dumfries, who rode the distance in 9 days 4 hrs. 40 mins., thus beating the previous record by nearly four days.

On July 7 two of the Union Championships were held at Aston Lower Grounds, Birmingham. The Five Miles Bicycle Championship fell to F. Sutton, A. C. Auster second, and G. H. Illston third in slow time. C. E. Liles easily secured the One Mile Tricycle Championship from M. J. Lowndes in 3 mins. 18½ secs.

In July the London T.C. organised a great twenty-four hours race on tricycles, the course being from Caterham Junction near Croydon to Brighton, thence along the coast to Fareham, thence *via* Romsey and Salisbury and on through Stockbridge and Alton, as far as the riders could go in the twenty-four hours; no less than 74 entries were obtained, of whom 67 started at midnight on Friday, July 6, and it was truly a marvellous sight that met the eye, as 67 tricycles bearing one or more lamps, together with a great crowd of cyclists who were present as spectators, moved off at the word 'Go' along the dark glade of Smitham's Bottom. Ripley, distant some 202 miles from the start, was regarded as likely to prove the destination, especially when the breeze freshened as the day broke, and several men arranged to ride down on Saturday to see the finish. Those who went down early, however, were startled about a quarter to nine in the evening by the receipt of a wire from Mr. T. Griffith, who was checking at Alton, announcing that Marriott had passed there at 7.1 P.M. At 9.30 John Keen on a bicycle dashed into Ripley and ordered tea, and at 9.39 T. R. Marriott, the first man, rode up, going strongly and well. After a mouthful of tea, he pushed on, and riding out the time, reached Merton, 218¾ miles, at 11.50 P.M. Nixon was the second man to reach Ripley, which he did at 10.23, and having no friend to keep him going, he went to bed, and whilst he slept Vesey, who arrived at 10.29, pushed painfully on to Wisley Common and back, and took second place with a score of 205¼ miles, the last 5¼ miles taking him 1 hr. 15 min. to cover. Gosset, arriving at 11.41, rode a quarter of a mile further up the road and back, and thus took third place, the score at the expiration of the twenty-four hours being:

			hrs.	min.
1. T. R. Marriott .		$218\frac{3}{4}$ miles	23	50
2. C. D. Vesey .	.	$205\frac{1}{4}$ ”	23	33
3. C. H. R. Gosset	.	$201\frac{1}{2}$ ”	23	42
4. Alfred Nixon .	.	$201\frac{1}{4}$ ”	22	23

As will be seen, Nixon's was without doubt the second best performance, and had he had an energetic friend to have kept him going, he would have easily taken second honours. Thus ended the great road ride which did a great deal for the sport in one way, whilst setting a very bad example in another. It is needless to add that Marriott's time was a best on record, whilst all the four men beat Gosset's record of $200\frac{3}{4}$ miles in twenty-four hours.

In July, Lord Bury, whose efforts to bring about an amicable arrangement between the B. U. and the T. U. had been frustrated by the executive of the latter body, who repudiated the arrangement they had empowered him to propose, resigned the Presidency of the Tricycle Union, and was subsequently unanimously elected President of the B.U. (now N. C. U.), his acceptance of office marking a new era of increased prosperity and success for the Jockey Club of the sport.

On the 14th, the One Mile Bicycle and Ten Miles Tricycle Championships were competed for on the Crystal Palace track, the mile falling to H. W. Gaskell, who was followed home by Alfred Thompson—F. Sutton, who was much fancied, falling in the second lap; time, 2 mins. $55\frac{2}{5}$ secs. The Tricycle Championship fell to C. E. Liles in 33 mins. 45 secs., M. J. Lowndes being second.

The Crichton B. C.'s evening meeting on the following Thursday was notable for the fact that the four miles record was twice beaten. H. F. Wilson covered the distance in the fifth heat in 11 mins. $37\frac{3}{5}$ secs., whilst in the final H. W. Gaskell won in 11 mins. $34\frac{1}{5}$ secs., Wilson declining to start. Wilson won the Fifty Miles Championship on the 21st in 2 hrs. 46 mins. 26¾ secs. from F. R. Fry of Clifton.

M. Sinclair won the Fifty Miles Tricycle Championship of Scotland on the 25th in 4 hrs. 45 mins. 35 secs., Laing being second and D. H. Huie third ; whilst on the 27th F. R. Fry of Clifton beat all bicycle records from 51 miles to 100 on the Crystal Palace track, covering the full distance in 5 hrs. 50 mins. 5⅗ secs., which still remains at time of writing [1] a best on record. On July 21 another Birmingham cyclist, Mr. Alfred Bird, beat the 24 hours tricycle record (Marriott's 218¾ miles), covering 221½ miles in all.

The Twenty-five Miles Bicycle Championship fell to C. E. Liles in 1 hr. 22 mins. 42⅗ secs., the race being run at Taunton on August 2. On the same day James Lennox beat the existing 24 hours bicycle road record by covering 229 miles in the specified time.

The Harrogate meet was once more a pronounced success, being favoured with excellent weather, and everything passing off in the most satisfactory style. Lennox's record was not long permitted to stand, as Mr. J. W. M. Brown on August 16 covered 255¼ miles on the road in 24 hours, a grand performance.

On September 8, the Tricycle Conference promoted what proved to be the last Fifty Miles Road Championship Race. For some considerable time the more far-seeing members of the cycling body had recognised the fact that the practice of holding open races on the road was illegal and likely to prove detrimental to the credit and interests of the cycling sport, and as a consequence much opposition was manifested. The Tricycle Conference, however, rather braved the matter out, inserting advertisements, not only in the cycling, but in the sporting press. A few hours before the race the managers were notified that the police were on the *qui vive* on the chosen route, so at the eleventh hour the course was changed, the start taking place at Caterham Junction, and the line running through Oxted,

[1] Dec. 1887.

Westerham, River Head and Ightham and back. The men were despatched at minute intervals, and no police interference took place at the start, nineteen men in all being sent off. A number of riders went out to meet the returning competitors, some of whom awaited them at the top of the hill out of Godstone, and here Marriott was sighted—hatless and smothered in dust. Mat Sinclair, the Scottish champion, set a fair pace for him on a tricycle, whilst Messrs. G. L. Hillier and C. E. Liles rode quietly along some few yards in the rear, when within a mile of home an approaching pony carriage was suddenly drawn across the road and a constable in blue and another in plain clothes stopped the leader and the accompanying trio and took their names and addresses, Marriott going off at top speed the moment he was released, to the intense disgust of the officers, who hastily jumping into the trap made an unavailing effort to catch him. Marriott won by 25 minutes from George Smith, W. Bourdon being third. No further action was taken by the police except the issue of the following notice :—

Persons using bicycles, including tricycles, are hereby cautioned that such vehicles are carriages within the meaning of the Highway and Metropolitan Police Acts. Furious driving (Taylor *v.* Goodwin, decided by the Judges, March 25, 1879). The Metropolitan Police Acts impose a penalty on any person who shall ride or drive furiously, or so as to endanger the life or limb of any person, or to the common danger of the passengers in any thoroughfare. The police are directed to ascertain the names and addresses of persons about to take part in any bicycle or tricycle race within the metropolitan police district, or to proceed against, and, if necessary, to take into custody, any persons violating the above law. The provisions of the law as to obstructions are independent of the above.

It will be easily seen that the road race, being obviously an illegal contest, even if it had done no more than necessitate the issuing such a notice, had already accomplished more harm than good to the sport of cycling.

C. E. Liles won the Surrey Cup at the autumn meeting in 34 mins. $69\frac{1}{3}$ secs., W. Brown second, and H. W. Gaskell third.

In the month of September Mr. Alfred Nixon rode from London to John o' Groat's in 8 days 23 hours on a front-steering tricycle; distance about 750 miles.

'The Times' contained in October a letter signed D.C.L., in which the writer stated that although he had suffered for twenty-five years from a spinal affection which rendered it impossible for him to undergo a journey by train or vehicle, he '. . . . had just undertaken a tricycle tour through Sussex of 115 miles.' He added that, throughout the trip, he had not only felt better in health, but had absolutely been in less physical pain than at any other period during the previous quarter of a century. Without doubt the affection in this case must have been partly nervous, the novelty and excitement of the exercise taking the sufferer's attention somewhat from his troubles.

W. F. Sutton made an attempt upon the twenty-four hours bicycle road record with success, covering 260¼ miles in that time, whilst a few days later J. S. Smith and his wife on an Invincible sociable rode ten miles on the Palace Track in 41 mins. 40⅗ secs.; best on record.

Lengthy discussions on large wheels *versus* small wheels brought '83 to a close, and 1884, destined to be an important cycling year, opened with a meeting of lady members of the C.T.C., who discussed *in camera* the details of a suitable costume. Of course the 'Rational' enthusiasts attended, but in the end a decision was come to mainly based upon the practical experiences of Mrs. J. S. Smith, Miss Choice, and several other well-known lady riders, the result as tested by C.T.C. ladies being in every way satisfactory.

In March the Birmingham Local Centre of the N.C.U. initiated the very valuable agitation for improved roads, which has been so energetically followed up. A great meeting was held under the presidency of the Mayor of Birmingham, at which cyclists, horse-owners, and horse-users banded themselves together to promote the agitation, and subsequently action was taken against sundry road surveyors with satisfactory results. As a consequence the Union has now some very convincing precedents to lay before road surveyors who object to a demand on the part of cyclists for improved highways.

The Hampton Court meet was finally abandoned in this year, although a young and unknown club called a second meeting to discuss the matter, the general view being that 'monster meets' had served their purpose and were not likely to do the sport further service. At the end of May a Cyclists' Camp was held at the Alexandra Palace on the same lines as the Harrogate Camp, but proved a complete failure. The one redeeming point was some excellent racing.

On June 21 the first two of the Championship contests were held at Lillie Bridge (new track), the mile falling to H. A. Speechley, after a waiting race, C. E. Liles being second, and H. W. Gaskell third; time, 3 mins. $30\frac{2}{5}$ secs. The Twenty-five Miles Tricycle was won by C. E. Liles, H. J. Webb second, Sidney Lee third; 1 hr. 28 mins. 58 secs.; best on record.

Chambers walked over for the Five Miles Championship at Cardiff, time 15 mins. $36\frac{1}{5}$ secs., on June 28. On the same day the official timekeeper at the West Kent B.C. meeting returned Alfred Thompson's mile time in the fourth heat of the open mile as 2 mins. $39\frac{3}{5}$ secs, giving the $\frac{1}{4}$ mile times, which he had been specially requested by Mr. G. Pembroke Coleman (who was away at the Championship) to note, as Thompson's private form pointed to his doing something good. A dead set was however made at the record, and it was not put upon the book. Thompson ran a trial the next week, but was very nervous at the start, and when the pistol went, one of his pace-makers fell and upset him altogether. Thompson held at this time the half-mile record, and had only a week or two before been deprived of the starting quarter record. The same evening G. L. Hillier made record for a flying quarter; time, $35\frac{2}{5}$ secs., thus beating J. S. Whatton's $36\frac{2}{5}$ secs.

HISTORICAL.

The Ten Miles Championship of the North, run on the Wallsend track on July 12, fell to R. H. English in 30 mins. 14½ secs., and caused that sterling rider to take a foremost place in the opinion of amateur cycledom. On the same date the Five and Twenty-five Miles Tricycle Championships were run off on the Crystal Palace track, C. E. Liles winning both, H. J. Webb finishing second in the mile—time, 3 mins. 29½ secs.; and Sydney Lee in the five mile—time, 18 mins. 8⅗ secs.

On July 14 the Fifty Miles Amateur Championship fell to F. R. Fry of Clifton, after a splendid race with C. S. Wadey; F. J. Nicolas third; time, 2 hrs. 51 mins. 16¾ secs.

On July 26 the holding of the Twenty-five Miles Amateur Championship brought to the front R. H. English of North Shields. The race was run on the North Durham track, a small and by no means fast path, Speechley, Robinson, and Nicolas representing London; they waited at the start, but English was off like a shot out of a gun, and fairly left the lot, lapping all his opponents and winning anyhow in 1 hr. 22 mins. 0⅘ sec. on a wet and heavy track; D. H. Huie was second, and J. Tough third.

M. Josef Kohout, of the Cesky Velociped Klub, Prague—a splendid specimen of the Continental cyclist—rode 220½ English miles (355 kilomètres), from Hamburg *viâ* Kiel to Flensburg, and back to Bönningstedt, in twenty-four hours, and as he had to lift his heavy old-fashioned roadster over innumerable gates in the dark, this performance becomes the more remarkable.

On September 11 R. H. English made his *début* on a London path in the Crystal Palace Challenge Cup race, distance fifteen miles. A fairly good field opposed him, but he dashed off the mark at a tremendous pace, and covered the first mile in 2 mins. 42 secs., or only a fraction outside record; twenty yards short of the mile William Brown, who had hung on to him up to this point, cracked, and English went right away, and beat every record from two to twenty miles—keeping on after winning the race for the purpose of securing the records. He established the following record times :

	English min. sec.	Cortis min. sec.	Falconer min. sec.
2 miles	5 $32\frac{2}{5}$	—	5 $36\frac{3}{5}$
5 ,,	14 $33\frac{3}{5}$	14 $40\frac{2}{5}$	—
10 ,,	29 $19\frac{2}{5}$	29 $30\frac{2}{5}$	—
15 ,,	44 $29\frac{3}{5}$	44 $37\frac{2}{5}$	—
20 ,,	59 $6\frac{3}{5}$	59 $20\frac{1}{5}$	—
20 ,, 560 yards	60 0	—	—

In the five miles race for the Kildare Cup, run at Lillie Bridge on the following Saturday, English pursued the same tactics, and though not riding nearly so fast, the first mile taking 2 mins. $48\frac{1}{5}$ secs., he left Speechley in the first quarter of the second mile, and won again anyhow. The big Tynesider has never done better than he did on this occasion; some severe falls, and a desire to spurt fast for short distances, decidedly did him no good subsequently.

On September 25 there was a Colony race meeting at the Crystal Palace, the frequenters of the path having a go at the records all round, with the following results. J. S. Smith and W. Brown on an Invincible tandem made the following records :

	min. sec.
1 mile	2 $59\frac{3}{5}$
3 miles	9 23

H. J. Webb tried to beat the single tricycle record for two miles, and succeeded by $\frac{2}{5}$ sec., doing 6 mins. $23\frac{3}{5}$ secs.

G. Lacy Hillier tried to beat the bicycle records for five miles, and secured the following :

	min. sec.
3 miles	8 32
4 ,,	11 24
5 ,,	14 18

On September 27 a curious contest was decided between Major T. Knox Holmes, a veteran tricyclist of seventy-eight, and Mr. G. Lacy Hillier, a bicyclist of twenty-eight, the latter conceding the former the start of one mile for every year's difference in their respective ages in a ten hours' race. The veteran only dismounted for a trifle over five minutes, whilst the bicyclist stopped for over thirty-five minutes. The scores at the finish were, Major Knox Holmes 115 miles, 101 to 115 being records, and G. L. Hillier 146 miles, 51 to 54 and 101 to 146 being records. The Major thus won easily. The day was very unfavourable, being windy and wet.

1884 closed in a somewhat perturbed manner. Several road performances were being openly questioned in the public press, and the Union was engaged in investigating the *bona fides* of the various claims. An agitation was also in progress concerning the way round for racing paths, which ultimately resulted in the almost universal adoption of the left-hand inside practice of riding. The annual meeting of the C.T.C. was held in London, and certain revolutionary doctrines with regard to the internal management of the club, which had been demanded in a blustering and ferocious manner in all of the papers, were advocated at the meeting in mild and mellifluous terms, singularly in contrast with the earlier steps of the dispute; the voting, however, showed a large majority in favour of the *status quo ante*.

In 1885 commenced the great struggle between the N.C.U. and the A.A.A., the dispute being originated by some of the most prominent of the supporters of the dissolved Liverpool Local Centre. After a struggle the Union obtained all the points for which it had felt obliged in the interests of cycling to contend, thus becoming without any question the sole ruling body of cycling.

About this time the news arrived of some of those marvellous records claimed by American riders which have from time to time reached England. The makers of those records were subsequently beaten by the strong English contingent which visited America, and the times have not been generally accepted. We do not, however, propose to enter into the newspaper controversy which took place on the subject, though some of it was amusing—and the whole of it was fierce.

S. Sellers won the One Mile Championship at Lower Aston Grounds, Birmingham, by six inches from W. A. Illston, on June 13, time 2 mins. $47\frac{1}{5}$ secs. ; and R. Cripps the Five Miles Tricycle Championship in 16 mins. $53\frac{1}{5}$ secs., G. Gatehouse being second.

Webber won the Five Miles Amateur Championship on June 27, at Jarrow track, in 14 mins. $22\frac{2}{5}$ secs., after one of the finest races ever seen in a championship contest, D. W. Laing being second, and R. Chambers third. July produced another crop of records. On July 6 Mrs. Allen of Birmingham covered 200 miles on the road in 23 hrs. 54 mins., and C. H. R. Gosset covered $231\frac{3}{4}$ miles inside 24 hours.

On July 11 the N.C.U. held its One and Twenty-five Miles Tricycle Championships on the Crystal Palace track, and the contests proved most exciting. P. Furnivall won the One Mile Championship after a dead heat with P. T. Letchford in 3 mins. $5\frac{2}{5}$ secs., having however made a best on record in his heat; time, 2 mins. $58\frac{1}{5}$ secs. The most remarkable fact about the race was that it was absolutely the first single tricycle race in which Furnivall had taken part. The Twenty-five Miles Championship was won in splendid style by George Gatehouse, who made most of the running; records were made for two and three miles, and from eleven to twenty-five miles. The full distance he covered in 1 hr. 26 mins. $29\frac{2}{5}$ secs.

On July 9 Webber beat the mile record on the Crystal Palace track, doing 2 mins. $39\frac{2}{5}$ secs. On July 18 R. H. English won the Fifty Miles Championship from G. Gatehouse in 2 hrs. 45 mins. $13\frac{4}{5}$ secs., record being beaten by English, Gatehouse, and Nicolas from 29 to 38 miles inclusive. English also won the Twenty-five Miles Championship at the Ayleston Road Grounds, Leicester, time 1 hr. 20 mins. 13 secs.; R. Cripps second, and W. Terry third. The Harrogate Camp was again a marked success, whilst a southern camp at Tunbridge Wells was also fairly successful.

G. Lacy Hillier visited Leipsic in September, and defeated the amateur champion of Germany and others in a 10,000 mètres scratch race, beating the German record at the same time, and bringing back one of the finest prizes ever given for a cycle race.

An effort was made to establish a vigilance committee of race-giving clubs to deal with the question of the 'Makers,' Amateurs,' a name given to a class of riders in amateur races who are suspected of being paid for riding certain makes of machines; the vigilance committee failed owing to want of cohesion amongst the most prominent race-giving clubs.

In November the C.T.C. accepted with much regret the resignation of its Chairman, Mr. N. F. Duncan, who had done good service to the club during his period of office. Mr. Duncan resigned as he was just about to take holy orders in the Church of England.

'Kangaroo hunts'—i.e. paper chases on bicycles—were very popular during the winter. The N.C.U. agitation concerning the mending of roads was organised and pushed on, and a very eventful year was closed by the usual festivities, accounts of which filled the pages of the cycling papers well on into 1886.

On January 16 the A.A.A. meeting at Anderton's Hotel, Fleet Street, passed a resolution by which 'the war,' as it was termed, which had created no end of trouble and annoyance, was put an end to. Since this time the two associations have worked side by side and hand in hand for the benefit of amateur sport.

In February the cycling world was startled by the receipt of the sad news that Herbert Liddell Cortis, the ex-amateur champion at all distances in 1879 and three distances in 1880, was dead. One of the most popular of men, and in the opinion of many good judges the best rider that ever crossed a wheel, the memory of H. L. Cortis will always remain green in the annals of cycling.

In March came the welcome news that the League of American Wheelmen had taken action against the Makers' Amateurs on their side of the water, and suspended a number of the best men who were known to be employed to ride for the two leading bicycle-making firms. The L.A.W.'s action eventually drove the best of this class into the professional ranks.

H. A. Speechley won the Surrey Cup for the third time, thus making it his property, as Cortis had done before him, P. Furnivall finishing second, and A. E. Langley third; time, 41 mins. 44⅓ secs.

The International Tournament, promoted by Mr. F. Cathcart, the lessee of the Alexandra Palace track, which was held in May, proved a sporting, and it is to be hoped also a financial, success. Belgian, Scotch, and Irish cyclists competed, and some excellent sport was witnessed, the English team winning the challenge shield. W. A. Illston made a new record for half a mile, 1 min. 16½ secs.; whilst A. E. Langley covered the mile on a Marriott & Cooper tricycle in 2 mins. 55½ secs.; E. Kiderlin on a Beeston tricycle making record for 2 miles. The Tournament is to become an annual fixture.

The tricyclists foregathered at Hampton Court in May, the meet including nearly 500 riders of the broad-gauge machine, and proving highly successful. At the Gainsborough meeting H. A. Speechley cut his own starting quarter record, doing 38⅗ secs., this time being tied later on by E. M. Mayes. The Society of Cyclists visited Colchester, considerable preparations having been made by the hospitable townsfolk to welcome and accommodate the anticipated visitors, who, however, arrived in such meagre numbers that much disappointment was caused. A rose-coloured account of the visit, which appears to have had little or nothing to do with cycling, is to be found in the organ of the Society.

The first of the championship meetings was held at Weston-super-Mare on the new track on July 14, 1886. The One Mile Tricycle Championship fell to Percy Furnivall, A. E. Langley second, and P. T. Letchford third; time, 3 mins. 5⅖ secs. The Twenty-five Miles Bicycle Championship fell to J. E. Fenlon, W. Ratcliffe second, and G. Gatehouse third; time, 1 hr.

19 mins. 29⅗ secs., the fastest Twenty-five Miles Championship ever ridden.

On June 19 the North Road Club promoted a fifty miles race open to all sorts of cycles; some mischievous persons sent letters to the police authorities signed with the name of a cyclist who was known to object to these races, but no trouble ensued. The ordinary bicycles were set to concede the tandems a start, but were not in the hunt. The race was handsomely won by C. E. Liles and A. J. Wilson (time 3 hrs. 16 mins. 58 secs.), J. Lee and G. Gatehouse second (time 3 hrs. 23 mins. 16 secs.), both couples riding Beeston Humber tandems. E. Hale on a Premier safety bicycle was third in 3 hrs. 29 mins. 55 secs., and O. G. Duncan was the first man in on an ordinary bicycle in 3 hrs. 31 mins. 22 secs., though a severe cropper through a collision with a Safety rider doubtless had a great deal to do with the failure of this excellent wheelman.

The One Mile Championship was run on June 26 on the Jarrow track, and proved in every way a success, victory resting with Percy Furnivall, H. A. Speechley second, and W. A. Illston third; time, 2 mins. 46 secs.; one of the finest races ever seen for what is practically the blue ribbon of cycling. F. W. Allard, on a Marlboro', made a record for the tricycle mile at Long Eaton on the same day—time, 2 mins. 54 secs.; whilst F. J. Osmond and S. E. Williams, on an Invincible tandem, at the Crystal Palace, covered 2 miles in 5 mins. 47⅗ secs., which is the accepted record for this distance.

On July 3 F. W. Allard pushed his Marlboro' Club to the front in the Five Miles Tricycle Championship at Hampton Park, Glasgow; P. Furnivall being second, and G. Gatehouse, who most unwisely rode a waiting race, third; time, 24 mins. 42⅖ secs.

One of the most astonishing feats of the year was performed by George P. Mills, of the Anfield B.C., who, leaving Land's End at midnight on July 4, reached John o' Groat's in 5·days 1 hour 45 mins., beating T. R. Marriott's record by 1 day 6 hrs. 40 mins. Mills rode a 53-inch Beeston Humber bicycle. The distance is 861 miles, and he only slept for ***six hours in all*** during the journey.

On July 10 F. J. Osmond, on a 60-inch Invincible, beat M. V. J. Webber's three-quarter mile record of 2 mins. 0 secs., doing 1 min. $58\frac{3}{5}$ secs. On July 17 the Twenty-five Miles Tricycle Championship was run at the Alexandra Park track, the weather being very bad, rain falling almost without intermission all the afternoon. G. Gatehouse (the holder) preferred the waiting game, and was beaten in the run home by the Irishman, R. J. Mecredy; time, 1 hr. 55 mins. $40\frac{4}{5}$ secs.

On July 24 the Five Miles Bicycle Championship was run off on the Long Eaton track, and resulted finally in a win for the champion short-distance man of the year, P. Furnivall, W. A. Illston second, and G. Gatehouse third; time, 14 mins. $44\frac{1}{5}$ secs.

The Fifty Miles Bicycle Championship was run at Lillie Bridge on August 14, and fell to J. E. Fenlon, W. F. Ball second, J. H. Adams third; time, 2 hrs. 47 mins. $21\frac{1}{5}$ secs. Fenlon, who rode a Premier racer, made a waiting race of it until a little over a lap from home.

Records continued to fall like autumn leaves. George P. Mills rode a Beeston Cripper tricycle from Land's End to John o' Groat's in 5 days 10 hrs., thus beating the tricycle record by 30 hours. Furnivall and Gatehouse also did some marvellous times on the bicycle and tricycle respectively; but owing to the inaccuracy of the official watch the records claimed were rejected. On the road E. B. Turner and S. Lee cut the fifty mile tricycle record, doing 3 hrs. 9 mins. 55 secs. on a Marriott Humber tandem; and Alfred Fletcher, on an Ivel Safety, did the same distance in 3 hrs. 9 mins. $56\frac{4}{5}$ secs. On August 28, in the North Road Club's one hundred mile race, E. Hale made a road record on a Premier for fifty miles, 3 hrs. 6 mins. $25\frac{3}{5}$ secs.; and J. H. Adams and R. V. Asbury a one hundred miles record on an M. & C. Humber tandem of 7 hrs. 29 mins. 5 secs. George Gatehouse was credited with no fewer than nineteen records on the tricycle, being an unbroken string from two miles in 5 mins. 37⅖ secs. to twenty miles in 59 mins. 10¾ secs., all made on a Beeston Cripper Tricycle.

At the end of 1886 it may be safely asserted that the sport of cycling was fully established in popular estimation, and its progress has been quite as rapid since that date as it was before.

The more recent history of cycling is a matter of common knowledge. Papers, daily and weekly, have given an increasing amount of space to the racing and other branches of the sport, and the developments have been steady in all directions.

The Jubilee year was made the occasion of a very singular demonstration. The cyclists of the United Kingdom, acting on the suggestion of Mr. Henry Sturmey of Coventry, subscribed sufficient money, over 800*l.* in all, to present a lifeboat called 'The Cyclist' to the port of West Hartlepool, where the boat was formally launched at a public ceremony on December 17, 1887. The civic dignitaries of the 'The Hartlepools,' headed by the Mayors of Hartlepool and West Hartlepool, and accompanied by deputations from all the public bodies, the clergy and ministers of various denominations, the member for the Hartlepools, and a contingent of cyclists, amongst whom was Mr. Henry Sturmey, the founder and honorary secretary of the movement, marched in procession to the Quay, where Mrs. Richardson, the Mayoress, christened the boat 'The Cyclist.' Since then the lifeboat has done good service, and the cyclists of the United Kingdom have paid the expenses, amounting to some 70*l.* a year. Over 6,000 individual subscribers supported the fund; one club, the London Social C.C., collected over 31*l.*, whilst Mrs. Blurton, London, collected over 22*l.*, the largest individual collection. The movement was discussed in the press, and the public spirit of the rapidly increasing army of wheelmen was commended in many quarters.

The 19th June, 1886, was an occasion to be put on a par, from a racing man's point of view, with a certain race-meeting of the Wanderers B.C., near Caterham, held on the 16th of the same month in 1877, at which the late H. L. Cortis made his *début*—for at the Brixton B.C's. meeting at the Crystal Palace a tall pale boy named F. J. Osmond won his first races on the track. His style very strongly resembles that of Cortis, though somewhat neater and more effective in the ankle work, and it is even possible that Osmond is a finer handicap rider than was his predecessor. In 1890 Frederick J. Osmond accomplished, for the third time on record, the feat of winning all the four bicycle championships, which has been done but twice before—by the late H. L. Cortis in 1879, and by G. Lacy Hillier in 1881. Osmond has made many records and has held many cups and championships; had he chosen to go for records, he could without question have accomplished some very fine performances at the end of his championship year. A rider of the Ordinary bicycle, he owes much of his success to his physical advantages, for he is tall, with an abnormally lengthy leg-reach, his 58-inch wheel being apparently quite small for him. In the opinion of many who are competent to judge, Osmond is the finest all-round cyclist we have yet seen, and he was the first man who, upon the type of machine ridden by Cortis, Keith-Falconer, English, Furnivall, and other giants of the past, has ridden one mile inside $2\frac{1}{2}$ mins., his time being 2 mins. $29\frac{4}{5}$ secs., figures he shortly afterwards reduced to 2 mins. $28\frac{4}{5}$ secs. His wins in the Surrey, Kildare, and other cup races, and his other performances, will be found fully recorded in the appendix.

Another development which has without question done the sport much service is the encouragement of military cycling. As early as June 1882 a suggestion had been made in the press, by the Hon. R. G. Molyneux, to form a volunteer *corps d'élite* mounted on cycles, but nothing came of it, the ordinary bicycle being decidedly unsuitable for this purpose. With the advent of the perfected Safety the matter again became prominent, mainly owing to the efforts of Colonel A.R. Savile, of Farnborough, Hants, who threw himself into the movement with enthusiasm. On October 7, 1887, some remarkable experiments were made at Aldershot, where Major Fox and others interested in the gymnasium work saw a number of energetic gentlemen do a number of absurd things—riding at logs and such-like. The climax was reached when, after several riders had charged the obstacles and fallen, one of the cleverest of our wheelmen started at top speed, and, by simply dismounting and lifting his safety over each obstacle in turn, did the course in considerably over half a minute faster time than his rivals. Late in the year the War Office appointed a committee to go into the subject of military cycling, composed as follows :—Colonel Savile, chairman ; Lieut.-Colonel E. D. Drury, 2nd V.B. Royal Kent Regiment; Lieut. E. J. A. Balfour, London Scottish R.V.; Lieut. H. Stapley, Major G. M. Fox, G. Lacy Hillier, Henry Sturmey, Robert E. Phillips, and E. R. Shipton. This committee sat in the levée room at the Horse Guards, and went at great length into the subject, inspected many machines in the St. Stephen's Hall of the Royal Aquarium, placed at their disposal by the directors of that establishment, and fully threshed out the subject, the result of their labours being embodied in an official report, which had more than the usual share of success.

Since then military cycling has advanced most rapidly, and has unquestionably established itself in public estimation as a useful branch of the Volunteer service. Those enthusiasts who went to work, not wisely but too well, in the earlier days have 'burnt out,' and the less imaginative but more practical men have come to the front. The movement has grown out of leading-strings, and bids fair to take a reasonable place in the service. Perhaps the most singular and significant of developments is the existence of what is really a body of Volunteer military cyclists within the ranks of the regular army. This remarkable corps has been formed by Major Edye, of the Royal Marine Light Infantry, at Walmer, assisted by Lieutenants Anderson and Connolly, and it has proved very successful, despite the fact that the authorities, beyond giving permission to Major Edye to make the experiment, have done nothing towards helping the corps to purchase machines or fittings; and as the men have to devote what would otherwise be their leisure to attaining perfection in cycle drill, it can safely be said that any services which may in future be rendered by the cycle-mounted soldier will have been made possible to a very great extent by the labours of Major Edye and those who have worked with him.

It is singular, at first sight, to read of a Marine Cycle Corps. The 'Horse Marines,' beloved of the fabulist, could hardly seem more incongruous; but as a matter of fact the cycle should prove a really serviceable 'horse' for the use of marines, inasmuch as many cycles could be stowed aboard ship, and would need neither care nor food till wanted for active service.

Colonel Savile, Captain Balfour, Captain R. E. Phillips, and others devoted themselves to the subject, and there can be no question but that it will continue to spread, and that the sport on the one hand and the Volunteer movement on the other will be mutually benefited. In the appendix will be found such additional items of information as may seem likely to prove of value to the prospective Volunteer cyclist.

The more active branches of the sport have continued to grow apace. Touring, watched over by the Cyclists' Touring Club, has spread further afield, and when Messrs. G. W. Burston and H. R. Stokes, the Australian round-the-world tourists, arrived in England, they were loud in praise of the gigantic organisation which had smoothed their path. Periodical attacks upon the secretary and editor are made, sometimes from outside, sometimes from within the C.T.C.; but Mr. Shipton has so often shown that he labours heart and soul for the big club, that there is always a solid majority of sturdy and undemonstrative members to back him when need arises. On the last occasion when this became necessary, in connection with the special meeting held in London in 1889, the outside wire-pullers suffered a most crushing and decisive defeat. The cycling tourist is now to be encountered all over the Continent, and the Cyclists' Touring Club has done a great work in educating the public, and especially the hotel and inn keepers, up to the proper appreciation of the army of touring wheelmen and women, an army daily recruited from all classes of society.

The National Cyclists' Union continues to do good work in a quiet fashion, and, considering the meagre support accorded it by the cycling world from a financial point of view, it is astonishing how much it has effected. The discipline of the sport has been carefully maintained, the annual series of amateur championships contested, and the interests of cyclists carefully watched. A full return of the amateur championships to date will be found in the appendix.

It is worthy of note that the universal by-laws for the regulation of cycle traffic, so long an important feature in the Union's programme, have at last become an accomplished fact, after years of labour. At one time every local authority exercised its own sweet will in the matter of cycling by-laws. A bell was required in one place, a whistle in another, lamps must be lit at sunset or earlier, and many other absurd regulations were enforced. All this has now been changed, and the hour of lamp-lighting—one hour after sunset—is the same all over the country, whilst the wheelman is also required to give audible warning of his approach. These and many other smaller matters have received attention, and the Union continues to labour successfully for the benefit of the sport.

On the racing path advances of a most significant kind have been made. The records of the giants of the past sink into insignificance as compared with those of the riders of to-day. New tracks of vastly improved construction are laid or being projected, and the whole section has made a step forward.

With the advent of the rear-driving Safety the dangers of mixed races became very apparent. The unequal heights of the machines, the unsteady steering of the Dwarf, and the fact that a novice on the small machine did not fall off, but simply swerved all over the path—a danger to those behind him—led the leading riders to take action. The best men, with but one or two exceptions of any moment, pledged themselves not to enter or ride in 'mixed' races. For reasons not necessary to detail, the movement met with opposition of the most unscrupulous character from a number of men who never raced; but the cracks stood to their guns, and in 1890 there was scarcely a single race meeting the programme of which did not include one or more races for 'Ordinaries only,' or for 'Safeties only,' and the separation movement, as it was called, was triumphant. This is not astonishing, inasmuch as handicappers are able to make much more satisfactory allotments when the classes are separated; to secure closer finishes and better sport, whilst the safety of the riders in both classes is

GOING FOR A RECORD.

most materially increased. In short, the advantages of separation are many, the disadvantages non-existent, and every sport promoter who desires to secure the best entries and the best sport will in the future separate the classes.

Ordinary bicycle racing still holds its own in popular favour, the tall and graceful machine having a decided advantage from a spectacular point of view over its dwarf rival. To ride this class of machine with success upon the racing path requires certain physical gifts. A man must be above the average height, with a long reach of leg, in addition to those other qualities necessary in any athlete—sound lungs, plenty of strength, and plenty of courage. Possibly 10 per cent. of our cycling youths are big enough to ride an Ordinary with a fair chance of success, *but* every one of the remaining 90 per cent. can ride a geared-up Safety bicycle; thus the ranks of the riders of the Dwarf machines are certain in the course of time to outnumber those of the riders of the Ordinary, who will, however, to quote a neat expression, always form the aristocracy of the racing path. 'Ordinary' racing has fully held its own. The Ordinary-riding champions are known to the crowds who attend race-meetings, and the interest is vivid and sustained, and it will be many a long day before any description of cycle racing will oust the bicycle from the place it holds in public opinion.

Safety racing was steadily making its way up to the middle of 1890. The public began to know the best men, and the meetings of the cracks excited much interest. In July 1890 the best of the Safety men suffered defeat at the hands of an Irish rider, who, having trained himself to spurt some 600 to 800 yards, was able to repeat Bob English's victories in 1884, as the Safety men were only in the habit of spurting from 80 to 120 yards. This, combined with the difficulty of handicapping the solid and inflated tires with any degree of accuracy, upset Safety racing to a great extent, and detracted a great deal from its interest, the races in many cases resolving themselves into the most tiresome and uninteresting of processions; and some of the best and most intelligent of the promoters of sport took the very wise step of separating solid and hollow tires, thus ensuring a good and well handicapped race for the delectation of their patrons.

The advances made in the racing department, the innumerable records made to-day, to be beaten to-morrow, the difficulties of the handicappers, and the step by step development of the various types of machine upon the racing path, the best trial ground—the trial ground whereon almost every important cycling advance has been primarily tested and eventually developed—would take too long to detail at length in this chapter. The final result can best be gauged by the 'common measure' of time, and the latest recorded times will be found in the appendix, though even this test fails to convey in all cases the exact results arrived at, inasmuch as in the instance given above a faulty system of training—training to sprint without training to stay—may for the time being, at any rate, give to certain figures a fictitious importance. In this connection the tricycle records credited to Dr. E. B. Turner may be instanced. Dr. Turner is a gentleman who made a name for himself as an amateur runner some years ago. At a time when many men give up athletics he took to tricycling, and he has reduced the art of training and riding with pacemakers to a science. In 1890 he accomplished, upon a solid-tired tricycle, times which, in some cases, were then world's records for any sort of cycle !—a feat unique in itself, and particularly well timed as affording proof that, with pacemakers, a man trained to stay can make mincemeat of the fastest sprinter's time over any distance which is a little further than the sprinter is accustomed to go. Tricycle racing holds its own; the tricycle is not the fastest machine upon the path, but it is a machine which suits men of a certain physique, men with plenty of power, who like relatively hard work. The tricycle racing of to-day is of great interest, but it is confined very much to first-class tracks such as Paddington, it being almost impossible at the pace they go nowadays to race with safety on a flat track. Thus the home of tricycle racing may be said to be at Paddington, and this branch of the sport will without doubt grow in popularity as soon as other well-banked tracks are established. On the whole the racing side of cycling shows a great advance. Promoting bodies should bear in mind that the finer shades of cycle-racing tactics only appeal to the *cognoscenti*, and that what the public like is a short sharp race, with a close finish, or a contest of champions from scratch ; and with this end in view they should plan their meetings on certain lines, the most important of which may be said to be the separation of Ordinaries and Safeties into absolutely distinct races, and of solid and hollow tires in the Safety contests. Should either class fail to respond with sufficient entries, that class can be dropped. For the rest, the latest developments in the racing section will be found in the appendix.

An historical occasion, and one which cannot be passed over in silence in connection with anything purporting to be a history of cycling, must not be left unrecorded. It was arranged that on July 5, 1890, H.R.H. the Prince of Wales, to whom 'The Badminton Library' is dedicated, and the Princess of Wales should visit Paddington Recreation Ground, and for the first time on record witness a series of cycle races. The arrangements were placed in the hands of Lord Randolph Churchill, Mr. Melville Beachcroft, C.C., and Dr. E. B. Turner; and the latter gentleman practically took the whole of the cycling work upon his shoulders, and made the three 'royal handicaps,' which were really masterpieces in their way. Unfortunately the chosen day turned out wet, and, somewhat unwisely, the meeting was postponed till the succeeding Wednesday, July 9, when the weather was scarcely any better. The track was wet, but happily not flooded, and the arrangements were very complete indeed. Punctually to time the royal party drove into the enclosure, their Royal Highnesses being driven to a daïs placed inside the running track, opposite the finish, and as soon as the address had been read by Lord Randolph Churchill and the Prince had made a suitable reply, the sport began. The One Mile Tricycle Handicap fell to Lewis Stroud, Oxford U.B.C., 10 yds. start; A. H. Tubbs, 30 yds., 2nd; B. W. Crump, 20 yds., 3rd; H. H. Sansom, scratch, Notts Castle C.C., 0; B. W. Scheltema-Beduin, scratch, Trekvogels, Amsterdam, 0; E. Dervil, 20, Paris, 0; W. Ward, 20, Stanley B.C., 0; A. J. Watson, 40, Catford C.C. The handicap was made for 2 mins. 41 secs., and Sansom, who had joined his men, would have won but for the fact that he pushed one of his cranks off in the straight for home, and of course failed to get up, Stroud winning in 2 mins. $42\frac{1}{5}$ secs.

The One Mile Safety Handicap was shorn of much of its interest owing to the absence of H. E. Laurie and W. C. Jones.

E. Leitch, on the scratch mark, having no one to help him, it resulted as follows :—

W. Price, Polytechnic C.C. . . .	30 yds.	1st
A. Du Cros, Irish Champion Club . .	20 „	2nd
G. L. Morris, Polytechnic C.C. . . .	45 „	3rd
C. W. Schafer, Kildare B. and T.C. . .	50 „	0
S. H. Pearce, Kildare B. and T.C. . .	50 „	0
J. E. L. Bates, Surrey B.C. . . .	40 „	0
E. Leitch, Polytechnic C.C. . . .	scratch	0

Time, 2 mins. 33⅗ secs. The handicap was made for 2 mins. 34⅘ secs.

The *pièce de résistance* was unquestionably the One Mile Bicycle Handicap—the original Ordinary bicycle, and the royal party were treated to a piece of handicapping and an example of handicap riding such as had never been seen upon a track before. The race resulted as follows :—

Fred. J. Osmond, Brixton Ramblers B.C. .	scratch	1st
Frank P. Wood, Brixton B.C. . . .	35 yds.	2nd
F. J. B. Archer, Catford C.C. . . .	35 „	3rd
J. H. Adams, Lewisham B.C. . . .	50 „	4th
Herbert Synyer, Notts Boulevard B.C. .	scratch	5th
F. Weatherley, Speedwell B.C. . . .	45 yds.	0
W. H. Bardsley, Hounslow B.C. .	60 „	0
Douglas McRae, London B.C. . . .	80 „	0

Every man did his best to secure the result aimed at when the handicap was made, viz., the establishment of a record. Of the scratch pair, Synyer most loyally assisted his co-marksman, riding the first quarter in 37⅖ secs. Osmond then dashed away, reaching the half-mile in 1 min. 13⅘ secs., *a record*, and three-quarters in 1 min. 55 secs. Here the whole field were bunched, and rounding the bottom corner Osmond found his way through, and, riding with tremendous determination, won by six feet in 2 mins. 31⅘ secs., tieing his own record. The handicap was made to beat 2 mins. 31⅘ secs., and but for the wet, which made the track rather holding, Osmond would doubtless have created new figures.

In the above account the name of every starter at this

HISTORICAL.

now historic gathering has been recorded, and for the sake of completeness the list of cycling officials is appended.

Judge: G. Lacy Hillier, Stanley B.C.

Referees: Robert Todd, Vice-President N.C.U.; H. Du Cros, President Irish C.A.

Umpires: M. D. Rucker, London B.C.; Charles E. Liles, Ripley R.C.; Major Thomas Knox Holmes, London T.C.; Harry J. Swindley, Ripley R.C.; A. V. Puckle, Brixton B.C.

Handicappers: 'Royal' handicaps, Dr. E. B. Turner, Ripley R.C. For other handicaps, S. T. Brown.

Timekeeper for Cycling: G. Pembroke Coleman, London B.C., official timekeeper N.C.U. since 1878.

Starters: G. H. Green, Brixton B.C.; Fred Jenny.

Telegraphist: Carey.

At the conclusion of the 'royal handicaps,' Her Royal Highness the Princess of Wales graciously intimated that she would present the prizes to the fortunate winners, which she did, and the royal party shortly afterwards left the ground amidst loud cheers from the assembled crowds.

On this occasion certain Irish riders competed on the inflated tire, their times appearing very good; subsequent developments, when the English riders were able to obtain these contrivances, showed that the enthusiasm was misplaced, the times accomplished being really very moderate.

The failure of the few earlier users of the contrivance to get even these moderate results out of it was due to the fact that they were afraid to blow their costly tires up to bursting-point, whereas the more experienced persons connected with the Tire Company blew them up very hard indeed. Messrs. Jones, Parsons, Edwards, Lloyd, and other *habitués* of the Paddington path, when they were able to obtain machines so fitted, very soon established records far in advance of those over which the uninitiated had been gasping with astonishment, and as 'inflated tires' are at present in a very crude and unimproved state, there is no doubt that in the near future some compressed-air contrivance will be invented which will produce even better results.

For the average cyclist the present contrivances possess few attractions. The effects of vibration at an ordinary pace over average roads on an average cycle have been absurdly exaggerated. A careful rider using a ⅞-inch rubber tire secures ample isolation for all ordinary purposes. The inflated tires slip badly on wet and greasy roads; they puncture easily, burst spontaneously, whilst the application of adequate break-power is somewhat of a difficulty, and, to crown all, the cost is excessive, a fact which is made of more importance by the want of durability which characterises the tire. In time all these drawbacks may be satisfactorily obviated, and future developments will be fully dealt with in the appendix as they occur.

In this chapter the history of the cycling sport has been traced from the beginning of the century to the end of 1890. The development of the various modern types of cycle, from the Hobby Horse and the Draisnene, has been related, and the gradual increase in pace from the days of Tomes' mile in 3 mins. 5 secs. to the 2 mins. 28⅘ secs. of Osmond has been recorded. Much of the earlier history of cycling was forgotten when this volume first saw the light, and many a writer has availed himself of the information therein contained.

In the future developments will, it is to be hoped, continue, but they will be more developments in detail. All such forward steps will be found duly recorded in the appendix.

The sport is full grown, and waxes daily in public favour; recruits of both sexes are flocking to the ranks of cycling, and the practical every-day use of the wheel as a means of locomotion is becoming more and more general. The sportsman, the cricketer, the rowing man, the tennis player, reaches his destination upon the cycle; the tourist finds in it the acme of suitability as a touring vehicle; the tradesman adopts it vicariously for despatching his wares to his customers. In short, the uses of the cycle are numerous and varied, and will doubtless be added to.

Like all sports in their youth, cycling has its drawbacks and its dangers. The free use of the highways at present accorded to the velocipedestrian is in many cases grossly abused. Week after week, in the summer months, races at various distances, from one mile (?) upwards, are held upon the public roads, whilst several large organisations exist solely for the purpose of promoting road races. Public opinion is slowly but surely being roused to hostility by the course taken by a relatively small section of cyclists—the road-racing men—and it remains to be seen whether the Jockey Club of cycling—the N.C.U.—will take the necessary steps to check the abuse, steps fully within the power of that body, or whether it will remain supine until some mischance causes other interference, which will be certain to seriously curtail the freedom which the average cyclist has upon the highways.

The sport is now fully and finally established in public favour; its organisation is approximately complete; it maintains a special press of a magnitude which astonishes an outside inquirer; its literature is extensive, and its popularity steadily extending. It is a sport which bids fair to be more international than national, albeit there can be no question that Great Britain, with its excellent roads, was and is the home of cycling.

A COUNTRY POSTMAN.

CHAPTER III.

RIDING.

RIDING a bicycle is, for obvious reasons, more difficult than riding a tricycle. There are, however, points in common between the two classes of machine, and for this reason many of the instructions are equally applicable to either. Thus the directions with regard to pedalling, holding the handles, attitude when riding, &c., may all be applied with little, if any, variation to the bicyclist as well as the tricyclist. The first necessity for the learner of the art of bicycle riding is a machine on which to make the early efforts—so well remembered by every active rider. This should be one of that class of original velocipedes known by the derisive titles of 'bone-shakers,' 'timber-trucks,' and other facetious names, relics of a past age. The frames were of heavy solid square iron rod, in many cases coiled and curved in a clumsy attempt to break the jars of the roads; the wheels generally of hickory wood, with a heavy hub faced with a brass plate, and tired with iron, of course rattled tremendously over stones. The head was a long and heavy socket turning on a curved shoulder which was unpleasantly liable to fly right round, and either strike a heavy body blow or catch the leg between the tire and the backbone. At the top of the head was an elaborate bracket, bearing a 16-inch handle bar, which was about on a line with the rider's chest. The whole fabric was absurdly heavy, and, if it had seen service, loose in every joint. The cranks were very long, perhaps eight or nine inches, and the pedals of the most primitive construction. It speaks volumes for the conscientious efforts of the early builders of velocipedes, that so many of their machines have so well and so long withstood the heavy work to which they have for years been subjected; generations of novices having wrestled and fallen with the faithful timbertruck in their efforts to master the mysteries of the sport. Riders who have had ten or twelve years' experience will recall with a feeling of pleasure the day when, after many struggles, they really acquired the art of riding, and purchased the brilliantly coloured hickory-wheeled bone-shaker which

EARLY STRUGGLES.

they now lend to their friends who wish to become cyclists in their turn.

There is even now nothing so satisfactory as this old pattern machine for learning to ride; it is very low, in fact the rider should be able to touch the ground on either side; the long spring diminishes the effects of contact with the kerb or a brick —and it is remarkable with what pertinacity the beginner will make for a brick or any other awkward looking obstacle which may come more immediately within his agitated purview when there are acres of clear road around him at his disposal. The beginner cannot in his nervous trepidation minimise the shock of an inevitable collision as the experienced cyclist can, and it is consequently a distinct advantage to him to have the safeguard of a long and flexible spring. The shape, make, and general type of the original machine will therefore be found to offer special advantages to the learner; and a point in its favour must not be lost sight of, that is, that it affords to the attendant who is instructing, plenty of places which he can conveniently grip while steadying the novice; the long horizontal spring, and the heavy bracket of the high-pitched handle-bar being equally convenient for the purpose. It is not difficult to procure one of these bone-shakers should the intending cyclist not live near enough to a riding school. The best way is to advertise in one or other of the cycling papers, when the necessary hack will be obtained for from 2*l.* to 3*l.*

Here it will be well to put in a word of warning to those who wish to learn or to those who desire to teach, and this is to observe that none of the new dwarf bicycles known as 'Safeties' are suitable for purposes of instruction. Every practical rider is aware of the added difficulty of steering these new machines when of the ordinary bicycle type with the big wheel in front. They are by no means so easily managed as an ordinary bicycle, owing to the fact that the wheel centre is generally placed some inches in front of a vertical line dropped through the steering-head centres, whilst the pedal centres are carried still further back, instead of being coincident with the wheel centres as in the ordinary bicycle. For these reasons, although a practised cyclist can very soon attain proficiency upon this dwarf type of machine, unless the learner has a very strong aptitude for the task his novitiate will be notably lengthened if he is put upon one of these sensitive steering machines. The other variety of safety bicycle has been described as having the big wheel a little one and the front wheel behind. These are machines in which the rear wheel is the larger and is driven tricycle wise by a chain, whilst the front wheel is a small one used only for steering, and they are even more erratic in the matter of steering, until properly mastered by constant practice. So the beginner will be wise if he avoids 'Dwarf Bicycles' and 'Safeties' and adheres to the use of a hack of the original bone-shaker pattern, or adopts as small a bicycle of the ordinary type as will permit the free action of the legs, so that when riding his limbs do not come in contact with the handle-bar. Of course, should circumstances confine the rider to the use of a Safety, he can learn on it, but his struggles would be much shortened by avoiding that class for his initiatory efforts.

The practical assistance and advice of a friend or attendant will go a great way to getting over the more serious preliminary difficulties of the work. Instructors are to be found in most big towns throughout the country. There are schools and agencies, where cycle-riding is taught in a complete and satisfactory manner, and this is, without doubt, by far the best method of acquiring the art; for the attendants and instructors have had in most cases plenty of miscellaneous experience in the task which they undertake, and are thus enabled to bring their charges safely through the ordeal without any serious or unnecessary damage. Some pupils, of course, are more clumsy than others, and although we do not give much credit to the oft-told stories of men who simply take a bicycle, jump upon it, and ride off without any previous experience of the machine, yet, on the other hand, we do know of many cases in which a careful and painstaking instructor has taught a beginner to ride, mount, and dismount in three separate lessons of half-an-hour each. For this reason we advise the would-be bicyclist, if possible, to go to a properly qualified teacher. The charges for instruction vary in different places, but a complete course, enabling the learner to mount, dismount, and ride sufficiently well, can generally be obtained for about half a guinea—whilst, if the learner decides to purchase for subsequent use a new machine of his teacher, instruction in its use will often be a part of the bargain.

It frequently happens, however, that the cyclist *in posse* does not reside near enough to any of the cycling academies to undergo the regular course of tuition, and is constrained to fall back upon his own resources to acquire the desired accomplishment; and, arduous as the task may appear, many men have triumphed in a very short time over all the difficulties which present themselves. As actual experience is always the best guide, it will be well to relate the course taken by a well-known rider, who taught himself enough in the course of a few hours to make bolder and more practical essay upon a convenient and quiet piece of road. Procuring a bone-shaker over which he could just stand, he took it into the garden, where, on a level and smoothly kept lawn, a horizontal bar had been erected. Standing beneath the bar he, with its assistance, got across the machine with one pedal in a convenient position, and then, steeling himself for the effort, let go of the bar—which he had been firmly grasping with one hand—thrust wildly with his foot at the descending pedal, grasped the handle, and, shooting a couple of yards or so away from the bar, fell ignominiously sideways upon the turf; the small rosewood handle, owing to the weight of the clumsy vehicle, each time punching a neat hole about one and a half inch in diameter and three inches deep in the neatly-kept lawn. These holes sorely puzzled the gardener next morning, and he was furbishing up his mole-traps to capture the strange and destructive animal which had caused them, when he learned the truth.

These struggles went on for nearly three hours, off and on, a white stone being used to mark the farthest point reached until the whole length of the lawn was covered without a mishap, and the 'hill' at the other end (a grassy slope of about eight feet) successfully surmounted. A modification of the same plan may be successfully adopted by the solitary learner. A stout rope stretched between two trees, the lintel of a conveniently placed doorway, or in fact any overhead point on which the learner can secure a firm hold, which will enable him to sit upon his machine, and place himself comfortably in position for a fair start, should be at once devised or taken advantage of. The rider who teaches himself should do his best to secure a very small machine, as this will minimise the chances of injury in case of falls. Should the learner be able to secure the assistance of a practical friend, however, he will be very much better off; or two beginners can materially aid one another by following out carefully the suggestions and hints appended below. Supposing them to have obtained a sound and serviceable machine of the old type. A cycle maker or repairer, or in default of these skilled workmen an ordinary blacksmith, should be got to run his eye over it so as to see that no serious defects or damages exist, and then the learners, if everything is right and the machine quite safe, can proceed to give one another lessons in turn. A few minutes at a time will be ample, say five or ten at the outside, and then the second man should take his turn, as at first the limbs tire very rapidly, and the tyro apparently goes backwards instead of progressing. The running and walking beside the machine stretches the legs, and enables the dismounted man to recover himself by the time he is called upon to mount again. A stout piece of rope about a yard long should be firmly fixed to the left-hand crutch of the handle, and it should have two or three knots tied in it to afford a good hold and preclude the possibility of its slipping through the attendant's hands. The saddle, which should of course be firmly fixed so as not to slip, should be put well back in the middle of the spring, great care being taken to see that it is even, and set straight. A saddle put on crookedly, or a little higher on one side than the other, will often mar a man's efforts to a serious extent when he is in the early stages of his task. Beginner number two should then stand in front of the machine on the left of the driving wheel, and grasp the head firmly with his left hand, steadying it at the same time with his right hand on the left-hand handle of the machine (he will be facing backwards, of course), with the end of the piece of rope in his left hand. Beginner number one will then stand across the machine (looking forwards) and taking hold of the handles with both hands, will place his left foot upon the step, raise himself thereon, and seat himself in the saddle. The piece of road chosen should be slightly down hill. The assistant (*pro tem.*) should then, whilst carefully holding his friend up, remove his left hand from the head to the left-hand handle, and his right hand from the handle to the spring or backbone behind the rider. He will then of course be facing forward, and will try to hold the learner up on the machine, always doing his best to prevent his falling away from him, i.e. over to the right, while, should the learner at any time so fall, the attendant must pull with all his strength on the rope so as to prevent the weighty and clumsy machine falling heavily to the ground with the rider. Several cases have been known in which a broken leg, and in one case a very bad fracture of the thigh bone, have resulted from such a fall with a solid iron-framed bone-shaker, and this danger is obviated to a very great extent by the use of the rope, as suggested above, which also subserves other purposes. The mounted man should not attempt to pedal at first, but should simply sit upright upon the saddle with a firm grip on the handles, and try his best to keep his balance by their use. The rule for steering is exceedingly simple, but its difficulty to the novice lies in the fact that, despite its extreme simplicity, it requires the rider to take instantaneously the exactly opposite course to that which his natural impulse suggests. Supposing a rider feels himself falling to the right, the natural impulse will cause him to turn away from the direction of the threatened danger—a course which is instantaneously fatal ; the rule, which is emphasised by italics, runs as follows :—

'*Turn the steering wheel towards the side to which the machine is falling.*'

For example, if the rider feels himself falling to the right, he should pull the right handle towards him, and push slightly at the left handle, and after a swerve or two, and a stagger towards a calamity on the opposite side, the balance is regained.

Of course, at first there is a strong and natural tendency to overdo this corrective action, so that the beginner who turns his wheel sharply to the right to counteract an impending fall to the right finds himself the next moment falling to the left, owing to his having overdone this turn; and then, getting into a wild and flurried state, of course he falls. A capable and expert rider keeps his balance by following exactly the same

HIS FIRST LESSON.

rule, but the corrective turn of the wheel is infinitesimal, as the balance of the body of course co-operates to a very great extent with the maintenance of the equilibrium by means of the steering. The natural tendency of the beginner, as pointed out above, is always to turn his wheel the wrong way; so the attendant should keep on repeating to the rider the maxim, 'Turn the wheel towards the side to which you are falling.'

During all this time the mounted man should keep his feet off the pedals and concentrate all his attention on the steering, the attendant for the time being pushing him along at a fast walking pace, say four to five miles per hour. After a short time the rider will acquire the knack of steering sufficiently well to warrant his placing his feet on the pedals. This will momentarily upset all he has learnt, as from the position of the saddle any power he may consciously or unconsciously exert will tend to thrust the wheel out of its direct course, and thus to throw a severe strain upon the hands and arms, which are called upon to steady the steering wheel. It is an admitted fact that practical tricyclists are by far the best subjects amongst the learners of bicycle riding, more particularly those who have ridden the Humber type of tricycle. They have of necessity mastered the art of correcting the lateral thrust of the leg by means of the handles and careful pedalling, and they are thus quite capable of correcting it in the early stages of their career as bicyclists. Even those riders who have only ridden the bath-chair pattern tricycles are better off in this respect than the absolute beginner, for they have acquired at least the knack of moving their feet in rotary action, and are thus able to propel the machine without awkwardness even if they cannot balance it. The complete novice, on the other hand, as often as not pushes at the wrong time, awkwardly throws his weight on the ascending pedal, thrusts the wheel out of its course by jerky lateral efforts to propel it, and frequently misses his pedal, with, of course, disastrous results to his cuticle. A course of careful and intelligent tricycling (necessarily on a rotary-action machine) before commencing the initiatory stages of bicycling is for this reason most emphatically recommended.

The beginner's two great difficulties will be found first in the steering, as detailed above, and then in the pedalling. The position of the rider on the bone shaker, so far behind the pedals, converts all the pedal action into a lateral thrust: this increases the tendency to unsteady steering, and the beginner must use both arms in concert to overcome, by means of the handles, the strong tendency to lateral thrust of the leg action.

Of course, when the more modern type of machine is in due course mounted, the thrust of the leg approximates more closely to a vertical than a horizontal line, and as a consequence the tendency to irregular steering is very largely modified, whilst the strain on the wrists and arms is reduced to a minimum.

Having sufficiently mastered the art of propelling and steering the machine, the beginner will have to learn to mount and dismount; and here again the services of the assistant and the rope are very valuable. The most dangerous fall which a man can have is that which occurs at the moment of mounting or dismounting, as the sufferer not infrequently falls into, or on to, the machine, and very serious injuries may easily be inflicted by contact with the sharp angles of the iron frame, the edges of the step or the pedals, or with the handles. To learn to dismount, the rider, very carefully watched over by his friend, should begin a long curve to the left, so that the machine leans slightly to that—the getting-off–side; then reaching back carefully with the left foot, he should feel for the step, taking care not to put his toe amongst the spokes—which would of course result in a severe fall. Having found the step—and the assistant will do well to advise him by word of mouth in which direction to move his foot—he should rise upon it fairly at once, then throwing some of his weight upon the handles and the rest upon his left leg, turning the machine still more to the left and throwing more weight upon the left-hand handle, the right leg is brought sharply over the hind wheel and the rider drops easily and quickly to the ground, his right hand leaving the handle at the last moment as soon as some degree of proficiency has been acquired, and falling on to the back of the saddle. In after experiences, when higher machines are used, this dropping of the right hand upon the saddle will be found a great assistance in easing the drop of a dismount. The dismount should be assiduously and carefully practised until the rider feels perfect confidence in the execution of the manœuvre.

When this stage has been reached, and this is determined by the amount of practice the novice is able to give, he may go a step further and learn to mount. This is most easily accomplished in the following manner :—The beginner should practise a few dismounts on the lines laid down above. Then dwell for as long a time as possible on the step ere descending to the ground, until after a few experiments he finds he can stand on the step and keep the balance of the machine for several yards at a time. The next stage is to stand thus on the step, preferably on a slightly down-hill road, and while so doing, to bend the left knee (holding firmly on to the handles at the same time) and just touch the ground with the right foot, immediately afterwards straightening the left knee and regaining the saddle. This exercise may be continued, with intervals for rest, until the rider feels quite confident of his own proficiency. And now comes the crucial test—that of mounting from the ground—a feat for which the above recommended exercises have gradually prepared the learner. On the oft-mentioned piece of slightly falling road, with the wind behind if possible, so as to make everything as easy as circumstances admit, the learner should place himself astride the hind wheel and put his left foot fairly on the step, the handles being firmly grasped. Throwing most of the weight upon the left foot, several hops should be made with the right foot until a sufficient pace is attained. Then, holding well on to the handles, the left leg should be sharply straightened, and the rider should get into the saddle. This should prove an easy task after the necessary pace has been got up if the exercises set forth at length in the foregoing pages have been carefully and completely carried out.

At first, of course, from nervousness the beginner will be in a great hurry, but as soon as he gains confidence by frequently repeated executions of this movement, he should seek to perform it slowly and with the utmost care and deliberation. This caution is extremely necessary, for many bad habits and tricks are learnt in this stage of a cyclist's practical experiences, and many an otherwise good rider may be seen whose method of mounting a machine is simply ridiculous. One, for example, will get on to the step of his machine with any amount of lightness and grace, and from that point spring into his saddle with a sort of jerky leap which occasionally takes him over the front wheel into the road, and which always strains the spring and frame of the machine in a violent and perfectly unnecessary manner. Another may be noticed whose mounting is a painful and arduous undertaking, necessitating many struggles and entailing frequent failures If the beginner will only take the trouble to study carefully the right way, he may hope to avoid the many faults of bad mounting.

A large machine may be as easily and safely mounted from the step as a little one if the rider will follow out carefully the following hints. Having got fairly on to the step with the left leg, the right should be placed over, or rather round, the right-hand side of the saddle, the weight being thrown a trifle to the left and well forward. Then, carefully avoiding any spring from the left foot, the rider should pull himself by means of the handles directly forward, at the same time thrusting his right knee downwards and forwards (taking care to keep the right foot out of the spokes). If a steady force be exerted without any jerky action, the rider will glide into his saddle with the utmost ease and comfort. As soon as the left foot has been removed from the step, the leg should be swung sharply but evenly forward into the same position as the right limb, and then—and not till then—the beginner may make a careful effort to catch his pedals. It is well once more to emphasise the vital rule: Do not hurry. A very deliberate and careful mount may, by steady practice, be converted into an adequately rapid mount—sufficient for all practical purposes—which will always, with care, retain the very important quality of safety. The jerk or spring off the step is the fatal flaw in many a rider's method of mounting, although only a little care is necessary to overcome the fault whilst the habit is young. The spring will be found, more especially in the case of heavy men, to severely damage the machine ridden, the backbone of which will often become twisted, unless it has been especially made extra strong (which of course also necessitates extra weight) to withstand the strain. The rider who takes the trouble, therefore, to cultivate an easy and scientific mount, will never be very nervous should occasion arise for him to mount a very light machine, for fear of that most dangerous of all accidents, a forward pitch before he is quite settled in the saddle.

It is frequently the case in modern close-built machines that the handles come so low as to interfere with the forward passage of the right knee in the course of the mount as suggested above. Where this occurs it is advisable either to have the handles made cowhorn fashion, or else to raise the step about a couple of inches; either of these expedients, the latter being in most cases the least expensive, will prevent the rider from acquiring an awkward habit of mounting, which might result from his having been baulked in his earliest essays by striking his knee against the bar of the handles.

Mounting, riding, and dismounting having thus been explained, and, it is hoped, brought within the capacity of the beginner, he may at once begin to study the real art of bicycle riding as distinguished from what, for want of a better term, may be called the mere rule of thumb of riding the wheel. The cyclist should from the first aspire to be something more than a mere straight-away rider; he should seek to be a clever and expert master of his machine. For this reason, and with this object always in view, he should carefully study the various methods whereby he applies his power, should seek to acquire an effective, comfortable, and easy style, and to develop by careful and constant practice that dexterity of limb which is so necessary to pace. The cyclist is not recommended to take up that branch of the sport known as 'fancy riding.' Such tricks of balance may well be left to the circus performer and professional athlete, whose business it is to risk their limbs in these exercises and feats of skill. The average amateur cyclist should simply seek to acquaint himself with the qualities and peculiarities of the machine which he uses. The first point, when sufficient confidence has been acquired by a course of steady and continual practice, is to try and acquire an easy, and, above all, comfortable style; and as this requisite is as indispensable to the tricyclist as to the bicyclist, the two classes may be taken under the one head. Readers will remark that an easy and *graceful* style is not spoken of, inasmuch as the latter cannot always be learnt, and the effort to gain it might in some cases prove an absolute drawback ; for it may not be possible for a cyclist to be graceful and at the same time exert his full powers, just as in the same way many a first-class racehorse has not perfect action, and many a fast running man has progressed in the most ugly style. In the same way many

COASTING—SAFE AND RECKLESS.

a good cyclist, in adopting an easy and comfortable attitude, suited to his individual idiosyncrasies, is often found to indulge in a habit which may be considered extremely awkward and ugly by the more hypercritical of the observers. A very sharp line must, however, be drawn between mere laziness as opposed to actual necessity, as very often the former is the true cause of the awkward style and clumsy action of many a young rider. The beginner should therefore seek to cultivate a style based on the very best models, and then, when his experiences are somewhat enlarged, he may modify it in one direction or another to suit himself, always of course taking care not to fall into any error whereby he may unnecessarily lose any of the good points which he has by careful practice acquired.

For ordinary road riding, either on the bicycle or the tricycle, a fairly upright position should be assumed, although in ninety-nine cases out of a hundred the bolt upright attitude is as inconvenient in practical cycling as it would be in foot running, when the best efforts of the rider are to be made. So the novice will bear in mind that when hurrying or riding against the wind, the body may be advantageously carried rather forward, always supposing that the saddle has been rightly placed, and that the leg reach has been properly studied, of which more anon. This forward inclination of the body tends to throw most of the weight upon the pedals and the driving wheel, and, when not exaggerated, it is most suitable, as it presents less surface to the wind and at the same time increases the grip of the wheel upon the ground, thus steadying the steering. The position of the handles is a point which requires very careful consideration, as it very often happens that a mistake in this detail will permanently injure a rider's style. A very old and favourite

FIG. 1.

theory with cyclists has been embodied in the oft-quoted phrase 'a straight pull,' and bicycle handles (which are as a rule not adjustable) have been put lower and lower to afford the rider the full advantage theoretically supposed to be thus obtained, until the extreme point of efficiency has been passed, and the style of the rider cramped and seriously damaged through his having to reach after his handles in a noticeable and consequently awkward manner. This is, in this connexion, absolutely the most serious error that can be made, and both the bicyclist and the tricyclist will do better to ride with a short reach and bent arms rather than have the handles so low as to cause the

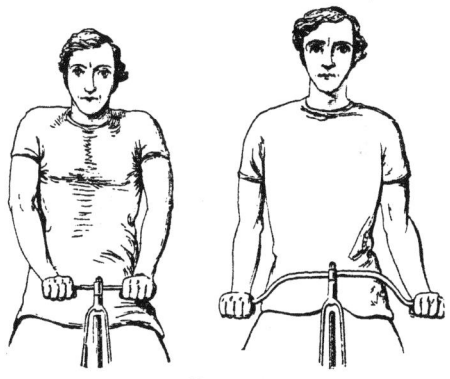

FIG. 2.

rider to crane over with rounded shoulders to reach them, which very soon bows the back, pulls the shoulders forward, compresses the chest, and generally alters the comfortable pose and set of the body; added to which the rider must, at any rate if he be a bicyclist, retain a firm and steady grip of the handles, and cannot therefore, in a sudden emergency, throw his weight backwards by straightening his arms, as in the case of a shorter reach, and the danger of serious accidents, especially down hill, is thus very largely increased.

In the case of the tricyclist who suffers from a too lengthy arm reach the difficulties are less important, although they equally tend to spoil the style, added to which in the case of a well-poised machine the rider will find himself constantly slipping forward on to the peak of the saddle, and as constantly having to recover himself by raising himself on the pedals—an irksome and annoying task which can be at once obviated by altering the adjustment of the handles, or, if they are raised as high as possible (which sometimes happens with very long-legged riders in certain patterns of tricycles), a fresh pair of handles with longer standards should at once be purchased from the makers, as the added comfort thereby obtained will amply repay the rider for the expenditure. A short arm reach, therefore, is very much to be preferred to an overlong one. The correct and most comfortable position of the arms can only be satisfactorily determined by actual experience and practice in each individual case, as the length of the arm is variable; but the best guide is to ensure a slight flexion of the arm at the elbow when the handles of the bicycle are held with the undergrip, or a slight inward bend of the wrist on the ordinary pattern front-steering tricycle. This bending of the arm on the bicycle will ensure an easy and comfortable position of the body and shoulders, and the rider's weight can in a moment be carried back by straightening the arms and throwing back the shoulders. These remarks, as will be seen, apply in a great measure to both bicyclists and tricyclists, but only a practical experiment can satisfactorily determine the exact and proper position of the handles on either class of machine.

How to hold the handles is a much discussed point, there being three recognised styles amongst bicyclists, all of which have been also adopted by tricyclists. They may be best described as the over-grip style, the under-grip style, and the end, or cap, grip. The over-grip is when an ordinary parallel horizontal handle on the end of the handle-bar is held with the knuckles and back of the hand upwards and the thumb underneath at the inside end of the handle. This is the way ordinarily adopted by the beginner, and is a sound and serviceable method, very popular amongst the upright class of road riders. It should in most cases be used in descending a hill, as it affords especial facilities for applying the break, and also compels the rider to hold himself fairly well up, whilst it allows him also to sit a bit back, and to shift his shoulder weight to the rear in case his hind wheel becomes unsteady; at high speeds, with a steady shoulder and a straightened arm, the machine can be held straight by pressure on the handles, whilst, if the rider prefers to descend the hills with his legs over the handle bar, the over-grip is still more suitable as enabling him to lift himself away from his machine in case of a fall over any obstacle which may be encountered.

The over-grip must, however, give way to the under-grip for level and up-hill work, and also more especially for racing. In the under grip the hand grasps an ordinary parallel handle with the knuckles and back of the hand turned downwards, the nails on the top, and the thumb upwards on the outside of the handle. This method of holding the handles is generally identified with the 'grasshopper' fashion in racing, and—as can be easily proved to demonstration by any reader—it throws the shoulder blades well back and opens the chest completely for the full inspiration of the air, obviously a most important matter for race riders.

For racing men, as suggested above, the value of the under-grip cannot be over-estimated. Its effects are simple, yet efficacious. The rider's weight is thrown forward over the front wheel, which is thereby steadied, whilst its hold upon the ground is increased. Very little of the weight is carried by the hind wheel as long as the course is straight; the rider can, however, by slightly bending his back, carry his weight suddenly to the rear, and almost instantaneously increase the pressure upon the hind wheel so as to give it the necessary grip for steering purposes round corners or in case of any sudden emergency, and this rapid retrograde action is most conveniently made when the hands are held in the under-grip position.

The end grip or cap-hold is that position taken by the hand when it grasps the handle over the end, the rounded end of the handle being pressed against the palm, or when the horn handle is affixed in the Portsmouth fashion at right-angles across the end of the steering bar. The back of the hand and the knuckles are turned outwards, the thumb coming over the top of the handle to secure the grip, and the fingers folding round it from underneath. This position is a compromise between the over- and under-grip, and finds much favour with some practical riders. Anyone who likes it can of course easily adopt it, but it has some drawbacks which will prevent its becoming altogether very popular. The shape of the handle and its fittings preclude the possibility of any change of position, and in the course of very long journeys or over very rough roads, when the vibration is severe, the absence of this possibility would in most cases be found very irksome; and for this reason the fitting of these cross-handles to the small-wheeled 'Safeties' now in vogue is to be very strongly deprecated. The varying positions which the hand can take with ease in succession on an ordinary handle gives the latter a distinct advantage in most riders' opinion over the transverse or cross-fitted handle, and it is therefore suggested that the beginner should carefully limit himself to the use of the ordinary horizontal handle.

The rider should accustom himself to the various methods of holding the handles pointed out above, and the bicyclist should mostly confine himself to the under-grip for fast work, taking, of course, every care not to get too far forward; he should also, when opportunity occurs, practise shifting his hands from one position to another as occasion may require, at the same time steadying the machine with his feet, so as to be ready to meet any emergency. Whilst the learner is in the throes of mastering these minor points he will find, as suggested above, that with a little care with his feet he can control the course of the bicycle by their aid alone; and although he should at first exercise the utmost caution in so experimenting, yet, as he gets more expert, he may devote a certain portion of his exercising time to trying to see how far he can go without touching the handles. He will soon discover that nothing so soon obliges him to grasp the handles afresh as the uneven thrust of the leg that he acquired in the early days of his novitiate, which deflects the wheel from the straight course, and has in actual riding to be counteracted by a pull on the handles, an obvious waste of muscular power. With but a very little careful practice the beginner will acquire a varying amount of control over the steering with his feet, and this is the first crude step towards that mastery of the pedal action, the art of ankle work, which makes all the difference between a good and an indifferent rider.

To clearly appreciate the point at issue—and this is of primary importance—let the rider seek the nearest grindstone or coffee-mill, or in fact any apparatus fitted with a handle of the type usual in such machines. Taking hold of it, the experimentalist should move it to its highest point and then turn it slowly round, standing fairly behind, and, if possible, over it, so that the arm may be brought when straight in the position of the leg on a 'bone-shaker,' and he will find that the power he exerts can be roughly broken up into a series of direct forces. Supposing he is standing behind and a little above the grindstone, he first thrusts the handle away from him, the force being a forward horizontal one, roughly speaking Then he presses it down, this being a downward vertical force. Then, before it quite reaches the lowest point, he begins to pull it towards him, exercising a backward horizontal force, and finally he lifts it over the relative dead centre. exercising an upward vertical force; and then commences the forward thrusting action again. Having carefully studied this action with the hand, the principle of keeping up the application of the power all round should be adapted, as far as possible, to the action of the feet when riding a cycle. It will be necessary to have a pair of shoes fitted to the pedals with deep slots, to give the feet the necessary grip and prevent their slipping; and if the machine can be placed on one of the 'home trainers' or otherwise raised from the ground so that the first ankle work may be done on a free wheel, the task will be all the easier. The 'Home Trainer' patented by Mr. Milbrowe Smith of West Bromwich is a valuable assistance in this connexion, whilst the art of pedalling is of equal importance to every cyclist road rider and racing man, whether he ride bicycle or tricycle, safety or full-sized, front- or rear-steerer. The theory will be best understood if the rider momentarily supposes that he has gone a few steps backward in the Darwinian line of human descent, and that he is once again quadrumanous or four-handed, after the style of our Simian ancestors, his feet being replaced by hands. Were this four-handed being asked to sharpen an axe on a grindstone, he would probably grasp the conveniently arranged double handles of the grindstone with his nether hands, and perform the pull and thrust action illustrated above, whilst with his normal hands he held the blade he wished to sharpen. Supposing he had much of this exercise, a Simian man would be likely to do exceedingly well upon a bicycle or tricycle; for, steadying himself upon the saddle with his normal hands on the handle-bar, he would, with the others, grasp the pedals and not only push them down but pull them up, thrusting, pressing, pulling, and thrusting again in regular sequence. This would be practically the whole art of pedalling, and were man so formed as to be able to grasp as firmly with his feet as he does with his hands, his pace on the wheel would undoubtedly be greater. But the foot grip is wanting, and the next best plan must be looked for. This is supplied by a careful and intelligent cultivation of the use of the ankle-joint, which, by proper practice and constant exercise can be brought into a sufficiently skilful state to effect with consummate ease nearly all the various actions which a quadrumanous cyclist might perform; the main idea, as will have been gathered from the foregoing, being to exert throughout almost the whole revolution of the pedal a force or forces which shall tend to propel the machine, whilst ankle work, even in its weakest and least developed stage, prevents the rider from holding the pedal down when the lowest point is reached, a trick which very often has much to do with the notable slowness of a promising-looking rider. It is well therefore for the learner, as soon as he has mastered the rudiments of the art of riding, to begin to practise, however incompletely, the art of ankle work, as he will thereby modify and lighten his action and obtain a full return for all the exertions he may make.

It is a necessity in artistic ankle work that both legs should work equally, and the rider who begins to cultivate ankle-pedaling is advised to commence the education of his left foot first. It is usually found that the left leg takes longer to acquire its full share of skill in this direction than the right. Sitting upon the machine placed as suggested upon some sort of stand so that the driving wheel or wheels run free, or upon a 'home trainer,' the rider should put the left foot upon the pedal, being careful to see that the pedal bars are fitted into the slots in the soles of the shoe. Then let the pedal drop to its lowest point, and from the stationary position start the wheel—using the left foot alone—by grasping downwards with the toes, raising the heel and bending the foot downwards from the ankle, and (to use the only expressive word available) 'clawing' the pedal backwards and upwards. This should be done fairly from a dead stop half a dozen times, and then the break may be very lightly applied, and the same performance repeated. This course will initiate the beginner into the nature of the precise action required, and it must be carefully practised for a time both on the home trainer (if available), and also as far as the action is concerned in active riding on the road, until the knack or trick is fully mastered. Then, with a certain amount of break check on the trainer, or in the actual work out of doors, the rider should carefully carry out the following exercises, keeping them up as long as possible despite aches and pains (except cramp, which necessitates an instant dismount and a sharp friction of the muscles affected), so as to educate the joints and muscles up to the work required.

The appended diagram, fig. 3, although at first sight it savours of Euclid, is not by any means as learned as it looks. It is only intended to illustrate clearly the course of a rotating crank and pedal attached to a machine travelling in the direction G C as marked by the arrow. The pedal drawn at A will describe around the *axle* centre at J a circle as shown. Practically the reader is only concerned with the circumference of this circle, the diameter of which is equal to twice the crank-throw, as it is round the circumference that the foot placed on the pedal travels, and with it therefore it will be convenient to deal to

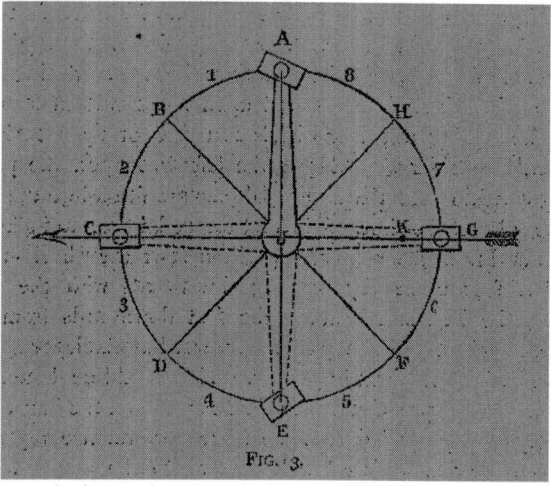

FIG. 3.

further simplify the description. There are shown in the diagram eight equidistant radii, as A J, B J, and so on, which may each in turn be taken to represent the crank. These radii divide the circle into eight segments, numbered in the order in which the pedal will pass through them in a complete circuit. Thus A to B, 1—B to C, 2—C to D, 3—and so on. It is assumed for the purposes of illustration that the rider is seated vertically over the point K, some few inches behind the centre of the driving wheel (taking an ordinary bicycle as the most convenient illustration, though these remarks apply equally to other cycles).

Seated then vertically above K, suppose it assumed that the rider only exerts a downward pressure by simply straightening his leg in the direction A E, it is obvious that he cannot effect very much in the way of propulsion whilst his foot is passing through segment 1, from A to B. From B through C to D, traversing segments 2 and 3, the force would be at its maximum of efficiency, after which whilst traversing section 4 from D to E its value as a propulsive power would rapidly decrease until it reached F, where if the force acting in the direction A E were kept up, *i.e.* the pressure downward on the pedal maintained, it would actually retard and stop the machine—a source of frequent falls to the novice. Supposing, however, that the downward force of the leg were stopped at E, and the foot simply lifted with the pedal *viâ* F, G, and H to A, the downward thrust would again become effective. This raising or lifting of the foot with the rising pedal from E to A, by a distinct and intentional muscular effort, is one of the earliest signs that the student has at length passed out of his novitiate. It is, however, obvious that a rider merely moving his feet straight up and down is effective only from A to E, and only really effective, to any material extent, from B to D, or through just one-fourth of the entire revolution of the pedal, an obvious loss of power if of nothing else. Supposing, for example, a rider were so placed as to be well behind the crank centre, say for argument's sake on a level with the line C G produced backwards, if he were to attempt to propel the machine by straight thrusts, as in the foregoing example, then it will be clearly seen that he becomes effective through the semicircle G H A B C, having the maximum power from H to B, whilst he would be also quite ineffective during the return half of the stroke from C through D E and F to G. What an advantage it would be if the rider, instead of driving but half a revolution of the crank, and that not effectively, could by a little practice drive throughout nearly three-quarters of the entire revolution of the crank? This tremendous increase of power can be secured by cultivating the proper use of the ankle-joint, and is in short the result of a careful mastery of the art of ankle work. By the aid of a few simple diagrams it will be easy to explain the whole mystery, and although a mere perusal of the theory of the art will not teach it practically, yet if the learner will carefully carry out the instructions appended there is little doubt that he will soon understand the principle of the thing, and it then becomes simply a question of sufficient practice to make him an adept at this most valuable accomplishment, whatever may be the class of cycle the learner uses, always supposing that it has a rotary action, or something very closely akin to it. Seated either on

FIG. 4.

a bicycle slung so that the wheel may revolve, or upon a hometrainer, the beginner should raise the pedal to its highest point, and then, steadying the wheel with the break, place his foot upon the pedal, carefully fitting the slots in his shoes into their places, and seeing in any case that the foot is straight. Then, using the thigh muscle for the most part, let him thrust the foot (and pedal) forward in a horizontal direction, in fact a sort of sharp forward kick, having the heel dropped as low as possible, the toes well up, and the foot firmly set on the pedal, which will be at an angle as shown in fig. 4. This should be practised carefully with the break slightly on, and for this purpose, though

RIDING.

a bicycle can be used, a tricycle will be found much handier, if no home-trainer of the West Bromwich pattern is available, as the break can be put slightly on by means of a piece of string or a strap to the lever, tied to any convenient point, and the novice can spend a few minutes daily practising this exercise; in carrying out which programme the left foot should at first be used more than the right. As soon as the usual awkwardness of the ankle-joint has been worked off this action will be found remarkably effective in starting the machine, as the force is applied in a direction approximating to the line taken by the

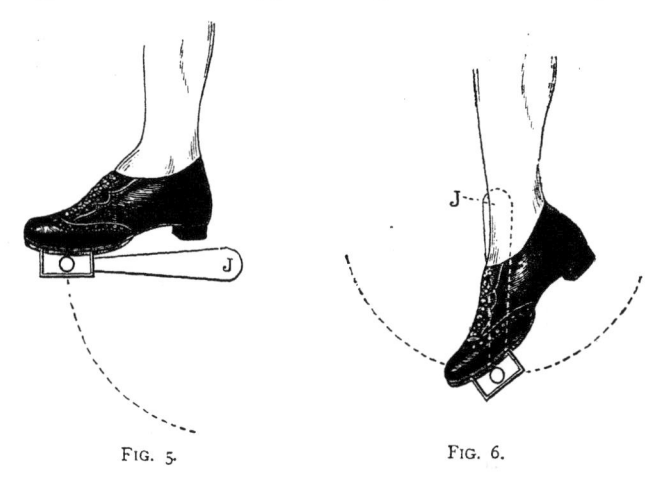

Fig. 5.   Fig. 6.

pedal through segment 1, fig. 3; after a time the ankle muscles, and those of the calf, will become stronger, and a sharp straightening of the ankle, as the pedal passes from A to C through segments 1 and 2, will materially aid the propulsion of the machine. This straightening of the ankle will be continued until at C the foot is brought into a position at right angles to the leg (fig. 5), the muscular effort of which should now have by equal gradations become directly downwards. The pedal will now assume a horizontal position, and the power of the leg with the weight of the body and the pull of the arms will all be exerted to force it downwards—at this point the crank throw is in the most effective position and the hardest work is put in. Passing C, the pedal begins to follow a backward course to D and E, and here the ankle action becomes of the greatest value. The toe is gradually dropped, and the heel raised as the pedal gets nearer and nearer to the lowest point E, when the foot will have assumed a position shown with some exaggeration in fig. 6, the action having at length reached the backward or 'clawing' stage. To secure the full advantage of ankle work this '*clawing*' action must be very carefully practised; the toes should be sharply pressed upon the sole of the shoe as if they were trying to grasp something, whilst the ankle should be straightened as much as possible, the foot being almost in a line with the leg, the calf muscles being strongly retracted, and the backward pull (which of course requires fitted shoes) can be made practically effective through segment 5, and also of service well into segment 6. The ineffective portion, which exists on either side of the point G, is soon reduced to a very small part of the circle, for as soon as the point G has been passed, the heel should be sharply dropped, and an upward and forward kick or thrust as described in the directions for the first position, will lift the pedal forwards and upwards to A, when of course the whole series of actions will be repeated.

No rider can pedal properly in a week, only a very few are passably proficient in a month, whilst a master of the art takes years to develop, and never claims to be perfect, for not one man in a thousand can be found with equal power and equal action; so the beginner will see at once that he has plenty of scope for work and also for improvement. Constant, careful, and intelligent practice is not only absolutely necessary, but is the only way in which the thing can be fully mastered. At first a good deal of stiffness and some pain will be caused, especially in the knees, calves, and front of the shins, whilst the lower abdominal muscles are occasionally painful in common with those of the upper thigh; this is sometimes caused by over-work, or by attempting to practise up-hill. Elliman's embrocation can be recommended as a complete specific in such cases, but if the stiffness is very bad, warm fomentations or a warm bath may be taken, the embrocation being afterwards carefully applied, whilst after each spell of work the rider or his attendant should carefully rub the legs for ten minutes or so with the bare hand, which will assist the circulation of the blood through the muscular tissues, and enable them the more rapidly to accommodate themselves to the novel task imposed upon them. As pointed out above, these exercises may be carried out upon a bicycle, tricycle, or home-trainer.

As suggested above, the left foot should first be carefully schooled (except, perhaps, in the case of those persons who are left-footed as well as left-handed), then the right, which latter should be put through the same exercises, though for a time less frequently than the left. As soon as some precision of action has been acquired, the learner should attempt a little slow and painstaking road riding, on a level road, not down hill or before the wind (as being likely to cause inadvisable rapidity), or up stiff hills or against heavy wind, because this will unduly tire the limbs and muscles. The right foot being taken off the pedal and put on the foot-rest, or swung backwards, taking care, of course, not to get it in the spokes, the left should be carefully exercised alone, the machine being driven as straight as possible at a moderate pace. This strengthens and develops the muscles, and at the same time affords the rider or his attendant a practical opportunity of testing the actual amount of force exercised by the leg, a material point, as ankle action without a little power to back it is practically useless, albeit a very small amount of power can be made to go a very long way by the possessor of a good and well-studied ankle action. In fact, to this one accomplishment, possessed in a very high degree of efficiency, may without doubt be ascribed the successes on the path and the road of riders who, regarded merely from the muscular power standpoint, are by no means pre-eminent as athletes. As soon as the left limb has been fairly started, and has developed some little proficiency in the steady and even propulsion of the machine, that more promising pupil, the right leg, may be exercised in the same way ; but care should always be taken, for months after the commencement of the work, not to forget the left leg, or to throw all the labour—as so many riders unconsciously do—upon the right, as an uneven ankle action is possibly worse than no ankle action at all, seeing that the machine is always being driven to one side, necessitating of course extra exertions on the part of the rider to keep it in a straight course, so that power is lost all round, and literally thrown away, for no possible good of any kind is derived from it.

The rider who follows out closely the above instructions will soon begin to appreciate the value of the art which he is acquiring, but he will do well to curb his impatience, and to adhere to his plan of daily practice at a slow pace for a considerable time. It is very bad policy to hurry, at any rate for some time after the rudiments of ankle action have been fully mastered, for if the rider gets up a high rate of speed he is almost certain to fall into some faults which will cause him to slur over some material portion of the stroke ; it is therefore necessary that a rider who desires to gain a thoroughly irreproachable ankle action should devote daily a certain specified time to practising it at a slow pace, which may gradually be increased as proficiency is acquired, until at the highest speed of the racing path the all-round ankle action of the accomplished rider is seen in its highest development. Whilst learning, say for the first couple of months, an exaggerated action is recommended, the heel dropped as low as possible, the toes alternately being pointed as high up and as low down as the ankle-joint will permit, and the forward thrust and claw back carried out as far as possible. These actions, thus carried to the extreme, effect the same purpose as the skipping or jumping of the sprint runner:

they stretch all the muscles and increase the freedom of motion in the joints, and thus assist materially in the development and freedom of the action; but when at length it has been fully mastered, and a lengthy practical experience has taught the rider that even at the highest speeds he does not slur or shirk the work, it is well to modify the action of the ankle as far as is compatible with the full use of the joint. The true art is to conceal art, and this modification properly learnt in no way impairs the effectiveness of the ankle action; in fact, it really increases its value by adding to its rapidity all round, and thus allows more scope for the use of the powerful muscles of the calf and thigh, whilst the easy smart rhythmic action of the ankle keeps the work alive, to use an expressive if somewhat technical metaphor. The real point is that the pull and thrust action, going on simultaneously with both feet, practically does away with the dead centre, and keeps the wheel running between the full throw strokes, a point which will be fully appreciated by all practical cyclists, and may be likened to that portion of the sculler's art which enables him to keep his boat running between the strokes. The rider must bear in mind throughout all his work that the downward thrust is of course his most valuable point, and that it should be fully taken advantage of, and not lost sight of in the course of the all-round action; but at the same time the quick clawing recovery prevents any hang of the machine at the dead point, and therefore materially aids propulsion. Nor is it right to suppose, as some riders have done, that ankle work is only of service on the racing path, and of no value elsewhere; as a matter of fact the very greatest value is to be attached to the art on the road. All our best road riders excel in a sound and straight ankle action. Mr. Harry Osborne, for example, is a splendid road rider, and especially good at hills, and his excellence is due to a very great extent to a natural ankle action, backed by plenty of physical power. Mr. Charles E. Liles is another skilful exponent of the advantages of true ankle action, inasmuch as he always uses rubber pedals when racing, yet he seldom or never slips his pedal, even in the excitement of the closest of finishes, owing solely to the fact that his ankle play always keeps his foot in the safest of positions, behind the pedal in the direction of the force applied. John Keen, the well-known professional ex-champion, is pre-eminently an ankle worker, and he shines now, as he always has done, on the road and up hill; indeed, all the modern racing men, amateur and professional, have cultivated this style with a greater or less degree of success. The road rider should therefore study and practise the art with as much care and assiduity as the racing man, as he will always find it of the very greatest service in all branches of active cycling.

The accurate arrangement of the reach of the machine is an important point, and has a notable effect upon the success or otherwise of the rider. The question, as far as it deals with racing machines, will be found fully treated in the chapter devoted to this branch of the subject. The choice and arrangements of a roadster will, however, interest a much larger section of readers, and is therefore described at greater length here. It is an absolute necessity that the machine for use on the road should be well under control, so as to ensure the complete safety of the rider, and this desideratum can only be secured by having the roadster machine as nearly as possible an exact fit.

Too long a reach on a bicycle is dangerous, as the rider loses his pedals at the bottom of the stroke, and is thus unable to steady the machine with his feet at high speeds, whilst too short a reach, though infinitely preferable to the other extreme, is also likely to cause trouble, as the cramped position prevents the free action of the limbs, and as high-speed pedalling is thereby rendered very difficult, the result is unsteadiness, together with bad and irregular steering. To meet these objections the bicyclist who has passed through the novice stage must make an effort to secure a machine which exactly suits him, and although he may possibly get suited by chance, it is very much better to try a few machines as occasion serves, and also to get the assistance of a practical friend, before he finally decides on buying any one mount.

It is characteristic of the novice that he wants to ride a high wheel, but he will do well to curb this aspiration. Another idea which often takes this class of aspirant is that because an old and experienced cyclist of five feet nine inches rides a certain height of wheel, the novice of the same height can do the same. Putting aside the possibility of the older rider being abnormally long in the leg, there remains the undoubted fact that the effective length of a cyclist's leg is, up to a certain point, increased by practice. This is to be accounted for by the stretching and great freedom of the muscles : and the beginner will do well to remember this. The measurement to decide the right size of wheel which a novice should adopt must be taken down the inside of the leg, from the fork to the ball of the foot. The most convenient method of measuring is for the rider to put the inside of the front sole of his boot either on the end of the tape or on a piece of wood over which the tape ring may be slipped ; the tape should then be drawn tightly over the first finger of the right hand and pulled well up to the fork, along the inside seam of the trousers. This will be the theoretical reach of the leg. For example, say it is 35 inches. From this certain deductions must be made, say $5\frac{1}{2}$ inches for crank throw, inasmuch as the pedal drops that much below the centre of the wheel at each revolution, whilst another $2\frac{1}{2}$ inches must be deducted to allow for the set of the saddle above the backbone and the wheel. These deductions will give the rider 27 inches as his effective reach or radius, and this being doubled indicates approximately the correct size of his wheel, viz. about 54 inches. A rather smaller size may suit one rider, a slightly larger one another ; but the above measurements, if carefully carried out, will give very fair and convenient results, at any rate for the guidance of the beginner. After a time the effective reach of the rider becomes longer; the muscles act more freely, the limbs are used with greater boldness, and then a compensating increase in the size of the wheel used may be found advantageous, or the spring may be altered, or a more open Arab cradle spring adopted, and the reach of the original machine thereby lengthened. Those riders who do not intend to tempt fortune upon the racing path will do well to content

THE REAR-DRIVING SAFETY BICYCLE.
'Jog on, jog on the footpath way.'—*Winter's Tale*, Act iv. Sc. iii.

themselves with a machine which has an easy reach, although, as pointed out above, care must be taken not to adopt so small a mount as to cramp the action of the limbs. For winter riding, or for use in very rough or hilly country, a machine with a relatively smaller driving wheel is recommended, and should the user desire not to get out of his stride he can easily have the winter machine built with the same reach, &c., as his summer mount; others, again, who desire to use the same machines, but who find the work rather laborious in winter, will find very great benefit from having the cranks so arranged as to allow of adjustment from five to six inches—tricycle cranks, on central-geared machines, have mostly this arrangement. Riders who have not practically tested the matter can hardly appreciate the power, ease, and comfort obtainable during the worst and most inclement season by the use of the longer crank throw. The new class of Safety bicycles just introduced afford added facilities to the winter rider, as he can have his summer mount geared down for winter use, and a machine which has been used all the summer geared up to 58 inches will be found a model winter roadster when geared down to 50 or 52 inches during the inclement season.

Tricyclists are of course much better circumstanced as regards both winter riding and the arrangement of the leg-reach, whilst the practical success of the two-speed gears has placed almost unlimited powers at the service of tricyclists, as they give a lower power for use when, by stress of weather or badness of the roads, it is required. As pointed out above, adjustment is easily obtained on most tricycles, and the rider should not shirk the trouble of frequent alteration and readjustment until he has found out, by practical experience, exactly the reach which suits him. The careful tricyclist, having discovered this exact adjustment, will cut with a small file a very slight nick on the standard to mark the correct point, so that should the bolt by any chance slip, or the standard be altered to suit a taller or shorter friend at any time, he will at once be able to replace it at the most effective position for his own use—a hint the value of which will be found to lie 'in the application thereof,' like the aphorisms of the great Jack Bunsby.

The proper adjustment and placing of the saddle is another very important point in the curriculum of the cycling novice, as on this one thing depends to a very great extent the personal comfort of the rider; and there is no one item in the whole arrangement of the fittings and accessories of any class of machines on which so great a diversity of opinion is to be found. In fact, the rider, whatever his mount may be, must suit himself; but practical experience teaches that, by the exercise of a little judgment, he can find exactly what he wants, and at the same time so fashion his seat that it may assist him in forming a good style of riding.

The main point to be studied is to place the saddle as nearly as possible in a horizontal position. The cyclist, on the path as well as on the road, should sit upon his saddle, and not cling to it by means of the handle, or slide off it because of its awkward position, as so many riders may be noticed doing every few yards. A theory which once found a great many practical supporters was that if the saddle was raised high up behind and tipped well forward the rider was thrown on to his pedals continuously, and was thus kept at, or on, his work. Nothing could, in truth, be more fallacious, as the awkward pitch of the saddle threw almost all the bodily weight upon the wrists, and thus tired them, and at the same time defeated the very object it was supposed to attain, whilst back action and ankle work became practically impossible; and this error has been recently revived in the Safety bicycle of the rear-driving type. At the same time, many racing men have their saddles very sharply curved up at the back, but on inspection it will be found that the front part of the saddle affords ample space for sitting on, the curved-up back being simply a sort of steadier for cutting round the sharp corners of a cinder path. If the saddle is bodily pitched forward it entails endless annoyance, as the rider is himself thrown forward, and he has to lean very much to the front to carry his weight on the saddle with any approach to comfort, whilst the temptation to get off the saddle and on to the handles is very great, but if adopted, cramped and strained wrists, awkward and constrained leg action, and last, but by no means least, erratic steering owing to insufficient weight on the hind wheel, must inevitably follow. Experienced riders are nearly all able to recall instances in which a saddle so pitched was used by a novice, and they will recognise as characteristic the frequent assertion of the user that he could surmount hills better with his saddle in that position than when it was placed in any other. To the expert the reason was obvious. For going up a hill the pitched saddle becomes nearly, if not quite, horizontal, and the rider for once in a way sits at ease and can use all his muscular power for the propulsion of the machine. The opposite trouble, when the saddle is raised unnecessarily high in front, is possibly quite as annoying and objectionable. It was a very favourite arrangement on the old class of single-driving rear-steering tricycles, the object doubtless being to throw the rider's weight well back on to the steering wheel, and to prevent his falling out of the open front when the single-driving arrangement allowed the machine to swerve round on greasy roads. A high peak is exceedingly awkward for the rider, likely to prove very injurious, and to bring about accidents similar to that which caused the death of William the Conqueror. The victim of this error in the arrangement of the saddle has to cling with great tenacity to his handles to overcome the constant tendency to slide off his work and over the back of the saddle, whilst every bump on a rough road shoots him backwards, causes him to lose his pedals, and, in fact, generally prevents him from doing the full amount of work he is capable of. All these errors clearly point to one conclusion, viz., the panacea suggested above, a horizontal saddle.

The saddle on bicycles should never be put close up to the head, as, although this secures for the rider more vertical action, it also diminishes very materially his safety, by bringing him much nearer the vertical line from the centre of the driving wheel, and thus taking the weight off the hind wheel, making it more liable to fly up, and also very unsteady at high rates of speed.

The proper position is some five or six inches back on bicycles built without any rake on the front forks. For very

160 *CYCLING.*

nervous riders it is a good plan to have the roadster bicycle built with a good rake on the front fork, as this increases the steadiness and safety of the machine. This plan has been exaggerated with marked success in the "Xtraordinary' bicycle made by Singer & Co., which is without doubt one of the safest of the old class of machines.

In the case of all springs, great care should be taken to

THE 'XTRAORDINARY BICYCLE.

keep the nuts fastening the pins well screwed up, as any side shake or looseness in the spring attachments will very soon cause irremediable damage if not at once taken up, and a loose spring will sometimes injure an incautious novice's style very materially, especially if, as is frequently the case, he is riding a relatively small machine, in which for convenience sake the spring has been raised some considerable height above the backbone. The looseness of the attachments is magnified by the height of the spring above them, and the rider rolls slightly from side to side; this unsteadies his steering and gets him into the bad habit of slightly swaying from side to side to maintain his balance, which of course prevents him from using his legs or ankles truly, and soon leads to awkward and clumsy action. It is the fact that the wear is practically *nil* as far as the attachments are concerned that so strongly recommends to all practical riders that very best of cycling inventions the Arab cradle spring. Its dual construction allows of a limited amount of vertical play, and a gentle and equal oscillation which tends to ease the rider without unsteadying him; the action being in marked contrast to the jerky and uncomfortable movements of an ordinary spring with worn fastenings. A careful adjustment of the head or centres of bicycles and tricycles is also an absolute necessity, as a loose head will inevitably cause the steering to become very unsteady and erratic down hill or at high speed, whilst in the case of a bicycle the backbone will be wrung, and the wheels will not 'track' or follow accurately one after the other. Moreover, the machine itself is sure to be very seriously injured if the carelessness of its owner allows the mischief to continue for any length of time; for the loose head plays backwards and forwards in the top and bottom sockets or centres, which are thus very soon cut oval-shaped instead of remaining accurately circular, with the obviously inevitable result that they can never be subsequently satisfactorily adjusted owing to this irregular wear. By far the larger number of heads now fitted are of the 'Stanley' pattern, consisting of a backbone head carrying two coned ends, one upwards and one downwards. These coned ends fit into two coned sockets, one a fixture in the fork head, the other cut in the end of the adjusting screw fitted into the top of the head; and the adjustment is effected by screwing the top cone down upon the upward cone of the backbone head. Too much pressure at this point may possibly prove a serious danger to the head itself, as it will sometimes cause it to break off at the base of the opening just above the shoulder, so the rider will do well to take especial care to keep this vital part of his machine very carefully adjusted. To effect this satisfactorily the lock nut, which fixes the top or adjusting screw, must be loosened, and the latter screwed down upon the top of the backbone head until the backbone moves stiffly in the head; the adjustment may then be unscrewed half a turn at a time until the backbone moves quite freely; then, when this point has been reached, two tests may be applied: (1) the backbone may be lifted up and down, the rider standing a little above the machine, on a chair for example, and if it appears to move up and down in the head it requires further tightening; or (2) the backbone being held firmly with the right hand, the left thumb may be laid across the opening of the head so that it touches both the sides of the slit, and also the backbone head within: if the machine is now shaken backwards and forwards the slightest looseness in the adjustment will be felt by the ball of the thumb and can be taken up with care. Before either of these tests is applied the top lock nut should have been screwed up tight, as it often happens that an accurate adjustment before this is done is found quite tight and immovable after it has been locked up. As pointed out above, and again emphasised here, the rider should be very careful to ascertain that the adjustment is accurate and not over-tight, otherwise the strain on the head may injure the machine itself. At the same time the beginner will do well to remember that there is a point of perfect adjustment which can be attained, provided that the machine has not been ill-used and that the centres have been fairly worn, although he will find it necessary sometimes to exercise a good deal of patience and some little care before the required point is reached.

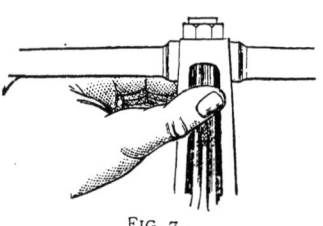

FIG. 7.

Without neglecting the machine, if it obviously requires attention, it is well to let the head alone as much as possible, and perhaps at first to get some experienced friend to do the needful job, especially in the case of an expensive new machine, as it oftens happens that such a machine requires considerable adjustment at first, but after a little steady wear it settles down and remains in a practically satisfactory state for a long time with very little further attention.

The next points that will require looking to will be the wheels themselves and their bearings, and the axles and bearings of tricycles. These may require a little screwing up, though the anxiety of the novice to do away with any side shake in his bicycle wheel is not to be encouraged; a very little looseness at this point does no harm, and shows that the bearings are not screwed up too tight, whilst it often happens that to readjust the bearings of an old and well-worn machine causes the balls to break, owing doubtless to the alteration of the positions of the coned surfaces on which they run presenting some irregularity which has been worn there by constant and careless use. Obviously untrue wheels are necessarily unsafe to begin with, and also a serious detriment to the rider who desires to steer a straight and steady course; and thus it is always well to have such wheels at once put right by a competent repairer, who should be also asked to run his eye over the cranks and see that they are straight. This fact being established, the pedals should be put on. These should be preferably rat-traps which afford a good hold for the feet, and tend to prevent the rider from slipping his pedal. They should be true and straight, and if they are bought second hand they should be carefully examined. If any suspicion of untrueness is entertained the pins should be taken out and put between the centres of a lathe and rapidly rotated, when any bend will be easily detected, and should be at once put right, as a crooked pedal pin gives a very uncomfortable twist to the ankle joint, and very soon tires the rider, whilst constant use will give the cyclist a permanent bad habit of screwing with the foot, a most unfortunate habit, and one which causes the action to look particularly ugly. The step, if not an adjustable one (some excellent adjustable steps are made by Messrs. Hillman, Herbert & Cooper, of Coventry; these can be arranged at any desired height, which is something of a desideratum for a beginner), should be conveniently placed not too far off the ground, but at the same time at a fair reach from the saddle, whilst if there is any difficulty in the matter it is better for the step to be convenient for the saddle and rather higher than is quite comfortable from the ground than *vice versâ*, as the rider will be more likely to get from the ground on to the step than from the step to the saddle, under adverse conditions. In every case the edge of the step should be frequently rounded off with a file, as the constant friction sharpens it up to such an extent that it inflicts a very ugly wound should the rider be so unfortunate, from wet shoes or other cause, as to miss it in the hurry of mounting or dismounting. The teeth of the step, as well as of the rat-trap pedals, should also be kept moderately sharp, at any rate at first, until the rider has arrived at that stage of his experiences in which he recognises the necessity of watching with care all these minor details of his steed's accoutrements, every one of which has a direct bearing upon his comfort and, what is still more important, his safety.

ACCIDENTS.

Falls on the road or path are of course of occasional occurrence amongst cyclists. Although their frequency has been much exaggerated, a skilful rider will escape many an accident where an unskilful cyclist is certain to come to earth.

Many accidents are caused by the failure of some part of the machine, and are practically inevitable and unavoidable; beyond, of course, the exercise of a certain amount of care and supervision, an examination of all parts of the machine for cracks and flaws and so on will obviate many falls.

The habit of flying hills at a reckless pace, or run-aways

through inadequate break power, will often be found at the bottom of some of the most serious accidents on the wheel; and though caution may add to the time taken on the journey, it vastly improves the rider's chance of completing the trip in safety. A sound and well fitted break is of course a *sine quâ non* to the road-riding cyclist. A stout pair of gloves is a great protection to the hands in the case of a header, and when a cropper at high speed seems inevitable the rider should avoid as far as possible falling *against* banks or similar obstructions. A fair fall on the road, especially if the shoulder can be made to come first to the ground, generally results in a series of somersaults, which, though damaging to the cuticle and the angles of the frame, is nothing like so serious in its results as a dead stop against a bank or wall. It may seem absurd to offer hints how to fall, but it is quite an art of itself, for which many riders develop quite a peculiar talent. If the rider can by any little ingenuity twist or turn on to his back, the resulting injuries will be very slight. A case in point occurred, when a well-known rider came into violent collision with another on the track; throwing his shoulder forward, he managed to fall flat on his back, and beyond the shaking felt no ill effects. Down hill on a bicycle the safest position is without doubt that in which the legs are placed on the handle-bar, as not only will a sharp application of the brake bring the rider over the front wheel and on to his feet, a somewhat jerky method of dismounting, but singularly serviceable in cases of emergency; but in cases of a bad fall the rider gets at once clear of his machine, and all practical cyclists know that the most painful injuries are caused by the handle-bars striking the front of the legs, so that, provided the rider has full confidence in his break, the legs-over-handles position is the safest. Should a rider fall on the road, as soon as the first pain has gone off he should essay to move. If his machine is uninjured and the cause of the cropper—a stone for example—clearly apparent, he should get on at once and make for the nearest doctor. If, on the other hand, he suspects a broken spring or a damaged bearing he will do well to walk, but in any case he should move off at once ere his wounds get stiff. Careful bandaging and the application of vaseline on lint will enable him to get home, and warm water and a soft sponge should be courageously employed to extract the grit and dust from the wounded surfaces; their subsequent treatment should be left in the hands of the doctor.

The path falls are decidedly the most serious in one respect, for if a rider has the misfortune to fall on cinders the results will be very disfiguring, blue marks exactly like tattoo and much of the same nature being the results of cinders being left in the wounds. Some of the best racing men have been sadly disfigured about the face, elbows, and knees in this way. It is therefore necessary for the rider or his friends to take instant action after an accident on the cinder path. Warm water if possible should be used, and the wounds superficially sponged over quickly to remove the surface cinder, then the edges of the wound which resemble a series of parallel deep scratches should be pulled gently apart and the cinders which lie in them gently removed with the corner of a towel or a bit of sponge, frequent washing with water being necessary. The pain in some cases is considerable, in others the force of the blow temporarily dulls the nerves, and advantage should be taken of the fact. In cases of insensibility similar steps should be taken. On one occasion within our knowledge a friend seized a stiff nail-brush and brushed out a deep wound, with the double result of bringing the patient to by the combined effect of pain and blood-letting and of extracting all the cinder at the same time. Heroic reminders like these should however be gently used, under the eye of a doctor if by any means possible. Face wounds should always be well cared for, and the victim should be encouraged to permit the painful process as long as possible. If a companion will firmly grasp both wrists it will be found of assistance in the more painful moments. As in the case of road falls, vaseline should be freely applied and a handkerchief tied round to prevent rubbing, and then the rider should be sent home as quickly as possible. Gentle fomentations with warm water will assist in keeping the wound open and extracting the foreign matter. Dr. G. B. Partridge, of Anerley, in a letter on this subject says :—' The best treatment undoubtedly is copious washing with warm water ; it need not to be desperately hot, and much of the foreign matter may thus be got rid of with the aid of a soft rag or a sponge. Very often larger fragments more or less imbedded in the skin may be removed at the time with a needle point, and this will be a considerable gain as to speed of recovery, and subsequently large soft *linseed-meal* poultices will materially hasten the separation of the particles too deeply imbedded for such mechanical treatment. I do not think anything else can be done in aid of Nature's own process of cure, which is in itself fortunately a fairly rapid one, the superficial layers of the skin undergoing frequent removal.'

Rest is a very great assistance to convalescence, and it is imperative in the worst cases. Of course broken bones need the surgeon's care, as also do more serious wounds than those alluded to above. The great thing is not to desire too rapid a recovery, and to give Nature time to re-establish the disintegrated membranes.

Cyclists, being usually in good health, and fair condition, recover rapidly. There are numerous nostrums in the market, some of which are very successful in removing stiffness, sprains, and bruises. Elliman's embrocation should be found in every dressing-room.

CHAPTER IV.

RACING.

THE racing section of the cycling sport presents both advantages and disadvantages to the rider; but there is no doubt that on the whole racing has done good service to the sport, and that cycling owes much of its success to the racing man. He is in fact largely responsible for its phenomenal development: a development which is far in advance of any parallel growth of a sport in this country. Nor is the reason difficult to discover: the successful athlete uses his head: his mental, as well as his physical, powers are called into play. The successful cyclist, as well as the runner and the jockey, must think as well as act. It is only when sound judgment co-exists with suitable physical powers that excellence in any branch of athletics is obtained. The racing cyclist very soon decided that it was necessary to demand from the manufacturers an improved vehicle. Mr. Frederick Cooper, the ex-professional champion, was among the earliest of these reformers. He was fortunate enough to find

GOING IT!

an able seconder in Mr. Thomas Humber, of Nottingham, now one of the best-known manufacturers. Finding that the machines then made were unnecessarily heavy, the present head of the well-known Nottingham firm was soon convinced that improvement was imperative and possible. The result of considerable labour was a vehicle which was then considered a marvel of lightness and strength. The existence of a demand very soon created a supply. The makers vied with each other in their attempts to meet the requirements of their customers, and in due course produced the thirty-five pound machine of 1879. This was generally considered as light a machine as it was possible to make consistently with the strength and stability required: yet in 1884 that weight was practically approached by roadster machines of sound and serviceable pattern. Once having discovered the advantages derivable from a saving in the weight of a machine, the racing men incessantly clamoured for further reduction and obtained it. As a matter of fact the craze was carried to the opposite extreme, and machines very much too light for any but feather-weight riders were sold to heavy men without any consideration on the part of their constructors. The heaviest of our racing men got across the flimsiest of racers, with the only possible result: breakdowns and consequent injury to both rider and machine. A reaction followed, and racing machines of from twenty to twenty-six pounds weight are now made amply strong enough to carry men of nearly twelve stone weight over the beautifully prepared cinder paths on which cycling contests are run, whilst the weightier racing men have learned by somewhat painful experience that they *must* have their machines built of sufficient strength and solidity to withstand the strain of their weight and power in the course of a long and severe race.

The manufacturers, thus constrained to cut down the weight of the racing machines, were enabled, by the practical experiments they made, to arrive at some rather startling discoveries as to the amount of unnecessary metal hitherto introduced into the frame and fittings of their roadsters, and ere long the experience thus gained enabled them notably to reduce the weight of that very much larger class of machine represented by the roadster cycles. Heavy joints, clumsy tubes, and preposterous solids were eliminated from the standard patterns, and tube frames of light gauge, ingeniously curved and fitted, replaced the haphazard constructions of the dark ages of cycling; thus the road-riding contingent, on whatever style of vehicle they disported themselves, were actually benefited by the practical and sometimes painful experiences of their racing *confrères*.

This gradual development and improvement in the machine was almost entirely confined to the bicycle, and it was not until after that machine in its roadster form had been thus benefited by the experiences of racing men, and cut down by successive steps to a wonderfully light weight, comparatively speaking, that the attention of the makers was directed to the hitherto almost unnoticed tricycle, a machine which, as we have shown, was really very much older than the bicycle. The original velocipedes were clumsy and heavy, and at first the adapters of bicycle construction to the three-wheeler followed too much the old lines, and attempted to secure success with a lever action; this phase did not, however, last long, and the modern tricycle with its balance gear became an accomplished fact. At first it seemed as if tricycle making had sprung at once to perfection, for the novel materials were introduced after complete and exhaustive testing in the bicycle, and all the 'latest improvements' as fitted to the bicycle were adapted to its new and popular congener, which thus 'on paper' seemed abnormally advanced for so new an introduction. This, however, was not an unmixed blessing, this adaptation of bicycling details to the tricycle, inasmuch as many of the additions to bicycles proved inadequate or unsuited to the requirements of the tricyclist. Thus the spoon break, much employed by some makers of tricycles in the earlier days and persistently affixed even now to the most dangerous samples of rear-steering machines, was, and is, by no means suitable for use in connexion with the tricycle, whilst in many other minor

LAST LAP.

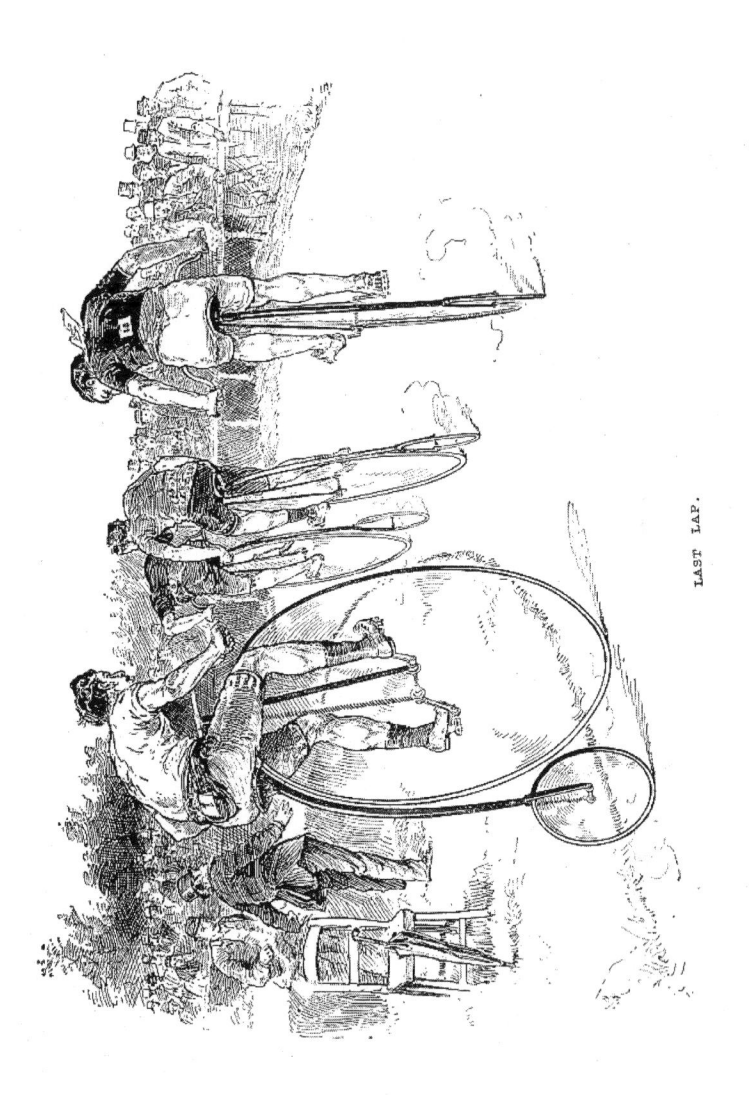

points inadequate contrivances were adopted, solely because they had been found suitable and sufficient upon the bicycle of the day. Thus those cyclists who imagined that the suddenly developed tricycle was 'improved' beyond improvement were considerably mistaken.

An opportunity occurred not long ago of comparing the 60-inch Humber tricycle upon which Mr. Lacy Hillier trained for the 1880 championship with the 44-inch Humber racer constructed in January, 1885, for Mr. George Gatehouse, the C.U.Bi.C. man; the difference between the original type and its improved 'descendant' is very marked, more marked in fact than is the variation between the earliest 'spider-wheeled bicycle' and the 'racer for 1886;' and tricyclists may feel assured that the development of their favourite mount will in point of rapidity compare favourably with that of the bicycle, inasmuch as scarcely six years have elapsed since the tricycle began to assume a position as a practical vehicle side by side with the bicycle. We venture to credit the comparatively small section of racing men with being the 'original cause' of the rapid improvement which has been made in both classes of velocipedes. Possibly the manufacturers would tell us that the racing men gave them more trouble, and were more difficult to please, than any other section of their customers, and doubtless this would be quite true; but it is particularly this fact which has brought about a desire on the part of the manufacturers to meet these particular gentlemen, and in that endeavour they have vastly improved the machines they manufacture, not only for the small class of racing men, but also for the much larger body of general riders.

The very first thing that a man who decides upon taking up bicycle or tricycle racing should do is to take competent medical opinion as to his physical capabilities for the work. And we would venture to suggest that the intending racing man should ask the opinion of some medical man who is also either a rider or an athlete in some way or another. We say this simply because some medical men set their faces against the sport without taking the trouble to consider the question at all. They arbitrarily assert the danger of cycling and threaten the would-be cyclist with all sorts of pains and penalties if he rides. Some medical men—their numbers are becoming daily fewer— assert that the sport is especially productive of hernia, although long experience has shown not only that this is seldom or never caused by cycling (unless a severe fall produces it), but that persons suffering from it can yet ride and cover long distances without any trouble or suffering. It is for this reason, therefore, that it is suggested to the novice that he should go to a doctor who has some knowledge of athletics. There are many, unfortunately, who cannot stand the mild strain of a ride upon the road, and such men would not of course venture to tempt fortune on the racing path; there are others also who, although they are free from disease, *might* possibly damage themselves by a vigorous course of cycling, and they also should avoid the path and its concomitant excitement and exertion; but there are men— many of them—to whom the hardest physical exertion is, or would be, of the greatest practical benefit. These are men with good physical powers, sound in wind and limb, without any heart or lung trouble, and with an active digestion. Such men, unless they can take a sufficiency of exercise, absolutely suffer from those very physical advantages which they enjoy. They grow fat and unwieldy, and in the train of the abnormal development of adipose tissue follows any number of ailments which might have been avoided by exercise. 'But,' one of these physically favoured individuals may say, 'I cannot take exercise enough. I have got to work, and the time at my disposal for recreation is limited.' To such a one the obvious reply would be, 'Although your time *is* limited, you can take quite enough exercise therein to keep you fit and well. Remember it is the pace that kills, and if instead of a slow walk, or a quiet ride, you go in for a rapid run or a sharp burst upon a cycle, you will put into a few minutes the equivalent exertion of hours of slow exercise with equal advantage to yourself; always supposing, as premised above, that some competent and unbiassed medical man has said that you are physically fit for the exertion you propose to undergo.' It is well for the prospective racing man to consider whether there are any other drawbacks which may prevent his success. Varicose veins do not seem so seriously to interfere with the pursuit of the sport as they do with running and walking. The reason is obvious. There is an absence of any direct *vertical* jar such as is experienced in running each time the foot comes to the ground, whilst the action is necessarily smoother, and with the aid of an elastic stocking a person suffering in this way may in most cases ride without injury or discomfort. In the same way, as was pointed out above, hernia, if properly supported, is no bar to riding or even racing, although the latter is by no means an advisable recreation for those who have the misfortune to be thus afflicted. Myopy, or near sight, is sometimes a great bar to success on the path; the sufferer, being afraid to wear glasses in case of a fall, yet being unable clearly to see his opponents, is always nervous when near them. This is the best explanation of the unsatisfactory performances of some of our racing men, who can do good work when alone in practice, but who, after overhauling their men in open races, seem nervous or afraid to pass them. The only remedy is to wear glasses, and the danger in case of a fall would be very slight, as the glasses would be flat to the eyes, and these are in nearly every case protected by the nose, frequently to its serious disfigurement. Many good men in the past have constantly ridden in glasses, and although occasionally they have fallen badly, no injuries to the eyes have been recorded as a consequence.

If after a careful examination a rider has ascertained that he is physically fit for the severe exertions of the racing path, and can undertake the labour without injury to wind or limb, his first step should be a little preliminary work upon the road on his ordinary roadster machine; and here once again the necessity must be urged of cultivating carefully, at the comparatively easy pace of road riding, that skill of ankle action without which a rider is always at a disadvantage. On the road the rider, whether bicyclist or tricyclist, should try and remember the rules laid down for successful pedalling, and should, so as to get every muscle properly set in place, have his racing machine as nearly identical as possible in pose and measurement with the roadster he is accustomed to ride. It is a very good plan for a beginner to race a few times upon his roadster, as he will be well set to the machine and thus will be enabled to 'feel his feet,' so to speak, without the dangers which must always attend anyone who makes his first essay on the path as a racer. When, however, he has gained a little experience and can keep his head during the few exciting moments from the crack of the pistol to the crossing of the tape by the winner, he may purchase a racing machine, and this he should use in all his practice spins upon the path, so that he may get well set to it ere he ventures upon it in an actual contest.

The choice of a machine which is to carry its owner at the highest possible rate of speed through a contest on the path is a serious matter, inasmuch as the slightest flaw or unexpected weakness in any part may lead in a moment to a serious if not fatal accident, and it is therefore a necessity that the would-be racing man should exercise great care in his selection of a mount. No complete novice at the sport would contemplate purchasing a racer, but even a fairly accomplished rider may be warned against purchasing a racing machine entirely upon his own responsibility. Some of the best makers of roadster machines do not make satisfactory racers, and therefore when a rider decides upon buying a racer he will do well to obtain the assistance and advice of a competent and able friend, who must of necessity be a racing man. In the choice of such a friend avoid the rider who is known or rumoured to be interested in any one or other of the manufacturing firms; his advice is naturally not free from bias. The machine chosen should be of a make which has secured a reputation for trustworthiness upon the path; for, as we have pointed out above, a reputation for the construction of sound and serviceable roadster machines does not of necessity imply that the firm shines as brightly in the construction of path machines. It is only by the severest of all tests, *a practical one*, that the merits of a racer can be gauged, and the disinterested advice of an old and experienced racing man will, therefore, be of the very greatest value.

We regard with the sincerest sympathy the adventurous rider, and there are a few such, who for the first time ventures upon a 'racer' of phenomenally small weight, constructed by a new and untried maker. The frame in such vehicles is cut down

RUSHING A RISE.

as light as it can be, the lowest possible effective strength being relied upon, and a very slight and probably undetectable fault or flaw will bring about very serious results. It may be that the new maker who has ventured on the experiment of constructing a racing machine has overlooked, in his heavier work, the bad quality of one particular casting, or other part of the rough material. This fault, when the casting, only just *finished*, and still with plenty of extra metal about it, was used in a roadster machine, was not apparent, but when cut down to the extreme of lightness, so as to compare favourably *on sight* with a similar fitting in a well-tried and popular make of racer, its weakness declares itself, of course, at the wrong moment, and a dangerous accident probably ensues. Then there is another class of maker—the firms who simply make up machines *for sale.* The main features of their manufactures are an exact similarity in design and construction throughout, and they supply a machine of just the same weight for the rider of thirteen stone as for the rider of eight stone. Such machines are invariably ill-fitted, and inadequate in ninety per cent. of the cases in which they find unsuspecting and unfortunate purchasers. *The machine, to be successful, should always be built for the rider*, and with a careful consideration of his weight, proportions, and style of riding. The maxim above is closely adhered to by every rider of note, and also by every trustworthy firm of racing machine makers, and no novice can hope to be really suited unless he takes some trouble to inform the makers to whom he gives his order as to the especial points which he requires modified to suit his individual peculiarities. Thus the effective reach of his leg can only be ascertained by practical experiment, and it is for this reason that an adjustable crank is fitted to all racers. Many men on the racing path use too short a throw. Five inches, except in the case of particularly short-legged riders, should be the minimum, whilst men of lengthy reach may well avail themselves of their physical advantages, and by using a five and a half or even a five and three-quarter inch throw, make the work proportionately easier without any inconvenience to themselves as soon as the first novelty has worn off. A wild theory once obtained amongst racing men that a very short throw (as short as four and a quarter inches in some cases) tended to assist and improve the sprinting powers of the rider. This error was due to the relatively slower action of the limbs with so short a throw, and as the pioneers of path-racing were mostly heavily muscled road riders there is little doubt that they really could go faster by exerting their strength, in place of undergoing the exhaustion of a rapid light action, just as now-a-days a weighty tricyclist finds it easier to propel a geared-up machine with a slow action requiring more power, than a low-geared mount which requires not so much muscular exertion, but a more accelerated action of the limbs. When in due course the path 'flyer,' as distinguished from the steady road rider, became developed, the light, compact, and easily moving muscles of the trained racing man found ease and comfort in increased leverage in the throw. Heavy muscles, if put into unduly rapid action, are soon exhausted, but the light and flexible muscles of the path rider can more easily meet the strain of rapidity of action, as opposed to the slow yet powerful exertions of the road rider. Then again very much depends upon the position of the handles; nothing conduces more to an easy and effective style than a properly adjusted length of arm-reach, nothing will sooner destroy a rider's style than an awkwardly placed handle-bar, or an ill-arranged pair of tricycle handles. The position productive of the best results is that in which the rider has his arms just flexed whilst sitting upright upon his saddle in a free and unconstrained position, and albeit men may, and often do, assume very awkward-looking positions when engaged in a race, yet, whatever attitude they may take, the position of the handles suggested above will usually be found the most suitable; this therefore is another point which should be studied by the maker of the machine. If the rider when racing is given to leaning very far forward,[1] the maker will provide for this by putting a slight rake on the forks, or else the rider will do well to move his saddle some little way back from the head, thus putting a sufficient weight on the hind wheel, and at the same time carrying it forward when in action by leaning over the handles in the manner known as the 'grasshopper style.' One of the most successful of our racing men—Fred East—set this fashion in 1879; his racing machine was made with upright forks, and his saddle was placed some inches back, this at that period

[1] The illustration on page 168 shows just how a racing man should *not* sit.

being a noticeable fact, inasmuch as most riders then put their saddles close up to the head of the machine, following an example set by the then champion, John Keen. All these little matters require a certain amount of consideration, and that rider will succeed best who has most fully gauged his own requirements in all the above points, whilst he should not hesitate a moment about having any alterations or modifications made which, after a practical trial, may appear to him advisable or necessary, for 'a good fit' is as necessary to a cyclist on a racing bicycle as it is to a runner in the matter of shoes, or to a rowing man in the shell which is to carry him in a race. Unless a man be fitted and suited, and unless he himself believes that he is fitted and suited, he cannot expect to ride with confidence or courage, which can only be cultivated by having every little item throughout exactly to fit his ideas and experiences as to comfort and safety.

The choice of a maker, then, should not be unduly hurried, and the order for a racing machine should only be entrusted to a firm whose manufactures have already made a name for themselves amongst practical and *disinterested* racing men. The best and most convincing testimonial an independent racing man can give a maker, is to ride the machine he makes, and when an intending purchaser finds that a largely advertised machine is ridden by only a few inexperienced *bonâ fide* amateurs, outside the circle of 'salaried representatives' or 'employés' of the firm, he may feel assured that the machine, as made for the ordinary purchaser, is not good, and that for that reason it does not find favour with the genuine independent amateur, who invariably consults solely his own comfort and safety. Any racing man can tick off on his fingers the names of the few firms who have made and kept a reputation as makers of racing machines, and a beginner on the path will do well to compare notes with the disinterested section of path-riders before he gives his order. This important point decided, let us say a word of warning to the would-be racing man himself. First, let us urge him not to run to extremes, and to permit the maker, who has had much experience in the matter, to decide as to what ought to be the weight of the proposed machine. A craze for lightness is one of the earliest symptoms of the racing fever, and the rider, oblivious of his actual bodily weight, his clumsy strength, and his general inability to properly 'nurse' his machine, insists upon having a cycle so light that it would need all the accurate pedalling of a Hamilton—the Prince of Pedallers—to keep it from injury. In most cases where the novice makes this absurd demand an experienced maker acquiesces for comfort's sake, and then sends home the machine of a reasonable and safe weight. Perhaps the purchaser does not weigh it. He finds that it suits him, and is satisfied, and perhaps long after he has got the fullest confidence in it, he is surprised to discover that it is three or four pounds heavier than he imagined. But, if he is wise, he will be content with the clever combination of lightness and strength, the happy mean between unnecessary weight and undue weakness, so successfully struck by the experienced, though often sadly abused, manufacturer. A well-known rider writes as follows in the editorial columns over which he presides. It is valuable as the opinion of a practical man whose authority is acknowledged among cyclists:—

We can give from our own experiences (experiences which are bound to be accurately recorded if somewhat egotistical) a case in point. In the early days of our racing, without a mentor to advise us, we demanded from the makers of our racing machine *lightness*, and lightness only. Despite the remonstrances and sound arguments of the firm's most practical chief, we still reiterated our request, threatened to put the machine in the scale immediately on its arrival, and, if it weighed over thirty pounds, to return it. In due course we got it, placed it in the scale, and found it just a shade over twenty-nine pounds (this occurred some years back of course). Duly satisfied, we commenced to ride it, but it was by no means satisfactory; it did not run rigidly at all, the forks whipped at the corner—in fact, at our then weight (nearly twelve stone) it was eminently unsatisfactory, so much so that we complained to the maker, whose reply may be easily supposed. We had asked for, nay demanded too light a machine. In due course the twenty-nine pounder was replaced by a vehicle of exactly the same measurements and proportions, which weighed thirty-one and a quarter pounds, and this proved in every way eminently satisfactory—in fact, we won all our championships and many other races thereon in 1881. The extra weight had not been put on at any especially weak spot, it had been introduced generally into the frame, and thus enabled it to bear our weight and withstand our exertion.

In the same way may be instanced the machine ridden a few times in 1882 by the Hon. Ion Keith-Falconer. This, though a beautiful specimen of the bicycle-maker's art, was not sufficiently strong to carry his relatively heavy weight, and no sooner did he begin to spurt on it than the deflection of the forks caused the bearing balls to bite, and made the work very hard; a very slight additional weight, scarcely two pounds we believe, made a machine amply rigid enough for the fifty mile record-holder of 1882. We could multiply instances if it were necessary. Mr. F. L. Adam, for instance, once came out on a really beautifully finished racer by a very prominent firm of makers. There was but one fault to find with it—it was too light for so strong and heavy a man. The backbone sprung beneath his weight, and try as he would he could not get any pace out of it. He replaced it with a racer of another make some three or four pounds heavier, and immediately did well. Thus the novice will do well to avoid undue and excessive lightness, and as the question is not solely one of bodily weight, but of weight and skill considered together, he will, in the first instance at any rate, be well advised if he allows the more experienced maker to decide for him the actual weight necessary to carry him safely and satisfactorily. That important point being decided, the rider must next consider what shall be the size of his machine. It is obvious that, to do his best, his machine must be comfortable, he must have full confidence in it as well as in himself, and it must of course correspond very closely with his roadster machine, unless he has found in the latter any points and peculiarities which he would prefer to have altered in the new machine, whilst it will be vastly to his benefit if the roadster is altered at the same time, so as to bring the measurements as nearly as possible together. Thus if a man is riding an ordinary fifty-eight inch roadster, it is clear that a closely built fifty-eight inch racer will be noticeably too short in the reach for him, and he will feel that he is what cyclists call 'tucked up,' 'cramped,' or 'going short.' To meet this trouble the rider should carefully measure, or rather get carefully measured, while on his roadster machine, the exact reach from the *saddle* to the pedal at its lowest point, and then have the racer constructed as nearly as possible to fit that measurement; if he can measure in the same way the reach of a close-built fifty-eight inch racer by the same maker, it will assist him in his decision; for should the racer reach prove shorter than that of the roadster by one and a half or more inches he can, without danger of over-reaching, have his racer built an inch higher than the roadster. So, in the instance given above, the user of the fifty-eight inch roadster would probably get the nearest 'fit' by having a fifty-nine inch racer. Thus each item of the order should be compared with the roadster, and where the latter has been found unsuitable, the racer should be modified to meet the ideas of the prospective user; but, as has been once or twice suggested, the roadster machine should, if possible, also be altered so as to correspond pretty closely with the measurements of the lighter machine. The relative positions should as much as possible be the same all through. The saddle should be put in just about the same place and just as far from the head, or, should the roadster have a good deal of rake on the front forks, put the same distance back from a vertical line drawn through the axle of the driving wheel. The saddle will then be in each case in the same relative position to the pedals, a somewhat important point. The arrangement of the handles must also correspond as regards the saddle and pedals, and so on. When all these points have been carefully studied the practical rider will benefit by his work on the road as well as by his practice on the path.

THE MANAGEMENT OF A RACE MEETING.

It should be first noted that race meetings, whenever and wherever held, must, if they include amateur cycling events, be held under the rules of the National Cyclists' Union, and in the case of clubs not affiliated to that body, the committee must obtain a special permit to hold such a meeting. Unless this is done, any amateur riding at the gathering will be liable to suspension. A great many incompetent persons are too often to be found assisting, or attempting to assist, in the management of race meetings, especially in the country, where gentlemen are chosen to officiate in important posts who have not the slightest practical knowledge of the duties they are asked to perform. For example, at one race meeting, wherein one good rider beat another by a foot, the mayor who was judging admitted he did so, but gave it a dead heat, 'because the other one had ridden such a plucky race.' Such little incidents as these disgust the riders, and they stay away another year.

Great care should be taken to avoid that fruitful source of trouble—Local or Committee handicapping. One of two faults is almost always committed. The locals are so tremendously underrated that they win the open events anyhow, or else the Committee so far over-estimate the merits of local contestants, and allot such short starts to their own men as to put them out of it altogether, which is just as serious a mistake.

The handicapping of open events should always be placed in the hands of the National Cyclists' Union official, who should be given as much assistance as possible by the local authorities. Certain rules have been drawn up by the executive of the National Cyclists' Union for the guidance of those who essay to manage race meetings, and they will be found of the very greatest value. The officials most necessary to the complete success of a race meeting are the honorary secretary, the judge, the time-keeper, the starter, the dressing-room clerk and the telegraph-board steward. The honorary secretary must, of course, be energetic and untiring. He should be a well-known man if possible, and one in whom racing men will have confidence, and he should be backed by a small practical committee. Have as many good names as possible connected with the thing, as President, Patrons, and Vice-presidents, but avoid having any but the practical section on the working committee. The meeting should be announced as long beforehand as possible, in the Cycling and local Press, and moderate advertising should be arranged for some six weeks or so before it comes off. The duties of the honorary secretary will be various. He must write to the best riders, and press them to come; he must obtain all the addresses he can of racing men who are likely to compete, and send them prospectuses : he will see that the cycling editors are supplied with copies of the same document, and also that a supply is sent to all the training tracks, the latter lots having a piece of string tied through one corner for the convenience of the attendant, who should be asked to hang the forms upon a hook in the dressing-room under his charge. The secretary should be in charge of the affair on the day, outside the ring, within which is the domain of the judge, wherein that official rules absolutely. The judge, as the Union points out, is a supreme official, and should be most carefully chosen, for if he is incompetent all will go wrong. There should be only one judge, and his decision is final and absolute, and thus the choice of the right man is a *sine quâ non*. The judge takes absolute charge inside the ring, and should work with the secretary in timing the calling out of the heats and the general run of the meeting. The time-keeper is another vastly important official, and should also be selected with very great care, as it is very annoying to have a grand performance done at the meeting and then to find it disallowed because the time-keeper was not sufficiently reliable. There are a number of trustworthy clockers with public reputations to uphold, and one or other of these gentlemen should be secured even at some expense, so that in future years good men may be induced to enter and run by the knowledge that, should they do a good performance, they will get the credit of it. The starter is another official of importance from every point of view, as with an incompetent starter men may take an unfair advantage, and any amount of heartburning will be caused thereby. When athletic events are also included in the programme, a professional starter is a great attraction, but it is always advisable in the case of a newly employed man to give him a word of caution not to hurry the pistol, as it often happens that a starter accustomed to starting sprint races is very much too quick in starting bicycle races. He should be asked to substitute 'Are you ready?' for his habitual 'Get ready,' and to give time for any one of the competitors to answer ere he fires his pistol, otherwise the men will be hurried unprepared off their marks, and accidents are bound to ensue. Perhaps the most thankless task of all is that of the dressing room clerk, who is compelled to stay in the room or tent throughout the meeting, and to look after the men for each heat. This official should set his watch with that of the secretary, and by that should send the men out in due course. He should have three copies of the programme, one fastened to the table with drawing pins, for his own especial use, and two to be handed alternately to the telegraph-board steward, with the starters in each heat marked. He should also see that every man has his number, and should call out at least twice the names of the contestants in the next heat. The telegraph-board steward should be specially detailed for the job, and should be unmolested throughout the afternoon, as on him depends the information of the spectators, which, if not satisfactorily accomplished, will disgust them, and cause them to stay away in future. The telegraph steward should see that he has all the necessary appliances ready at hand, and should, as soon as a heat is over, get up the numbers of the next. In the case of extensive grounds, two telegraph boards are an excellent institution, and if worked competently assist much in popularising the meeting. The telegraph stewards should be allowed the assistance of a smart boy, or under-steward, to run for the list of starters during each heat, and also for the times accomplished. In the case of big meetings this task may well be entrusted to a professional, and some have made quite a name for themselves for reliability, and as has been pointed out above, the spectators round the track depend entirely upon the services of the board official for their information in many cases. Umpires are a necessity, and should be very carefully chosen, the judge being consulted as to the men to be asked; whilst lap scorers and clerks of the course must also be selected. It is also advisable to appoint an official to keep the enclosure clear of unauthorised persons, and as this is somewhat of an invidious task, it would be well to give such an individual the assistance of a police officer, who should take his orders from the appointed official. This is a particularly necessary appointment at country meetings, but needs much tact on the part of the person appointed; still it is necessary for the comfort of all concerned. A very ingenious plan was successfully adopted at a certain meeting. A number of gentlemen connected with a cricket club, whose field had been duly hired and paid for, forced themselves into the centre of the ring, and insisted on staying there, despite the remonstrances of the official that the public who had paid could not see the finishes because of the crowd. Suddenly a happy thought struck him. It had been raining heavily, and he suddenly gave the order that all inside the ring should lie down; the youthful cyclists did so, but the rheumaticky elderly gentlemen, after a moment's consideration, sought seats in the grand stand as a safer resort, and the public viewed the races with comfort. The enclosure should be carefully cleared of unauthorised persons after each heat, and attendants and starters should be got outside as soon as their men have finished. Some racing men fancy they have the right to stroll about inside the ring, but they should be at once disabused of the idea, as they interfere with the view. A certain section of press men also fancy that their journal is entitled to any number of representatives within the charmed circle, but this should be at once put a stop to, one representative being ample and all that can properly be allowed, whilst it is an excellent plan to reserve a space outside the track, properly fenced in and provided with seats and tables, for the accommodation of the representatives of the fourth estate. They can from this position see all the incidents of the racing, and a special messenger should be told off to keep them posted with the times, and so on.

Great care should be taken to keep up the character of the meeting in every way ; the prizes should be of full value, and a special effort should be made to secure good dressing accommodation for the competitors. In country towns the local lights should be invited to present a good prize, which should be called by some appropriate name, 'The Mayor's Cup,' for example, and the precedent once established, the prize will become an annual one. A 'Ladies' Prize' should also be arranged for, or a 'Town Cup' may be secured by judicious canvassing amongst the tradesmen and others. If the competitors enjoy the meeting, they and others will revisit the town, and the racing will be kept up to the mark, and each year will attract more and more attention and consequent gate-money. In a great number of provincial towns the cycle races are regarded as an annual event, and the possibilities of the amateur champion coming to contend for 'The Cup,' or the chances of the local favourite, are the subjects of lengthy discussion for weeks before the date of the fixture.

The rules and regulations of the National Cyclists' Union bearing upon amateur race meetings will be found in the chapter devoted to that institution.

CHAPTER V.

TOURING.

There is little doubt that by far the largest number of active cyclists find their pleasure in touring on their machines. The racing man has to undergo an elaborate and strict preparation marked by many rules and precautions, and although his enthusiasm may carry him through, yet it must be admitted that for the most part the work is very severe. On the other hand, the pottering cyclist who never ventures far from home has no idea of the enjoyments to be found in country rambles on the wheel. Many men are precluded by business engagements or physical incapacity from indulging in the fierce joys of competition, but the touring field is practically open to any rider who has the time to devote to it, and the number of quiet cyclists who thus spend their holidays is yearly increasing, as the records of many an old wayside inn on the more favoured routes will abundantly testify. These holiday tourists, guided by the experience which they have obtained in previous years, or by the advice of their more practical fellows, plan out their trips with an eye to personal comfort, and after a few days of enjoyable riding return home invigorated and instructed. If they wield the pen with facility they fight their battles over again in the pages of the wheel press, and the short summer tour becomes a fund of lasting amusement, an event to be looked back to with pleasure or anticipated with delight.

To this important and daily growing section of cyclists it is intended to offer a few hints on the proper methods of planning and carrying out a tour. As to the machine which should be adopted, this will be best answered by a reference to the chapter on cycles of various kinds, always, of course, bearing in mind that too light a carriage, or one not fitted with adequate break power, is merely a source of trouble and annoyance for the purposes of legitimate touring. Dress, too, will be found duly considered elsewhere.

The first step a tourist should take after he has acquired a sufficient knowledge of his vehicle and confidence in himself is to join the Cyclists' Touring Club, an association formed especially to promote the interests of tourists in every way. The subscription is but 2s. 6d. with an entrance fee of 1s., and the rider having filled up a form will have to wait a longer or shorter time for his ticket. He should then purchase the 'C. T. C. Handbook,' which contains an infinity of valuable information. This preliminary is given a foremost place in the present chapter as there is some delay in election, owing to the name of the candidate having to appear in the monthly gazette of the club, and it is therefore highly desirable that the intending tourist should lose no time in putting up for election. This matter having been duly arranged, the next thing necessary is to plan out the tour and select the route to be followed. This can best be done with the aid of the various maps, road-books and guides, a number of which have been placed before the public. In general, some objective point is selected ; the tourist, perhaps, has friends in a distant town towards which he makes his way, or else he takes a circular route, which will eventually bring him home over new and unridden roads. Maps are of course of great service, especially for the purpose of learning the general direction of a place or a district, and shaping the course of the proposed tour accordingly. The 'Cyclist's Pocket Road Guides,' published by R. E. Phillips of Selhurst Road, S.E., are very useful, whilst the 'Cyclists' and Wheel-World Annual,' and the earlier 'Bicycle Annuals,' those especially for 1879 and 1880, together with as modern a copy of 'Paterson's Roads' as may be obtainable, will, with the aid

THE 'ANCHOR,' RIPLEY

of a decent map, enable the tourist to work out his route with sufficient completeness. This task having been accomplished, it becomes necessary to decide as to the average day's journey, and on this point it is necessary to utter a very emphatic warning against the error into which so many tourists fall, of fixing a ridiculously high standard which they find it practically impossible to accomplish. A large number of beginners fancy that they can ride with ease from sixty to a hundred miles daily for a week at a stretch, and on this basis they arrange their tours, with the result that they either break down utterly and are compelled to take the train home, or else they spend a miserable 'holiday,' riding hard against time during the whole of the trip, thus converting what should have been a pleasant outing into a period of hard labour and discomfort. The experienced tourist, on the other hand, does not attempt to fix arbitrarily the distance to be covered each day or the places where halts shall be made. He rather shortens the day's journey, being quite satisfied with forty or fifty miles at the outside, and generally has a spare day in the middle of the week as well, thus letting himself off as lightly as possible with a view to the more complete enjoyment of the tour as a whole.

For the beginner even shorter distances are advisable. From twenty to forty miles, more or less, as occasion serves, will be found quite enough to count upon, at any rate until the rider has gauged his powers for road work day after day. This is a serious point, for a man who can ride sixty or seventy miles right off will find forty miles a day for a week rather a task, until by lengthened experience he has learnt how to economise and save his physical powers. The next necessary point, if the tour is to be a long one, is to fix upon one or two inns (headquarters of the C. T. C., as set forth in the Guide, to be preferred of course if the traveller desires, as it were, to identify himself with the interests and followers of the sport), where changes of underclothing should be forwarded, with a request that they may be aired and laid by ready for the tourist on his arrival.

Except in the cases of some few peculiarly constituted riders, a solitary trip is a very slow performance, and the presence of at least one companion brightens things up materially; yet the rider had better go alone than journey with a disagreeable companion (though this is a truism applicable to every step in life), or a man very much slower than himself. Two fairly equal riders greatly assist one another in maintaining a good rate of progression, as when one is a little tired the other brings him along, and when this man tires the other has perhaps again got into his stride. Large parties are scarcely so satisfactory, especially where club rules are rigidly enforced, as the men are then required to keep together, and this of course means that the whole party proceeds at the pace of the slowest rider, which after a few miles becomes very irksome to the faster riders. Under such conditions loose riding should always be permitted, and, if possible, the slower men should be persuaded to start somewhat earlier than their more speedy companions. If a man can find no one to travel with him among his immediate friends, and if he is so bent on companionship as to be willing to take his chance of finding a congenial spirit, a notification may be put in the 'C. T. C. Gazette,' asking for a consort. It is always well for riders who put in such a request to state as clearly as possible their social position, so that the associate chosen may be suitable. Under these circumstances many a pleasant tour has been made and many a hearty friendship established.

The intending tourist should not start upon his fortnight or more of active work without some sort of training and preparation, as this course very often produces most unfortunate results. The mere task of sitting in the saddle for several hours per day is painful to a rider who has not taken the precaution of undergoing previous practice and seasoning for the work contemplated, and it is for this reason that at least a fortnight's preliminary work is strongly recommended. Of course, if a cyclist has been on his machine daily for a time, he will soon get into sufficient condition to undertake a moderate tour without any extra preparation ; but where riders only get out for the Saturday's spin, it is advisable that for

LUDGATE HILL.

some time before the advent of the looked-for day they should ride at least three times a week, either early in the morning or in the evening, whichever is most convenient to them; this riding should occupy as nearly as possible an hour, and should include a bit of hill climbing as well as some sharp dashes along the flat. Nothing like high training is needed, but still something more than the easy dawdling which so many riders are fond of indulging in during ordinary rides. It is an excellent plan for the prospective tourist to fix upon a given route, say eight or ten miles for a tricyclist, and ten or twelve for a bicyclist, and to ride over it at the most convenient period of the day, say three or four times a week. The trip should of course be carefully timed, and the rider should try to do better time on each occasion; this will seem somewhat of a task, but it will vastly develop the muscles and increase the powers of the rider for average work. For this training the rider should put on some old flannels, and devote himself steadily to the business in hand. If this course be carefully followed out for a fortnight or three weeks before the tour, it will make a vast difference in the rider's capabilities, and, as a natural result, will decidedly add to his comfort, for of course it is scarcely necessary to remark that when touring the highest possible pace should not be attempted, but a fair, easy, and regular rate of going should be adhered to throughout. This steady and regular pace will be all the easier if the rider has learnt, by means of the training advised above, the knack of going a great deal faster, and it is just this theory of training which has succeeded so well upon the path.

This precaution having been taken, and the rider having fairly developed his powers by careful practice, it will next be necessary for him to seriously consider what are the necessaries which he will have to take with him, or to send on, to the various important places where he will stop *en route*; and here again great latitude must be allowed, as tastes in these matters differ most notably. Thus one rider may regard a tooth-brush and a piece of soap as an ample equipment for a trip from Land's End to John o' Groat's, whilst another rider may be seen laden with packages cunningly contrived and ingeniously fitted, all of which contain 'necessaries' from his point of view.

The bicyclist is in this matter obviously less favoured than the tricyclist, who has ample facilities for carrying the greatest comfort a tourist can wish for, viz., a 'complete change.' But the ingenuity of riders of the narrow gauge machine has met the obvious want, and many cleverly designed bags and carriers have been placed upon the market, some remarks upon which will be found elsewhere under the head of accessories. One general caution is absolutely necessary, and that is that luggage should never be carried on the spring. Several of the newly-invented carriers and bags are designed especially to be attached to the very tempting little loops placed at the back of the saddle, or to the upper bow of an Arab cradle spring, but the result is obvious and inevitable. If the saddle has been properly and carefully adjusted, and is absolutely comfortable without the luggage attached, it is clear that to hang upon the back of it a heavily laden bag must necessarily disturb its poise and cause it to rise awkwardly in front, a result which disturbs altogether the pose of the saddle, and, as a natural sequence, the comfort of the rider, supposing him to have been comfortably seated at first. Touring riders, therefore, will do well to avoid all such contrivances, and to adopt only those which do not interfere with the set of the spring or saddle. All the luggage to be carried should be carefully affixed by means of one or other of the carriers described elsewhere to the solid frame of the machine, although a strap may be run through the lower curl of an Arab cradle spring on a bicycle to prevent the load from slipping backwards. This, however, should not be done unless there is an actual necessity for it, and the strap should in no case be put through the saddle loops or through the top loops of an Arab spring. These cautions are absolutely necessary, as anyone can easily see who will cast a glance at the bags, &c., carried by many touring cyclists, which he will note are often affixed in such a way as to utterly nullify the effect of the spring as far as the rider is concerned. On a tricycle the difficulty of carrying luggage is very much lessened, nearly every maker of a machine of this type designing and fitting a sound and well-planned carrier, which will accommodate any reasonable amount of luggage : and although it is not advisable for the tricycling tourist to unnecessarily load his machine with impedimenta, yet this possibility gives him the opportunity of carrying a small but well-chosen selection of convenient garments, and so being to a very great extent independent of the troubles and annoyances which always environ the sending of clothing by railways, owing to mistakes and difficulties as to the carriage and delivery of luggage, drawbacks which every tourist has experienced.

Elsewhere carriers are fully discussed, and it will therefore be only advisable here to specify the various necessaries to be taken say for a week's tour. The bicyclist will in many cases fly light in the matter of luggage, and trust to chance for those changes which may be necessary, whilst he has always the option of retiring to bed should he be unable to obtain dry garments in which to sit up. But the cautious rider, be he bicyclist or tricyclist, who has once suffered from the inconvenience and discomfort experienced by the man who travels without a change, more especially of such articles as are made of cotton fabrics, will take care to provide himself with at least one complete change of undergarments, one of the best and most convenient forms of which will be found in the long pure wool Combination Garments, now placed upon the market by the Sanitary Woollen Company, of 42 Fore Street, Messrs. E. Ward, of Eldon Buildings, Bradford, and some other firms.

A medium thickness Combination will roll up into very small compass, and when put on it completely clothes the body from neck to ankles in dry woollen attire, over which damp woollen things may be put on again without danger, if not without some little discomfort. The Combination garment in short affords that complete change which will ensure immunity from colds and chills, and it can be carried with ease, even by the bicyclist, as it will roll up into a small package and

A CLUB TOUR

can be placed along the handle-bar of the bicycle with a couple of straps. As it is of a very soft texture most riders can sleep in it at night, instead of using an ordinary nightshirt, always a bulky matter to pack up when space is limited. The fact of the woollen underclothes being a notable protection in case of damp sheets is also a strong recommendation for its adoption by the tourist. At the outset the bulk of the kit is thus materially reduced by making one article serve in place of two or more; and if the Combination garment be only used in the evening and at night, and, of course, not ridden in, it will serve very well for the week. The kit carried must include toilet requisites, such as tooth-brush, hair-brush, comb, and razor. Of these the hair-brush is often omitted, as the rider wears his hair short, and the comb suffices. Some very excellent little cases known as the 'Cyclist's Pocket Dressing-Case' are obtainable from the 'Cyclist' office, 12 Smithford Street, Coventry. This miniature dressing-case is $4\frac{1}{2}$ inches long, $1\frac{1}{2}$ inch wide, and 1 inch thick, and so takes little space in the bag or package, and it contains a very cleverly arranged telescopic razor, a looking-glass, a tube of shaving soap, a comb, and a tooth-brush. Some handkerchiefs of small size, not too thin, and carefully marked with the full name of the rider, are very useful for anyone who is given to touring a great deal, as, if left to be washed at any hotel, they are easily identified. These handkerchiefs will roll up in the Combination garment. One neck wrap should be either worn or carried in the pocket to put on when stopping, and another may be with great advantage carried in the luggage for use in the evenings. Clean stockings will also, of course, be necessary.

The articles required will easily roll up into a long bundle in a piece of waterproof, purchasable at any waterproof or india-rubber shop. The Combination should be folded till it is about twenty inches across. The bundle thus made may be held together by a couple of stout india-rubber bands, wrapped in the square of waterproof, and then affixed with straps to the handle; the whole will make a sausage-shaped parcel, which will ride safely anywhere if properly strapped on or placed in a Nagel carrier, care, of course, being taken that it does not interfere with the action of the break. This parcel will also be found to answer a double purpose, as it affords a very comfortable rest for the legs when they are put over the handles for down-hill work. The rider who ventures far afield with this limited outfit will have to exercise a little care in his proceedings; as soon as he has quite finished his work for the day he should get out of his damp underclothing and get into his dry Combination as quickly as possible; over it he may, if necessity requires, safely put his damp shirt—of course supposing it to be flannel—whilst the dry neck wrapper should be put on under the band of the shirt. The dry and clean stockings, which should be kept for this purpose and not used for riding in, will prove an immense comfort. They should be long, and the wearer should draw them up as far as they will come over the knee; thus next the skin all over he will have a dry change. Next morning his convenient little pocket-case will enable him comfortably to conduct his toilet.

The tricyclist, as was pointed out above, is decidedly better off in this matter, and can easily carry more luggage; at the same time the weight carried is decidedly a factor to be considered in studying the convenience of the rider. Even the strongest and most steadygoing of cyclists will do well to take care not to overweight himself in this direction. The following will be found to be the best and most useful additions to the kit, which may also be carried by a bicyclist with a little extra trouble and care. The Combination garment will still be found of the greatest service, and should, of course, be taken; but a flannel shirt, preferably with a collar, should be added and used solely for the evening wear, whilst the riding shirt is being carefully dried. The pocket dressing-case will also be still used, but a stout sponge-bag should be carried with a rubber band round it, containing sponge, tooth-powder, and brush. A soft cloth hat of the deer-stalker shape, which folds up flat, should be added, and the handkerchiefs, neck wrap, and stockings, as before. One or other of the larger bags used by tricyclists will generally hold this outfit.

The bag should be fastened when packed on to the carrier, which will of course have been fitted to the machine. If the Clytie or Humber bag be used, it should be so arranged that it can be easily unlocked and opened without removal from its fastenings on the machine, as this will be found a great convenience when riding. For a longer tour, especially if the direction is uncertain, the baggage must, it is hardly necessary to say, be increased, or the rider must make up his mind to stop for at least one clear working day to have his things washed ; but, wherever possible, arrangements should be made to avoid carrying much more than the outfits detailed above. To do this it will be necessary to forward the requisite changes, preferably by parcels post, to various points *en route.* Half a dozen of the squares of waterproof mentioned above should be purchased, and when the tourist has decided on a lengthy trip, the route should be approximately fixed upon and certain houses picked out, to which changes should be sent. A parcel should be made up for each week of the tour : thus, if the rider is going away for five weeks, he will need to send on four parcels, including, in each, Combination garment, flannel shirt, handkerchiefs and stockings. These, having been well aired, should be tightly rolled up in the waterproof or otherwise securely packed and the fastening sealed, and a label should then be attached bearing clearly the name of the sender thus :

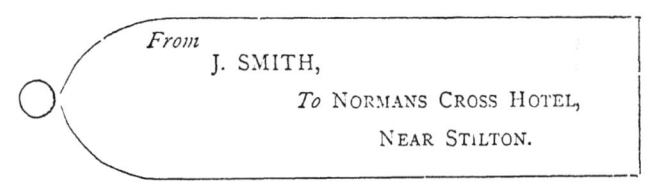

From
J. SMITH,
To NORMANS CROSS HOTEL,
NEAR STILTON.

On the back in smaller characters should be carefully inscribed Mr. Smith's name and home address, whilst it is always a good plan to have the same name and address clearly written on the inside of the bag or piece of waterproof used. The hotel people should be advised by letter and asked to keep the parcel in a dry place, and a couple of days before the rider gets to the hotel he can (in the case of a parcel) send on a note asking the people to open the package, and get the things therein aired. The parcels can be sent on to the C. T. C., or other houses, either before the rider starts on his tour—which is the best plan for a single man in lodgings or otherwise situated in such a way that he cannot be sure of his orders being attended to at once—or else from home on receipt of instructions as to when and where they are to be sent. At the end of each week the rider will get his change of clothes, and will send the used ones home in the same package by parcels post (which is in many cases quicker and more certain than the railway carriers' delivery), and they can, if necessary, be washed and aired and sent on again to another point on the route followed. The more luxurious of our tricycling tourists go even further in the matter of changes which they carry, as they not only take a complete suit of underwear, but also a complete change of outer garments; this is of course the acme of sybaritism, but it is doubtless a great comfort to a good many riders. Some take a pair of trousers made of the same material as their riding suit, but without any linings, and they generally choose a cloth hat of the same stuff, constituting the traditional 'suit of dittoes' of the British tourist. The advantage of making the wearer inconspicuous as a pedestrian is gained, although the cycling uniform is now so common an object in all towns during the riding season that it may be worn without annoyance almost anywhere. Others, again, have a suit made for the purpose of carrying with them whilst on tour. This suit will pack up into a very small space and is very light, and, if put on immediately on arriving at the hotel, it will soon lose the creases due to close packing. A pair of woollen socks, a dry flannel shirt, and a pair of shoes, complete the costume. The extra shirt should in most cases be of flannel, preferably a thin flannel, but in the heat of the summer and for short trips, the lounging shirt—as distinguished from the working one—may be of light cashmere or stockingnette, some of the garments of this type being excellent.

Whatever may be the class of shirt chosen, these points should be insisted on: it should open down the front, come well up to the throat, and have a good-sized lay-down collar as a part of the shirt. A long stocking cap, or sailor's cap, of knitted material is a very useful addition to the kit. It can be used for night riding, being drawn down well over the ears, whilst, should the tourist entertain the slightest suspicion of the dryness of his sheets at night, he can obviate cold in the head or worse dangers by sleeping in this cap. For campers, whether it be a hot summer night or not, the stocking cap, which is light and takes up very little space, is almost a *sine quâ non*. For those who when touring will insist on carrying an immense amount of luggage there is no excuse, as any amount of baggage can be sent on to various points through the usual channels, and a rider is not supposed, even by the most punctilious of his friends, to carry an elaborate wardrobe with him. If a host really expects this, the guest had better either go by train himself, or forward his portmanteau before him. On the other hand, it is not necessary for the cycling tourist to be always in *déshabille*; a very small amount of forethought will enable him to appear carefully and appropriately dressed if nothing more. For further remarks upon dress as applied to touring the reader is referred to the chapter on dress.

The tourist, with his luggage arranged and his route chosen, is ready to start; but before he gets away from home he will do well to look over his machine, and in fact the careful rider will do this a day or two before the start, so as to allow time for the rectification of any little breakage or damage which may be discovered. The machine should be carefully overhauled; the head should be adjusted, not too loosely or too tightly, but just at the happy mean; the break fittings should be cleaned up and scrutinised with a careful eye, the hinges oiled, and a very strict search made for any flaw or crack or unexpected wear—

the slightest weakness in this important point may endanger the life or limb of the rider. If the break of a tricycle does not seem to act with sufficient strength, the band should be carefully removed and the black shiny places on the leather lining cut away with a rasp or rough file. If a little powdered resin is then dusted over the leather, it will add to the efficacy of the break. The bearings throughout the machine should be carefully adjusted if any looseness is apparent; but it is never right to screw them up so that there is no side shake at all, as the balls are thus liable to be broken, and any slight stiffness which may result from the closer adjustment should be worked off some time before the start for the tour. The bearings should be dosed with paraffin, which should be put in with an ordinary oil-can and the wheels rotated rapidly, when the coagulated oil will be liquefied and the grit brought out with it. After the exudations from the bearings have been wiped off they may be carefully oiled up anew with good oil. The spring screws should be looked to and tightened, and the saddle firmly fixed in a comfortable position; if the saddle itself is very hard, it may be washed with soft soap, which should be rubbed quickly on and off, carefully cleansed with a sponge full of warm water, then dried with a cloth and left for some hours to get quite dry. The wallet should be looked over carefully and the necessary spanners placed therein; unless they fit *every* nut (a most unusual occurrence with most firms in the cycle manufacturing trade), a good adjustable wrench should also be carried. The spanners, &c., should be wrapped up in a stout piece of rag to prevent them from rattling; the oil-can should be rinsed out with a drop of paraffin and the nozzle carefully cleansed with a bit of wire, and then a pin may be put down it and the cap screwed on, after which it should be filled with a good sound oil with plenty of body; some string and a couple of feet of fine copper wire will often come in useful, and an extra nut or two may be added to fill up an unoccupied corner. A spoke-tightener is necessary with some machines, but it is not a good plan to ride the class

A MID-DAY HALT

of vehicle which requires this appliance; the tourist's wallet will therefore contain the following items:

The spanners supplied with the machine.
One adjustable wrench.
One oil-can carefully filled.
A piece of copper wire.
A yard or two of string.
A piece of rag to wrap spanners in.
Some nuts and other odds and ends.

The lamp will next require attention; the bicyclist will of course examine the fittings to see that they are sound, especially if it be a hub lamp, as any failure of the rivets will be certain to cause an accident, which will involve the ripping of a good many spokes out of the machine as well as very serious results to the rider. It is well to take a bit of wick in the wallet if the tour is to be a very long one, whilst the lamp should be charged with colza or some other easily obtainable oil, so that there may be no trouble in getting the lamp refilled, a serious drawback to the use of some fancy oils for lamps. The lamp being found all right, the bell or gong should be seen to, and any alteration that may be necessary having regard to the luggage carried on bicycles or any other matter in connexion therewith should be made. The tires should be examined all round to see that they are firmly cemented into the rim, and should any portion however small prove to be loose, it should be at once refixed and made sound to undergo with safety the work before it. The man and the machine being ready, the baggage packed and the route selected, it only remains for the tourist to jump upon his carriage and depart upon his journey.

CHAPTER VI.

TRAINING.

TRAINING, as applied to athletics, may be defined as the preparation of the body for new and unaccustomed strains, and the gradual fitting of the human frame to undergo the severest physical exertion. The systems whereby this result is sought to be obtained vary greatly in character; some are sensible and practical, some—and it is to be feared the greater number—are very much the reverse. Even now many of the authorities who superintend the preparation of our athletes are ignorant and illiterate, and work by rule of thumb without any accurate knowledge, guide, or intelligence. In former times this was even more conspicuously the case. Till a comparatively recent period the only persons who underwent serious training were men who made the sport they practised a profession—'professionals,' as by the colloquial employment of the adjective they are ungrammatically called. An amateur who competed with other amateurs in boxing, running, walking, and similar exercises, rarely trained at all. He took the matter much less seriously than his successor at the present day, who knows that to have the smallest chance of success he must be fully prepared. As a result, most of the training lore that has come down to us is of the professional stamp, the outcome of much hard and sharp experience, largely diluted with ignorance and absurdity. The professional athlete was in many cases a very vulgar creature, whose idea of recreation and relaxation was indulgence in unlimited liquor, and whose habitation was among the lowest class. His patron, or master, backed him, made a match for him, or laid a wager on his prowess, as he might on a horse or bulldog in his possession, without greatly troubling himself about the feelings or desires of the human animal he controlled. The patron when he had made a match sought not the athlete himself, but the trainer, the professional

A PRACTICE SPIN.

manager of such refractory creatures. The trainer, acting on instructions, dislodged his promising charge from his favourite haunts, and in all probability found him—if the last match had been won, and the patron had 'behaved handsome'—fleshy, dull, and ill, with physical powers degraded by debauchery. Under such circumstances, no half measures were possible. The trainer, having got his charge in hand, forthwith dosed him with aperient salts until he had half killed him; that, indeed, was the usual practice, even in a higher class of life when health failed in the good old days. A course of drastic treatment soon brought the unlucky gladiator down, and reduced him to a humble and tractable state of mind and body. Having thus overcome to a certain extent the active effects of his excesses, the trainer commenced the 'building-up' process, which culminated, if all went well, in the delivery of the athlete, as 'fit as hands could make him,' at the appointed spot on the day of the match. Not only had the sorely-tried mentor to train his man, regulate his diet, watch over his work, and keep him at it, but he had to guard night and day against an outbreak of drunkenness, which destroyed in a few hours the careful preparation of weeks. Knowing from long experience that his charge was certain to transgress if not closely watched, the main idea of the trainer gradually centred on the best means of keeping him from drink. It may readily be supposed that such a system was wholly inapplicable when the subject was no longer a mere animal, but an intelligent and well-educated man. A few years ago a great revival of athletics took place. English youths began to recur to the example of ancient Rome, and to fashion themselves as did the Romans of old—

>   . . . . decoræ
> More Palæstræ.

The enthusiastic amateurs, with all the energy of men following hotly a new idea, sought assistance from the only guide at their disposal, some old-fashioned trainer, who could see no difference between the ardent young athlete and the men on whom he had formerly operated. Sauce for the goose, argued the ancient gladiator, was sauce for the gander. The disciple who hung upon his words did not dream of suggesting that the system which had been found necessary and efficacious for so many generations was inapplicable in his case. The new pupil did not urge that he was a well-behaved young man, that he had no sort of inclination to excess of any kind, and that from previous habits he had no acquired maladies to shake off.

The trainer felt sure, from long experience, that, whatever he might prescribe, his patient would be sure to drink enough, if not decidedly too much ; and so, when the rules and regulations laid down orally by these athletic fossils were reduced to print, the prohibition of liquid refreshment was found to be absolute. Thirst was utterly ignored, or was treated as an enemy to be resolutely defied. A man in training, said the ancient trainer, must drink nothing. He did not recognise the fact that, whereas his charge of the past had to be coerced into doing what he was wanted to do, and watched and prevented from doing what he was not wanted to do, his charge of the present—the young and ardent amateur—was as likely as not to go to the other extreme, and to overwork himself, over-diet himself, nay, 'starve' himself for want of a reasonable amount of liquid, out of deference to Draconic laws laid down in the faith that whatever a trainer said would be only partially obeyed.

But experience keeps a hard school, and, after a somewhat lengthy thraldom, amateur athletes began to exercise their own common sense and to emancipate themselves from the Spartan regimen of work, diet, and drink laid down for them by their earlier mentors. When once intelligent medical attention was directed to the system of training, very little consideration sufficed to show that the old rules were only made for men who were expected to carry them out half-heartedly, whereas the new school of amateurs carried them out to the letter, and even exceeded them, with very evil results. So after a time the old system fell into desuetude, its professors became discredited, and a style of training more appropriate to the new circumstances and surroundings rose in its place. The old athletes who still survive sneer at the men of to-day, whose training, from their point of view, is no training at all ; but the fact is undoubted that amateurs to-day get into better condition and go faster than the best of the old-time professionals, who, with dosing and work, were often 'done to death' by the time their match was over. Of course, once in a way an athlete is found who not only can stand, but actually requires, the very hardest work. On the other hand, we have plenty of instances of men who, with but little training in the truest sense of the word, and with only a slight amount of careful practice, can show their very best form at very short notice.

The racing cyclist of to-day should avoid the old system altogether, and do his best to get the assistance of a modern adviser who works upon reasonable and rational lines. The main idea of the modern school is that every precept laid down is to be carried out to the letter. Preparation of the frame and the physical powers for severe exertion is not a task which should be undertaken in haste. If a man has but a few days in which to prepare for an important contest, his mentor will do well to keep him off the track altogether, and thus let him start quite unfit, so that his miseries may cause him to desist early in the struggle.

To start in a contest when out of condition is a very serious matter, both to the novice and the rider who has once been highly trained. The novice, unless he has undergone an adequate preparation, may very easily damage or strain himself. The once highly-trained rider is in still greater danger. There is no doubt that in athletics a mental training goes on side by side with the physical development—a quickening of the mind, an enlarged nervous control over the limbs; in short, a reflex action of the mental over the physical powers, which has very much to do with success. Physical training is easily lost; a very short spell of idleness will cause the rider to lose much of his power for sustaining prolonged exertion; he gets fat, and his wind gets short—in fact, all the results on his bodily functions of hard and careful training pass away, and he is 'unfit' in every sense of the word. But, although the subject is left with but little of the muscular fitness that once distinguished him, and with skill impaired by want of condition, the mental training remains, and is to a very great extent permanent. That supreme command, which the mind in a moment of highly-strung excitement—such, for example, as the sharp finish of a race—brings to bear upon the physical powers, takes considerably longer than mere physical powers to develop; but, once developed, is very rarely altogether lost. Though the athlete may be physically unfit and out of training, the tyrant mind remains imperative. The flaccid, fat-laden muscles, the stiff, unexercised limbs, the clogged and unexpanded lungs, when called upon for a tremendous effort, like the soldiers of Hannibal after their stay in Capua, are not ready for the task. The result is an inevitable breakdown. Lucky is the athlete who, under such circumstances, only strains a ligament, or ricks a joint, and escapes heart-disease or other insidious ills. A very keen observer, a splendid athlete (and a tricyclist also) —Mr. Horace Davenport—who has so long been the champion swimmer, in a letter to a journal that has now disappeared—the 'Athletic Review'—says: ' I fancy that in all competitions where staying power is required, the mind has far more to do with keeping going than has the body, though, of course, the latter must be in good condition to answer the call of the brain, otherwise there is a breakdown, probably with permanent consequences. Training undoubtedly gives the mind a great power over the body, and my experience goes to show that, after training has been given up, the mind retains the power it has developed far longer than does the body; and this is where the danger of athletics comes in, for many a man who has trained is induced, on the spur of the moment, to make some foolish match. His body is out of condition, yet it is likely his mind enables him to pull off the event; but the feat will probably be followed by prostration of the system. There would not be nearly the same danger to a man who had never trained were he to try his level best at anything, for in his case most likely the body would decide when it had had enough, and would " cave in " accordingly.'

This opinion, coming from so practical an authority, should carry weight. Unless an athlete is well prepared he should exercise a wise discretion, and abstain from entering on any sort of competition, even if he only goes in for the purposes of exercise; in fact, it is always safer for one who enters any contest with that object to choose one outside his *spécialité* at which he does not mind being beaten. Say, for example, a once prominent cyclist desires to keep up a certain amount of exercise, but does not intend seriously to train. Let him take as much exercise as he pleases upon his machine; but, if he is pressed to enter in some open competition, or at the sports of clubs to which he belongs, let him take up some other branch of athletics; for, if he rides in any contest half-trained, he will assuredly find himself in an awkward and uncomfortable predicament. Perhaps, for example, half a mile from the winning post he will be racing side by side with some old rival. In a moment all the old Adam stirs within him. There is the old familiar whirr of the wheels, the well-remembered shouts of the spectators, and the encouraging cries of friends. His caution and the determination to give up when he has had enough are forgotten. The clang of the bell as he enters the last lap strikes his ear. His mental training involuntarily calls upon the physical powers for the old spurt, the old well-timed muscular effort. What though he be exhausted, if giddiness and sickness almost overcome him? He simply sets his teeth the firmer, grips his handles, and makes the fierce and final effort as of old. Muscles and lungs are not fit or ready for the task, and, unless he stops from sheer exhaustion, *something must go*, and injury, perhaps for life, ensue. This is what should be most carefully avoided, and a once trained athlete should exercise the greatest caution in after years as to the exertions he sets himself to undertake.

Bearing all these facts in mind, the rider, when commencing to train, should seek to develop, not only his mere animal or physical powers of wind and limb, but his mental powers as well. His trainer, if he has one, should study as much as possible his temperament and peculiarities. Should he, however, decide to train himself, some observant and experienced friend must be persuaded to watch him, and, as far as possible, point out his errors. There is nothing more beneficial to the beginner than the care and treatment which a competent trainer can bestow. The very things which a rider does not want to do are frequently the particular exercises most necessary to his success. Racing men, like race horses, have their tempers and their peculiarities. Some horses must lead all the way, others prefer to wait; some are lazy, others too fiery. So with the racing man. One cannot 'make the pace'—i.e. go fast—when in front; another cannot go fast when alone on the track; others go fastest when they have an adversary 'dogging' their hind wheels. Some riders feel compelled to wait behind the leader, and only come out for the final rush; others like to ride first, and race from start to finish. All these varying temperaments are represented upon the path, and their various exponents show the highest quality an athlete can possess—judgment—when they succeed in winning on their own preconceived plan. It would be easy to name individual riders whom the descriptions given above would fit. Mr. R. H. English, of Newcastle, is a type of the rider who simply 'goes all the way.' He puts down his head and never looks behind him. Mr. H. W. Gaskell was a typical 'waiter'; whatever the distance of the race, he never led until the last 300 yards, and then he threw all his energies into one supreme effort. Of late years we have had perhaps too many 'waiters'; and scratch races—that is, races in which men start level—have, in consequence, been very slow for the spectators—the one mile championship of 1884 occupied three minutes and thirty seconds. Sometimes, in an important contest, such as a five-mile scratch race, all the men who have a chance for the race wait upon each other, and leave an unimportant outsider to make the pace. They start, but no one wants to go in front; they literally crawl round the path. Presently an ambitious rider—an outsider—without the ghost of a chance, dashes to the front and takes the field along for a mile or two at an improved pace; then another outsider takes his place, and makes the pace for another mile; the two or three 'crack riders' stick close together for some sixteen or seventeen minutes. Suddenly there is a change. 'Two more laps!' shouts the judge. The ambitious outsiders suddenly collapse, and the three cracks draw out from the ruck and race to the front. One of them secures a momentary lead, the others in close pursuit; they close up; wheel overlaps wheel; the three riders are nearly abreast as the tape is reached for the last time round; the bell rings, away they go for a furious spurt of 440 yards, and the speediest sprinter wins what is nominally a long-distance race. Nearly all our men during the last few seasons, if indeed there are any exceptions, have trained for sprints and sharp finishes only; as a natural consequence beginners have followed in their footsteps, and a good final spurt has been regarded as the great object of a racing cyclist's ambition. Happily a change has already begun in this matter, and a more careful preparation for long and well-sustained effort is being undertaken by some of the best men. Among professionals several well-known riders, such as Battensby and Lees, go long distances in training. Profiting by the example of the former rider, Mr. R. H. English, the sturdy amateur from Newcastle, set a grand example by 'going all the way' in the Crystal Palace and Kildare Challenge Cups in 1884; and our amateurs, more especially those whose forte lies in staying, as compared to sprinting, will do well to study the successful system of preparation undergone by Mr. English and other long-distance riders.

In the following notes we shall treat of the riders in two classes: short- and long-distance men. In the immediate future these two classes of racing cyclists will probably become more and more distinct. The long-distance man, as distinguished from the sprinter, will stick to distance races. The 'sprinter' will go in for what Americans aptly call 'dashes.' Of course racing cyclists are as diverse in their powers as are running, walking, swimming, or rowing men. Amateurs of running would be surprised to see Mr. J. M. Cowie, the 100-yards amateur ex-champion sprinter, start in a one-mile race, yet no one seems to think it at all surprising that a bicyclist like Mr. Gaskell, who is extraordinarily speedy for a single mile, should start for the 25-mile championship. In the same way when George, the distance running champion, enters for a short race for the purpose of improving his pace, he gets a long start—and a beating; yet in cycling Mr. H. F. Wilson, a man who held many records over 30 miles, persistently enters and runs for one-mile handicaps. The whole theory and system on which cyclists have been working of late years have been vitiated by this effort on the part of the riders to succeed at the distance for which their physical powers most unfit them. Cyclists must look to it: the 'stayer' must stick to distance riding, and the 'sprinter' to short 'dashes.' The sprinter, when training, should never ride either a long distance or a long race, as it is certain to stiffen his muscles and make him slow. The long-distance man on the other hand may in moderation ride in short-distance races to improve his pace, always taking care not to train for short distances, and to keep his attention fixed upon long work.

A fatal error into which many racing men fall is over-work, or rather over-competition. Anyone who carefully considers the principles of exercise and training will see that it is impossible for a man to be actually in perfect condition for a long consecutive period of time. Many riders, by careful and judicious training, maintain a wonderfully high average of condition, but this falls short of their best form. Without doubt the better times accomplished in running and cycling by 'professionals,' as compared with those of amateurs, are due to a very great extent to the fact that the professional never thinks of running or riding a serious race at frequent intervals. For each serious match in which he is engaged he undergoes careful preparation, preceded and followed by a period of complete relaxation. On the other hand a file of the sporting or cycling papers records the regular appearance, week after week, of many prominent riders, who are to be found every succeeding Saturday—with an occasional mid-week meeting thrown in—riding very hard, in open races. These riders probably regard the races in which they engage as a sort of training; but the cyclist who calmly and deliberately winds himself up for a great effort on some important occasion is likely to do better than one who is constantly racing.

In Chapter VII. of this work will be found some notes on dress, and especially on the shoes to be adopted. A couple of pairs of soft and rather thick merino socks will be necessary, to be used alternately and very carefully dried by the attendant on each occasion; a stout pair of plain white flannel drawers, of the same cut as the racing drawers, or a pair of elastic web pants of stouter make than those worn for racing; and finally a jersey, or singlet. A cap may be worn and also a woollen neck wrap if the throat is very delicate, but this is not much to be recommended. The novice must at first depend very much upon himself, and it is an excellent thing for a young racing man to train himself for his first season under the mentorship of some candid friend. He thus, if he is at all observant, learns his own peculiarities, and is as a consequence able to tell his trainer, when he engages the services of such an assistant, what are his especial requirements.

One piece of advice is important: always train with an object. Thus if the novice fancies he can stay, let him decide to go for the ten-mile championship of the club he belongs to, never mind even if the amateur champion himself belongs to it as well, go for it and it will be an object to train for; if on the other hand the novice thinks that his forte lies in sprinting, let him enter for a club mile race, or an open contest for that distance on some safe track, and then train for that particular race. The first thing every trainer does when he takes a man in hand is to weigh him: the novice should get weighed and make a note of his exact weight, stripped. He should then consider whether he is fat or not; if of spare habit he will not require, nor indeed endure, so much hard work as another who carries a superfluity of adipose tissue. He should begin work for the chosen event at least a month before it is fixed to take place. If the event he has pitched upon for his first venture is a one-mile open handicap, he should consider that he will have to possibly ride in two rounds and a final, and that he will have to ride all through the race to win. The track chosen for his work should be easy of access, safe, with easy corners; and, if possible, he should secure a companion or two—who would in most cases be his fellow club-men—to assist him and ride with him. A stop-watch is also useful to gauge the progress. Of course he has done some road riding and is in sufficient rough form for that work. Should it be possible for him to visit the track twice a day, he should after breakfast take a sharp walk for half an hour or so, not too heavily clad, and then returning home or to his office rest quietly, attending to business or other cares until 11.30 or 12 o'clock, when he should visit the track and take half-an-hour's steady work at half speed. Rattling along at a smart pace, but carefully refraining from spurting, a healthy perspiration will be induced, and the pace may be slightly accelerated for the last mile. As soon as the half-hour has expired, let the rider dismount and, without loitering, go straight into the dressing-room and sit in a corner out of the draught, put a towel round his neck and remain quiet. In a few moments a profuse perspiration will follow, which should be encouraged by a gentle friction with a towel folded over the hand, whilst if an attendant is present he may, by more vigorous rubbing, set up a glow over the whole surface of the body. A good many attendants hurry the 'rubbing down' process, especially those who have a number of men to look after, and thus defeat the very object they are desired to accomplish. In nearly every case under these conditions there is a second flow of perspiration after the man has been completely dried; when this has been removed, and not till then, the rider may guard against cold by taking a showerbath of cold water, an appliance which should be found in every training dressing-room. This closes the pores of the skin and precludes the possibility of catching cold; the rider should then dress, preferably in flannel, at least with some thin flannel garment next the skin, and go about his business, dining about 2 o'clock. In the evening he should revisit the track between 5 and 7 P.M., according to the season, for the real work of the day. This in the case of a short race will consist of 'short' work with a view to the improvement and knowledge of pace necessary for a one-mile race. A second set of flannels should be put on, and the rider now more especially needs the services of his friends to clock, or ride with him. His work should consist of quarter-mile spurts, with an occasional half-mile spin, and perhaps once a week a regular mile trial against the watch. A 'pacemaker' is of the very greatest service at this juncture, and on most of our tracks, especially in London, there are generally at hand amateur riders who will so far assist a novice, if he asks them, as to give him a lead and even some valuable hints. In doing his work the rider should be very careful to note the following points and see that he is carrying them out :—

(1) *Always to look where he is going.*—This is very essential, especially for a man who trains much alone, as such riders often get unconsciously into a trick of guiding themselves by the edge of the track, and thus in actual competition may run into a man before they can avoid it.

(2) *Always sit straight.*—When a man is riding on a small track, or on a path with bad corners, he often picks up a trick of sitting all on one side, and thus 'throws' his outside knee very awkwardly. It is essential that a beginner should think of it when at work. The saddle should, of course, be set quite straight.

(3) *Pedal evenly and use both legs.*—Those who have no practical experience will hardly believe how often a rider 'favours' one leg more than the other. A blister, a strain, or a bruise will often start it, and it is only when an experienced rider, who has been 'hanging on' behind the other man, notices and mentions it that the victim becomes alive to his defect. A bad or incomplete ankle action with one leg is often the cause, and therefore, when at his spurting work, the novice should be constantly watchful to keep up the same power with both legs.

(4) *Pedal straight.*—This is also a point which must be watched. Very often a rider pedals beautifully on the road, but throws his knees very awkwardly out or in when on the path. This fault is often traceable to the difference in *the width*

HARD AT WORK

of the tread of his roadster and racer machines, or to an unconscious sympathy between the arms and legs, the former limbs being often bent outwardly when leaning forward in the grasshopper style. The novice, therefore, should watch his knees in the manner suggested in our chapter on learning to ride, the action in each case being exactly similar.

(5) *Keep the foot straight.*—This is usually effected by mechanical means. The wriggling action of the foot is often caused by a crooked crank, or pedal pin, and in any case it must be corrected. The racing shoes often tell the tale by the slots in which the pedals fit being found worn to unequal depths on either side; and the rider will find that this denotes a bad foot-action, which must be carefully corrected ere he can hope to do good work.

(6) *Hold the handles naturally.*—If the rider can race nearly upright, he may hold his handles either way—'over' or 'under'; but, if he rides 'grasshopper' fashion, he must hold them 'under.' If anyone will put his hands in the position described, about twenty-six inches apart, on the edge of a table, and then lean forward in the 'grasshopper' style, he will discover that, awkward as it looks, it fully opens the chest and permits full play to the lungs, whilst the position allows of a very nice adjustment of the weight.

(7) *Don't wobble the shoulders.*—Some men seem to think that pace is developed by moving the shoulders as if they were throwing all their bodily weight on the pedals. This is a very grave error. Without too rigidly setting the muscles of the trunk, the shoulders should be kept comparatively steady. This will assist very materially in keeping the machine straight. A very little up and down movement may be allowable, but beyond this nothing of the sort should be permitted.

(8) *Hold the body still and sit down.*—A great many riders get up off the saddle when spurting. This is a serious fault; it unsteadies the steering and diminishes the available power. The arms should assist in keeping the body steady, and the saddle should touch always. A very slight grip of the peak of

the saddle between the legs will be found of notable assistance in steering round awkward corners.

(9) *Don't shake the head.*—Some flyers of note do wonderful things with their heads when spurting. It is hardly possible for the rider to watch his opponents and judge his course when his head is in constant motion. The head, in the 'grass-hopper' style of riding, should be thrown back, the face to the front, almost in the position of that of a swimmer; it should be held still right over the driving wheel, with the eyes directed well forward. Some riders turn the head a little to one side, so as to listen for the opponent behind them; and this may be done, if the above caution is carried out. But in this case, in practice, the rider should turn his head away from the inside of the path, and should stop the ear which is directed forward with cotton wool, as the wind blowing in often sets up a cold. Owing to this fact a large number of well-known riders are a little deaf in one ear.

Always supposing that the tiro has given a fair amount of time to acquiring a good ankle action, the above hints will assist him in forming his style on a good model. It is essential that he should not get over the front of his wheel too much, or, the weight being taken off the rear wheel, the steering is sure to become erratic and the danger of a 'header' is thereby vastly increased.[1] For this reason hint No. 8 should always be kept in view. Bearing all these precepts in mind, the tiro should turn out for his evening work. After a quiet paddle for a lap or two, he should mentally resolve to spurt, say one lap; and here it is necessary to point out that the mental training alluded to will have to begin. Having resolved to go the one lap, or even if very new at the game the half lap, the novice must ride it out however exhausted he may feel. This will not, perhaps, be possible the first time, owing to the insufficient development of the mental power, and the consequent inability

[1] The illustration on page 168, entitled 'Going it,' shows a rider placed so close to the head of his machine that his hind wheel would be in the air before he had gone a hundred yards.

to push the muscular powers to the utmost. But nevertheless, the rider should set his teeth and struggle on to the point on which he mentally decided before starting. Here he should ease up and ride round quietly until he has regained his breath. When he feels all right he may essay the same spin again, and do this half-a-dozen times or so during the half hour he remains on the path. He should then finish up with an easy pace mile or so, and retiring into the dressing-room, follow out with equal exactitude and care the proceedings of the morning. After each of these exercises, the rider, or preferably his attendant, should rub the legs, especially the front of the shins and the calves, with his bare hand, the rider relaxing the tension of the muscles whilst this process is going on. This assists the muscle in throwing off the fat which may lie in its tissues, and also strengthens it by aiding the flow of the blood through the vessels. This hand rubbing is the secret of training success, and the attendant who gives most time to this portion of the work when his charge has got rid of superfluous flesh will assuredly turn out better men than the trainer who shirks the necessarily irksome task. It may be well here to insert a caution against too much faith in the times made in the early stages of the work. Many a novice has been disappointed to find that after a week's hard work, he is going decidedly slower than he went in his half-trained state. This of course is very natural; he has exhausted and used up his rough muscular power, and sufficient time has not elapsed to allow of its natural replacement by the development and training of his powers for the special work contemplated. But although he is momentarily a worse man than he was, yet very shortly nature will respond to the call and supply him with muscles, or rather muscular developments, which will fully atone for his disappointments. Should the rider's trainer or friend find the time compare badly with earlier efforts, he will do well to put the watch in his pocket and make an excuse to the rider, or else explain to him the why and wherefore, and encourage him to keep on, carefully watching his progress until the sudden improvement of the times points to the fact that the muscles are becoming accustomed to the task. During all this period our typical novice must be studying himself and trying to reason out the various surroundings of the exercise. He must be continually thinking and making little changes and alterations such as he may fancy will suit him. Time and trouble should never be grudged when devoted to getting the racer exactly right, and it is only those who take an infinity of trouble to have everything comfortable that can hope to succeed. A thousand and one aches and pains will probably trouble the tiro, but unless he feels very sick and faint after his work, or detects any sensation of lung trouble, he need not go to a medical man; and, as we have said before, if he does experience such sensations he should go to some doctor who has had experience of athletics and athletes. Pains in the calf of the leg, the thigh, or the back, due to straining or cramp, will mostly give way before easy work, Elliman's embrocation or 'Thilum,' whilst a good hand-rubbing will ease the stiffness of the limbs in the earlier stages; and all this time, as suggested above, the beginner must be studying and gauging his own powers, and storing up information to aid his judgment when the actual contest arrives.

A very good rule for a beginner to carry out (and for a veteran, too, for the matter of that) is to try seriously to succeed in the special point in which he fancies himself deficient; thus, if a rider fancies he cannot stay, let him try a distance spin merely for his own instruction. If he thinks he cannot spurt, let him essay spurting; if he cannot negotiate corners, he should go and train for a little while on a track with bad ones; whether the plan is successful or not the rider will begin to know all his own points. The period of efficiency depends of course upon the recovery of the muscles from the first strains of the novel exercise, and this will be much influenced by the previous use to which they have been put. If they have been abnormally developed in any other direction, the time may be considerably lengthened; for example, running or gymnastics will often develop muscle of no service in cycling and a considerable time may therefore elapse ere the limbs get fitted to the new work. Only one sport 'nicks' with cycling, and that is fair toe and heel walking, doubtless owing to the strengthening of the legs generally, and the ankle work. Rowing, when the sliding seat has been used, makes the legs powerful enough for cycling, but very slow, whilst the development of the upper pectoral muscles by gymnastics is sometimes so great as to cause them when set to interfere with the rapid respirations of a spurting cyclist, an event which does not noticeably occur in the intermittent, and above all, slower exertions of the gymnasium, but which asserts itself somewhat emphatically when the gymnast on the bicycle sets his chest muscles, by gripping his handles in the fierce rush of a final spurt; we remember at least one rider whose apparent 'softness' in a sharp finish was undoubtedly to be attributed to this cause.

Es gingen drei Jäger wohl auf die Birsch;
Sie wollten erjagen den weissen Hirsch. —*Uhland.*

CHAPTER VII.

DRESS.

EXHILARATING and enjoyable as is the sport of cycling, and healthy as it has proved itself to be, its enjoyment and its health-giving qualities are wholly dependent upon one very important point: a correct and suitable costume. It must not be forgotten that cycling is, after all, an athletic exercise, that it causes perspiration when ardently followed out, and for that reason alone it requires its votaries to be properly costumed in a dress suitable and convenient for the work in hand. It may be well to say a few words on this question of appropriate attire, as a good many riders are even now doubtful about the propriety of donning a regular cycling dress. In the earlier days of the sport, a pedestrian or a rider in cycling garb was sufficiently a novelty to attract a good deal of annoying attention in any town he might visit. But this is no longer the case, and a correctly dressed cyclist, more especially if he adopts the C. T. C. costume, is so common an object, that he passes without special notice. One reason for the protection which ladies undoubtedly find in the C. T. C. grey uniform lies in the fact that it is so little remarkable, and so closely resembles that ordinarily worn by the wife of the parson or doctor, and therefore the bucolic intelligence sets down the passing stranger in his mind as probably a friend or acquaintance of the local lady. Every day the public outside the sport become more and more used to the sight of a correctly dressed cyclist, and the familiar grey dress of the lady rider, and the knee breeches, stockings, and short jackets of the sterner sex, occasion no remark.

That every rider who cycles, whatever his age, should wear a cycling costume appropriately cut needs no proof. The rider of a cycle who ventures out in an inappropriate costume is regarded as one who does not know the right thing to do when pursuing the sport, and proclaims himself as either an ignoramus or a novice. The cyclist therefore should seek to be comfortably and scientifically clad, making the mere ornamental question as it affects the costume subservient to the necessity of having a practically useful dress in which to ride. The essential points are few and simple; they should be carefully studied by every cyclist who wishes to ride in comfort.

1. The dress must be fully protective—that is to say, it must afford an even and adequate warmth all over the body, without unduly confining the action of the limbs; and there must not be too much of it.

2. It must be of some very sound and serviceable cloth, which can stand hard wear. Loosely woven cloth holds the dust; so the material chosen should be a wiry and closely woven stuff of some medium colour, and the costume as a whole should be neat and quiet in appearance.

A practical costume, meeting all the requirements of the rider, requires the experiences of many riders under varying conditions to bring it up to the point of practical perfection, and the ingenuity of cyclist after cyclist has been exercised on the many minor points which go to make it a complete and comfortable whole. Not only must the outer garments be suitable to the work and its surroundings, but the under garments must correspond. This remark applies with peculiar force to the clothing worn by ladies.

OUTER GARMENTS.

These consist of the uniform, or cycling costume proper, viz., the coat or jacket, the waistcoat (if worn), the breeches or knickerbockers, the stockings, and the hat or helmet. No cheap material can withstand for any time the hard usage to which a cycling dress is of necessity subjected, and the truest economy is to pay a fair price for some tested material which experience has proved in every way suitable for the purpose.

The solitary cyclist might spend his life and a small fortune trying and testing various goods which would be highly recommended to him as suitable for cycling, and the lady rider would probably find that any garment which the shopkeeper had in stock was pronounced to be eminently adapted for her purpose. Happily for cyclists generally, expert assistance has long since been called in, and materials suited to all classes of riders are now supplied.

A cloth which *par excellence* finds acceptance amongst a large class of wheelmen is that sold by the Cyclists' Touring Club. It was originally decided upon by a jury of experts, who also happened fortunately to be cyclists. It is a West of England tweed, a very small check pattern in grey; it is excellent in wear, does not show the dust, and will stand any amount of knocking about; it will also wash, which is a great point, as a cyclist is apt occasionally to come in contact with oily parts of his machine. The C. T. C. cloth, as it is usually termed, cleans remarkably well.

When braid is worn, it should be sewn on the inside of the seams: the primary object of braid was doubtless to strengthen the seams, and also to strengthen the garment generally. Flat bars of broad braid sewn inside, across the chest of a military or cycling uniform, are remarkably efficacious in preventing the jacket from stretching, and losing its shape. This fact was clearly proved by a well-known cyclist who had two jackets of the same material and shape made at the same time, one braided and the other plain; the braided one, though decidedly shabby, still keeps its shape and is usable, but the plain jacket has long since been destroyed as shapeless and unwearable. Those, therefore, who wish to get the greatest possible amount of wear out of a costume, will do well to have it braided, but in place of braiding it outside, which looks conspicuous, it should be braided *inside*, the braid being run down the seams and across the breast to the buttonholes on the inside of the coat throughout. The jacket thus treated will be found to wear for a very long time, and it will in most cases retain its shape to the end, a point worth consideration by those whose means are limited.

The material having been chosen, the make and shape must be decided upon ; and here again experience has laid down certain principles which have been established by the slow process of discussion and trial. The result of these practical discussions has been the establishment of a few points as imperative rules for the comfort of the cyclist, and first and foremost stands the dictum : ' That every garment worn whilst cycling should be of flannel or woollen material, without any admixture of cotton or linen in any form.' The past experiences of many well-known and prominent riders in the early days of the sport taught them in the most emphatic manner, and sometimes with unpleasant emphasis, the imperative necessity of doing away with every atom of cotton or linen used in any one of the garments worn, as these materials when damp from perspiration or rain are found to strike very cold and chilly wherever they may be situated ; and this becomes more particularly apparent should the rider sit about after a hard day's work, when he feels chilled to the bone, and in many cases catches a very severe cold, if nothing worse, whilst some very bad cases of inflammation of the kidneys have been traced directly to the wearing of a linen waistband in the knickerbockers or trousers. As a number of elderly tricyclists will insist on riding in trousers, and will of course equally insist on riding in an old pair of ordinary nether garments, they often suffer as above described, and cycling is blamed for an illness which can be directly traced to the folly of the victim himself. Sore throat is often to be traced to the linen band which so many tailors and shirtmakers will fit round the neck of a flannel shirt, whilst there is often in addition a little square of linen marked with the maker's name and address, which, when it is damp, can be readily felt, especially if the wind blows up coldly after a long run as evening falls. Throughout the whole list of garments used by cyclists the same fault extends, the merino or woollen vest has a strip of linen down the front right over the throat, and so placed as to be likely to produce the very worst results; the drawers, if worn, have a linen waistband and a linen front, the knee-breeches or knickerbockers are lined round the knees and at the waist with Italian cloth or some other 'cold' material; the coat is strengthened with a linen stiffener wherever necessary, and the arms are lined with linen or some kindred material. The waistcoat is backed with cotton and lined with cotton, and is altogether about as bad as it can be in this respect, seeing that the cold-giving material is stretched over the loins and round the stomach. The flannel shirt, especially of the non-shrinkable and fancy class, contains a large proportion of cotton, and the result is that the rider after a long run is cold, clammy and chilly, loses his appetite instead of improving it, feels quite out of sorts, and may consider himself lucky if, in addition to all these discomforts, he does not get a heavy cold, or, worse still, a local chill. More especially is this likely to occur if the victim has a few hours of night riding at the finish of his day's work, when his only chance is to button his coat right up to the neck and keep moving until the very end of the trip; standing about, or trying to get warm by the fire, will only add to the chances of illness. On the other hand, the rider clothed from head to foot in complete flannel, or pure woollen garments, is comparatively safe. He may get wet through half-a-dozen times, and although the situation is in no wise comfortable, it is at any rate the next best thing to being comfortable, viz. it is safe; and every rider, whatever his age, who values his health and wishes to avoid the very worst results that can follow from cycling, will do well to see that this all-wool programme is fully carried out. Some young or inexperienced cyclists will scoff at the above views, but experienced riders will simply advise them to wait until two or three weeks on a sick bed shall have convinced them of the folly of casting aside as useless the experiences of their predecessors.

In the earlier days of cycling it was difficult to procure all the articles which a modern practical tourist looks upon as actual necessaries of the most ordinary type ; but now, a number of well-known firms specially connected with the cycling trade are laying themselves out to meet the requirements of the touring riders and to supply guaranteed pure woollen goods and materials for the use of the riding public, who are thus spared the trouble of looking for them, and the suffering of the pioneers has not been without fruit. Riders desirous of availing themselves of the resources of civilisation in this direction will therefore have no difficulty in getting the necessary garments when contemplating a tour. It is needless to add that these remarks apply with even added force to the clothing required by lady riders, who are at any rate quite as liable as men to chills and other evils, and should of course take equal precautions.

The 'body garment,' the coat or jacket, is the first item to be considered, and there are plenty of designs and shapes to choose from. A jacket for bicycling should not be too long, but when the rider is seated upon the machine it should just reach below the saddle. For tricycling, and especially in the case of elderly riders who use an ordinary pattern front steerer, the jacket may be cut a little longer. The usual type, and one most popular with the general run of riders, may be described as follows: it should be single breasted, buttoning up with not too many buttons, it should be cut pretty high up round the throat, and fitted with a good wide lay-down collar, which should be finished in front with a small lappel, so arranged that when the collar is turned up the lappel may button across the throat. If a triangular 'tab' which can be buttoned across the opening of the turned-up collar be also fitted, and its lower corner hooked or buttoned over the lappel itself, it will be found a very complete protection for the throat and neck. For bicycling the bottom of the front of the jacket should be cut away in two curves, so as not to rub against the head and get oily, and the same plan should be adopted in costumes for tricyclists who ride Humber pattern machines. For the other class of tricyclists the front may be left square as affording more protection, especially in the case of rain. Two pockets on either side, in front of the hips, and a breast pocket, are ample provision in this direction, but a watch pocket will be found a convenient addition, and should be put very high up on the left-hand side, when, if it has been properly arranged so as to come just below the projection of the collar bone in front, the watch will lie safely and will not disturb the set of the coat. The arms should be rather looser than ordinary, and the armholes cut a trifle larger to allow for extra garments at night and in the winter, and also to facilitate the putting on of the jacket over woollen underclothing. This enlargement should be very slight, not more than one inch at the most, but in actual practice this makes all the difference between comfort and discomfort. The sleeves should not be too long, or they will worry the rider very much, especially in case they get wet with rain or perspiration, and the cuffs should be fitted with a couple of buttons so that they may be opened and turned back in hot weather. An ordinary link button is a capital thing to carry when on a tour, as with its aid the coat can be unbuttoned and then just linked across the chest to prevent its flying about, and at the same time there will be plenty of freedom and fresh air for the chest and arms. For winter use the coat may be lined throughout with thin sound flannel, but in the summer this will be found oppressive unless very little underclothing is worn. For a summer jacket the very smallest amount of lining and stiffening, which should invariably be all of woollen material, should be used. The armholes, button-holes, and the backs of the buttons, together with the collar, are practically the only points which will require lining, and a summer coat cut as we have suggested has the additional advantage of being quite as serviceable in winter, as owing to the slightly enlarged sleeves a considerable addition can be made to the underclothing without any inconvenience being felt when the coat is put on. This type of jacket may therefore be considered the main stay of a cycling uniform, and will in most cases be found the very best style which can be adopted.

Next in order of merit as a useful garment for ordinary wear comes the 'Norfolk jacket.' This shape is well known to most sportsmen; it is light and easy, and commends itself particularly to those who are inclined to be stout. The same rules, as far as cut and make go, will apply to this jacket; it should be made to fit loosely, and the belt should be fixed to the jacket above the hips; the pockets are usually put in the breast folds, and when the Norfolk jacket is made in C. T. C. cloth it looks exceedingly well. It is particularly suitable for couples upon sociables and tandems, as it is a type of jacket which suits many ladies excellently, and the couple being in the same cut of jacket undoubtedly adds to the neatness of the turn out. The arrangements as to the collar, &c., will be the same as in the case of the ordinary round jacket. Another type much affected in some quarters is the military collar, on one or other of these jackets. In this case the jacket buttons or hooks right up to the throat, and is finished off with an upstanding collar all round the neck. This looks neat and may suit some people, but in general it confines the throat too much and prevents the air circulating around the neck, more especially round the nape of the neck, and this is liable to cause sunstroke and headache. In any case it must fit closely to look well, and if it fits so it is bound to be stuffy and unsatisfactory, and is not therefore to be recommended. Some of the newest cycling jackets now in the market are woven or knitted, and they are very comfortable, but in some cases lose their shape rapidly. Some of the webbing jackets, however, withstood the severest tests, and they are very good for touring work, as they prevent the wearer from catching cold, and yet are by no means so stuffy as thick cloth garments. For winter use a jacket which comes right across the chest and is buttoned under the left arm and across the top of the left shoulder may be recommended. This construction effectually prevents the wind from blowing in, whilst the even distribution of warmth all over the body, without an undue thickness in one place, makes it very effective in warding off colds and chills. For winter riding and night work it has proved practically useful. Of the same class is the 'Weather Defiance' made by the Sanitary Woollen Company of Fore Street, though the double thickness over the chest seems scarcely necessary in a garment made like this one, of a very thick camel's-hair rug-like material. This also protects the throat, and is a most serviceable garment for those who go in for much night riding, which is always attended with some danger, as the wind is often very chilly even in the middle of summer. The 'Weather Defiance' is very well made and very light, whilst at the same time it is warm and porous, allowing the free escape of the perspiration. All the garments mentioned are specialities which find favour with various riders, but the general choice for all-round use will be either the ordinary round jacket or the Norfolk jacket. The waistcoat is a garment not much worn by active cyclists, although the tourist will in many cases find it a most useful addition to his outfit. There is nothing special about the waistcoat except that it should be cut high, in fact the square clerical cut may be best adopted. The back and lining of such a waistcoat should always be of flannel and need not be so heavy as it is ordinarily made. A combination garment has been suggested combining the waistcoat and jacket, by having an all-cloth waistcoat fitted with arms and cut a trifle longer than usual, and then putting on over it a sleeveless coat, which, when the rider gets out into the country, could be taken off and easily packed away. The idea seems practical, and might be adopted.

The nether garments may be either knickerbockers, knee-breeches, or trousers; the latter are the least suitable, as having no support at the knee they are sure to slip downwards, and drag if the rider assumes the only proper position, viz. the vertical, whilst any scheme for looping them up or fixing them, though it may effect its object so far as to allow the rider to use the machine without fear of accident, invariably makes them look awkward and uncomfortable. The gaiters adopted by the

C. T. C have their advocates, but they are hotter than stockings, and if a rider wears gaiters there seems no good reason why he could not as well wear stockings. This brings the matter to the much-vexed question, knee-breeches or knickerbockers? and there is much to say on both sides. Riders with abnormal calves will do well to tone them down with wide and somewhat baggy knickerbockers, but the youth with attenuated limbs should encase them in pretty closely fitting knee-breeches. In general the bicyclist will be found to adopt the tighter knee-breeches, whilst the tricyclist will affect the loose knicker-bockers. The reason is obvious, as a fold of loose cloth has been known before now to throw a bicyclist, whilst the tricyclist is quite safe from any such accident.

Knee-breeches require careful making; they must fit without being tight, and they must not grip the limb at any time during the action. When a rider goes to his own tailor for knee-breeches, it very frequently happens that they are very nice as long as the rider only walks in them, but the moment he begins to ride he finds them tight, stiff, and awkward. For this reason it is always best to go for these special garments to some firm which thoroughly understands the requirements of the cyclist in the matter of freedom in the muscular action. Breeches should never be tight round the knee, a remark which applies to all classes of leg gear, but they should just fit and no more at that point, as if they are accurately adjusted they will uphold the stockings without the necessity of garters, a somewhat valuable point, and one which should be carefully attended to. Knee-breeches should be lined where required with thin flannel, and the stiffening which may be necessary should be effected with all-wool stiffener in place of the linen material which is so usually used now. A strap and buckle should not be necessary, as a wise cyclist will invariably wear braces (of which more anon). Knickerbockers require careful cutting to look well, and the same remarks apply to them as to knee-breeches. Flannel linings should be used throughout, and the garments should be very carefully fitted, and not cut too high. They are best fastened with a cloth strap and buckle at the knee, which should not be drawn too tight ; they should be made with a view to the position assumed by the rider when on his machine.

Knitted or webbing breeches are very suitable for work of all kinds, though in the winter they may require supplementing with some sort of underwear ; they are cool, and though rain goes through them at once, it gets out of them with equal rapidity, as they dry very fast indeed. They should be all lined with flannel around the waist, and should be worn with braces. Double seating for cloth breeches was at one time much insisted on by riders, but it is not now quite so popular, as the edges of the sewing have been found to give rise to blisters, and the great thickness is also clumsy and awkward. Single seats are therefore now most popular, though in the case of the webbing garments above alluded to, the seat is strengthened by the running of an extra thread through the stuff at this point, which notably strengthens it. Washleather seats were also once in great favour, but they have not proved on the whole satisfactory. When sewn into ordinary breeches the leather soon stretched and then went into rucks and folds which hardened, and, as a natural consequence, produced great discomfort. The only practical way in which the washleather seat can be successfully used is to have two or more, made entirely independent of the breeches they are to be used in, and then after getting them washed and pulled into shape, having them either stitched in, so as to be easily removable, or else buttoned in, to some permanently fixed buttons. In any case it is a question whether the game is worth the candle, as a carefully finished pair of breeches, with the seam neatly sewn down, and if necessary rubbed over with a bit of soap at first, will soon become quite comfortable.

In all cases the breeches should be worn well braced up, so as not to hang in a loose and baggy manner, which may cause an accident, especially to a bicyclist, as a fold of the loose garment will catch upon the back of the saddle and cause the rider to fall when trying to mount. On the other hand, too tight bracing up will cause endless discomfort, and induce the cyclist to stoop in an awkward and constrained position.

Pockets in the breeches are not much recommended, but if they are adopted they are best placed high up in front, close under the brace buttons, and they should not be too large. A side-seam pocket is liable to gape when the rider is mounted, and unless made very deep, and consequently clumsy to get at, the articles contained in it are liable to be lost. If the rider wears a loosely cut jacket, say a Norfolk jacket, a breeches pocket on the back of the hips is a very good addition; this should be moderate in dimensions, the opening being diagonal, so as to admit of the easy insertion of the hand, and it should have a button to fasten it. If there be no watch pocket in the jacket, it can be very comfortably added to the breeches, put close up to one of the brace buttons, and having a hole in front of the pocket to pass the chain through.

There are several very dangerous ideas which some practical riders have adopted; thus one rider has a long pocket just inside the opening of his jacket in which he carries an adjustable spanner. Were he to fall heavily on his chest, the chances are that this spanner would break one of his ribs, or inflict other serious injuries. The same remark applies to those riders who carry a bell in their breast pocket when not in use. All jacket pockets wherever placed should have flaps fitted, as in the case of wet the flap will protect the contents of the pocket for a considerable time; in the case of the breast pocket, it is sometimes an excellent plan to have a small flat black button to fasten it with. An inner pocket can be made in fully lined garments inside the right breast to take the C. T. C. ticket, but overloading a suit with pockets inevitably spoils its look, and eventually its shape, so it should be avoided as far as possible.

Possibly it may not strike a casual observer that there could be much variety in the matter of stockings, but the ingenuity of hosiery manufacturers has supplied the cycling world with a pretty extensive choice in this important item. Well-fitting leg gear is a *sine quâ non* in the outfit of a rider. The most usual error into which cyclists, as well as manufacturers, fall, is the wearing or making of too long stockings. Thus stockings reaching half-way up the thigh have been offered as suitable for cycling, whereas the less stocking a rider can wear with comfort and decency the better, always supposing that the breeches or knickerbockers are well cut, and reach, as they should do, well below the knee. Some of the more elaborate double-kneed arrangements are hot, heavy, clumsy, and decidedly uncomfortable, whilst they seriously interfere with the free action of the knee-joints, and should be avoided. If adequate arrangements are made for holding the stocking up, the less strained it is the better, so long as it does not fall into creases or folds. For all round wear an ordinary fairly stout ribbed stocking will be found the best.

In the case of new stockings, put on for the first time, it is an excellent plan to soap the joints and edges carefully with a piece of common yellow soap, as this will prevent the stocking from rubbing the foot in any part, and abrading the skin. Attention to this little point will often save a rider hours of painful work. In the summer time, and for short runs, a much thinner stocking may be worn. Thread stockings, to say the least of it, are unwise. The tourist should therefore adhere rigidly to wool, and wear fairly stout stockings of that material.

The great question with all stocking wearers at all times has been how to hold them up, as although a new pair if well made will cling to the limb, and look smooth and neat, yet as soon as they get a little worn and loose they will slip down and look very bad indeed.

The various slings and kindred arrangements are by no means suitable for the use of cyclists, as they are arranged for the upright position of a man when standing, and are not a success when used by a rider in active work; moreover, most of them merely transfer the drag from the knee to the waist or shoulder, and they are therefore to be avoided. The constant motion, too, causes the metal clips or fastenings to rub the skin, thus setting up an annoying soreness, and in some cases causing worse troubles. The garter, though by no means wholly satisfactory, seems to be the only practical plan. Non-elastic garters should in no case be worn. The slight drag of the stocking causes the hard and unyielding garter to press tightly upon the muscles and vessels at the top of the calf, and may give rise to varicose veins. Some of the spiral wire arrangements, if carefully adjusted so as to be exactly the right length and no less, are very good, as the slight gaps between the wires permit circulation, and are more likely, when in action, to shift a little, so as to alter the points upon which the pressure comes. The most frequent error in using these garters is having them much too tight, and this should be most carefully avoided. The broad flat elastic garter made for ladies' use is fairly good, but the buckle or latching arrangement is altogether too elaborate, and might possibly cause a severe injury if driven into the leg, in the event of a fall. After a careful testing of every contrivance in the market, it is probable that the practical cyclist will eventually come back to the original plan of a plain broad elastic garter, which, if carefully made, will be found the most comfortable and serviceable.

Double heels and toes are a mistake in cycling stockings, and in fact in stockings used in any athletic sport, as the double portions have a very marked tendency to stretch unequally, with the obvious result that they go into rucks and creases, and cause endless trouble. There should be little or no actual friction, that is if a well-fitting shoe be worn, properly laced up over a well-fitting stocking. The main idea in all sorts of cycling work is to allow the foot plenty of play, and to keep it as cool as possible.

The next point to be considered in the outer garments is the head gear, and here again the individual fancies of the rider must be consulted. The hat or cap most identified with cycling is that most unpractical and unsuitable of head gears, the so-called polo cap, a little circular cloth saucer which is of literally no service at all. The wideawake, deer-stalker, and others of this class will be found of more general service than any other.

A good wide brim is an essential in a cycling hat, and it should also be light, well ventilated, and durable. If a felt be chosen, it should be a soft one, of a colour either matching the coat worn, or very distinct from it. Some of the lighter greys and browns are very suitable for summer touring. They should have a moderately high crown, which should be fully ventilated by means of a number of metal-edged eyelet holes, and a hat guard is a necessity, as if the hat is crammed on tight, when the wind is blowing it is almost certain to cause headache and similar troubles. The brim should be wide, but not too wide. It should be just stiff enough to retain its shape against an ordinary breeze, as to have one's hat brim flapping over one's eyes, perhaps when half-way down a hill, or at any other similarly awkward time, is troublesome or even dangerous. For winter riding a plain black felt wideawake may be recommended. A high-crowned hard felt affords a very great protection from the rays of the sun, though it is hardly so useful in wet weather, and catches the dust. The helmet is perhaps the very best head gear for touring work in all weathers. In this alone will be found those proper provisions for complete ventilation which are usually so conspicuous by their absence in ordinary hats and caps, whilst the protection afforded to the nape of the neck, and the freely ventilated space between the top of the head and the top of the helmet are all of the greatest value to the rider who goes a-cycling in the hot sun of summer. The practical tourist need look no further for a head dress than the C. T. C. helmet of the hard pattern. The soft type of C. T. C. helmet, which is simply a small cap with peaks before and behind, is by no means to be recommended. The ventilation, owing to its close fit, is practically *nil*, and the protection it affords is very limited. There are, of course, other designs besides that sold to its members by the C. T. C. The Canonbury Cycling Club have had made for them a very good shape rather different from the C. T. C. The Canonbury helmet is considerably wider and lower in the crown, and it is also lighter in weight. The Stanley C. C. have also a very good type of helmet. The best of these are made upon cork bases and are light, but their durability is open to question. Except in the hottest weather the neat, light and comfortable cricket cap may be worn with safety and comfort, and its use is daily becoming more universal. The cap should be of flannel, unlined, and with a stiff peak also of flannel, which may be stiffened with a piece of leather not too thick. This cap has many points to recommend it for ordinary wear (except in the hottest part of the summer); it is very light, fully ventilated, seeing that it is of thin and very open flannel, without lining. The peak affords protection to the eyes, and can be turned round to shade the back of the neck, whilst it can never be lost, seeing that it can be rolled up and put in the pocket with ease.

The great question of boots *v.* shoes was for a long time debated, but time which settles all things has most decidedly settled this question in favour of shoes. At one time a theory was strongly advanced that it was necessary to wear boots to support the ankle, and the sport of skating was adduced as evidence of the necessity of that support being given. It did not occur to the advocates of the boot side of the argument that on a cycle the bodily weight of the individual was carried by the machine, and that the muscles which carried the body in ordinary case were, whether strong or weak, available for the support of the ankles and the propulsion of the machine; added to which the tendency of the pedalling was to keep the foot and ankle straight, and the theory of support for the ankle was thus absolutely negatived by facts. It is interesting when considering this fact to remember that medical men are now prescribing tricycle exercise for children who suffer from weak joints, either at the knee or ankle, as they find that as the weight of the body is not thrown upon the joints, the exercise they thus obtain tends to gradually strengthen them. The theory that weak joints require support for cycling work is consequently untenable, and those who are victims of this evil will do well to undergo a short course of tricycle or bicycle exercise, which will strengthen the muscles and joints without the otherwise unavoidable strain of the bodily weight upon the tender parts.

Foot gear, however, to return from this digression, becomes simply a question as to what shoes shall be worn, and it will be well to consider the uses to which the foot is put. It is an absolute necessity that the foot should be free to extend itself and to carry out untrammelled all the varied actions described in the foregoing chapters on ankle action and pedalling generally. To secure this desideratum the shoe must be light, flexible, and easy. The sole, too, must be of sufficient thickness to preserve the bottom of the foot from feeling the bars of the pedals, and should be as stiff as possible, as in this case the rider practically gets the whole surface of the sole whereon to apply his power, instead of having to push at two narrow bars of iron. The sole of the shoe may with advantage have a piece of steel run up the middle, that is the middle of the front sole from the waist to the toe, not from the waist to the heel. The piece of steel should be flat and broad, and it will be found of the very greatest assistance in keeping the sole flat, and thus precluding in most cases the possibility of cramp in the toe joints, especially in that of the great toe. The rider should be very careful to see that the shoemaker uses a flat piece of steel, as many shoemakers, to save themselves trouble, will use a bent waist spring which invariably bends the sole very awkwardly in time.

This stout sole is the mainstay of a sound shoe; the toe should be made rather wide, the 'uppers' should be cut rather high up over the instep, and the grip of the shoe, whereby it is retained on the foot, should be arranged to come just round the waist of the foot, about three or four fingers broad at the most. The waist of the shoe itself should be as light and flexible as possible, as light as a running-pump. Shoemakers generally have a strong objection to making so light a waist behind so comparatively heavy a front sole, but the rider who wants to be well shod should insist upon this part of the plan being fully carried out. The whole of the back part of the shoe may be as light as possible, the upper heel, however, being stiffened; whilst on to the pump-like heel of the shoe may be affixed one thickness of stoutish sole leather in the shape of a broad flat heel, so as to protect that part of the foot from injury in case of a dismount on rough ground. For touring and men's wear, hooks all up the front are the best method of lacing the shoe, as the laces are thus kept from pressing on the delicate bones and muscles of the front of the foot. It is also a good plan to have the shoes to open a good way down, as by adopting this fashion the shoe can be easily and comfortably put on even when wet, and can be wiped out and quickly dried. This is another of those minor points the value of which will only be appreciated after a tour of some duration. These points are all fully carried out in Norris's 'Lacy-Hillier' shoe.

It is, as has been pointed out before, always advisable to go for these specialities to some maker who is acquainted practically with the reasons which guide their construction, as in many cases the maker who is not so informed is very obstinate in his ideas, and refuses to make the necessary changes in his usual methods. One point, for example, which has been alluded to above, may be cited; many ordinary shoemakers steadily refuse to make a light running-shoe waist to a shoe with a stout sole, whilst the effort to make the shoe look well by having it narrow in the toe is fatal to a good cycling foot-gear, which should be especially broad and roomy at that point to allow of the natural play of the foot.

There are many other very good patterns of shoe which possess especial points to recommend them to riders, whilst there are as many more which show no practical acquaintance with their wants. Thus a shoe very much cut out, so as to make it as light and open as possible, would perhaps be cool and comfortable once in a way, but for riding over dusty or muddy roads, and more especially if worn when many hills had to be walked, it would prove a terrible drawback, owing to the easy access provided for grit and dust, which is fatal to comfort when it gets into the stockings, from which it is not easily dislodged.

Thus far the outer garments suitable for men, the larger section of cyclists, have been described; but before passing to the next section it will be well to say a few words as to ladies' dress for cycling purposes; and it is also advisable to note that in the main the divergence between the appropriate cycling costume of the two sexes is confined solely to the outer garments, as the under-wear is of necessity very similar in either case, ladies having taken advantage of the experiences gained by their husbands and brothers, and adopted with but slight modification the underclothing which they have found most suitable for wear whilst indulging in the sport. A well-designed tricycle costume will allow of the greatest freedom of action, and thus enable its wearer to ride a machine without the troublesome and tiring drag which is always felt if an ordinarily dressed woman mounts a velocipede. On the other hand, the would-be dress reformers seized upon these undoubted facts and desired to use the tricycling ladies as a medium whereby they might introduce to the public their crude notions of a suitable and hygienic dress. Seeing that the spectacle of a lady on a tricycle was at that time a novelty sure to attract remark, it was somewhat unreasonable that those who were courageous enough to ride should be asked to render themselves doubly conspicuous by putting on a novel and *outré* costume. But, although the reform was not adopted in its entirety, the ladies interested took up the question, and at a meeting called by the C. T. C. the matter was carefully discussed, and the following decisions arrived at, which embody a full description of a cycling dress for ladies, and which is reproduced from the official gazette of the Touring Club.

Ladies :—It has already been announced that in addition to the thin cloth specially manufactured for their use—which weighed 16 oz. per yard run, 58 to 60 inches wide—a new substance, identical in pattern and width, is preparing to weigh 12 oz. only. This we conceive to be as light as in any case desirable, for a lady who dresses from a practical hygienic point of view, invariably discards the majority of the garments usually worn, and assumes those more in consonance with the taking of healthy athletic exercise, with its concomitant need of freedom of movement—the result being that the few articles assumed have to compensate for the inevitable loss of warmth which must otherwise ensue.

A considerable amount of latitude must necessarily be allowed, and the rules may in some respects be considered recommendatory only, *i.e.*, any lady who upon principle objects to implicitly follow them is at liberty to introduce any reasonable modification. It may not, however, be amiss to remark that the most careful consideration has been given to the question in all its bearings, and the result has been arrived at only after consultation with, and receiving the openly expressed opinion of hundreds of the best known cyclists of both sexes. The uniform designed and strongly recommended embraces the following.

(1) A combination merino or woollen garment to be worn next the body.

(2) A pair of dark grey woollen or merino stockings.

(3) A pair of loose knickerbockers, of the Club cloth, fastened with elastic, or by a cloth strap and buckle, under the knee; to be suspended from the hips or the shoulders at the option of the wearer; or

(4) A pair of trousers cut loose to just below the knee, and thence tighter just down to the foot; to be suspended from the hips or shoulders at the option of the wearer.

(5) A plain skirt, of the Club cloth, without kilting, and of sufficient fulness to admit of absolute freedom of movement without undue bulk.

(6) A bodice or jacket, at option of wearer, cut either to fit the figure, or of 'Norfolk' shape, lined throughout (including sleeves) with the Club flannel, and provided with an adjustable belt if so desired.

(7) A helmet or hat of the Club cloth, or of straw, with a special and registered ribbon, in any of the shapes that may be provided by the Club from time to time.

(8) A pair of soft 'Tilbury'd' doeskin gloves.

Cost of Special Items.

	£	s.	d.
Knickerbockers or Trousers	1	10	0
Skirt	1	15	6
Coat Bodice, or 'Norfolk' Jacket	0	18	6
	4	4	0

This costume, adopted in February 1884, has since been worn by many practical and successful lady riders with complete satisfaction, and it embodies all the necessary points of a hygienic riding costume. The cloth should be closely woven and not fluffy or rough, as in either of these cases it will hold the dust and defy brushing; neither should it be too thick, or too heavy, and it should be neither too light nor too dark in colour, a happy grey medium being undoubtedly the most serviceable. That ladies generally will be fully competent to suit themselves in this matter there can be little doubt, but a very large consensus of opinion is at present in favour of the lighter class of C. T. C. cloth for ladies' use. As with the bicyclists' costume, the ladies' tricycling dress was not designed at once, but was gradually perfected by active riders in constant work. The all-flannel, or rather the all-woollen, costume is even of more moment in this case, as the danger of colds is possibly greater with those who do not so frequently indulge in exercise, and no rider should wear anything but wool. One drawback which has existed for some time in this connexion has now been removed, as all-wool corsets are obtainable as well as every other requisite for a lady's cycling costume.

The choice of a body garment is not a difficult one, but unfortunately lady riders are very fond of a tight-fitting bodice or jacket, which, however well it may look, must of necessity be hot and uncomfortable, and a 'shaped' jacket should be carefully avoided if the rider means to ride in earnest and not to play at cycling. Of all the different styles of jackets, nothing touches the Norfolk jacket for all-round use. If nicely cut it looks well, is comfortable, and appropriate, and as it can be worn by either sex, it is a most serviceable garb. In all material points, the instructions laid down for cutting the ordinary Norfolk jacket should be observed. Some of the closer fitting jackets with a military collar are suitable for cold weather.

When ladies first began to ride they were constrained by prejudice to ride upon a seat placed low down and some distance behind the pedals, and this position, besides being awkward and uncomfortable, was also exceedingly dangerous. The dress in this case was constantly riding up over the knees, each alternate stroke lifting it higher, and many attempts were made to design some method of keeping it in place. Some riders sewed a considerable weight of shot into the lower edge so as to keep it down, whilst others fastened the front of the skirt to the front of their boots or shoes, with the very obvious result that the skirt dragged tremendously over the knees and rapidly tired the rider. Many cyclists of both sexes made experiments to see how best to overcome this serious difficulty, and a remedy was found, although not quite in the direction anticipated. Instead of altering the dress, it was the position of the rider which was altered; instead of sitting low down, and a long way behind the pedals on a rear-steering tricycle, she was placed upright, well over the pedals, upon a front-steerer. At first many ladies so placed insisted on still using the seat instead of the saddle, and were proportionately uncomfortable; but in due time they were converted to the use of the saddle, and at once found their troubles were over. The knees, instead of awkwardly rising and falling in front of the body, were simply moved in a manner closely resembling the action of walking. The skirt was simply thrown out by either knee alternately, and still hung gracefully and comfortably in front of the rider. This was the solution of a difficulty which bade fair at one time to prevent many ladies from following the sport.

The skirt should be just long enough for walking purposes, and no more. It should be of sufficient size to admit of the freest motion of the knees, and should be of some closely woven and wiry material which will not cling unduly to the figure. It may be a part of the jacket, or may be worn with a belt or suspended from one of the under garments, the latter plan being the best, as doing away with any tight cinctures around the body. It should be simple in design and not loaded with braiding.

The stocking should be of thin and soft merino, as the extra garments worn make these somewhat oppressive if unnecessarily thick. They should be treated in all cases as advised for the bicyclist above ; but a special caution may be here given against tight garters, as the exercise of cycling requires that the limbs should be as free as possible from tight ligatures, which may give rise to serious troubles. On the question of the head dress the ladies again will exercise their own choice, but in general a smallish hat is advisable, with some provision for the adequate protection of the neck and eyes. With the general caution not to have too large a hat to catch the wind, or too small a one, which would not afford adequate protection from the sun, this point can be dismissed. Ladies will of course adopt shoes when riding, and these should be light and of thin leather, with a thin waist as flexible as possible. Eyelet holes should replace the hooks which the bicyclist is advised to adopt, as the latter catch in the front of the dress and tear it, besides sometimes tripping up the rider. From a similar cause the shoe should open a good way down, and if it is neatly made this will cause the foot to look all the smaller and be of great service to the wearer. The steel in the sole is not an absolute necessity, but should any lady rider suffer from cramp, or be continually missing her pedal, a steel and grooves to take the rat-traps pedals should at once be fitted, as this will enable her to keep her foot straight, and at the same time will correct the error into which she has fallen. The garments worn under the skirt may be practically regarded as outer garments, as they are usually made of the same cloth and assimilated as much as possible to it. A choice is offered between trousers and knickerbockers, but the latter are much to be preferred, as trousers will inevitably drag very much over the knees and fatigue the rider. A carefully fitted pair of knickerbockers, with a cloth strap and buckle at the knee, will be found the most useful garments to wear under the skirt, and if the stockings be either of some dark colour or else match the dress, and the skirt be cut the right length, it will both look well and prove comfortable, regarded merely as a cycling costume. Here again it is scarcely necessary to point out that ladies should go to a practical ladies' tailor for cycling clothes, as unless the maker is aware of the particular purpose for which they are wanted, and has some special knowledge of the requirements of the case, the garments when made will not be likely to prove successful.

Outer garments being thus disposed of, the next section is the under wear, and it is of the very greatest importance that the under garments should be of an appropriate description, as unsuitable underclothing is certain to cause the wearer annoyance, which might easily have been obviated by taking a little trouble in the selection at first. Nothing but wool should be used, and this is more than usually important in the case of anything which is to be worn next the skin. The commonest error into which riders fall is putting on too many things. For short sharp runs too little clothing is infinitely preferable to too much, and for long journeys too much clothing will weaken and tire the rider terribly. When he arrives at his journey's end, moreover, every one of his numerous garments is wet through and of no use at all; whereas, if he had but tied one or two dry vests, &c., to his handle-bar, they would have come in well at the end of the day. In ordinary summer weather, and when the rider can get home without riding long into the night, he will find that one good woollen sweater will be quite enough under an ordinary riding jacket, or a good and not too thick flannel shirt will be ample protection; and if he be a cautious man, he will perhaps take a dry vest with him to put on whilst dining in the middle of the day. The tourist who does not mean to unduly hurry himself, but at the same time intends to have a few days' holiday, will perhaps wear an extra vest under the shirt as a preventative of cold, but even this in hot weather will be transferred to the luggage bag.

The variety of undergarments is enormous, and the cyclist has a large selection from which to choose. It has been observed above that the woollen goods sold by the Sanitary Woollen Company of Fore Street are excellent, especially some of the vests, which are considerably longer than the ordinary vests, and are thus usable as both shirt and vest in one. This, if worn beneath a buttoned-up coat, will be found ample for summer riding. The flannel shirts usually sold for cycling purposes have one or two faults; they are much too voluminous and much too long. The shirt of the future will be just shaped to the figure without fitting tightly, whilst the tails will be notably shortened so as to get rid of some of the extra material; the sleeves will be made rather tighter and the neck band of woollen material, and not the linen or cotton now usually employed, this small piece of linen being responsible for many a sore throat. The flannel shirt should preferably button up the front and should be of a uniform thickness all over, made of the very best flannel, not too thick and just a nice fit. Pockets in the shirt are a failure, as they tend to pull it open when in use, and should not be adopted for that reason. A good many riders of both sexes prefer those excellent garments known as 'Combinations.' They are especially useful for cold days and winter work, as they secure that great desideratum an even distribution of warmth all over the body, and at the same time combine the various advantages of many garments in one. For those who habitually wear under drawers, or other similar garments, the Combination is a great boon, and is certain to grow steadily in public favour. Cashmere neck handkerchiefs are to be preferred to any others, though a somewhat thicker woollen comforter may be used with advantage for night riding in the winter. There are also some cashmere collars in the market which are decidedly better than the waterproof goods, as the latter condense the perspiration in little beads upon the collar, and this strikes very cold to the neck. But a flannel collar attached to the shirt is much the best for all purposes. Ladies' underclothing should be constructed very much on the same principles, the main idea to be carried out being to secure good fit without undue tightness, a point which may be attained by the use of merino and stockingnette carefully chosen. If the fit of each garment is carefully studied, the result will be satisfactory in every way, and the costume will as a consequence sit well.

Having thus set forth at length the various details of dress which are necessary, it may be well to recapitulate the whole of the items needed for a cyclist's outfit, together with the price as charged by the C. T. C., which may be taken as a very fair average cost :—

	s.	d.
Jacket	32	0
Breeches or knickerbockers	16	0
Waistcoat	10	0
Shirt	11	6
Gaiters	8	6
Helmets, any size	6	6
Soft knockabout helmets, do.	4	6
White straw hats, rough or smooth plait, with registered ribbon, complete	4	6
Straw hats, without ribbon	3	6
Registered ribbon, without hat	2	0
Polo caps, do.	2	9
Deerstalker or wideawake	5	9
Puggarees, for helmets	2	0
Cap covers	1	9
Stockings, any size	4	0
Gloves, any size	3	3
Silk handkerchiefs, or mufflers, in Club colours (grey checked ground, worked into amber and gold border) registered, 24 in. square	6	6
30 in. ditto	9	0

It is also advisable to conclude with the oft-repeated bit of advice, viz. when cycling clothing is wanted, go to a practical cycling tailor, who will appreciate the reason of the numerous little variations required from the regular model, and as a natural consequence will carry them out with accuracy and intelligence. The introduction lately of sound woollen stiffeners and other necessary materials for a garment, guaranteed all wool, have lightened the task of those who desire to ride in comfort and safety, as they will find all such things ready to their hands, whereas the pioneer cyclist had to go and seek for them all over the country.

The final maxims therefore are: (1), wear nothing but pure woollen garments ; (2), have them cut by a practical cycling tailor ; (3), study the even distribution of warmth ; (4), do not over-clothe the body ; and (5), in the event of a longish ride, always take a dry under-vest in case of accidents. By following out the above few precepts, the cyclist, lady or gentleman, will be enabled to ride in comfort and safety whatever may be the state of the weather.

CHAPTER VIII.

CYCLING FOR LADIES.

WHEN the first edition of this work was issued the tricycle had already been taken up by ladies in a manner which augured well for the future of the sport. In 1878 tradition told of a lady cyclist who, in company with her husband, made an extended tour along the south coast; and in quiet lanes and private gardens feminine riders began to initiate themselves into the pastime which presented itself, very soon arriving at the conclusion that the novel vehicle was singularly suited to their requirements.

The sport of cycling, in which ladies had hitherto taken but little interest, now became of considerable importance in their eyes. Of course there was a great deal of opposition to be encountered. At first medical men, without any practical knowledge of cycling, tabooed it, and any number of ills were confidently promised to ladies who rode the new machines. Progress, thus checked, was further retarded by the fact that the most unsuitable machines in the market were labelled 'ladies' tricycles.' If any machine possessed points about it which would inevitably have secured its rejection by a practised rider, if it was a single-driver, with inadequate break power, rear-steering and generally impracticable, that was the machine a lady was recommended to ride, and as she was usually provided with a seat placed too close to the work, the pioneer lady cyclist did not have a fair chance. It followed naturally that the progress made was very slow;

still, a few ladies were found who disregarded criticism, and pursued the sport with vigour and enthusiasm. Some of these had the good fortune to possess male relatives who were themselves practical cyclists, and gave the learners valuable aid and advice. In one case the gentleman did his best to persuade his fair companion to adopt a saddle, vertical position, and a full easy reach, but she declined the trial, although the man she had promised to obey nearly ordered her to attempt it. At length one day, far in the country, away from the busy hum of men, the lady, much against her will, consented to the experiment. The seat was exchanged for a saddle, and the standard which carried it was raised some inches. For a few hundred yards she averred that she was going to fall on her nose every moment, then she became more comfortable, and for some hours rode in the new position with considerable satisfaction. On nearing home, though it was late in the day, she insisted on having the standard lowered again, as she was under the impression that her skirt was not quite long enough for the city ; and then, and not till then, did she fully recognise the advantages of the new position and the saddle, the two miles or so in the old position being an ample and convincing proof of its fallacy.

By far the larger number of our lady riders began their cycling experiences upon sociables or tandems with their husbands and brothers, and thus gained by degrees the experience and confidence necessary for the fullest enjoyment of a cruise upon wheels, eventually attaining the self-reliance necessary for a trip upon a single machine. It is perhaps upon a tandem with a gentleman companion that the lady rider looks most at home, and when, clad in a well-fitting and becoming costume, she flits by on the front seat of one of these light and speedy machines, the most sceptical observer is converted to the same view.

This fact is fully recognised by the general public, who have been quite educated up to the sight of lady tricyclists perambulating the roads, and gaze upon them with the same

WOMEN'S RIGHTS

CYCLING FOR LADIES. 249

sort of indifference with which a nineteenth-century horse gazes upon a railway train or a steam roller. In many crowded districts which would be more prolific of deterrent circumstances than quiet and out-of-the-way country corners, the efforts of individual riders have had very much to do with

THE LADIES' TRICYCLE.

popularising the sport amongst ladies. To these pioneers cycling owes very much. Ladies who now enjoy an unmolested spin upon the highway will think with gratitude of these first lady cyclists—several of whom were identified with the South London T.C.

After a transition period, in which these ladies whose names are now well known to cyclists courageously took the lead, the sport became popular among the sex, and they are to be found joining club runs, touring, and making short excursions in all parts of the country in search of fresh air and exercise. Many are amateurs of sketching, painting, or photography, and for these the tricycle soon becomes an almost indispensable adjunct—a convenient beast of burden which carries the impedimenta as well as the artist herself.

Thus far the history of cycling for ladies had been identified solely with the tricycle, and the idea that lady cyclists would ever use a bicycle never occurred to anyone. Yet there can be no question that for their use the tricycle is the machine of the past; the rear-driving Safety bicycle is the machine of the future.

The Ladies' Tricycle.—This should be of light weight, with smallish wheels well clothed with rubber; it should have an effective break, fitted preferably with a double lever, one for each hand. The spring should be carefully calculated to the rider's weight. The saddle should be comfortable, and the foot-rests within easy reach. A foot auxiliary break is a specially valuable addition; nowadays most of the cycle manufacturing firms cater intelligently for ladies in this direction.

The advantage of the tricycle lies in the fact that it stands up without balancing, and it may be safely said that this one point represents the alpha and omega of its merits. On the other hand, it has numerous inherent and ineradicable disadvantages, which may be summarised as follows:—

1. Its weight.
2. The difficulty of mounting.
3. The impossibility of dismounting when moving.
4. The three tracks.
5. The lateral jars and twists.

The extra weight is an important consideration. The mounting difficulty is a serious one, the rider having either to wriggle over the axle or squeeze in between the driving-wheel and the handle bar. Dismounting is a very awkward performance, the lady's skirt making a backward dismount an impossibility. The three tracks on stony or bad roads often necessitate a dismount, and possibly a long and tiring walk. A still more serious drawback is found in the fact that one of the three wheels may be thrown up higher than the others, thus jarring or twisting the rider.

The one and only disadvantage of the rear-driving Safety as a ladies' cycle is the necessity of keeping the balance. It may be well, therefore, to investigate the matter rather more closely.

Those persons who assert that the difficulty of learning would prove too great to permit ladies to become successful riders of the rear-driver pay them but a poor compliment. In the days of Clarissa Harlowe and 'book-muslin frocks' the young ladies of the period might possibly have been horrified at the suggestion that they should attempt to ride a bicycle, but nowadays happily all this is changed, and the girls of to-day scull, play lawn tennis, swim, walk, and practise athletic exercises in a complete and thorough manner, and it is absolutely ridiculous to assert that any girl of average physique could not learn to balance a Safety bicycle with quite as much confidence as any other young rider. When once this point has been reached—and it should be easily attained in a week if learnt under a competent instructress—the lady cyclist is certainly no worse off than the masculine rider, whilst one point is very decidedly in her favour, namely, the unquestionable fact that skill is of more importance than mere physical strength.

When once the initial difficulty has been overcome—and it should be easily mastered—the advantages of the rear-driver are indisputably very great; and, except for the small minority who are condemned to ride in towns or over long stretches of cobbles, and who would of necessity prefer the tricycle, there is no doubt that in due time the vast majority of lady cyclists will adopt the rear-driving Safety.

It possesses the following advantages :—

1. It is lighter than a tricycle, has fewer working parts and no balance gear, and is thus more easily driven.

2. The method of mounting is very much simpler, more easy, and decidedly more graceful than the tricycle mount.

3. The method of dismounting is equally easy, even when the machine is moving.

4. The machine makes but one track, a most important point, as it enables the rider to pick her way for miles along stone-strewn or rough roads where a tricyclist must walk.

FIG. I.—PREPARING TO MOUNT.

5. The absence of any lateral jars or twists, any obstruction being encountered in the central line of the machine.

6. The possibility of applying adequate and ample break-power, if necessary, to both wheels.

The one point of disadvantage has already been alluded to. It is practically of no moment, for it has often been demonstrated that ladies, though possibly inferior in the matter of mere physical strength, can hold their own with men at almost any sport requiring skill, and there is not the slightest valid ground for believing that, if the former are properly taught to ride, they will be to any material extent behind the average cyclist in the skilful management and control of their single-track steeds.

The Safety, when this point is reached, is immeasurably superior to the tricycle; whilst, as to its safety, it is as safe *if not safer*, when ridden at the same rate of speed. If, by any mischance, a lady has a fall from a tricycle, it is almost impossible for her to fall upon her feet, as the driving-wheels would be in the way and anything like a free escape impossible. On

FIG. 2.—MOUNTING: FIRST POSITION, RIGHT FOOT ON RIGHT PEDAL (STATIONARY).

the other hand, in the case of a side slip, or any similar accident on a Safety, the chances are very much in favour of the rider alighting on her feet.

The method of mounting is simplicity itself, and it can be acquired in one lesson. The rider stands on the left side of the machine, holding the handles firmly and inclining the machine slightly to the left. The right-hand pedal is brought to the front about two inches (see the ankle-action diagram, fig. 3, p. 146), and the rider puts her right foot firmly upon it; then, simply springing from the ground off her left foot, she raises her weight partly on the pedal and partly on the handles, and seats herself with the greatest ease in the saddle. Though at first hurried, before the rider has quite mastered it, this mount, when once perfectly acquired, is deliberate and graceful, much more simple and graceful than the lady tricyclist's climb over the axle, or the still more awkward task of squeezing in between the handle-bar and the driving-wheel. The dismount, again, is simplicity itself, the rider merely stepping out on either side of the machine at pleasure.

FIG. 3.—MOUNTING, SECOND POSITION; WEIGHT THROWN PARTLY ON HANDLES AND ON RIGHT PEDAL.

The rear-driver calls for less physical exertion than the tricycle, and a skilful rider will obtain much better results from a rear-driver than a merely strong rider.

In the early days of cycling, when machines were heavy and clumsy, the vertical position was a necessity, with a straight arm, so as to enable the rider to exert to the fullest the propulsive powers; but, as soon as machines were lightened, this necessity passed away, and an attitude depending for its efficacy more on skill than strength was adopted.

The adjustment of a lady's Safety is of great importance, as upon it depends both her comfort and her success as a cyclist. The saddle should be a broad one, placed upon an effective spring, and so adjusted that the rider can sit upon it without holding the handles or touching the pedals; if, then, she does not slip either forward or backward when sitting upright, the adjustment is correct. The front of the saddle should be from three to four inches behind a vertical line drawn through the centre of the crank-axle, and it should not be put too high, as a full reach will be found very irksome, and will also interfere

FIG. 4.—MOUNTED!

with the ankle action. The handles should be brought well within the rider's reach; this is most important. The arms should be just bent when the rider is sitting up. Many ladies' cycles are fitted with handle-bars very much too wide, the spreading of the arm being awkward-looking and uncomfortable. In a great many instances the handles are made too low, and are placed much too far away, throwing the riders into a most unsuitable position. A lady's pedals may be either rat-trap or square rubber, but in either case her shoes should be fitted with a couple of small blocks across the sole, as a necessary adjunct to accurate and satisfactory ankle work. A firm foot-grip on the pedals is a most important factor in the avoidance of accidents. Any shoes with rubber soles should for this reason be carefully avoided, as not only are they hot and heavy, but the rubber will slip or give under a strain at the particular juncture when upon its not doing either depends the safety of the user.

The lady's Safety should have smallish wheels shod with $\frac{7}{8}$-inch *floating* rubber tires: the inflated tires should not be adopted, as they slip very much upon greasy macadam, and a side-slip is the one thing to be feared. Ample break power should be fitted—preferably a front-wheel spoon-break—with two levers, so that one hand can relieve the other down long hills. The work should be put low, but the pedals should not come too near the ground. The chain should be fully protected by means of an adequate chain-guard, and the driving-wheel may with advantage be also covered with a guard if care is taken to give plenty of clearance inside the guard and in the forks.

An auxiliary foot-break, quite distinct from the other and preferably working on the back wheel, is a great gain in safety. The lamp-holder should project from below the foot-rest on the right hand side, as being more out of the way. A fair amount of baggage can be carried upon the handle standard, but when touring it is best sent on by post or rail, unless the gentlemen of the party will take charge of it.

As soon as the Safety becomes the acknowledged ladies' cycle the sport will see a further development of the tandem Safety bicycle, the possibilities of which machine have not by any means been exhausted. For a couple always riding together the tandem Safety presents many advantages over the tandem tricycle, and as soon as the great question of balance is fairly mastered and its present terrors discounted the tandem Safety will come into use.

The tandem tricycle will always be a popular mount, as the expert rider can thereon take a complete novice — his sister, his cousin, or even on an emergency a lady who is not a relation. The sport offers yet another opening for a sex which was for many years debarred from all healthful exercise. It was 'unladylike,' said Mrs. Grundy, to indulge in physical exertion. What wonder, then, that the Languishes of the period suffered from 'the vapours.' Nowadays all this is changed, and there is no more healthful or enjoyable sport for ladies than cycling, if undertaken under competent supervision at the start, and pursued afterwards with moderation.

'CAT'S CRADLE.'

CHAPTER IX.

RACING PATHS.

A FEW years ago there were no paths in existence which had not some serious drawback from a racing cyclist's point of view. All were in one way or another unsuited to the sport. They had been laid out solely for athletics, such as running, walking, and so on, and were not in any way calculated for the new and faster sport of cycling. The old Lillie Bridge path, which was always considered excellent by running men, proved absolutely dangerous for bicycle racing, and a new significance was found in the title of the lower left-hand corner of the track, which was termed 'the Hospital Corner' because it was close to the buildings of the hospital. Many a good man who has gone flying past his opponents in front of the grand stand, and rushed on to victory down the railway straight, has come a complicated cropper at the Hospital Corner, and brought down others in his fall. It would take considerable space to enumerate the names of all the riders who have escaped the railings only to plough up the cinders of the path.

The special points required in a cycling track are as follows :—

1. It must be as nearly level as possible.

2. It must be wide—not less than 18 feet, preferably anything more in reason.

3. It must be hard, with a solid basis of sound soil or of made ground, the softness of running paths being very much against the bicyclist. The improvement of the specially laid cycling paths in this direction has had much to do with the improvement in times recorded of late years; thus the Crystal

Palace cycling track is 30 per cent. harder than the Stamford Bridge running path.

4. The corners must be 'bevelled' or banked, the meaning of this being that the track must be made higher outside than inside, sloping from five feet or more on the outside edge to nothing on the inside (on the same principle as the set given to railway lines round a curve), to assist the rider in overcoming the centrifugal force which his twenty-five miles an hour dash down the straight has developed.

All these points and many other minor ones were entirely novel. They had never been raised before, and thus were not attended to by the layers and makers of running paths, and it was some time ere the requirements of the cyclists were fully met.

Even now, indeed, many of the cycling paths suffer from want of sufficient banking at the corners, or from inadequate care in keeping 'the bones' of the track fully covered with the hard surface.

Tracks are made of cinder alone, bound with unburnt coal and breeze; in very damp localities of cinder and burnt clay mixed; in drier places of gravel, which is never satisfactory; of clay, which is worse, except in the very driest weather; and of a combination of these and other materials. Much depends upon the situation of the track. If it is in a damp place it will often keep in condition longer during the active racing season, the summer; if, on the other hand, it drains freely, it will get loose and sandy under the same conditions; and, in short, it is impossible to lay down arbitrary rules, which would assuredly not be suitable in many cases. The attendant has to watch and nurse his path assiduously. The track which held for a long while pride of place amongst English cycling paths was that at *Cambridge*. It is composed of a whitish oolite mixed with gravel, but through want of attention is very seldom in good condition; there is usually a fairly smooth 18-inch path round which the training men ride, and once in a way it is got into good shape all over. When really in condition it was second to no path in the kingdom. It is situated in a field some little way out of Cambridge, is circular, 4 laps to the mile, not very wide. On one side it is raised slightly from the level of the field, on the other it runs through a sort of cutting. There is a dressing-room, but not much accommodation. Many notable races have taken place on this path, Ion Keith-Falconer's defeat of Keen, Cooper, and Cortis in a two-mile race in 5 mins. 36⅖ secs. being perhaps the most famous. It is a good path, and its excellence when in condition has had much to do with the great performances shown by Cambridge men.

The Oxford Path is situated a short distance outside Oxford, and is on a slight slope. It is a yard or two *over* 3 laps to the mile, is square in shape with the ends rather rounded, and narrow, excepting the straight finish, which is broad and well laid. The material used is cinder, which gets rather loose in hot weather, and always runs a trifle dead. The corners are fairly easy; the run down the back stretch is somewhat baulking to a stranger to the path, an obtrusive white post and rail fence being prominently placed on the turn. The dressing accommodation is excellent in every way. The ground is the property of the Oxford University Athletic Club.

One of the first paths which proved suitable for cycling in the metropolitan district was that laid down in the Recreation Grounds at *Surbiton*, although it was too slightly banked at the corners, a fact which caused a good many men to run wide since C. A. Palmer did so unwittingly in the Five Miles Championship of 1881; but the four corners, being only quarter-turns, were easy and well graded, and as no solid and permanent spike and-rail fence on the outside threatened the rider with injury should he make a mistake, he could go at his corners with courage and dash. Surbiton ranked second only to the Cambridge path for pace in the earlier days of the sport, but has now been broken up and built over.

The Stamford Bridge Track is laid out in the grounds of the London Athletic Club at Fulham. This path is of cinder, has two long straights and two semicircular ends, the half-turn of course requiring more negotiation than the quarter-turns of Surbiton; and as an iron post-and-rail fence stands just one foot from the outside edge of the path, unaccustomed riders have to be somewhat cautious how they make these turns, especially as the corners are but slightly banked. The dressing-room accommodation is excellent, with good shower bath, &c. The nearest stations are Chelsea and Walham Green.

Close to the Stamford Bridge track were situated the old and new paths in the *Lillie Bridge Grounds*, West Brompton. The old path was made of cinder, 3 laps to the mile; the new path was made of burnt clay and cinder, 4 laps to the mile, with two long straights; but the circular ends were of different radii, the top one being the smaller. The ground is closed to the public for good.

The Alexandra Palace Track was at one time of much greater size than it is now, being $2\frac{1}{2}$ laps to the mile. As this included a somewhat severe gradient, it was altered to an even 3 laps. In shape it somewhat resembled a reversed D. The dressing accommodation is good; the 'Palace Gates' and Wood Green stations are the nearest. This track is seldom or never ridden on nowadays.

The Crystal Palace Track at Sydenham was one of the first paths laid solely for cycling, and, the work having been done with consideration and care, it was one of the fastest in the kingdom. It was laid by the directors of the Crystal Palace Company, in deference to the representations of a committee of S.E. riders, headed by Mr. W. B. Tanner, and is placed round one of the lakes in the grounds, being carried through the water on two causeways. It is of cinder, with a very sound and solid bottom, which, however, is unfortunately bedded on clay, and this occasionally works through; but the path, on the whole, is an excellent one, much improved since the hydrants were laid all round it. As it drains very quickly, it has to be well watered to keep it in condition. It is circular in shape, $3\frac{1}{2}$ laps to the mile, the true circle being, however, a little flattened at the causeways, which are nearly straight. The dressing accommodation is good; there is a shower bath; and an extensive grand stand, so that the path is complete in every way. The Crystal Palace is easily reached from London; the Low Level and Penge stations are the most convenient for the path.

The Paddington Track.—This now famous path was laid out by Mr. Melville Beachcroft, L.C.C., in the Recreation Grounds, Paddington; it is $3\frac{1}{2}$ laps to the mile; two straights 90 yards long, and two semicircular corners. These latter are well banked; a fence is placed on the outer edge of the path. The surface is composed of burnt clay, brick-dust, and coal-dust, with a small amount of cinder, and it wears fairly well, though towards the end of the season it gets noticeably bumpy. There is a good bath; the dressing accommodation is poor, but this defect will shortly be remedied. The path suffers from a plethora of popularity, being decidedly overcrowded. The nearest stations are Kilburn and Maida Vale; omnibuses from the Marble Arch pass close to the ground. Inside the cycling track are a $\frac{1}{4}$-mile running and a 120-yds. sprint tracks.

Kensal Rise.—Another new track, 3 laps to the mile, with fairly well banked curved ends. Two long straights, with running and sprint tracks, as at Paddington. There is a fine grand stand and excellent dressing accommodation. The surface is burnt clay, brick, and coal-dust. The track is well found in every respect, with speaking-tubes between the telegraph board, grand stand, dressing-rooms, and judge's stand. Nearest station, Kensal Rise.

The London County Grounds Track at Herne Hill.—A new path, which lays claim to the title of 'the most accessible track in London.' It is situated close to North Dulwich and Herne Hill stations, and by a fast train a visitor can get from Ludgate Hill to the grounds in twenty minutes. The track is $3\frac{1}{2}$ laps to the mile; two 90-yards straights and two half-circle ends, with the heaviest banking in London. The track is protected from the wind from every quarter, and is laid on the very latest and most improved lines. In addition to making it of a good width, the proprietors are laying 4 to 6 feet of grass outside the edge, *inside* the fence all round the path; this will add immensely to the feeling of safety on the part of the riders. A very fine club-house, with the most complete accommodation for the training men, is also in course of erection, and it is confidently expected that the

Herne Hill track will be *the* track of the metropolis after its first season, and it is only 200 yards outside the four-mile radius.

There are several other more or less successful tracks in the metropolitan area, but none calling for special notice.

The Bristol Track is on the Gloucestershire County Ground, at Ashey Down, Bristol, the nearest station being Ashey Down. The track is three laps to the mile, four-sided, with big quarter corners, three having a radius of 165 feet and one of 120 feet. These corners are banked up nearly 3 feet, and the width of the winning straight is 30 feet, its length being 60 feet. There is a fine pavilion, with good dressing and other accommodation.

The Brighton Track is in Preston Park, Brighton; nearest station, Preston Park. Three laps to the mile; a four-sided track of irregular shape. Corners fairly well banked; dressing accommodation fair.

The Coventry Track, situated in the Recreation Grounds, Coventry. Four laps to the mile, half-circle corners; dressing accommodation poor, lavatory and storage accommodation *nil*.

The Long Eaton Track, between Nottingham and Trent, is of irregular measurement; about $2\frac{1}{2}$ laps to the mile. Square, with four heavily banked corners; was very fast and highly popular a few seasons back; has materially retrograded since the opening of Paddington. Dressing accommodation, &c., good; but the track is far away, and is not likely to regain its popularity with record makers.

The Torquay Track.—Four laps to the mile. Two 75-yards straights and two half-circle ends.

There are also good tracks, specially laid for cycling, at Weston-super-Mare, Paignton, North Shields, Birmingham (new track at Aston), and many more places, whilst others are in prospect.

THE LAYING OF TRACKS.

This is a large question, to which only a passing reference can here be made. The inquirer who takes up the matter of a local path always asks one question first, 'What will it cost?' To which the track expert makes reply, 'Where is it to be?

What is the subsoil, the price of labour, the cost of cartage, the supply of suitable material?' and a thousand other questions. Thus, it might be pointed out, that it would cost more to lay a permanent cycle track on the Goodwin Sands than on Paddington Recreation Grounds, which, though a *reductio ad absurdum*, is a very useful argument with some people.

A roller-made track is almost invariably a foredoomed failure. The roller is carried over the soft parts on the harder portions, and when the weather consolidates the path the soft place sinks in. The rammer, and the rammer alone, should be used in path-making. A golden rule in track-making is to make the foundation good. If the bottom be sound and solid all will be well; if, on the other hand, it is not so, has soft spots in it, and so on, the hardest working track man, with the best surface material in the world, cannot keep the top right, and the few pounds saved by careless laying of the foundations will cost many pounds in cash, worry, and vexation on the surface.

The bottom of the track should be built up with big solids, stones, bricks, clinker and such like materials, rammed well down, over this a layer of rather smaller materials of the same class, and finally a layer of finish matter well raked in prior to the putting on of the surface.

The most popular shape is two straights and two half-circle ends. The most popular sizes, four and three-and-a-half laps to the mile. Plenty of width should be provided. The fence around the track should not be put right on the inside edge. There should be three or four feet of grass between the outside of the track and the inside of the fence.

Special attention should be paid to the dressing accommodation, as unless this is good men will not care to train on the path, and it is, in most cases, the men training on the path who have most to do with its welfare and popularity with the public at large.

In the appendix will be found some special rules for the governance of tracks, and should any novel features in tracks or track construction present themselves they will be fully dealt with in the same place.

CHAPTER X.

THE NATIONAL CYCLISTS' UNION.

A SPORT such as this of cycling, so wide-spread, so valuable from a health-giving and economic point of view, so distinct from all the minor branches of athletics, which have their Alpha and Omega in the competitions on the cinder path, and moreover, so easily applicable to the stern business of life, was not likely to remain for any length of time under feeble control; and although at first promoters of ordinary athletic sports did not care to push forward the new pastime, the steadily growing interest in cycling gradually encouraged them to include races for bicyclists in their programmes, as these contests excited the widest interest and thus benefited the meeting in a pecuniary sense. Such clubs or bodies as then existed for the guidance of amateur sport were solely concerned with these path competitions, and the larger interests of cyclists were entirely overlooked. The Amateur Athletic Club of Lillie Bridge promoted a four miles championship, but beyond this nothing was done for the larger section of cyclists, the road riders; and these latter, together with a number of well known racing men, determined to create a governing body elected by cyclists to rule cycling.

This determination was preceded by many crude suggestions in the pages of the press devoted to the sport, some of them embodying in the proposed scheme the functions of the C. T. C. and N. C. U. combined, and others only touching on a small portion of the work to be done. There are not wanting cyclists who think that, had an association been then formed combining the C. T. C. and N. C. U., the result would have been for the benefit of the sport; whilst another section cling to the belief that the healthy rivalry which existed between our two great associations in their youthful days was the reason of their splendid development, as shown at present by the power and prestige which both undoubtedly possess.

In the year 1876 a flood of correspondence, notes, &c., appeared in the cycling and sporting press, advocating the establishment of a legislative body for the governance of the sport of bicycling chiefly as regarded touring, bicycling being the only branch of cycling then existing. Mr. Murray Ford of the Temple B. C. took a prominent part in the discussion, with a number of suggestions. A number of other well-known men, amongst them being Mr. Walter Cornell of the Wanderers B.C., M. D. Rucker of the London B.C., Mr. J. W. Beningfield of the Pickwick B.C., Mr. F. Jolly of the London B.C., and many more gave the benefit of their opinions and experience. In the press many advocates were found, amongst them Mr. Stephen Richardson, and others who still take an active interest in the sport.

The first definite move was made in the winter of 1876–77, and a debate was held at the head-quarters of the Temple B.C. in March 1877, in which a number of the most prominent riders of the day took part. In the result a draft scheme was unanimously accepted, and the hon. secretary of the Temple B.C. was asked to convene a meeting of delegates from every club in the kingdom to assist in the formation of a necessary association for the full control of the sport. Without doubt the successes of the Union may be traced to the fact that its origin was brought about at an open and honest meeting in which all who cared to be represented could take part, and thus the opinions of all who had any right to speak were obtained. The more formal meeting was called on April 30, 1877, and was well attended. It was perhaps natural that each of the larger bodies wished to claim the credit of having founded the great cycling association, and a good deal of care was necessary before this difficulty could be smoothed over. At length, however, a sub-committee was appointed, the first, but by no means the last, named by the then newly established body. This sub-committee did not make very much progress, and it was not until September 1877 that it issued its report, which mainly consisted of a resolution affirming that the London, Pickwick, Surrey, and Temple Bicycle Clubs had jointly agreed to establish the 'Bicycle Union' to meet an obvious necessity. The cycling clubs of the universities, the Cambridge, and Dark Blue (Oxford) Bicycle Clubs were consulted, and Mr. G. F. Cobb, M.A., of Cambridge (who must not be confounded with another well-known cyclist of the same name), whose able assistance and great influence were undoubtedly of inestimable value to the young association, took the chair at a meeting held on November 17, 1877, as the outcome of which the following circular was formally issued by the Hon. Secretaries of the now supreme ruling association of cycling:—

At a meeting held at Anderton's Hotel, Fleet Street, on the 17th of November, present Mr. G. F. Cobb, chairman, and Hon. Ion Keith-Falconer, C. U. B. C., Messrs. M. D. Rucker, junr., and F. Jolly, London B. C., Messrs. J. W. Beningfield and John Nixon, Pickwick B.C., Mr. F. Honeywell, Surrey B.C., and Mr. W. McWilliam, Temple B.C., it was unanimously resolved 'That a prospectus of the Bicycle Union be published in all the bicycle journals, and a copy of it sent to the secretary of every bicycle club in the United Kingdom, with the request that those clubs which may be ready to join an union formed on this proposed basis should communicate with the secretary *pro tem.* of the Bicycle Union it possible before the 1st of July, 1878, and further name a delegate or delegates to represent them.' I append the prospectus and await your reply. The first general meeting will probably be held in January next.

The prospectus, which was drawn up at some considerable length, ran as follows :—

1. *Objects of the Union.*

The Bicycle Union shall be a means by which bicyclists can co-operate together (by representation) for the following and other purposes :—

1. To secure a fair and equitable administration of justice as regards the rights of bicyclists on the public roads.

2. To watch the course of any legislative proposals in Parliament or elsewhere affecting the interests of the bicycling public, and to make such representations on the subject as the occasion may demand.

3. To consider the existing relations between bicyclists and the railway companies, with the view of securing, if possible, some modification of the present tariff for the carriage of bicycles, and greater security in their conveyance.

4. To examine the question of bicycle racing in general, and to frame definitions and recommend rules on the subject. To arrange for annual race meetings, at which the Amateur Championship shall be decided.

2. *Proposed Constitution of the Union.*

1. That the Union shall consist of all such bicycle clubs as may be willing to join it.

2. That the method of representation be as follows :—(*a*) Every bicycle club having thirty active members to be entitled to a representative. (*b*) Every club having more than that number to be entitled to an additional representative for every additional complete fifty. (*c*) That clubs with less than thirty members be invited to combine for the purpose of electing a joint representative. (*d*) That the delegate of a club shall not *necessarily* be a member of the particular club he represents. Provincial clubs can nominate some metropolitan bicyclist as their representative. But the delegate should be in all cases a member of some bicycle club.

3. That the representatives thus selected be called the Council of the Bicycle Union, and it shall be their business to discuss the above mentioned and other matters as occasion may suggest, and to pass resolutions, and take action concerning them.

4. That the Council of the Bicycle Union shall elect a secretary, treasurer, and executive, whose duty it shall be to carry out and apply the resolutions and orders of the Council.

5. That the secretary be, if possible, a member of the legal profession.

6. That every club joining the Bicycle Union shall contribute annually to the funds of the Union a sum equivalent to a capitation charge on each member of the club, the amount of such charge to be fixed annually by the Council of the Union, such charge for the first year to be one shilling for every member.

This was the first programme of the Union, and although its scope has been widened and its plan enlarged, yet on the whole, the policy so briefly outlined has been carried out as far as circumstances would allow. The influence of Mr. Cobb is to be recognised throughout, in the very wide and liberal lines on which this first prospectus is drawn. The most noticeable point about it lies in the fact that the Union then as now was so constituted as to admit professionals to membership, and thus secure a body representing not merely a section but the whole sport. This prospectus attracted but little attention in the provinces, where things were scarcely ripe for the new departure, but several London clubs joined, notable amongst them being the West Kent B.C., a club which gave to the legislative work of the cycling world Mr. W. B. Tanner, a gentleman whose good services both to the N. C. U. and C. T. C. cannot be overrated. The first formal general meeting of the Bicycle Union was held at the Guildhall Tavern on February 16, 1878, Mr. G. F. Cobb being in the chair, and at this meeting the general lines of the constitution were approved, and arrangements made for their complete establishment. Necessarily in a general scheme of such dimensions, especially when the minor points were settled by a number of men without any practical legislative experience in this particular line, there were many points which have required and received reconsideration during the course of practical work, and on one of these, the basis of representation, the first split occurred; the West Kent and other clubs seceding from the young body to its very decided detriment as far as prestige went, but to its advantage in another way, for those who were left in put their shoulders to the wheel even more vigorously than ever, with a determination to fight the thing through and make it a success.

On March 14 another meeting was held, and the constitution of February, faulty as it was, confirmed.

Almost at once the great 'amateur question' came to the front, and although it at one time threatened to wreck the little body, it proved in truth its salvation. There was no recognised athletic authority in the South, and the Northern Counties Athletic Association was more of a defence league, only interested in keeping the professional element out of the sports of the clubs which formed it. Thus it happened that the Bicycle Union was the only body ruling an athletic branch of sport which claimed paramount authority in its own sphere, as it still does, and which was ruled solely by the voice of the majority.

The action of the young body made a strong impression on the lovers of sport, and secured for it the respect of many who would otherwise scarcely have taken any interest in its working. It was soon evident that the first question which the Union would have to take in hand was that of the amateur definition.

On May 11, 1878, the Bicycle Union adopted the following negative definition of an amateur: 'That a professional bicyclist is one who has ridden a bicycle in public for money, or who has engaged, taught, or assisted in bicycling or any other athletic exercise for money, and that a bicyclist who shall have competed with a professional bicyclist for a prize knowingly and without protest (except at a meeting specially sanctioned by the Union), shall also be considered a professional bicyclist. Any person not included in the above definition shall be considered an amateur bicyclist.' This definition, ignoring as it did the social qualification as regards the amateur athlete, gave rise to an immense amount of discussion, and the cyclists were threatened with ostracism by some of the older followers of sport.

Two very important clubs, the Wanderers B.C. and the Temple B.C., both withdrew their support from the Union, and the movements of certain athletic clubs made confusion worse confounded, threats of protest being heard on all sides against the cycling division, who had thus taken this bold step in advance of the older branches of athletic sport. Like Lord Howard when he boldly chased the ships of the Armada without any powder, simply showing a 'brag countenance,' so the newly born association boldly faced the storm, and even left its intrenchments to encounter the foe in the open. Without altering its course or modifying its energy, the B.U., as it was conveniently termed, next attacked the Amateur Athletic Club Championship of Four Miles, declining to recognise it as a *bonâ fide* championship, and deciding to replace it by two championships of its own, the Two and Twenty-five Miles, which were duly brought off on May 11, 1878, at Stamford Bridge. Excellent contests ensued, the races being supported by the best riders of the day. The Two Miles fell to the Hon. Ion Keith-Falconer, of Cambridge, and the Twenty-five Miles to Mr. A. A. Weir, of the 'Dark Blue' or Oxford University B.C. The fact that the University men competed, owing doubtless to the influence of Mr. Cobb, had much to do with the ultimate success of the Union Championships. Up to this point the work of the Union had been nearly all internal amongst the cycling community, and comparatively plain sailing, but in July of this year the Highways Act, 1878, was brought before Parliament, and an amendment was proposed which would have entirely checked the use of the bicycle on the highways; consequently the Union was called upon to act promptly. Mr. Hutchens, a member of the London B.C., accepted the post of solicitor to the Union, and by instant and energetic action eventually secured the rejection of the amendment, mainly through the good offices of Sir Henry Jackson, M.P. for Coventry (the home of the wheel), and of the President of the Local Government Board, Mr. Sclater Booth. This action did the now growing association much service, and the support accorded to it rapidly increased. With characteristic boldness, the Union then authorised a contest between the best amateurs and professionals of the day. The event came off on October 23 at Cambridge, when the Hon. Ion Keith-

Falconer beat John Keen in a five-mile race. It would be ungrateful not to record the fact that the countenance accorded to the Union by the Universities was of great value at this period, as the University athletes were strong enough, numerically and morally, to give great aid to any cause they espoused.

The association was now at leisure to turn its attention to internal reform. It was found that there were many outside riders who would willingly join if they could, and a modification of the constitution was absolutely necessary. It was felt that to be a truly representative body it should be open to all interested in the welfare of the sport. Four championships were instituted, at 1, 5, 25, and 50 miles, and in the year 1879 the whole four were won by Mr. Herbert Liddell Cortis of the Wanderers' B.C., the contests being all run off at Stamford Bridge. The Union also decided to appoint an official handicapper, a very wise step, and Mr. Martin D. Rucker of the London B.C. accepted the office, an event which without doubt assisted the growth and development of the Union. In this year the Union promoted three races between John Keen, the professional champion, and Mr. H. L. Cortis, the amateur champion, the distances being 1, 5, and 25 miles; Mr. Cortis won the first race at Wolverhampton, the 25 miles, but Keen won both the 1 and 5.

Up to the end of 1880 the Union continued to gather strength, but the support was all, or nearly all, obtained from London men, the provincial cyclists looking on the cycling body as purely a London clique, despite frequent disclaimers on the part of the officials. One source of trouble was the general meeting of the Bicycle Touring Club, held in London. At this meeting the discussion grew somewhat warm, as the original constitution of the Touring Club, like that of the Union, was by no means equal to its after development, and it unfortunately happened that certain unpopular resolutions were put forward by London men and regarded by the provincial members present as an attempt to secure for the much objected to 'London clique' some of the power of the then B. T. C.

Thus a feeling of opposition to the Union was created which it took a long while to live down, but though the fears then entertained have since proved without foundation, the effect was the same as if they had been solid facts. It came to be daily more obvious that the Union required the support of the vast number of cyclists scattered throughout the country, and the activity of the newly-formed Amateur Athletic Association stirred the then officials of the Union to renewed action. In October 1880, therefore, Mr. G. L. Hillier, of the Stanley C.C., brought forward a scheme for the establishment of branches of the Union, under the title of 'Local Centres' in various important districts in the country. The scheme was of course very much modified when it was first considered, but it was eventually adopted, the provisions of the original plan having been in the main adhered to. The 'Local Centre' is a practically autonomous committee charged with the control of a specified district and subject only to the ruling of the executive, elected from the delegates of the local centres themselves. The scheme was soon put into practical working order, Mr. Hillier being the first local centre secretary, and strong branches of the Union have been established throughout the length and breadth of the land. Many details of the scheme were, of course, found to be incomplete in practical working, but the general plan has proved an unqualified success, and the accession of numbers to the ranks of the Union has been very great, whilst the centres have sent good men to the council and have also worked in the most commendable manner for the true interests of amateur sport. The following are the rules at present in force as regards the formation and management of local centres.

Rules relating to Local Centres.

1. The executive shall, from time to time, elect one or more of their members divisional secretaries for local centres, and shall allot to them such districts as shall seem advisable.

2. The divisional secretary shall (whenever it is desirable to form a local centre) nominate a hon. sec. *pro tem.*

3. The hon. sec. *pro tem.* shall call a 'local general meeting' of all cyclists in the neighbourhood, and a formal motion to form a local centre shall be proposed.

4. In the event of such motion being carried, the clubs joining shall each elect one representative to serve on the committee of the local centre.

5. Every club having 50 members shall also be entitled to a second representative, and every club having more than 50 members shall be entitled to an additional representative for every additional 50 members.

6. Members not represented through clubs shall be entitled to one representative for every 25 members who shall combine to obtain representation.

7. The committee at their first meeting shall proceed to elect a chairman and hon. sec., not necessarily from among their own number.

8. The hon. sec. shall, as soon as possible, forward full details of the formation of the local centre, together with names and addresses of the chairman, hon. sec., and committee to his divisional secretary.

9. The divisional secretary shall, at the next meeting of the executive, report the formation of the local centre for ratification.

10. The committee shall meet not less than four times in the year, and oftener if required.

11. The committee first appointed, and the chairman and hon. sec. elected by them, shall hold office till the 30th of April next ensuing.

12. Before the 1st of May in each year, every club belonging to the local centre shall send in to the hon. sec. of the centre—(*a*) The names and addresses of its representatives on the committee of the centre for the ensuing year (such representatives need not be members of the club they represent); (*b*) The number of members of the club. (*c*) The capitation fees for such members.

13. Between the 1st and 20th of April a general meeting of all members of the local centre shall be held to receive the report of the outgoing officers and committee, and for general purposes of discussion. Not less than fourteen days' notice of such meeting shall be given to the hon. sec. of each club (whose duty it shall be to communicate such notice to the members of his club), and to each unattached member of the centre.

14. The newly appointed committee shall hold a meeting as soon

as possible after the 1st of May in each year, at which they shall elect a chairman and hon. sec. for the year (not necessarily members of their own body), and shall appoint the delegates of the local centre to the Council of the Union.

15. The chairman and hon. sec. of each local centre shall be *ex officio* delegates to the Council of the Union. In addition, the committee shall elect delegates to the council (not necessarily members of the centre) in proportion to the number of their members, as follows: Fifty or less, two representatives; and for every further complete fifty, one additional representative.

16. The hon. sec. shall, before the 20th of May, furnish to his divisional secretary—(a) The names and addresses of the officers, committee, and delegates of the centre for the ensuing year. (b) A list of the clubs belonging to the centre, with their respective numbers of members. (c) A list of the unattached members of the centre.

17. The hon. sec. of each local centre shall make a report of the proceedings of all meetings to his divisional secretary, within ten days after such meeting.

18. Clubs joining a local centre after a general meeting shall appoint a representative or representatives to the committee, in accordance with rules 4 and 5, to hold office until the 30th of April then next ensuing.

19. Should the numbers of the centre increase between two annual general meetings so as to entitle the centre to an additional delegate or delegates to the Council, the committee shall thereupon appoint such delegate or delegates, and the hon. sec. shall forthwith forward the name or names of such delegate or delegates to his divisional secretary.

20. Clubs belonging to the Union shall have the option of appointing delegates direct to the Council of the Union, or of joining a local centre.

21. The hon. sec. of each local centre shall receive all subscriptions due from clubs and unattached members belonging to his centre.

22. The hon. sec. shall forward half such subscriptions to his divisional secretary every quarter, towards the general expenses of the Union.

23. The hon. sec. shall retain the other half of such subscriptions for the expenses of the centre, and shall forward a detailed cash statement to his divisional secretary on the 30th of April in each year.

24. The executive shall have power to make special grants to any local centre. A motion for such special grant shall not be brought forward without a week's written notice to all members of the executive.

25. The committee shall transact all the Union business for the district, as defined by the resolution of the Council as follows, viz. :—'Obtaining members, the erection of danger boards, the watching of bye-laws and local board action, the supervision of race meetings within the district, and the general conservation of cycling interests ; but any special business, such as assaults, legal cases, questions of amateur *status*, and applications in reference to amateur *v*. professional matches, shall be referred to the executive with full particulars of same.'

26. Any person feeling himself aggrieved by any action of a local centre, shall have the right to appeal to the executive of the Union, and from them to the Council of the Union.

27. The executive shall have full power over all proceedings of local centres, including their dissolution if necessary, subject to an appeal to the Council, and may add to or amend these rules as may seem desirable.

As will be gathered from a perusal of these rules, each local centre is practically a local union banded with other local unions for the purposes of more complete supervision and co-operation, and the local centres scheme, with the exception above alluded to, has proved a success.

These rules, with considerable modifications from time to time, have resulted in the establishment of a network of centres extending over the whole of the country, and have proved of notable benefit to the Union. The centre formed at Bristol, for Bristol and the West of England, has simply assumed the completest control over the whole of its very large district. Birmingham has also a local centre which has done good service to the Union. It started the agitation for improved roads, which has accomplished so much to bring the ruling body of cycling prominently and favourably before the general public, and has always worked energetically for the furtherance of union interests. In Liverpool the second local centre exceeds numerically the first one established in the district—

which for reasons which need not now be specified was dissolved —and the record of the body is excellent. In Newcastle, Edinburgh, Glasgow, Manchester, Nottingham, Brighton, Portsmouth, centres of the Union exist, and aid the cause of the sport. The organisation which has thus enabled the cyclists of the United Kingdom to work together in opposing any attempt to interfere with the government of their own sport has much to commend it.

When tricycling as a distinct branch of the sport began to come prominently to the front, the want of some ruling association for the tricyclist division was felt, and as the Bicycle Union was composed mainly of bicyclists, the tricycling section established a body of their own, under the title of the 'Tricycle Association.' As a number of the gentlemen connected with it had no practical acquaintance with the rules of sport, they were easily led into adopting a somewhat impracticable definition, and after a comparatively short independent existence, the Tricycle Association, led by its secretary, Mr. Boverton Redwood of the Finchley T. C., threw in its lot with the Bicycle Union, the combined associations being known by the somewhat cumbrous title of the 'Bicycle Union with which is incorporated the Tricycle Association.' The tricycling section at this time were mostly what are sometimes known as 'family men' and elderly riders, and these gentlemen were not sorry to relieve themselves of the necessity of attending committee meetings, and such like useful but irksome gatherings. The management naturally therefore fell into the hands of the younger men, mostly at that time bicyclists. Difficulties arose into the history of which, however, it would be worse than useless to enter. The election of Lord Bury to the post of president, which he has ever since held, was marked as an era in the history of the Union, the president being a practical cyclist who took an active interest in the questions of the day. The desirability of having one governing body for the two varieties of the sport was apparent, and ultimately the Bicycle Union, acting on the suggestion of its president, decided to change its name and to adopt a title which would cover all classes of velocipedes, to use an old but comprehensive term. Accordingly in June 1883, after a lengthy debate, the original style and title of the Union was changed to that under which it is now known, viz. the National Cyclists' Union.

This was both politic and necessary, as the Union at that time included in its ranks a large majority of tricycling clubs, and a still larger majority of tricyclists, who were attached to the various mixed clubs in the kingdom; and thus the word 'bicycle,' which had long been an eyesore to the tricycling section, was replaced by a name which will cover every sort of cycle which may in the future be placed upon the market.

From October 1883, when the present president of the N. C. U. assumed office, the work went on vigorously for 'the conservation of the interests of cycling,' to quote the oft repeated phrase. At this period the opening of the public parks to wheel traffic was attracting much attention, and the president of the N. C. U. was successful in securing an experimental extension of certain privileges to all wheels, with results which were in every way satisfactory. County government and highway bills and other enactments, which might directly or indirectly affect the right of wheelmen on the roads, were carefully watched and action was taken when required. Dangerous gratings placed in the streets were reported on, and notices were issued to the vestries responsible for the arrangement, that they would be held liable for any accidents which might result therefrom. Danger boards were erected, in conjunction with the C.T.C, at the top of dangerous hills; these 'boards' being solid plates of iron bearing the words 'To cyclists, this hill is dangerous,' and there is little doubt that these warning notices, which are now to be found all over the country, have been of material service to the large class of touring riders. A reserve fund for use in cases of severe emergency was established and taken charge of by Major-General Christopher, a member of the executive whose energetic efforts on its behalf are worthy of all

A DANGER BOARD.

recognition. The fund amounted in the spring of 1886 to some 300*l.*, and of course frequent additions are being made to it from time to time. Assault cases have been taken up with a considerable amount of success, due to a great extent to the care which is exercised by the members of the executive who belong to the legal profession, prominent amongst them being the Honorary Secretary, Mr. Robert Todd of the Stanley C. C. The question of road repair, started by the Birmingham local centre, has developed into a work of absolutely national importance. Many roadways, since the old coaches passed away, have been allowed to fall steadily into disrepair, and no effort was made to keep them in anything like a sound condition. This decay reached its maximum in the Birmingham district, and cyclists and others who had the misfortune to traverse the roads in question found them in a perfectly disgraceful state. The Birmingham local centre therefore called a meeting of persons interested in the question, over which the Mayor of Birmingham presided, and the strange spectacle of the hitherto despised cyclist heading a motion of reform and supported by a number of horse owners and drivers, showed how wise and politic a step had been taken. The road surveyors were at first inclined to regard the matter as a piece of impertinence on the part of the cyclists, some of them remarking that they were not called upon to make the roads good enough for that class of machine; but the result of an action brought on behalf of the Union against eight road surveyors at the Halesowen Court speedily convinced them that the cyclists were in the right, and held powers sufficient to compel them to do the work. Since then this fact has been brought home rather forcibly to the understandings of many similar officials, and the improvement in the roads in some places is very noticeable. Mr. H. R. Reynolds, of the London and Oxford Bicycle Clubs, has gone very fully into the question of the right method of road-making, and has in an able article in the 'Nineteenth Century' and in letters to the public and cycling press, pointed out how little the systems of Telford and Macadam are followed even on roads which are described as 'Macadamised.' In a pamphlet containing the gist of his remarks and advice, prepared at the instance of the N.C.U., Mr. Reynolds demonstrates clearly the saving in the rates which would accrue from an intelligent adoption of Macadam's system; and shows further the very expensive nature of the unsatisfactory methods now adopted. The result is that these facts are being daily brought before the most interested section of the public, viz., the ratepayers, and the day is not far distant when the persons who pay the piper will insist on the appointment of intelligent road surveyors, who are acquainted with the best and most scientific methods of road construction, instead of, as is too often the case, supinely permitting the election of any ignorant or careless person who will undertake to dump certain cartloads of rubbish haphazard over the highways. One of the surveyors who was interviewed by a Union official admitted that he had never heard of Telford or Macadam, and did not know who they were or what they had done.

In addition to these, and many other matters affecting the majority of the cycling community, the road riders, the Union also assumes control of cycle racing throughout the country. The most important item in the racing work of the N. C. U. is the promotion of the annual amateur championships, which are duly recognised in the world of sport, and have completely replaced all the previous competitions that claimed to confer the honour. The first championships were held at Stamford Bridge on May 11, 1878, the distances chosen being 2 and 25 miles. In the first heat of the shorter race Mr. G. F. Beck won somewhat easily from Messrs. W. T. Thorn and E. York, whilst the Hon. Ion Keith Falconer walked over in the second. In the final Keith Falconer led throughout, and holding Beck safe won in 6 minutes $30\frac{1}{5}$ seconds. Much regret was expressed at the absence of Mr. Wadham Wyndham, who was fancied to win right out. The 25 mile race fell to Mr. A. A. Weir of the Oxford University B.C. in 1 hour 27 mins. $47\frac{3}{5}$ secs.—a best on record at that date; 1878 saw the practical extinction of the 4 Miles Bicycle Championship hitherto promoted by the Amateur Athletic Club, and the Union then launched out in 1879, and established four bicycling championships at 1, 5, 25, and 50 miles.

In 1882 it was considered advisable to establish a tricycle championship, and one was run over a distance of 5 miles and won by C. E. Liles. In 1883 the championships for tricycling were increased to two, the distances being 1 and 10 miles; whilst in 1884 three championships were run, 1, 5 and 25 Mile Tricycle Championships being established. A complete record down to 1890 of all the championships run will be found in the appendix.

These events, the blue ribands of the cycling path, have yearly attracted more and more attention, and the best men of the year and of the country are usually to be found competing. In 1885, however, Percy Furnivall, who was no doubt absolutely the fastest rider of the season, for some reason refrained from competing in any of the bicycle championships, although he won the 1 Mile Tricycle Championship in a marvellous manner, beating record in his heat and winning, after running a dead heat with Percy Letchford of the Finchley T. C.; the wonderful part of the affair being that it was absolutely Mr. Furnivall's first race on a tricycle, on which he had ridden but very few times previously to the championship. As Mr. Furnivall subsequently beat the men whom he would have met in the shorter bicycling championships, in still more decisive style, there is very little doubt that, had he started for those contests, he would have held the 1 and 5 Miles Championships of 1885. One of the most interesting of the great races run has each year been the 25 Miles Tricycle Championship. On its first establishment in 1884 it was contested at Lillie Bridge upon the new track, and a very representative entry was secured. The race fell to C. E. Liles after a very hardly fought contest, H. J. Webb being second, S. Lee third, and George Smith fourth. The pace was very fast from the first, and record was beaten from the 12th mile.

Hebblethwaite cut out the pace, but Letchford, from whom much was expected, broke his machine and had to retire; in the 16th mile Liles drew away from Webb and established a long lead, and at one time looked as if he was going to lap his opponent, but in the 19th mile it was Liles' turn to become weak, and this, with a touch of cramp, made him go slowly. Webb's friends seeing this encouraged the latter, and he made a desperate effort to overtake Liles, who, however, got better in the 22nd mile, and riding with great determination to the end won by 19 seconds.

In 1885 the 25 Miles Tricycle Championship run at the Crystal Palace again afforded the spectators a rare treat, and as record was made the year before, so was record again beaten on this occasion. An excellent entry was secured, no less than 14 riders, comprising the pick of the cycling world, facing the starter. John Lee of Clay Cross dashed away as the pistol cracked, and was soon cutting out the running at a fast pace, whilst from amongst the crowd the brown headgear of the University man (Gatehouse), and the flaming red jockey cap of English, from Tyneside, were to be seen creeping cautiously to the front; Cripps, capless as usual, and Cousens, with a white handkerchief bound round his head, were also early to the fore, and this quintette raced rapidly away from the rank and file. John Lee secured the two miles record, 6 minutes 21 seconds, and Robert Cripps the three miles record, 9 minutes 38 seconds. But English and Gatehouse, though not letting their men get away from them, were yet riding carefully and without the sharp spurting which the others had indulged in. At six miles the pace had begun to tell seriously, Cousens, Cripps, Sid Lee, and others tailing off; whilst George Gatehouse, coached by his trainer Charley Wilson (the Crystal Palace track-man), was forcing the running at a fast but regular pace. Occasionally one or other of his opponents would spurt by him and get a few yards ahead, but his steady and powerful style very soon caused the leader to fall back and again resign the post of pacemaker to him. At 11 miles record again began to fall, Cripps beating the previous figures by 16 seconds, whilst Gatehouse without an undue effort secured the 12th mile; English the 13th, and then Gatehouse the 14th, 15th, 16th, and 17th miles. He covered 17 miles 986 yards within the hour, another best on record. The 21st mile fell to English and then Gatehouse scored every mile up to the finish. At 22 miles only English and Gatehouse had a chance, and both were riding with due caution, Gatehouse cutting out the pace and the North Shields man waiting on his hind wheels as lap after lap was reeled off. The spectators, who formed a goodly crowd, were worked up to fever heat. At three laps from home Gatehouse bent to his work, and to the horror of his friends appeared to make his effort, crowding a lot of pace on and riding as if he imagined that it was the last lap. English on the other hand, very cool and collected, hung on to him, and those who had been predicting a win for the Cantab began to feel rather uncomfortable. Two more laps were called, and still Gatehouse was swinging along as if he was bent upon settling himself before the final rush, but a very happy smile at Furnivall who cheered him from the rails, revealed the fact that he had not as yet overdone it. English, on the contrary, looked rather drawn; and the excitement grew in intensity as the men dashed round the far side and came rushing round by the dressing-room. 'Last lap!' is cried, the bell rings, when with a marvellous if ill-timed effort, English rushes up outside the leader, and the hearts of the Cambridge men sink as he slips past Gatehouse before the latter appreciates what has happened, and takes the inside berth. But for once in a way the big Tynesider has made a mistake. Gatehouse pulls himself together, and riding in possibly better form than he has shown all through, hotly pursues English. As the pair approach the wide clump of tall reed which momentarily hide the competitors at the Crystal Palace track from the occupants of the grand stand, Gatehouse is seen to be riding hard—they disappear and there is a momentary pause of expectancy, then a loud shout of applause, as Gatehouse emerges with a slight lead of

English. Neck and neck the two men ride to the entrance gate, 200 yards or so from the finish, English riding very wide by accident, and driving his opponent's off wheel on to the turf. Then, with a well-saved effort, Gatehouse draws out and wins one of the most exciting races by nearly 20 yards in 1 hour 26 minutes 29⅔ seconds, a best on record.

Such contests as these may be expected in the future in the championships promoted by the N. C. U., seeing that the best men from all parts of the kingdom are sure to compete, and the man who attains the highest honours of the racing path under the auspices of the Union will have to show to perfection every quality necessary in a racing man.

In its dealings with the racing path the N.C.U. was brought, early in 1885, into hostile contact with the Amateur Athletic Association. The Liverpool local centre of the Union had been for some time in a dissatisfied state, its rulers claiming for it the exercise of powers which would have made it practically independent of the supreme executive, and as such a policy could by no means be recognised, the executive felt bound to refuse the powers asked. These and other events produced an estrangement between the Metropolitan body and the first Liverpool local centre, whose members concerned themselves mostly with racing matters in the Liverpool district.

Into this bygone dispute, and the circumstances which led to the summoning of a general meeting of the A. A. A. Committee at Anderton's Hotel on January 16, 1886, it would be unprofitable to enter. On that date, however, important events took place. A treaty was duly agreed to, securing to the N. C. U. all the points it claimed. This treaty recognised the right of the Union to rule cyclists, as such, and this was and is the sole claim which the N. C. U. made in this matter, and the position of the N. C. U. is now most fully admitted on all hands. The rules of the body run as follows :—

Regulations for the Government of Race Meetings held under the Rules of the N.C.U.

It is strongly recommended that all Competitions be confined to Amateurs

ENTRIES.

1. All cycle races shall be held under the rules of the National Cyclists' Union.

2. The committee reserve the right of refusing to receive, and having received, of cancelling any entry before the start, without giving any reason for so doing. All entries shall be accompanied by the entrance fee, but in case any entry shall have been accepted without the fee, and the competitor shall refuse or neglect to pay it when called upon to do so, whether he actually ride in the race or not, he shall be liable to suspension.

3. Competitors in handicaps shall be required to send, with their entries, a statement that they are amateurs according to the definition of the N. C. U., and also full and definite particulars of their last three performances. Furnishing false, misleading or incomplete information shall be a ground for disqualification, and in the event of a prize being won, will render the winner liable to prosecution.

NOTE.—*It is recommended that the N. C. U. entry forms (obtainable at the rate of 2s. 6d. per 100 at the Offices, 17 Ironmonger Lane, E.C.) be used, as they suggest clearly what information is required by the handicapper.*

4. All entries must be made and races run in the real name of the competitor.

PRIZES.

5. All prizes should be purchased *prior* to the date of the meeting, and when practicable, engraved with the name and date of the meeting.

6. It is recommended that no prize be offered above the value of ten guineas; except for challenge cups or shields or the like, which have to be won more than once in order to become the property of the winner.

7. Clubs or others offering challenge prizes, subject to a guarantee for their return, must, if required, state explicitly to each intending competitor the exact nature of the guarantee required, and

in case any difficulty shall arise in arranging the terms, the decision of the N. C. U. executive in the matter shall be accepted by all parties as final.

ATTENDANTS.

8. One attendant only shall be allowed to each competitor in any race, but no machine other than a bicycle shall be started by an attendant.

9. The judge shall have power to act as he may think fit in cases of misconduct by attendants.

PROTESTS.

10. Any objection respecting foul riding, starting off a wrong mark, or other such like offence, committed during the race, shall be made to the judge as soon as possible after the heat, and before the distribution of prizes; and all other protests against competitors, respecting their status as amateurs or otherwise, must be lodged with the committee before the prizes are distributed, and if possible before the race is run.

11. All protests must be made in writing, signed by the objector, and accompanied by a deposit of 5s., which will be forfeited if the protest be considered a frivolous one.

12. In the event of a protest or objection being lodged against a successful competitor, his prize shall be withheld until the judge or committee, as the case may be, shall have decided whether he is, or is not, entitled to the same. In the latter case, the first prize shall be given to the second man, the second prize to the third man, and so on.

STARTING.

13. A bell shall be rung before each heat; and after sufficient time has been allowed for competitors to get to their allotted marks, a start will be effected.

14. No competitor shall be allowed to start unless he wear half sleeves and complete clothing from the shoulders to the knees.

15. Attendants, when pushing off competitors, must keep *both* feet behind the mark from which the competitor actually starts. Should the attendant cross such mark with either foot while starting such competitor, the competitor shall be liable to disqualification.

16. In starting, the *foremost part* of the competitor's machine

in contact with the ground, must be placed *on* that mark from which the competitor actually starts.

17. Any competitor shall be at liberty, with the consent of the judge, to start from a mark behind the one allotted him in the race; but in such case, as in all others, the point of contact of the foremost part of the machine with the ground shall be considered the starting mark, which the attendant shall not overstep.

18. Any competitor starting before the signal may be put back, at the discretion of the starter, not exceeding 10 yards for the race in question; and on a repetition of the offence, shall be disqualified. It shall be the duty of each competitor to see that he starts from his proper mark, and in default he may be disqualified for the race in question. A competitor, upon being disqualified, shall forfeit any fee or fees he may have paid.

19. As far as possible the times on the programme shall be adhered to, but no heat may be started *before* the stated time except with the consent of all the competitors in such heat.

20. In all races where more than one competitor starts from the same mark, lots shall be drawn by the competitors, who shall take precedence, counting from the inside of the track.

ENCLOSURE.

21. None but the officials of the meeting, the press, the competitors and attendants, shall be allowed within the enclosure, except by special permission of the secretary of the meeting.

22. Competitors and their attendants shall be allowed within the enclosure only during the time between the heats preceding and following that in which they are engaged.

GENERAL RULES.

23. The committee have no power to alter handicaps, after having received them from the official handicapper.

NOTE.—*It is recommended that the N. C. U. handicapper for the district be employed; and that entries for handicap races be closed 14 days before the race.*

24. Every competitor will receive, in the dressing-room, a ticket bearing a number corresponding with his number on the programme, which ticket must be worn by him in a conspicuous place during the race. It is recommended that in all cases the

ticket should be placed on the *back* of the competitor or of his machine.

25. Competitors may dismount during a race at their pleasure, and may run with their machines, but they must keep to the extreme *outside* of the track whenever dismounted.

26. A competitor overtaking another must always pass on the outside of the track (unless the man who is passed be dismounted or has retired from the contest), and must be a clear machine's length ahead before taking ground in front of his opponent. The inside man must allow room for his opponent to pass, and any competitor guilty of foul or unfair riding shall be liable to disqualification.

27. If a machine becomes disabled in the course of a race, the rider shall be allowed to use another, provided the substituted machine be not disapproved of by the judge.

28. The committee reserve the power of postponing all or any of the races in cases where they think it necessary. On no account will entrance fees be returned, or expenses allowed, to any competitor in case of such postponement.

29. The committee reserve the right of adjudicating on any questionable entry and on any other point not provided for, and of making any alteration in the programme that they may deem necessary.

30. All tracks shall be measured 12 inches from the inner side of the path, and all races shall be run left-hand inside when possible.

31. The finish of all races shall be judged by the *first part of the machine which touches* the tape, which shall be fastened flat on the ground, at the winning post.

OFFICIALS.

32. The officials shall consist of judge, umpires, starter, time-keeper or time-keepers, clerks of the course, lap-scorers, and the members of the race committee (including the secretary of the meeting).

33. It shall be the duty of the judge to declare the placed men in every heat; to instruct the umpires; to give judgment on protests received by him; to act as he may think fit in cases of misconduct by attendants, and to disqualify any competitors who have become liable to disqualification. His decision shall in all cases be final.

NOTE.—*As under these rules the duties of the judge are of a most important character, an experienced rider should be chosen for the post.*

34. The judge shall have the power of refusing to allow any person to act as attendant who has infringed the rules, or refused to submit to his ruling.

35. In starting scratch races, the judge shall give his instructions to the competitors and attendants, and shall see that the men are placed in position, after having caused them to draw lots; and every competitor shall go to the mark so drawn, and any refusing to do so shall be liable to be disqualified by the judge.

36. It shall be the duty of the umpires to watch the riding, and to report to the judge any competitor or competitors whose riding they consider unfair; and it shall also be the duty of the umpires to watch the starting, and to report to the starter any competitor or competitors whose starting they consider unfair.

37. It shall be the duty of the starter, when it has been reported to him by a clerk of the course that all the competitors are ready, to see that the time-keeper is warned, and before starting the men to say 'Mount,' in a few seconds after to say 'Are you ready?' and if no reply to the contrary be given, to effect the start by report of pistol.

38. The starter may, at his discretion, put back, to a distance not exceeding 10 yards, any competitor starting before the signal is given, and on a repetition of the offence shall disqualify him.

39. In case of a false start, the competitors shall be called back by the starter and re-started. Any competitor refusing to obey the starter shall be at once disqualified by him.

40. All questions as to starts in handicap races shall be in the absolute discretion of the starter.

41. It shall be the duty of the time-keeper or time-keepers to take the times of the first in each heat, and such other times as the secretary of the meeting may have previously arranged.

42. It shall be the duty of the clerks of the course to call over the names of the competitors in the dressing-room before the starting of each heat; to ring the bell shortly before the time that each heat should be started, and at the commencement of the last lap in each heat; and to see that the competitors are on their appointed marks, and have their numbers properly exhibited.

43. It shall be the duty of the lap scorers to check the number of laps ridden by every competitor, and to give the distance ridden

by any competitor at any point when requested to do so by time-keeper or judge.

44. It shall be the duty of the race committee to appoint the officers, to conduct generally the business of the meeting, and to adjudicate on any points not provided for.

45. It shall be the duty of the secretary of the meeting, under the direction of the committee, to see that the various officials are at their respective posts before the first race is started, to provide for any contingency that may arise, and generally to conduct the meeting.

46. The judge, umpires, starter and time-keepers shall not be permitted to compete in any race with which they are officially connected.

47. The judge and starter shall have the power to disqualify competitors without any protest being lodged by any other competitor.

The foregoing regulations are subject to revision by the executive of the N. C. U., which reserves to itself the right of adjudicating on any case of dispute or appeal.

NOTE.—*In all races stated to be held under the rules of the N. C. U., it shall be assumed (unless otherwise duly appearing) that the foregoing regulations are in force, and applicable.*

DEFINITIONS OF MACHINES.

The following machines are eligible for cycle races held under N. C. U. rules :—

1. *For Bicycle Races.* Any two-wheeled one-tracked machine, carrying one rider.

2. *For Tricycle Races.* Any machine three or more wheeled, two or more tracked, carrying one rider.

3. *For Safety Bicycle Races.* Any two-wheeled one-tracked machine, carrying one rider, and fulfilling the special conditions laid down by the race committee or promoters of the sport.

4. *For Tandem Bicycle Races.* Any two-wheeled one-tracked machine, carrying two riders.

5. *For Tandem Tricycle Races.* Any three or more wheeled, two or more tracked machine, carrying two riders, seated one directly behind the other.

6. *For Sociable Tricycle Races.* Any three or more wheeled two or more tracked machine, carrying two riders, seated side by side.

7. *For Double Tricycle Races.* Any three or more wheeled, two or more tracked machine, carrying two riders.

Note.—No machine which cannot be included in one of the above classes may be used in cycle races held under N. C. U. rules.

Any rider desirous of using a machine in any class of other than one of the patterns now ordinarily recognised in that class, must obtain permission to do so from the executive of the N. C. U.

DEFINITION OF A NOVICE.

A Novice, or person eligible to compete in a Novices' or Maiden race, is a rider who has never, up to the time of starting in such race, won any prize in any cycling race other than a race confined to members of his club. In any qualified novices' race such as a race open to those who have not won a first prize, the definition of a novice as contained in the foregoing definition shall still be held to apply, so far as circumstances admit.

CHAPTER XI.

THE CYCLISTS' TOURING CLUB.

THE Cyclists' Touring Club was originally founded on August 5, 1878, as the Bicycle Touring Club, being the outcome of a number of letters and suggestions which had from time to time found their way into the Cycling Press. The Bradford Bicycle Club and a number of north country clubs took up the idea with characteristic energy, and under their auspices Mr. Stanley J. A. Cotterell as honorary secretary was enabled to get the new association into shape, and to carry it on for some time. Its very rapid growth, however, soon caused it to outgrow the original scheme, and a certain amount of laxity having crept into the administration, troubles were frequent, and the Bicycle Touring Club, as it was called, was not growing at the rate which it should have done. Changes were tried; new secretaries were appointed, and many efforts were made to carry the club over the dead point, and at length, after some stormy meetings, the work was done, and the Bicycle Touring Club began to go ahead on the new basis. Walter D. Welford was for some time secretary, and under his care the club prospered, until history repeated itself, and the machinery was found inadequate for the full discharge of the business required of it, and there again occurred dissensions and troubles, until at length it became obvious that another move would have to be made. The club had long possessed an organ known as the 'Monthly Circular,' and this, after being edited by Mr. E. R. Shipton for some time, was on his suggestion named the 'Gazette,' enlarged, and made into what is practically a monthly club magazine. The work of the honorary editor soon became practically overwhelming, and Mr. Shipton, in justice to himself, was contemplating the resignation of the office, when the train of circumstances above alluded to brought matters to a crisis. A new secretary was wanted, and just when the council was at their wits' ends to find a suitable and reliable man, it was found that Mr. Shipton would be open to an offer. Seeing that this gentleman was already well known to the council for his very complete acquaintance with the work of the club, and also for his untiring energy in the discharge of his honorary duties, there need be little wonder that they soon came to terms with him, and he was duly installed as secretary and editor of the Bicycle Touring Club. Since then Mr. Shipton has conclusively demonstrated his fitness for the post, and the prosperity of the Cyclists' Touring Club may be dated from his accession to office.

As it at present stands, the Cyclists' Touring Club is the largest athletic association in the world. Numbering over 20,000 members, its objects are best set forth in the prospectus of the club, which runs as follows:—

As an essentially conservative nation, it is hardly a matter for surprise that Englishmen should have received with suspicion, which rapidly degenerated into factious opposition, the advent of the bicycle a decade and a half ago. Anything that tends to antagonise with the cherished traditions and old-fashioned habits of the average Britisher, is, by the more unthinking sections of the community, speedily condemned, aye, even without a semblance of a fair trial; and it therefore need hardly be wondered at that a mode of progression hitherto almost unheard of, and which ran counter to all preconceived methods, should have met with disfavour almost as soon as it was introduced. The dogged and unreasoning opposition of one section of society is, however, generally counterbalanced by the equally characteristic determination of a second section to adhere to its opinion 'though the skies should fall,' and it fortunately happens that the art of bicycle riding was no exception to the general rule. A few of its persistent adherents remained steadfast in the belief of the capabilities of the new invention, and when by a combination of fortuitous circumstances the wooden-wheeled vehicle of a dozen years since was superseded by the suspension and rubber-tired bicycle (which with countless improvements in detail remains in principle the same machine to the present day), the future of the two-wheeler was assured.

With the establishment of a new pastime or sport, it was not long ere the shrewder of the people became alive to the advantages that followed in its wake, and that might, with a little ingenuity, be diverted into their channel. Foremost amongst these was the hotel proprietor in the country town, whose receipts had gradually diminished since the octopus-like feelers of the railway had penetrated into the district, and diverted the traffic which formerly brought with it a handsome competence to himself, and to the keeper of each roadside hostelry. Recognising in the tourist on foot or on horseback a legitimate subject for the extortion of 'backsheesh,' the same generous line for argument was extended to the touring wheelman, who, with hundreds of followers, was scouring the country in every direction in search of the novel, the grand, and the beautiful, whenever opportunity offered. Nor was this drawback the isolated *bête noire* of the cyclist, for the ill-concealed antipathy, culminating at times in undoubted brutality, of the remainder of the road-using community, who knew little of the capabilities, and less of the advantages, of the new method of locomotion, was a patent and glaring concomitant. Added to these came the difficulty of obtaining reliable information of the nature of the route ahead—a route that often became treacherously unserviceable—so that, to commit a plagiarism as well as concoct a parody, 'The rider's lot was not a happy one.' The old adage, "'Tis a long lane that has no turning,' proved, however, to be applicable even here, and it was not long after the real resources of the steel steed were indubitably proved that there sprang into existence an organisation, the name of which is now a household word in every clime. Commencing with a desultory correspondence in the press which the new sport had called into existence for its own especial interest, a league or brotherhood, called the 'Bicycle Touring Club,' was, at the North of England Meet held at Harrogate, Yorkshire, on August 5, 1878, inaugurated.

The leading objects of its programme are :—

To encourage and facilitate touring in all parts of the world.

To protect its members against unprovoked assaults.

To provide riding or touring companions.

To secure and appoint at fixed and reduced rates hotel headquarters in all parts of the country.

To enlist the co-operation of a leading wheelman, who should act as a Consul in every town, and who should render to his fellow-members local information of every description.

To inculcate and encourage an *esprit de corps* among the followers of the wheel, similar to freemasonry in social life.

When the B. T. C. was formed, some four years and a half ago, the only pedomotive carriage which had approached such perfection as to warrant one in supposing that it would establish itself as a permanent means of locomotion, destined to aid, if not entirely revolutionise, the somewhat tardy movements of mankind, was the bicycle—a machine, as its name implies, of two wheels only ; but the pleasures of the new method of transit once partaken of, what wonder was it that the inventive genius of our mechanical experts sought to solve the problem of throwing open the practice of wheeling to every age and temperament, and to the able-bodied among both sexes? The difficulty once surmounted, it was still less a matter for surprise that the safer, if somewhat slower, machine — the tricycle — appealed irresistibly to thousands of gentlemen of mature years and methodical habits ; to the Clergyman, the Doctor, the Lawyer, and every professional man, any and all of whom would have deemed—without good reason, if you will, but still not unnaturally—that the bestriding of a bicycle added not to their dignity of deportment ; and to ladies of lethargic dispositions and retiring proclivities, to whom the art of cycling had hitherto been a sealed and unintelligible volume, beckoning each to share in the blessings Hygeia, the goddess of our pastime, was waiting to shower broad-cast upon all comers.

Cycling, as a national sport, to be indulged in by every class of the community, from the Queen upon the throne to the plodding artisan, has already taken a tenacious hold upon the sympathies of all unprejudiced people, and it is, perhaps, not too much to say that if the day has not already arrived, it is steadily and surely approaching, when, given a moderate endowment of health and strength, every soul within the confines of civilisation, where passable roads are by any means obtainable, may upon some one of the many modifications of the steel steed, in solitude or in company, participate in this health-giving means of locomotion. These postulates being admitted, it has recently been, by a large majority, decided that the B.T.C. shall adopt a more comprehensive title—that of the Cyclists' Touring Club.

The advantages of membership in it may be roughly summarised thus :—

1. An unattached cyclist, who, until now, has been unable to avail himself of the company of other riders on a tour, may reckon with certainty on getting a companion suitable to his tastes, should he desire one; whilst he will have the satisfaction of knowing that he is one of a large body bound together by the ties of good-fellowship—a body whose sole object is the encouragement of all that is admirable in the art of wheeling.

2. In small towns where there are insufficient riders to form a local club, it is becoming customary to seek admission to the Cyclists' Touring Club, when the members really form a kind of sub-division, and enjoy club privileges without the outlay attendant on belonging to a local club, such as cost of special uniform for a few only, rent of club rooms, &c. &c.

3. It is *par excellence* the club for professional men. It not only includes in its roll many of the nobility and gentry in all parts of the land, it is supported by some of the highest dignitaries of the church, by members of the legal, medical, military, and naval professions, and indeed by amateur riders of any and all of the numerous types of cycles now in daily request, who produce credentials showing that they belong to a respectable station in life. Membership in it combines all the manifold advantages of belonging to a local club with none of the disadvantages.

4. Clubmen readily join, not only to receive company on a tour, and guidance and advice from the local Consuls, but to avail themselves of the admirable arrangements the Council has made with hotel proprietors throughout the country, whereby any member can calculate with tolerable certainty the cost of any proposed run; and, better than all, can feel assured that at the different towns on his journey he will not only meet with civility and comfort, but he will be charged, at the hotels selected by the Cyclists' Touring Club, so moderate a tariff that he must inevitably save his subscription many times over on a run of only moderate length.

To follow the progress of the club, and inquire how far it has fulfilled its mission, is merely to quote facts historical in the world of wheels. Essentially an utilitarian institution, at the present moment it boasts nearly 23,000 members, 1,030 consuls, and 2,160

A C.T.C. HOTEL.

hotel head-quarters and recommended inns ; while added to this, it has successfully supported claims for redress in the case of its members who have suffered gratuitous insults and unprovoked assaults on the road, and combated the inequitable charges levied for the carriage of the rider's steed by the railway companies. Its feelers have penetrated the Continent, as well as encircled our island home, and it may be safely asserted that the time is fast approaching when the rider of the iron horse, in any of its manifold modifications, who has emerged from his novitiate without hearing of the Cyclists' Touring Club will be a living curiosity. The subscription to its funds is altogether incommensurate with the benefits it confers, and it behoves every lover of our sport to lend it his steadfast patronage.

The promises of this prospectus are most fully carried out, and the cyclist who only tours for a few days in each year will derive the fullest benefit from membership. Putting aside the question of routes, the mere fact of a cycling consul being found in every town is of the greatest service to the rider who wants assistance or advice. The hotels chosen are in the majority of cases the most suitable for the use of the touring wheelman, although, of course, mistakes do occasionally occur. A complete and exhaustive hand-book is published, containing all the information as to hotels, consuls, repairing places, and so on, and each member of the club is thus enabled to go through the country without any assistance but this valued little guide-book.

The Cyclists' Touring Club uniform, for both ladies and gentlemen, is a very popular costume with cyclists, as the cloth and other materials and articles of dress are all carefully chosen and of known quality. The Cyclists' Touring Club cloth is a most carefully chosen one, which has stood the test of several seasons' wear, whilst the Cyclists' Touring Club flannel is also very popular. The ladies' costume, which was decided upon at a specially called meeting of the lady members of the club, has proved very successful, and this is an especial boon to lady novices, who in the past were often sadly at a loss to know what to wear.

The consuls of the Cyclists' Touring Club, as the local

representatives are called, are now co-operating in the production of a road-book, and as each official will send to the editor a *résumé* of those roads only with which he is most intimately acquainted, the result cannot fail to be most satisfactory; and as the writers are all users of the lightest vehicles on the highways, their acquaintance with the roads is bound to be of a most intimate character. The Cyclists' Touring Club has also co-operated actively with the Union in the very necessary work of erecting warning notices at the tops of dangerous hills, and also in the great effort at road reforms which the two bodies have been carrying on with such vigour during the last two seasons. The Cyclists' Touring Club is thus doing good public work, but its main policy is to look after the interests of its members, and this it does most fully. The subscription is 2s. 6d. per annum, with an entrance fee of 1s. Or a life membership can be acquired on payment of 5l. 5s. The Cyclists' Touring Club has its offices at 140 Fleet Street, and is a body which every rider should support.

CHAPTER XII.

CONSTRUCTION.

PART I.—MECHANISM.

BEFORE a rider can be considered thoroughly competent for the pursuit of the sport, more especially as to the touring side of it, he must of necessity know something of the construction and mechanism of the machine he rides, and he should also possess sufficient general knowledge of the working parts and their functions to be able, on an emergency, to put them right enough to ensure at any rate a certain amount of safety in case of accident. The general intention of this chapter will be to describe the various parts of the machine and their uses, the proper methods of adjustment, and the commonest accidents which occur to them.

Before proceeding to dissect the various parts of the machine, the first thing will be to correctly name them, and for this purpose fig. 1, 'a roadster bicycle,' has been inserted. The first part marked is A. This is the head, a term applied generally to the hinge on which the whole machine turns (see fig. 2), but particularly to that portion of the frame which is continuous with the front forks, and which is distinctively called 'the head;' the top of the backbone, which enters the head, being distinguished as 'the backbone head.' The head A carries in front the bosses through which the handle-bar passes, and also the fittings of the break and the break lever; the handle is seen (endways) at K; the break lever, which runs along the right-hand handle, at J, and the break spoon and break attachment at O; B is the backbone, a hollow steel tube very light but very rigid, and often made oval in shape; at C the backbone B is split and carried down on either side of the wheel forming the hind forks S. These are, of course, for the most part made separately and shut into the backbone; but the effect, as far as

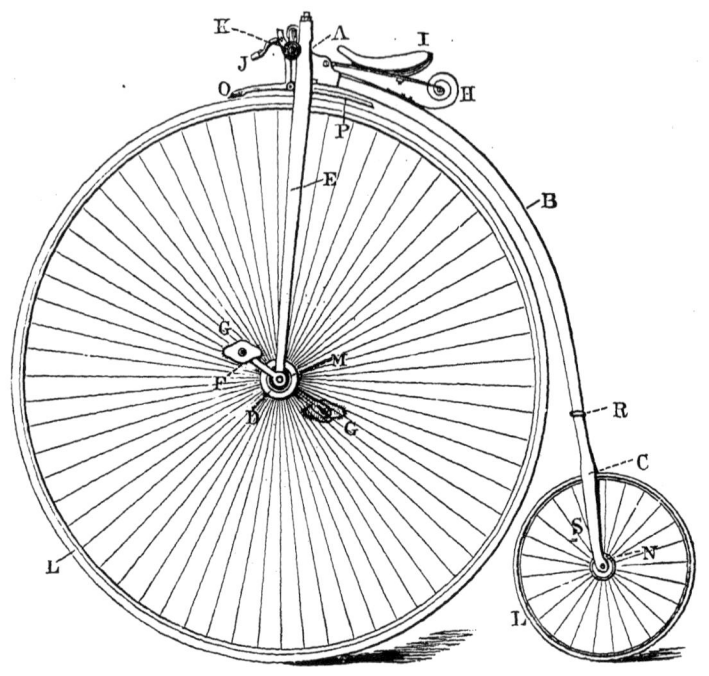

FIG. I.—A. HUMBER ROADSTER BICYCLE.

appearance goes, is the same. D is the hub of the front wheel, usually of gun-metal; N is the hub of the rear wheel, which generally contains the bearings, being in fact a hub and bearing case in one; E, the front forks, now almost invariably made hollow, passing down on either side of the front wheel from the head, with which they are usually homogeneous, to the front wheel bearings at M. Through these bearings runs the axle of the front wheel, and outside the bearings are placed the cranks F F carrying the pedals G G. On the backbone is placed the spring H (in this case a Humber coil spring), which carries the saddle I. Beneath the head and between the forks is placed the trouser guard P. The rims of the wheels L L are frequently hollow; R is the step for mounting. The various parts of the machine as illustrated, which will come under consideration, are as follows: 1. The frame. 2. The wheels.

The frame will include—

1. The head A, which has attached to it directly the handles K, the break and lever O and J, and the backbone head.

2. The backbone B, including the spring H, step R, hind forks C.

3. The front forks E, including bearings M, cranks F, and pedals G.

The wheels will include—

The front and back wheels.

As many of the parts of a bicycle as illustrated are either duplicated in the tricycle without any structural alteration, it has been thought desirable to treat fully on the simpler piece of mechanism first, and then to describe more particularly those points of the tricycle which materially differ from the bicycle fittings, or which are not represented at all. Thus there is no 'balance gear' in a bicycle, and the action and nature of that piece of mechanism will be subsequently considered.

THE HEAD.

The most usually adopted form of head, modified into many shapes but radically unaltered, is that known as the 'The Stanley Head,' invented by Mr. Thomas Humber of Beeston, Notts, and practically introduced by a firm in Sheffield, who manufactured a machine known as 'The Stanley Bicycle.' In fig. 2 is shown a 'Stanley Head' in section as regards the head proper, and with a backbone head drawn in the round *in situ*. This head is one of the latest types issued by Messrs. Thomas Smith & Sons, one of the largest stamping firms in the trade.

H H in the illustration is the backbone head, continuous with the backbone and shown in place. C C C C is the actual head homogeneous with the front forks, one of which is shown at E, the other of course being supposed to be removed with the other section. The hole K is for the front bolt of the spring. The hole D in the front of the head is where the handle-bar is placed, the front of the head being carried out in a neat boss to give it the necessary strength and support. O the small projection screwed into the front of the head to form a hinge for the second lever of the break, which carries the spoon upon its fore-end. The upright portion of the break is shown at N, whilst P is the hole into which in some cases the end of the handle lever of the break is put. In other cases the end of N is rounded, and enters a corresponding hole in the handle lever of the break, and several other plans are adopted. The backbone head H H, as will be seen, terminates in a solid piece of metal round and slightly taper with cones F and G at either end. The bottom cone G being rather larger than the top cone F, the bottom cone G drops into a corresponding coned socket cut in the solid portion of the lower part of the head, just at the shoulder of the forks as shown. A A is a set screw with a wide aperture up the middle, terminating in a cone, and into this the upper part of the backbone head and the cone F enters. This set screw is squared as shown at R, and has a very fine thread cut on it, and can thus be most accurately adjusted, as it is clear that by screwing the

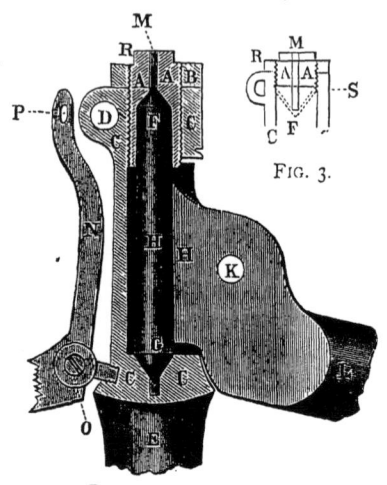

FIG. 3.

FIG. 2.—A CONE HEAD.

set screw A A farther into the head, *i.e.*, downwards upon the cone F, the cones both at top and bottom are pressed more firmly into their respective sockets, and as the head can be thus locked, so that with ordinary force the backbone head cannot be moved in the head proper, it is clear that a point of adjustment can be reached if the head is accurately fitted at which there should be absolute freedom of motion in the head without any looseness, always supposing that the machine is one made by a maker with a reputation for accurate fitting, as the slightest carelessness in fitting the head cones will of course cause them to grip at one point, whilst they may be possibly quite loose at another. M is an oil hole which will require a limited but frequent supply of lubricant, as the upper cone F being turned upwards the oil tends to drain away. The object in so placing the cone, instead of making it downwards in the old way as shown at S, in the outlined fig. 3, is to secure the greatest possible length between the centres without making a long and consequently ugly head, as it is evident that the greater the length between the points of the cones the greater the leverage of the head to steady the machine.

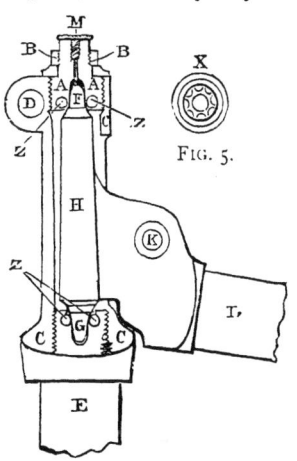

FIG. 4.—TRIGWELL'S BALL-BEARING HEAD.

B, shown in section, is the lock nut of the head, which is screwed down when the adjustment has been made to keep A A tight and secure. L is the beginning of the backbone. The wear of a head is of course considerable; the weight carried upon the lower cone and the general strain thrown upon the head tend to wear it out. If the adjustment is kept correctly tight, the wear will be even or practically so, but if a head is allowed to run for any length of time without adjustment, the cones will wear irregularly, and the correct adjustment of them will subsequently become almost impossible, as the circles of the cones being untrue, they will not fit when once again brought into close adjustment. Many ideas have been brought to a practical trial to remedy this defect, but none proved quite efficient until the Regent ball-bearing head was invented by Mr. Trigwell, of the firm of Messrs. Trigwell, Watson & Co. This is shown in section in fig. 4, lettered to correspond with fig. 2. But the additional points are as follows: in place of a plain cone at either end of the backbone head, there is a rounded end carrying a groove around which when *in situ* are placed nine steel balls of small size. In place of the coned orifice of the set screw there is

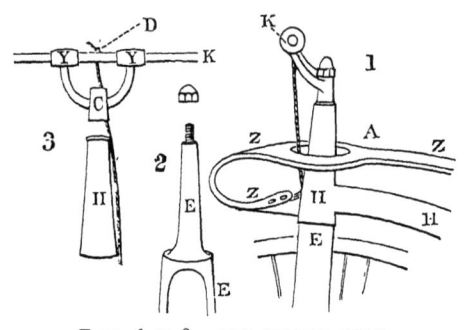

FIGS. 6, 7, 8.—THE SOCKET HEAD.

a groove, which, when the set screw is adjusted, presses upon the balls and keeps them in contact with the coned ends F and G, the adjustment and all other points being the same. If carefully adjusted the balls equally carry the weight and divide the strain, and also admit of considerable adjustment, with which a slight amount of irregular wear would not interfere, although if the adjustment is correct this irregular wear would be almost impossible. This head should in future be of still more value, and will doubtless be appreciated in due time. For Humber type tricycles, and especially for tandems, it should prove practically very serviceable. The Abingdon ball head, in which the balls and their adjustments are all fitted into the backbone head and removable with it, is also a singularly neat and useful fitting, with many good points to recommend it. Figs. 6-8 show the original head first used on velocipes and known as the 'socket head': (1) shows the head complete as it used to be turned out by the Coventry Machinist Company on the 'Gentleman's Bicycle.' H H is the backbone and backbone head. In this case the backbone head was placed outside, and carried in front a projection, on to which was fastened the old 'bow spring,' Z Z. The front forks E E, also shown in fig. 2, were continuous with a coned spindle, which passed through the backbone head, which was bored

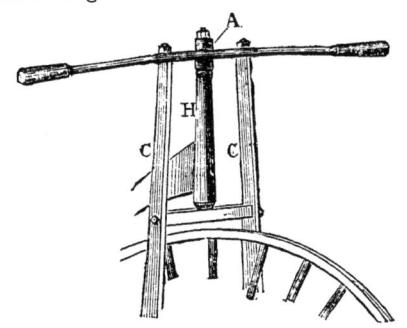

FIG. 9.—THE ARIEL HEAD.

with a conical hole to admit of an adjustment which was theoretically claimed, but hardly practically possible. The spindle head of the forks, having been well lubricated, was passed through the backbone head H. The bracket C (3) was then placed over the top of the spindle, and a nut being screwed down upon the bracket on the top of the spindle as shown at I, the socket head was complete. The handle-bar passed through the lugs Y Y, in which it revolved to wind up the cord of the break D. The old socket head allowed the wheel to turn right round, and when a fall occurred the wheel often did so, and nipping the rider's leg between the backbone and the rim, caused a very dangerous complication which sometimes resulted in a broken limb. At the same time the adjustment was found to be very inadequate, the coned spindle wore fore and aft, and would not admit of adjustment, which, if attempted, simply caused it to bind, and thus made it absolutely dangerous in practical work; and then some genius invented the 'Ariel Head,' fig. 9. This, as will be seen, contained the germ of the Stanley head in an undeveloped form, and even now certain firms fit a modified Ariel head to their machines, as it is a very strong and steady head, and is moreover easily cleaned and oiled. A is the adjusting screw, H the backbone head, and C the forks.

There are other steering heads in the market of varying pattern, several of which are impracticable and useless, whilst others possess conspicuous merit. The most notable departure from the general pattern is the American head, so-called, in which the backbone is hinged to projections behind the head proper, the idea being that as long as the wheel is driven forward, the head by a castor-like action will keep the rear carriage straight; and doubtless this is so, and the head therefore has its own peculiar merits for road riders, especially for tricyclists who use machines of the double-steering or Humber pattern.

The most usual and most annoying accident that can happen to a head is when it cracks around the lower end, from the corners of the opening where the backbone head is put in. This accident is frequently the natural sequence of an adjustment of the head in the spring, on the occasion of the first ride, as a very little tightness will often cause the casting to give way at this point. This accident is generally discovered when the rider notices that the pedals seem somewhat more to the front than usual, and the break remains steadily on in spite of his efforts to get it off, this being due to the forks going forward, whilst the head proper remains

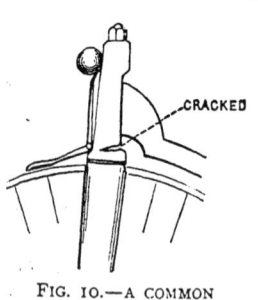

FIG. 10.—A COMMON ACCIDENT.

upright. Very often the cracked head will carry the rider many miles before it gives altogether, though of course great care should be exercised in descending hills and so on. Other accidents, or rather other dilapidations, are due to irregular wear through riding for a lengthened period with a loose head, which course if persisted in precludes the possibility of ever getting the head accurately adjusted afterwards. The adjustment of a Stanley head requires a certain amount of care and patience, but this should not prevent the young rider from giving them unreservedly to his machine, as on this point will depend much of his comfort and safety.

Having first undone the lock-nut B, fig. 2, the set screw A should be removed, the backbone head H taken out and all the grit, &c., carefully wiped out and the cones cleaned. Some fresh oil having been put into the lower cone and around the top of the backbone head, the latter should be replaced and the set screw AA screwed down until the backbone moves but stiffly in the hinge between the cones; this of course shows that the upper and lower head cones are gripping the backbone ends tightly and in close apposition.

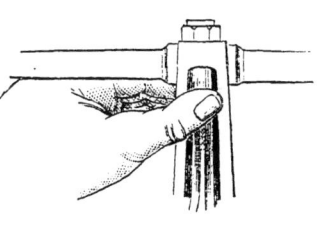

FIG. 11.—ADJUSTING THE HEAD.

A should then be carefully loosened until the backbone is found to move freely, and then the rider should place the ball of his thumb across the opening of the head just below C at the back, so that whilst his thumb touches both sides of the slit, the middle part of the thumb also touches the backbone head within (see fig. 11). The machine should then be shaken backwards and forwards by the backbone, and the slightest looseness will be easily detected. This plan is preferable to that of lifting the backbone up and down to see if there is any looseness there, though the latter plan may be used when adjusting tricycle heads. When the set screw A has been so carefully adjusted that the head moves quite freely, the lock-nut B may be screwed up tight, when in most cases it will be found that the head is then too tight, and a quarter turn of the set screw should be made, and the lock-nut being re-tightened, the head again tested in the manner above described, and this should be done just as often as may be necessary, until the head is found to be all right. With new machines it often happens that for a time the head requires frequent adjustment, and this should be seen to, as if it be kept carefully screwed up until it gets 'set' by wear, it will then run all right for a lengthened period. A head screwed up too tightly will be found an immense drawback to comfort, and it is quite worth while to keep this material portion of the machine carefully adjusted from the first.

Attached to the head and passing through the hole D are the handle-bars and handles, called generally 'the handles.' These are usually made of hollow steel tube, which is both strong and light and withstands the pull of the rider when racing or going up-hill. The fashion set some few years back by several well-known cyclists of having wide handles which give the rider a chance of breathing with comfort, has now become universal, and the machines of to-day are fitted with handle-bars some twenty-six to twenty-eight inches wide. The handle-bar is made of tapered tube in varying forms, and is fitted at the ends with bone or vulcanite rubber handles. The first handle-bars were straight, passing through the boss of the head and being continued out in a straight line on either side. At a very early date after the introduction of the longer bars they began to be bent in various ways, men going into raptures about the purchase which a 'straight arm' gave them. This was without doubt a mistake, as an actually straight arm proves

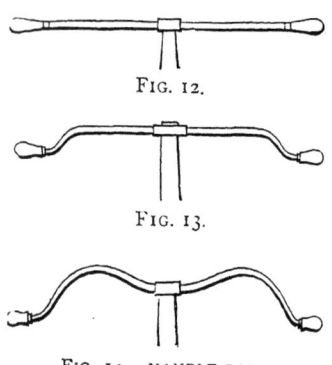

FIG. 12.

FIG. 13.

FIG. 14.—HANDLE-BARS.

very irksome and uncomfortable in practical riding, but at the same time 'cowhorn' handles, which took the hands lower down, possessed a decided advantage over the old high straight handle-bar. These variations were tested for the most part first on the path, and 'dropped handles' became the rage. In some cases the handles as they emerge from the boss of the head curve slightly upwards and then again rather further downwards, so as to allow the play of the legs under them and at the same time give the rider the advantage of a lower handle ; see bottom cut on p. 308. Others again, where the rider uses a full-sized machine, start out straight from the head horizontally, and then dip sharply at the end. In any case the rider, whether he be racing man or tourist, should be sure to have the handles conveniently adjusted. They should not be too low or too high, though the former fault is to be preferred to the latter. They should not touch the legs anywhere, and the handles themselves should be in a comfortable position. They should be arranged, in short, exactly to suit the arm reach of the intending rider, and he should be most careful in every case to see that they are rightly placed.

FIG. 15.

FIG. 16.—WHATTON'S HANDLE-BARS.

Once in a way very eccentric ideas are seen on the path ; thus Mr. J. S. Whatton, amateur champion of 1882 at five miles, used some extraordinary handle-bars, which started from just below the shoulder of the fork and passing in a wide curve backwards, came round under the thigh of the rider, and finished in handles placed just about in the same position as those of an ordinary machine, the idea being that the rider was more safe in case of a cropper, as he had an open front with no handle-bars to bother him. The idea was not followed up except by the Cambridge man's brother, the faults of the plan being obvious. The long bars not only added weight, but were even then exceedingly weak and afforded but little purchase; in fact, Mr. Whatton very soon bent them and pulled them out of truth. Despite these drawbacks the elder Whatton won a championship and showed some wonderful pace, making a flying quarter-mile record at Surbiton, and the only wonder of those who knew the nature and weight of the machine he was on, was, what he would have done had he been on an ordinary machine, with a stiff and rigid handle-bar at which to pull.

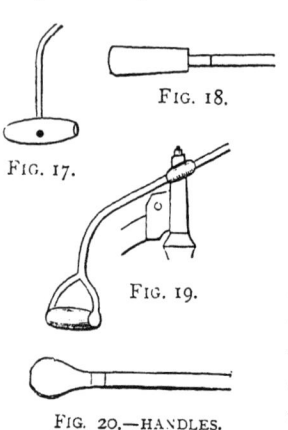

FIG. 17.
FIG. 18.
FIG. 19.
FIG. 20.—HANDLES.

All the varying types of handle-bar have their admirers, but for road work it is always well to have the head as long as possible, and this usually admits of a straight bar with dropped ends, the straight part being most comfortable for 'coasting' or going with legs over the handles down a hill. For tricycling, the handle-bar, when it is used, assumes varied shapes; thus the handle-bar of the Ranelagh Club is merely cow-horned to allow the legs to play freely, as is also the ingenious dummy handle-bar of the racing Quadrant. In Humber type tricycles, and more especially in Humber tandems, a bar, not only dropped but carried backwards a trifle, will be found of very great service in climbing hills and so on, whilst many of the safeties can be improved by adopting a handle more suited to the individual idiosyncrasies of the rider. In fact, on the adjustment of the handle-bar depends much of the comfort of the rider, and this fact will be found most clearly appreciated by racing men, who are always careful to have their handles placed according to their own predilections. The leverage exerted by a 26-inch handle-bar is obviously very great, and yet riders may be seen tearing first at one handle and then at the other in their efforts to surmount a hill; this is absurd, as the alternate pulls tend to deflect the forks and throw a crooked strain upon the bearings. On the other hand, by slightly setting the shoulder muscles, the strain is thrown equally on both sides of the bar, with the result that the machine runs easier and the course is straighter. An important item in this part of the machine is the kind of handle to be used. In the early days of cycling, ivory handles were fitted at a considerable extra charge as something particularly excellent, but the unfortunate purchasers soon discovered that nothing split easier than the ivory handles in case of a spill, and their popularity rapidly waned. At the same time rosewood (so-called) handles were most frequently fitted, but gradually horn took their place, and now it is quite the exception to see a racing machine fitted with any other handle, if the cork handles fitted by one or two firms are put aside. On the road, too, horn handles are by far the most numerous, though handles of vulcanite and other materials are also to be seen. The great fault of 90 per cent. of the horn handles is that they are too small, thus predisposing the hand to cramp, and similar troubles. The handle for road work should be of a good size, just large enough to fill the hand and to allow the fingers to touch round it, so as to secure a firm grip. This is a point which makers would do well to look into, as the horn handle has been getting smaller and smaller for two or three seasons.

The break fittings are a very important item in the economy of a bicycle, inasmuch as on their accuracy and soundness very often depends the safety of the limbs, if not the life of the rider. Fig. 21 shows the first lever of the break B, pivoting at D, a small socket screwed for the purpose into the head A; details of D are shown at G. H is a section of the spoon of the break; at the top of the lever B is a hole in which the end of the second lever plays. Fig. 22 shows the second lever in position. A A is the handle-bar, and B the handle, the lever E E is pivoted at D, and its end is inserted in the upright arm of the spoon lever. The details of the break should be often examined and any flaw at once remedied, as any breakage may bring about serious results.

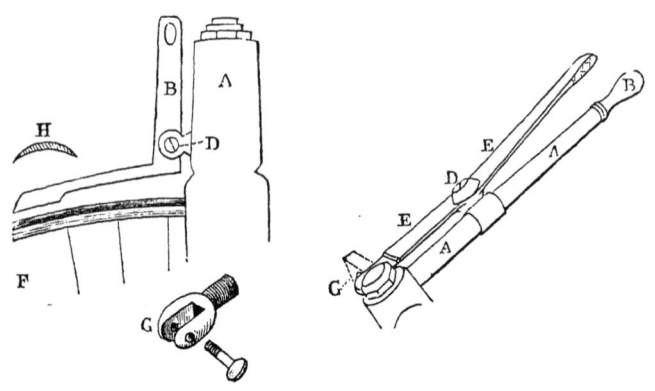

FIG. 21.—FIRST LEVER OF BREAK AND FITTINGS.

FIG. 22.—SECOND LEVER OF BREAK.

THE BACKBONE.

This part of the machine, whether it be the bicycle or the tricycle backbone, does not nowadays present any very marked variety of construction. Early in the history of the improved bicycle, square, fluted, and multitubular backbones were fitted by some makers, but they were all superseded by the marvellously light and strong weldless or seamless tubes, made by various companies for the trade, especially for the purpose. These backbones are circular or oval in section, and do not admit of much variety in their simple but effective pattern.

An ordinary ovalled backbone has a backbone head and hind forks separately fitted, the latter being in most cases rivetted and brazed in place, though sometimes made continuous with the backbone, the end being split into two half tubes, which are covered in with a flat piece of metal; whilst in the hind fork fitted by John Keen the backbone went simply undivided on one side of the hind wheel, the pin sticking out at right angles from the end, without any other support. The backbone heads are pushed into the tube, being of course very accurately fitted and then rivetted and brazed. The backbone head sometimes gives way, the most usual accident being a crack just behind the solid part of the head, and this should be looked for at any time when the pose of the rider seems to have slightly altered. 'Springing of the backbone,' as it is called, is another accident which sometimes happens, especially where a cheap make of backbone is used, or where the rider is too heavy for his machine. In both these cases the curve of the backbone straightens out. The part gives, thus taking the backbone off the front wheel and allowing the hind wheel to get farther away than it should do, whilst in cases where cheap oval backbones have been used, the straightening will sometimes be accompanied by a crooking to one side or the other, which of course makes the machine steer very awkwardly. The rider should therefore run his eye occasionally over the machine and see that the backbone, as compared with the rim of the front wheel, preserves the same relative curve. Should a backbone go in this way it will require watching; if it has been badly or carelessly bent to make it fit a particular wheel, it will perhaps only spring back slightly, but, on the other hand, if it is really a bad one it will go on straightening until it either breaks or places the hind wheel far away from the driving wheel, which not only looks ridiculous but also interferes materially with the running of the machine on the road.

The hind forks alluded to above are now usually simple stampings, the metal being convex to the outside, with a broad shoulder and a butt which is inserted in the backbone. The butt is carefully fitted into the end of the backbone, rivetted and brazed. At the tails of the forks are the holes through which the ends of the hind-wheel pin pass; these forks fully tested, light and strong, have almost entirely replaced the old-fashioned hollow hind forks. Hind forks may break, but such an accident seldom occurs with bicyclists. The tricyclists who ride Humber pattern tricycles, sometimes fracture the hind forks of their machines by the foolish practice of jumping into the saddle, which is good for neither the man nor the machine; the brazing of the hind fork sometimes gives way, and then it becomes loose and wears the rivet; this is however very soon detected, owing to the peculiar unsteadiness which it gives the steering.

The front wheel hubs take many forms; sometimes the flanges are of large diameter, and if used for direct spokes depending on hub tension, they are comparatively heavy; on the other hand they are sometimes made of very thin metal, the spokes being headed in a thin beaded rim with the tension in the felloe. Or again the hub flanges are small, with a beaded rim, and the spokes are passed through holes, hair-pin style, for tangent wheels with a tension in the felloe, as for example in the Invincible cycles; then, again, they are cup-like, with laced spokes sticking out well over the bearings. In racing machines with direct spokes and hub tension the hubs are made with flanges of small diameter but with enough metal to give the spokes a good hold, the bearing being buried in the hub, whilst for laced spoke racers the hub is of very light construction, being simply a collar on either side of the stout axle necessary for such machines; in short, the varieties of the hub are numerous; the day of very large and heavy hubs has gone by. Some hubs are so made as to lock the spokes after adjustment, and many inventors have worked upon the hub in various ways; but the plainer, simpler, and lighter a hub is, the better, always supposing that it contains strength enough to take without any failure the strain of the spoke tension. The hub axle has almost without exception remained a solid, and the strain of the cranks upon it is such as to make it most inadvisable to in any way weaken it. Gun-metal hubs have found much favour, as they set off a machine very much; but plain steel hubs are equally good, as far as actual service goes, and there is little chance of the simplicity of the hub being in any way modified. The hind wheel hub usually contains the hind wheel ball-bearing within it, and it will be found fully described under the head of bearings.

The front forks are usually made of a sharpened oval section, A, B, fig. 23; they are constructed out of tubing, which has

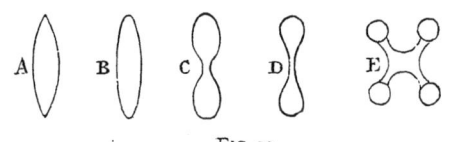

FIG 23.

been tapered, and are usually pressed into shape cold, in an hydraulic press. They are called bayonet-shaped forks, because they are tapered from the shoulder of the head gradually down to the bearings. The hollow fork A is fitted very carefully over the solid end B, fig. 24, which is made on purpose upon the head, and having been placed upon it the fork is rivetted and brazed. Sometimes, as in the Excelsior machines, the forks are simply flattened continuous tubes, running from the bearings to the handle-bar, having fixed upon them at the top a cross bar to take the lower cone of the improved Ariel head, and a corresponding top piece to which the handles are attached, this making a strong serviceable fork. The Premier double hollow fork bicycle has two circular tubes on either side placed side by side, running up to the head in the usual way, the result being a vastly improved edition of the old Ariel head E (see fig. 9).

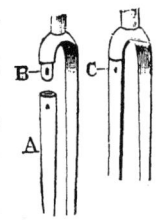

FIG. 24.

Forks, like other parts of the machine, have undergone many changes and variations; and many ideas have been tried to secure their rigidity or in other ways to improve them (C, D, fig. 23); but the simplicity of the hollow bayonet fork places it well above any others with the exceptions alluded to, and improvement except in quality, if feasible, seems almost impossible, although it is a bold thing to attempt to say where improvement in cycles will stop. A, fig. 23, is the so-called knife-edged bayonet fork, which was at one time very popular ; it was, however, given to cracking along the edge, and has been discarded in favour of section B, which is round edged ; C and D are sections of grooved and fluted forks, many styles of which have from time to time been tried ; the twin tube forks of the DHF (double hollow fork) Premier is the only important variation, and it is a sound, rigid and reliable fork. The B section fork is made by first carefully tapering a piece of stout steel tube and then pressing it flat in one operation by means of an hydraulic press—this method of construction has the merit of at once detecting any flaw in the material. The lower ends of the forks are sometimes made continuous with the bearing cases, or the latter are bolted on to them, the soundest way without doubt being to have them part and parcel of the forks, though for convenience of taking to pieces, should such a course be often necessary, the bearings fixed with a stout screw will be found most useful.

The cranks are placed on either end of the axle of the driving wheel in bicycles, and on either end of the lower pulley wheel axle in tricycles ; they are made from five to seven inches in length, have a long slot in them into which the pedal fits, and the length of the throw can be adjusted to the satisfaction of the rider. Some years back, James Carver introduced the idea of cutting grooves in the face of the crank, into which corresponding projections on the face of the inside of the shoulder of the pedal-pin fitted, and this idea has found favour amongst riders and makers. The crank is fixed to the end of the axle with a tapered pin which sometimes gives trouble by becoming loose. It is no good to try and tinker it up ; the machine should at once be taken to a good mechanic to be put right ; when once the crank pin has been loose, it will in most cases come loose again, unless remedied at once. Variable cranks are not altogether novelties, many inventors having from time to time tried their hands at this description of crank, the idea of course being that by making the length of the throw variable, the rider can so shift the pedals as to have a long leverage for up-hill and a short one for the level; whether in actual practice the variable crank will ever be found satisfactory is a moot point. The variation is wide, no less than two inches, and as a result the rider would never have a quite satisfactory reach; thus if he had the machine to fit his reach when working with the 5-inch crank, which is the speed crank, it is clear that he would be overreaching himself considerably with the 7-inch throw, and *vice versâ*, and moreover, without a great deal of practice, the alteration of a throw makes a practised rider feel all abroad, for a time at any rate. The variable crank bids fair to be of more importance upon tricycles than upon bicycles, as the tricyclist who does not want to hurry may possibly find a relief in a 7-inch throw up hill, whilst using the 5-inch on the level. It is, however, rather early in the day to judge with any certainty on this point, as it is only of late that the makers have put the variable crank commercially upon the market. The Surrey Machinist Company have a good variable crank, which should answer the purpose for which it was invented, and there are several more in existence.

The pedals are placed in the crank slots, and form the grip and rest for the feet. They are divided into two classes, rat-trap and rubber pedals. Rat-trap pedals are so called because they resemble in shape the old style of rat-trap or 'gin,' being made of two parallel iron plates, with saw teeth cut thereon, the sides being a little raised, with a pin running right through them, the pedal originally running on adjustable cones. The march of improvement has however made ball pedals most popular, the design being exceedingly simple, the ends of the pedal having in their centres two light cases in which are placed the necessary number of balls, with an adjusting cone fitted upon the pedal pin.

The 'rubber pedal,' as its name implies, consists of two or more stout rubber cylinders upon iron cores which replace the saw-edged irons of the rat-trap. A novelty in the shape of square rubbers made so as to revolve upon the iron cores, and thus adjust themselves to the set of the foot, has recently been brought out by W. Bown. Rubber pedals are most comfortable for long rides, but the rider is more liable to 'slip his pedal' when using them, especially in wet weather, and they are seldom used on the racing path. C. E. Liles, the mile champion in 1880, and Fred East, however, invariably used rubber pedals on the racing path.

The bearings are a very important item in the machinery of bicycle or tricycle, seeing that on them to a very great extent depend the easy running and practical working of the vehicle. The earliest bearing was, of course, simply a hole in the frame through which the axle ends were thrust, but the oil caught the flinty grit of the road, and soon produced wear, which upset the whole arrangement and necessitated the renewal of an integral part of the frame. This course suggested to the constructors of the earliest velocipedes that some arrangement would be necessary to provide against this wear, and so they hit upon the expedient of fixing two adjustable and removable blocks of steel or gun-metal on the ends of the forks, through which the ends of the axle passed. This simple plan, of course, possessed many disadvantages. The strain of the pedalling and the lateral twist of the bearings, but ill-supported by the thin and inadequate forks of that date, caused any amount of irregular wear, and plain or parallel bearings as they were called were soon improved upon. This time the coned bearing was introduced, which, as its name implies, was constructed of a coned shape, the axle ends being similarly arranged, the coned bearing had a successful run, and even now is used in cheap machines for hind-wheel and pedal-bearings, and in these cases the simple adjustment and general soundness of the plan make the coned bearing singularly appropriate. The disadvantages of a coned bearing are a tendency to run up and lock if carelessly manipulated, and the very awkward results of irregular wear, which can only be provided against by frequent and careful adjustment.

For some time bearings remained stationary and unimproved, but inventors were of course at work, and at length the ball-bearing was introduced to the cycling public.

The ball-bearing, as its name implies, is a device in which the wearing parts of a machine are so fitted as to run accurately upon a row of carefully made steel balls held in a suitable groove in the case.

The result of such an arrangement satisfactorily designed is obviously to make it very easy to adjust and take up the *equal* wear of such a row of balls, and at the same time to lessen materially the friction set up, seeing that in place of a grinding it is a rolling friction. The great desiderata are thus fully provided for in the ball-bearing, ease of running, minimum of wear, and simplicity of adjustment being all attained. Of course the first bearings were not in the main complete, and combined as they were at first with weak and inadequate forks, the tendency to a cross or twisting strain was very great; the single row of balls thus got thrown out of running, nipped, dented, or broken, and some of the pioneer wheelmen suffered so much annoyance from them as to entertain a determined and fixed prejudice against them for a long while afterwards. This obvious fault was met by the invention of the double ball-bearing, in which two rows of balls were placed, sometimes steadied by means of a cage, some fraction of an inch apart, and the adjustment being accurately and carefully made, the bearing resisted the tendency to torsion and twist which the single ball-bearing yielded to almost without resistance. The double ball-bearing in the days of weak forks was a decided advantage; nowadays as the forks fitted are infinitely more rigid in every direction, the merits of double ball-bearings are not so apparent, although they are of the greatest value and importance even now in minimising and directing the strains on the machines. This principle of double rows of balls has been carefully carried out by many firms. Messrs. Humber and Co., in a racer built in 1881, put the rows of balls very wide apart in a broad case which was buried in the hub, and thus secured great steadiness and rigidity ; whilst Messrs. Singer & Co. now fit an extraordinary double ball-bearing which really consists of a tube or sleeve some inches long, slightly expanded at either end and carrying in these cup-like ends the balls, one row in each. Needless to say this ingenious idea produces an immense degree of steadiness, and the same plan is also applied to the bottom bracket wheels of tricycles and Safety bicycles made by this firm. Simplicity combined with working efficiency is a *sine quâ non* in a ball-bearing, and the adjustment is the only patentable point. Messrs. Bown & Co. claim a patent which controls all ball-bearing adjustments by means of a cone ; and this adjustment, the simple screwing of a coned surface further into the bearing case, is without doubt one of the best—if not the best —method of adjusting ball-bearings. Happily Bown's Æolus bearings are excellent in design and construction, and are widely used by the makers. Other means are also used to procure adjustment more or less successful, as for example in the ingenious ball-bearing known as the Abingdon, in which a solid case contains the balls in a groove, and a slit is cut through it, closed by a block. The wear is fractional, but when it at length does become apparent the face of the closing block is carefully filed, and when the jaws are again screwed up tightly on it, the wear is taken up by their infinitesimal approach.

The hind-wheel bearings are most usually placed within the hub, although one or two makers have attached them to the rear fork-ends to secure stability. The hub bearing is, however, much the neater, and the radial leverage to be overcome is so small that this pattern has been adopted with satisfactory results by nearly all makers of the ordinary bicycle. In rear-driven Safeties the hind-wheel bearings are, however, often placed outside the hub, with advantage in the matter of added stability. Bown's hind-wheel hub, both for Safeties and ordinaries, is typical of the most popular method of fitting ball-bearings to the rear wheel.

THE SPRING.

Providing of course that the running parts of the machine are in perfect order, the spring is by far the most important adjunct to the whole machine, as on it depends to a very great extent the comfort and safety of the rider. In the days of the hobby-horse, the absence of a spring was one of the most serious obstacles which militated against the success of those vehicles, hernia being frequently produced by the serious jars which the rider suffered on the unprotected seat, and this fault was doubtless apparent in the very earliest velocipedes; but the first bicycle, the Boneshaker, was well provided in this respect. A long spring, running from the head to the top of the hind wheel, was employed in some of the first patterns, and this served to make the velocipede a luxurious vehicle compared with its progenitor. After some time, the machine having been improved, the long spring was considerably curtailed, and then the bow spring as fitted by the Coventry Machinist Company to their Gentleman's Bicycle was adopted; this was a spring attached to a projection in front of the socket head (see zz, fig. 4, p. 303) which passed backwards on either side of the head, and finished in a curve which was bolted to the backbone in such a manner as to allow some little play at the tail end. This was also very comfortable, but the craze for lightening the machine soon led to the reduction of the size of the spring, and then the 'clip tail' was adopted, that is, a spring bolted in front, and sliding on the backbone with a clip In various forms this spring is still used, although it is much improved in many ways, yet it still suffers from side shake, the bolts and bolt-holes get worn, and the spring rocks slightly.

Then came the Club spring, which consisted of a comparatively rigid bar of steel, slung in rubber loops and buffers, and this has proved fairly successful, although the rubber attachments often break, and to secure the necessary steadiness the buffers were supported by metal links and similar contrivances which to some extent conveyed the shocks of the road to the rider. Springs acting on rubber buffers by compression have proved fairly successful, as also have springs acting on coil springs by compression; but in most cases some arrangement has been applied to maintain the pose of the spring, and that arrangement will be found on examination, in nine cases out of ten, to be in permanent and sometimes in locked contact with the rigid plate of the saddle, which discounts to a great extent the work which the buffer arrangements are expected to do. In the original bicycles, and especially in the first spider-wheeled machines, the whole carriage became a spring owing to the want of rigidity which characterised it, and it is for this reason that many old riders still go into raptures over the old bow spring; but they would be considerably undeceived if one of the original springs was affixed for their instruction to one of the rigid machines of the present day. The fixing of the front end of the spring rigidly to the machine is one of those radical errors which are still maintained. The spring was so fitted to racing machines as long as those vehicles were furnished with springs at all, but the modern racing machine has no spring, and the spring fixed at the front end is out of place in a roadster. The play of all the clip-tail class of springs is radically wrong, the action tending to tip up the point of the saddle and induce dangerous strains, and in any case all the old forms of clip-tail, roller, and sliding springs should be discarded.

To note all the varieties in springs would fill up too much space, and it only remains to be seen what spring arrangements will best serve the purposes of the cyclist—the touring and road-riding cyclist that is to say—for the racing man has given up using a spring in any form, but has his saddle fitted right upon the backbone.

The main points required in a satisfactory spring are the following: it must fully and effectively break the jar of the road, between the points of the wheels in contact with the road and the rider's body; the rider, unless he adopts one or other of the anti-vibration handles now sold, will always transmit a certain amount of jar through his arms, if he rides with too much weight on the handles; but as far as his body is concerned the spring should absorb all the vibration, and break its effect upon the saddle and its occupant. The spring must also be calculated for special occasions, as for example, if whilst riding at night the rider comes into collision with a large stone, the result must be a bad shaking however good the spring; but, at the same time, a good spring will break the shock, a bad spring may break itself. Whilst performing these important functions, the spring must not give too much under normal conditions; it must not allow the pose of the saddle to be too readily affected, as any such variations must of necessity detract from the satisfactory application of the rider's power. It must be steady, strong, not liable to wear out, light, and easily adaptable to any machine; and these qualities are all to be found in one of the best inventions ever brought out in connexion with cycling, the well-known 'Arab Cradle Spring.' This spring was invented in 1878 by Mr. John Harrington, who was then residing in the Isle of Wight. Mr. Harrington is a most ingenious mechanician, and having turned his attention to the bicycle, he soon began to introduce improvements, some of which are now-a-days almost universally adopted. Prominent amongst them is the spring under notice, which has not only steadily grown in favour with the cycling public throughout the world, but has also been adopted by many of the leading firms of cycle makers for their standard pattern machines, this being without doubt the highest and most practical testimony to the merits of the invention. The spring has gone through a series of alterations and improvements since its first conception, but its main characteristics have by no means changed. It is composed of stout steel wire of a peculiar quality; the inventor experimented for some years before he was quite satisfied with the material he was able to obtain for the construction of the springs. As will be seen from the illustration (fig. 25), it has two sides alike, upon which the saddle is placed. Owing to this peculiarity in its construction, it drops freely on either side of the backbone, and so obtains a larger space for play without raising the saddle, thus increasing the length of the reach. The actual amount of play is small, but the practical length of the spring is very great; it is, however, cunningly coiled up into a convenient space—the double construction admits of a gentle and effective rocking action, which eases the rub of the saddle without in any way infringing on its rigidity and steadiness. The spring is peculiarly sensitive, taking up the small and great shocks with equal completeness, whilst in the event of an accident, one side will hold long enough to ensure the safety of the rider, although for the last few seasons breakages have been unknown owing to the quality of the material used. The spring is practically adaptable to any machine, bicycle or tricycle, and many riders never part with their cradle springs, as when they have got one to suit them, it can be easily adapted to any machine they may ride. Fig. 25 is an illustration of the newest pattern of the cradle spring. One other little idea of Mr. Harrington's in the shape of an adjustable tilt-rod is also shown, as also is a suspension saddle by Lamplugh & Brown, referred to further on. The rod I represents the usual saddle standard fitted to tricycles, at the top of which

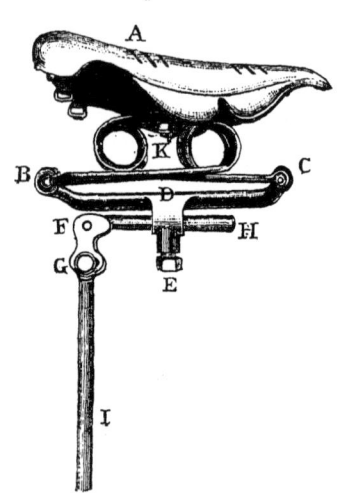

FIG. 25.—THE ARAB CRADLE SPRING ON AN ADJUSTABLE TILT-ROD.

the adjustable tilt rod fitting is shown. F is the hinge joint firmly fixed, whilst below at the point G is a locking nut and a segmentary slot; the horizontal bar H F can thus be adjusted at any required angle, and the necessity for packing the saddle to secure a comfortable position can thus be avoided, and what is more, the position of the saddle can be altered slightly from time to time, which will often be found a relief, especially on long journeys. D is the solid frame which carries the Arab spring, having at D a strong block through which the rod H F passes, and it can be locked in any desired place by means of the screw E. At B and C are placed short cross bars, which support the ends of the cradle spring, and the result of putting weight in the saddle at A is that the duplicate coils fall on either side of D vertically, thus producing an easy and reliable spring, with a modicum of side play but no unsteadiness. At K are to be seen the nuts which fix the saddle to the spring. The cradle spring and buffer saddle as shown will practically annihilate vibration in any ordinary case, whilst the tilt-rod adjustment is a minor but valuable invention. In these days when the small-wheeled Safety bicycles are finding so much favour, the most noticeable fault of which class of vehicle is the increased vibration to which the rider is exposed, the cradle spring assumes even greater importance; and one experienced cyclist who rode one of the earlier Safeties was to be seen for some weeks riding a bow-springed Safety, upon which bow spring was mounted, in addition, an Arab cradle spring. The cradle is a *sine quâ non* in Safety bicycle riding; it is also adapted to rocking and arm chairs, railway and ordinary carriages; and is, as was stated above, almost universally adopted by the trade, any manufacturer in fact being willing to supply it fitted to any of his bicycles or other machines. In ordering one of these springs from the original makers, it is only necessary to send name of machine, measurement round backbone, and exact weight of rider in his riding dress; the spring will then only require careful adjustment to give every satisfaction. It is of course necessary to mount the spring for bicyclists carefully, quite square with the backbone; when position and pose are found to be right by a trial the nuts may be given a final touch with the spanner, and the cradle spring will be found almost everlasting, the supporting bolts only showing any wear.

Of late years the spring has been combined with the saddle in various ways, and the latest novelties in this direction will be found fully treated of in the latter part of this chapter.

The foregoing practically closes the subject of the frame of a cycle, and although a bicycle has been specifically treated of, yet many of the points, such as cranks, bearings, steering-head, &c., are practically identical with those used in other classes of machines, and the description here given will be sufficient. Such further items of cycle mechanism not applied to the bicycle will be treated of under the heading of the class of machine to which they are fitted.

The foregoing as also the following sections are intended to convey some general idea of the mechanism of the machine the reader will use, but no particular machine is specifically described, because improvements are being introduced so rapidly that any minute description must of necessity become obsolete within a brief space of time. All that is required as regards the frame is a sharp eye for cracks and flaws. These are often only superficial, in the paint or the plating; but they should in every case be most carefully examined, as any breakage may lead to serious damage to the rider. Nuts should not be constantly undone, and such as may not be easily reached should be looked at specially, as a loose nut often causes an accident.

THE WHEELS.

In discussing this subject it would be impossible to go at great length into minutiæ, and as the various parts will all be duly considered separately, it is only necessary to allude generally to the various types. The bone-shaker, with its equal sized and heavy wheels, has been replaced by the lighter machines of to-day, the suspension principle being introduced and being mainly responsible for the wondrous lightening of the machine. Racers are now built weighing under twenty pounds, whilst a twenty-two pound machine is considered amply strong enough for an eleven-stone rider. The principle of the suspension wheel is best described by the means of a few simple diagrams.

Fig. 26 represents a simplified wheel. A A A is supposed to be a rigid rim, B is the hub, and C C C C the spokes, whilst W is the weight the wheel is supposed to carry. It is clear that hub, spokes, and rim would all have to be very stout and strong to withstand the wear and tear of the road. In the suspension wheel as applied to the modern bicycle, the rim is by no means so stout and rigid as the ideal rim A A A would have to be. The hollow rims fitted to many machines are both strong and rigid relatively, but nothing approaching in strength that of the ideal one. But the rim in its turn is supported by the spokes, themselves consisting of wire which under pressure would crumple up at once, but which under a tensile strain will withstand a 'pull' of many pounds. In the Crystal Palace Electrical Exhibition some two or three years back was exhibited a piece of very thin wire which looked scarcely thicker than a horsehair by which was suspended a

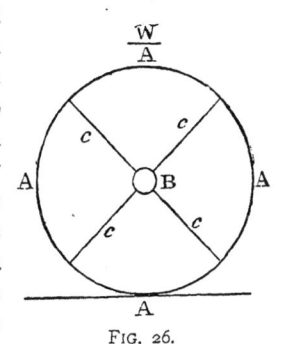

FIG. 26.

400-pound round shot; thin piano wire is used in some wheels, and it is clear that if the spokes of this wire simply went direct from the rim to a flange at the hub the danger of a lateral collapse would be imminent. To meet this obvious tendency the hub is spread until the spokes are carried alternately to flanges 5 or 6 inches or more apart, as shown idealised in fig. 27. Here the rim A A is shown in section, the spokes C C, as will be easily understood, being screwed up to a strong tension and tending to keep the rim true and in position whilst the strain on all the spokes is a tensile one; so fully is this principle carried out that the butt end of the spoke is sometimes headed through a plain hole, as shown in fig. 30 (representing an old lock-nutted spoke), so that were it possible for the rider's weight to so far overcome the tension of the spokes as to *press* upon those which happened to be below the axle, they would slide through the hub and carry no weight at all. It will thus be seen that the wheel is really a suspension wheel, and that the weight carried by it is hung or suspended on the spokes, although the tension put upon the spokes is much greater than any strain they may be expected to legitimately encounter. This principle has been very fully carried out, and the Surrey Machinist Company and Ellis & Co. have made wheels with hollow rims and spokes of marvellously thin wire, the last-named firm having made a 60-spoked 40-inch wheel for a Facile, the spokes of which only weighed five ounces. The spokes, however, were not at first drawn quite so fine as this, as nearly all the earlier wheels had direct spokes. Fig. 28 shows the method of fixing the direct spokes in the old crescent rim; the spokes having been cut to the required lengths, the end was

FIG. 27. passed through a countersunk hole in the rim as at C, and then its head B was made on the end of the spokes with a hand vice and a hammer. The head was drawn into the countersunk hole in the rim, in which it revolved as the spoke was screwed up. In the case of direct spokes, of which

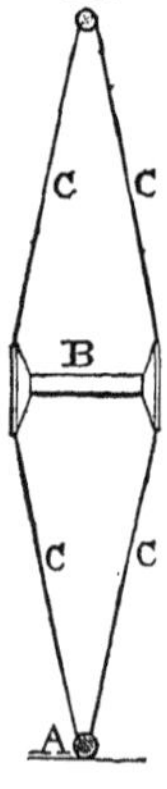

CONSTRUCTION.

fig. 29 is an example; H H being the hub, into which a hole with a thread in it is bored, and then the spoke with a corresponding worm cut upon it is screwed in until the necessary tension is obtained. Fig. 30 shows the earlier arrangement, a lock-nutted spoke. This spoke was headed at both ends, at the rim and at E inside the lock nut C C, which was screwed

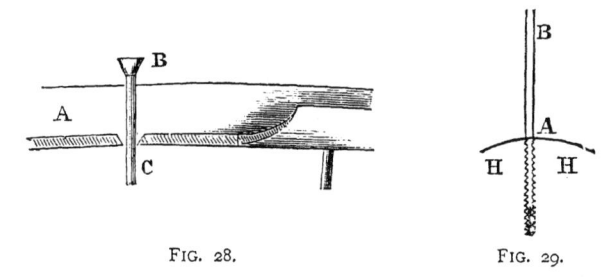

FIG. 28. FIG. 29.

further into the hub to increase the tension on the spoke, and when the wheel was true the lock nut D was firmly screwed down in its turn to fasten the whole. This plan proved cum-

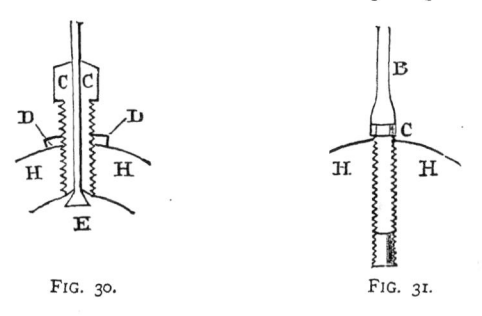

FIG. 30. FIG. 31.

brous and unsatisfactory, and has long since been discarded in the best machines. In the earlier direct spoked machines the cutting of the thread sometimes caused the spoke to break off just at the insertion into the hub, and this accident, now of less frequent occurrence, was met by the invention of butt-ended spokes, shown in fig. 31, the end of the spoke being thickened and made sexagonal to admit of adjustment.

330 *CYCLING.*

There are, of course, a number of other contrivances more or less ingenious in connexion with direct spokes, such as Andrews' plan of fitting a screw and socket in the middle of each spoke and securing adjustment in that way; but these are points into which it would scarcely be profitable to go at length. There is another very distinct type of wheel, divergent in many points from the direct spoke, and that is the Tangent wheel. As its name implies, the spokes, in place

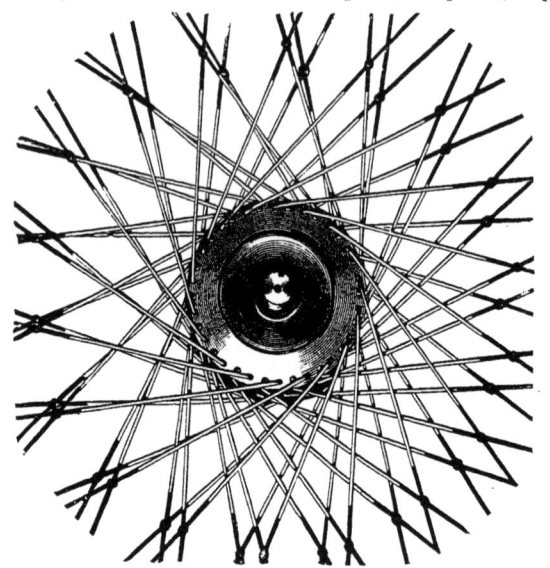

FIG. 32.—NEW RAPID TANGENT WHEEL.

of going direct from the rim to the hub, are arranged at a tangent, thus affording a more rigid connexion between the hub and rim, and in many cases the rigidity obtainable from this arrangement has been most ingeniously made use of. The racing wheels of Invincible and New Rapid bicycles may be instanced as cases in point. In many tangent wheels very fine spokes are used, and their most delicate point is at the bend in the hub, where the double spoke is bent 'hair-pin' fashion and again carried out to the rim, where, beneath the rubber tire, is a small screw, whereby the tension is secured.

There have, of course, been many other plans tested in the construction of wheels with more or less success. Thus we have tangent wheels, with binding rings of wire running round the spokes on either side, and many other schemes for producing a sound, rigid, and stable wheel; but for all purposes of description the details given of the direct and tangent spoked wheels will prove sufficient.

The rims, or felloes, of wheels were at first made simply of solid iron pressed into shape; they were called V rims, as their section was exactly like a wide V. These were followed in due turn by the U rim, also solid, and presently the crescent rim came to the front, this rim being U shaped, but thick in the middle and fining off to a comparatively thin edge when seen in section. Then came the hollow rims, undoubtedly the best of all. These rims are made in various ways: some, the Surrey Double Hollow rim for example, of strips of metal soldered into place; others from steel tube, stamped into shape; and others again from a long strip of fine metal, folded by machinery, and brazed.

There are half-a-dozen sound, tried, and tested hollow rims in the market, and there are many minor variations in detail, all designed to effect one purpose or another. The hollow rim is now used on the road as well as the path, and adds much to the stability and rigidity of some of the best types of roadsters.

The hubs, or bosses in the middle of the wheels, are also of very various patterns, to accommodate the various types of spokes with which they are fitted. Some are almost cup shaped, with small holes through which are threaded the tangent spokes; others are somewhat heavier and stouter, to take the threaded ends of the direct spoke. Some hubs have wide flanges, and others are almost rudimentary, being reduced to simple collars fixed or turned on the axle, and these again are deeply recessed, presenting in section a bell-like appearance to take the bearings which are put deeply into the hub, so as to keep 'the tread' of the machines, i.e. the width from pedal to pedal, as narrow as possible, this being illustrated in fig. 33, showing the hub in section and the bearing *in situ*, the

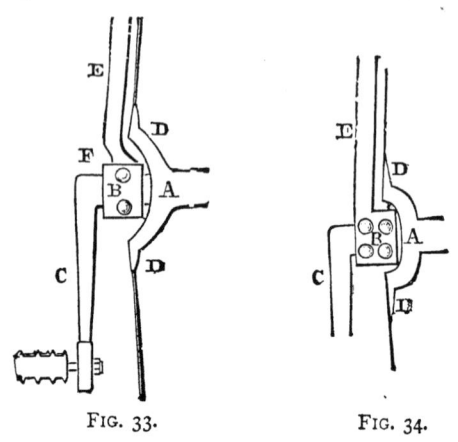

FIG. 33. FIG. 34.

arrangement being but little exaggerated from the fact. A is the hub of which D D is the flange, E is the front fork, which is run very close to the flange and then turned sharply in at F (a very weak point) into the deep recess of the hub, where it is firmly locked to the bearing box B ; C is the crank on the axle end—a similar idea, more neatly carried out, is shown in fig. 34, the broad bearing box B (homogeneous with the fork end) being sunk into the hub on its inner side, and thus finding room for a double row of balls without making the tread any wider. Many other ingenious little plans and adaptations have been made in hub fittings, but none are of sufficient importance to need a lengthy notice.

The remarks made at the end of the section treating of the frame apply here with equal force. The wheels used in tricycles are much the same as those used in bicycles. The hub in the former case is often wider, as giving more stability, and the spokes are thicker.

The care of the wheels is a material point in the life of a cycle. Never play tricks with them; if a spoke is loose, a spoke-tightener may be very carefully used, taking especial care to see that the rim is not pulled out of truth; and in fact the job, however small, would be much better left to a competent workman.

If a rider is compelled by adverse circumstances to try and adjust a damaged wheel, he should spin it rapidly whilst holding a piece of chalk against the fork so as just to touch the rim. This, if the wheel be untrue, it will do only occasionally, and the marks will guide the worker. At the same time, it is by no means a task which everyone succeeds at, and if it is by any means possible to put it in the hands of a skilled workman, it should be done.

In some makes the hub ends of the spokes are but poorly protected from rust; where the spoke runs into the hub a little cranny remains to hold the moisture, which rusts through the spoke. With a very small brush and some liquid 'Brunswick black' or enamel each of these crannies can be filled up. In a new machine rust will have little chance, for a time at least, of eating through the spoke and weakening it to breaking-point.

The wheels need care and watching, and they will then last a long time.

TRICYCLES.

The success of the improved bicycle drew the attention of makers to the hitherto despised 'velocipede,' which, though older than its narrow-gauge rival, had been quite distanced by it in the march of improvement; and some few enterprising individuals who aspired to the bicycle, but did not dare venture upon it, began to ask if it were not possible to construct a modernised velocipide, with all the advantages which the bicycle possessed in the shape of suspension wheels, hollow-tube frames, and so on, which should give a slow if comfortable method of travelling to those to whom the bicycle was denied. Accordingly very early in the history of the modern bicycle tricycles were made. Starley constructed one, so did Singer, and so did Messrs. Hillman, Herbert, & Cooper. Starley invented the Coventry tricycle, which resembled in general plan the present Coventry Rotary, but in place of the rotary action there were two long levers which drove the driving wheel by means of a cranked axle. Singer brought out the Challenge tricycle, a lever-driven machine. No sooner were these machines put commercially upon the market than practical riders discovered in them a new and valuable addition to the cyclist's stud. Some of the earlier successes on the path and road having been achieved upon rear steerers, Derkinderin's victory in the first road ride and Corbett's win at Leicester in the spring of 1881 being cases in point, popular favour leant to this type of vehicle, and as the earlier front-steerers were fitted with ridiculously small steering wheels, the rear-steerers were found to ascend hills and plough through rough ground with greater ease; but the many and insuperable disadvantages attached to the latter class soon made themselves very clearly manifest. Down hill the rear-steerer was utterly unreliable, as the rider's weight was taken off the steering wheel, whilst any application of the break simply lifted it clean off the ground at once. Moreover, the rider had to sit well back even on the level to secure a steady steering, and this brought him behind his work. So it is not wonderful that in a couple of seasons the rear-steering tricycle became obsolete, and the front-steerer took its place. The front-steerer was, however, by no means perfect, and it is only within the last few years that large front wheels, bicycle steering, and similar improvements have been introduced. The old bath-chair spade-handled front-steering tricycle is fast following the old rear-steerer into obscurity. The various types of tricycles, single and double, are alluded to below, the machines described being in each case typical of a class. The main divisions may be best described as follows: 1. the Humber type; 2. the Cripper; 3. the Quadrant; 4. the Coventry

CONSTRUCTION.

Rotary; 5. the Olympia type. All these varying types have been fully tested, and may be regarded as the digested and perfected outcome of a long course of practical experience.

SINGLE- AND DOUBLE-DRIVERS.

So numerous and diverse are the forms and construction of the modern tricycle, that it would be quite impossible to give even a bare description of their various characteristics within the limits of the present volume. Such a catalogue, moreover, would be tedious and uninstructive to the reader, and would probably leave in his mind simply a feeling of bewilderment at the almost endless variety presented to his view. Happily it is possible to indicate certain general principles under which all machines may be classed. Thus, the mode in which the muscular force of the rider is communicated to the tricycle at once differentiates machines into two distinct classes, viz.—

Single-drivers, and
Double-drivers,

the latter being again divided into two sub-classes, according as they are driven by

Two-chain clutch gear, or ·
Single-chain balance gear.

The systems upon which these different methods of construction are founded, and their respective advantages, may be thus explained. For the moment let it be supposed that, of the three wheels composing a tricycle, two, called for convenience the road wheels, are of equal diameter and placed at either end of an axle (termed the main axle), whilst the third wheel is used merely to give support, or as a means of steering (or both).

It is the road wheels that provide the means of propulsion, and according as one or both wheels are actuated by the rider, the machine takes its name of single- or double-driver. The method by which motion is imparted to the road wheels does not at present concern the reader. The question is, whether it is better that one or both of the wheels should be driven. No doubt can ever have been rationally entertained on this point. Clearly to perceive the effect of driving one road wheel only, it is only necessary to suppose the steering wheel to be at the same moment lifted from the ground. Obviously, the machine would at once swerve away to the side opposite the driven wheel. With the steering wheel on the ground, the actual swerve of the machine is prevented, but only at the cost of a large amount of force uselessly expended in producing side strain on the steering wheel. In point of fact, this side strain does by slow degrees cause the machine to swerve to the other side of the road, and it is necessary continually to correct this tendency by a slight turn of the steering handle. Another serious disadvantage attaches to the single driver—viz. that when great force is exerted by the rider, as in hill climbing, or when the road is loose or slippery, the driven wheel is apt to slip round for want of sufficient adhesion to the road. On the other hand, when both wheels are driven, the adhesion of the wheels is doubled and their liability to slip is practically prevented. The superiority of double-driving being so clearly apparent, it may be wondered why single-driving was ever had recourse to. The answer to this is, that in order to drive both wheels equally forward in a straight course, and yet admit of either wheel outrunning the other in passing round a curve, mechanical contrivances of considerable ingenuity are required.

It is the various means of achieving this double purpose that now come under notice. It will be obvious to the reader that when a machine describes a curvilinear course, the outer driving wheel must necessarily move both farther and faster than the inner wheel. From this it follows that both driving wheels cannot be rigidly fixed to the main axle (this latter being driven from the crank-shaft); nor, supposing both wheels to carry a toothed pulley on the hub and to run free on the axle (straight or curved), can the wheels even in that case be geared by chains to fixed pulleys on the crank-axle. For, in both of these supposed cases, the driving wheels would necessarily rotate at one and the same rate, and the machine could not be made to turn a corner unless the outer wheel were either lifted from the ground or forcibly skidded along it. The first of these alternatives is manifestly impracticable; whilst the second, involving as it does the skidding of a rubber tire sideways, would certainly lead to a sudden arrest and probably to the capsizing of the machine, with a stripping of the tire, and so on. Hence it follows that when each wheel is driven by a separate chain, a means must be provided for allowing either wheel to run on faster than the other. There is no need to describe all the various expedients that are or have been used for this end, the purpose of this chapter being, as already defined, not to catalogue varieties, but to explain principles.

The broad distinction between double-drivers with two chains and single-chain double-drivers is that the former are worked by means of a clutch action. That is to say, either the chain-pulleys on the crank-shaft are fastened to the shaft by means of clutches, or the chain-wheels on the wheel-hubs are so fastened to the driving wheels. The latter was the plan followed by the makers of the old Devon, two chains being made use of. The clutch employed was in effect the ordinary ratchet and pawl, the principle of which is so well understood as not to require explanation. A little consideration will show that this form of clutch has two drawbacks. (1) It does not admit of back-pedalling. For, if the wheels are, severally or together, capable of running on in advance of the crank-shaft, it follows that pedalling the crank-shaft backwards does not retard the wheels. Hence, the inventor of the Devon (Mr. F. Warner Jones) was led to add to the machine his ingenious and effective ground-break, actuated by the foot, which compensated for the inability to back-treadle. (2) The ratchet and pawl clutch unavoidably occasion a disagreeable clicking noise whenever the wheels run forward unactuated by the crank-shaft; as, for example, in running down hill, the treadles the while being held stationary. For these reasons, added to some other minor objections, this form of double-driving has never been in any great request, and it is now rapidly falling into desuetude. Its use is, in fact, now almost completely confined to machines of the Omnicycle and Merlin class, in which the action is reciprocating, not rotary.

The two chain double-driver must not, however, be dismissed from consideration without giving due attention to the form in which it has attained the greatest popularity; viz. that in which the chain-wheels on the crank-shaft are actuated through a friction-clutch. The best known friction-clutches is that adopted on the Cheylesmore rear-steerer, and is illustrated in the appended cut.

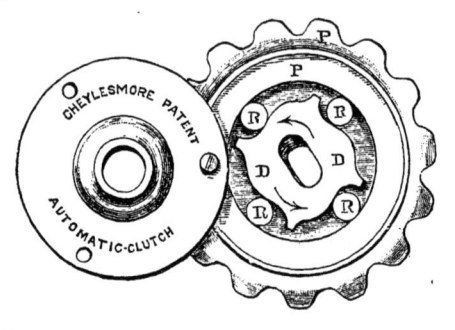

FIG. 35.—THE CHEYLESMORE TWO-CHAIN CLUTCH GEAR.

P is the chain pulley, one being placed at either end of the crank-shaft, and capable of freely revolving thereon, except when jambed by the shallow rollers, R. These rollers lie in a cavity formed by a circular recess in the pulley and a steel disc, D, which is shaped off on four sides so as to form alternately hollows and wedges. The disc, D, is a fixture on the crank-shaft. When the latter moves forward in the direction shown by the arrows, the rollers, R, are jambed between the disc and the inner surface of the pulley, P, and the whole of the parts, pulley included, run solid. The machine is then driven. On the contrary, when D is turned in the opposite direction, the rollers pass into the hollow spaces, and there simply rotate without jambing. This also happens when the crank-shaft, with the disc D, is held stationary as in running down hill, in which case the pulley P runs on, rotating the rollers in the hollows as already explained.

It will be observed that in this, as well as in the ratchet and pawl clutch, each of the road wheels is capable of running forward faster than the other, which must, of course, always happen when the machine is not running in a straight course.

CONSTRUCTION.

In all such cases, the wheels describe two concentric curves, the radius of which may be considered as a prolongation of the axis of the road wheels to a point which is nearer to the machine in proportion to the abruptness of the curve in which the machine is moving, as, for instance, in turning a corner. The wheel which describes the outer of these two curves is, obviously, the one which moves both faster and farther than the other. And here is brought out a cardinal defect in this class of double-driver. The outer wheel, from the conditions of the case, manifestly requires a larger share of the propelling force than the inner wheel; yet, as a consequence of its outrunning the other wheel, it and its connected chain-wheel move faster than the crank-shaft, the effect being that the latter expends its whole force in the driving of the inner road wheel—the one, viz. which at this particular juncture requires little or no propulsion.

It may be urged that this wrong application of power in going round a curve is but of slight importance, as, at the worst, it can only result in compelling the rider to make a wider circuit in turning a corner. This, however, is a mistake. It is but very seldom that a machine is running absolutely straight. To the extent that its course is curvilinear, its wheels are unequally driven. Furthermore, it may well be that for small periods of time only one wheel is driven. For let us suppose that the machine, after moving in a curve, is steered into a straight course. In describing the curve, the outer wheel has freed itself from the clutch, and run on. It is probable, therefore, that at the moment when the machine resumes a straight course this wheel is not in active connexion with the driving power. In other words, the clutch on that side has not yet 'taken up' its work; it has not yet overtaken the wheel, and by consequence the latter is not yet driven. The points of application of the power in the clutch under description are four only in number, and there is, of course, abundance of neutral space in which the clutch and driving power are non-effective. To make our meaning still more clear, suppose both the clutches—one at either end of the crank shaft—to be free, i.e. not yet to have arrived, in the process of a revolution, at the point at which each would take up its work. Now suppose that the crank-shaft is put in rotation, and that the near clutch engages and takes up its work before the off clutch has advanced sufficiently far to do the same thing. It follows that the off clutch, with its driving pulley, is not driving at all, and that it cannot do so until the machine has swerved, or been turned slightly to the near side, which will enable the off clutch to overtake its work. But observe, this very act may to a like extent have thrown the near clutch out of work. And so the see-saw may go on, varied only at the particular conjunctures when both clutches happen to take up at the same moment. When they do this, and so long as they continue conjointly to act, the machine is a true double-driver, and it is so at no other time.

Herein, without doubt, lies the true explanation of what has often been asserted to us by riders of this class of machine, viz. that on removing one of the chains the machine was found to work equally well. Though we cannot fully endorse that view, we certainly consider it open to question whether, the machine being but an imperfect double-driver, the extra weight of a second set of chain-wheels, clutch, and chain, is altogether worth carrying. In this connexion it is well not to omit to say that, in order to obviate the impossibility of back-pedalling with a clutch gear, a mechanical contrivance is sometimes introduced, by means of which the rider, by the slight movement of a lever, is enabled to lock the lower pulley to the crank-shaft. Practical experience shows that this arrangement is not very often applied to a machine, and that even then it is but seldom brought into use.

The last, and by far the most important, division of the subject must now be treated of, viz. that which treats of single-chain balance gear.

It is hardly an exaggeration to say that one of the most important steps made in the evolution of the modern tricycle was the application of differential driving gear to its propulsion. For this great improvement tricyclists are indebted to the late

CONSTRUCTION.

James Starley, of Coventry, who in the year 1877 took out a patent for the driving gear figured in fig. 36, which to the present time remains the type and exemplar of the various differential gears since brought out, and every tricyclist should have a clear idea of the principle on which it acts.

As already explained, the object to be attained is, to provide a means of driving both road wheels equally forward in a straight course, and yet to permit one of the wheels to outrun the other when the machine is going round a curve. The description of the particular method of achieving this end, adopted

FIG. 36.

A, bevel-wheel fixed to hub of loose driving wheel. B, bevel-wheel fixed to main axle. C, small mitre-wheel, revolving on a stud fixed in the plane of the chain-pulley, and gearing with A and B. D, main axle, running through from side to side of the machine. At one end is fixed the road wheel, which is driven by B; at the other end rotates the loose road wheel before alluded to, which is fixed to A. E is the chain-pulley, through which the power is brought from the crank-axle.

and applied to the tricycle by James Starley, will be clearly understood by reference to the appended cut.

It will be observed that the pulley E runs free upon the main axle, or rather that it would do so but for its connexion, by means of the mitre wheel, with the two bevelled wheels A and

B. But the mitre-wheel C is *in gear* with A and B at its opposite sides. Consequently when the pulley E moves forward, its little mitre-wheel encounters an equal and opposite resistance from A and B. Suppose the pulley E to be rotated towards the reader and the bevelled wheel A to be away; C would roll round B, i.e. it would rotate on its axis in the same direction as the hands of a watch; whilst, under the same circumstances, but with B away, C would roll round A in the reverse direction. From this it will be seen that when E is rotated (the resistance to A and B being supposed equal), the mitre-wheel C will exert an equal and opposite pressure on A and B. As a consequence C will be unable to rotate, but being carried bodily round by E, will drag A and B round with it; whilst A and B, being connected with their respective road wheels, will communicate to them the forward motion of the pulley. Readers will have noticed the important qualification introduced above, viz. that the resistance offered by A and B shall be equal. This can only be the case when their respective road wheels are running in a straight course, and on a similar surface. If one wheel is traversing a rough and the other a smooth part of the road, the resistance to A and B is unequal, the balance on the mitre-wheel C is destroyed, and the latter, rotating on its axis, rolls forward and imparts a larger proportion of driving force to the wheel which is less impeded than its fellow. This is, in point of fact, the besetting weakness of this and every other balance gear, considered as driving agents. Suppose the machine to be driven forward along a straight road of uniform surface. The action of the balance gear is then perfect; the power is equally expended on both wheels, the wheels, the balance gear, and the upper chain pulley revolve as one piece. But now suppose the near road wheel (for example) to be on a sudden impeded by some obstacle in the road, such as a large stone. The balance on the mitre-wheel C is at once destroyed. It commences to rotate on its axis, and in the same degree that the *near* road wheel is retarded the off road wheel is put forward, or *vice versâ*. In other words, the road wheel that requires a larger portion of the power to help it over the obstacle receives in fact *less* than the comparatively speaking unimpeded wheel. The result is that a side strain is thrown upon the steering wheel whenever there is an inequality in the resistance encountered by the respective road wheels. So long as this difference in the resistance is only small its effect on the steering wheel is comparatively unimportant. But all riders are familiar with the fact that if a serious impediment to one of the driving wheels is met with, the steering wheel is powerless to hold the machine in a straight course; the driven wheel runs forward, the steering wheel is forced sideways along the ground, the machine swerves suddenly to one side, and if moving fast not improbably turns right over. Hence it will be seen that an ideal balance gear, could such be devised, would be so constructed that the two road wheels, the main axle, and the driving gear should run as one piece so long as the machine is taking a straight course, because then both the driving power and the forward momentum would directly co-operate in enabling the road wheels to surmount the obstacles individually or jointly encountered. The side strain on the front wheel and the swerving of the machine would in this way be reduced to a minimum; and cyclists look forward with pleasure to the time when some efficient means of attaining this desirable end shall have been brought into use. Meanwhile, putting aside an ideal which is perhaps unattainable, they have in Starley's balance gear and its congeners a very excellent means of driving both road wheels straight forward, with the necessary provision for their separate and unequal motion when required, as already described. Starley's gear has attained a just celebrity as the first application of this principle to the tricycle; and though several varieties have since been brought out in which straight-toothed wheels are employed, there is not one which effects more than Starley's. Some, indeed, effect less than Starley's, inasmuch as they are not true balance drivers at all, but at every moment exert more pressure on one wheel than on the other The result is that the machine incessantly swerves to the side opposite to the wheel which receives the larger share of force. Riders have a ready means of ascertaining, even without riding, whether a machine is fitted with a true double-driving balance gear. Having swung or propped up the machine so that the road wheels are off the ground, fix the crank-shaft immovably in order that the upper pulley of the balance gear may be held fast by the chain. Then, with the hand move one of the road wheels round a complete revolution. If the balance gear is a true one, the other road wheel will also make a complete revolution, but in the *opposite* direction. Should it make either more or less than an entire revolution, the balance gear (improperly so called) is not a true and equal double-driver. Of this fact there can be no question, though opinions may differ as to the degree of importance to be attached to it.

As already mentioned, the aim in this chapter has been to explain the mechanical import of balance gear, not to describe in detail its varied construction. Those readers who desire to acquire a knowledge of the several varieties now in use will find full information in the valuable Handbook compiled by Mr. Henry Sturmey, a work which is strongly recommended to all cyclists.

The part played by the balance gear in racing is of equal importance, seeing that but for its intervention the sudden spurts and desperate efforts of the racing tricyclist would inevitably overcome the grip of his steering wheel on the path, and cause his machine to swerve and sway in a most dangerous manner. Any cyclist can demonstrate this fact easily by mounting a single-driving machine of any type and jerking the pedals; he will find that the driven wheel will exhibit a strong tendency to run round the loose wheel, and he can then appreciate what such a tendency might do at the final moment of a race.

The invention of the balance gear has not exactly made cycling possible, because it was possible under other conditions, viz. with two chains, and so on; but the application of the balance gear to tricycles has made high speeds on road and path safe ; it has given the tourist the power of back-pedalling with the same perfect action of the balance gear, and it has done much to encourage the lightening of tricycle wheels. The two-chain and similar methods had the disadvantage of throwing a great deal of strain upon the wheel which happened to be actually driven, and so in many ways the sport of tricycling has been benefited by its application. But, as pointed out above, there are balance gears and balance gears, and it will always be well for riders to ascertain for themselves the merits of the gear fitted to their chosen mounts. Of course Starley's is one of the best, and a large number of firms fit that gear under a royalty to the representatives of the original inventor. Amongst the firms whose balance gears are made on sound lines will be found most of the best names in the trade. The main feature which should be investigated is the relative size of the bevel wheels ; these, it is obvious, must have exactly the same radial leverage, i.e. must be of the same diameter to the outside edges of the teeth, otherwise the effect of the same amount of resistance on each wheel will become unequally operative in the gear-box, and that defeats the whole object of the contrivance. The results are sometimes attained in a most ingenious manner, as, for example, in the Sparkbrook balance gear, of which an entirely novel method is employed. The case becomes the equivalent of the cone wheel, and the action of this gear is as accurate and certain as can be wished ; whilst experience has demonstrated that it will stand lengthy and hard wear, it is fitted to sociables and tandems, in which it receives a very complete testing, and it has behaved admirably. It is invariably fitted to machines bearing the name 'Sparkbrook,' and the machine having that designation is much liked on both road and path. The Premier tricycle is fitted with another excellent pattern of Starley's balance gear which works satisfactorily, as also are the Humber machines. In the double-steerer of this type, the gear is fitted in a remarkably neat manner, the end of the axle-sleeve is enlarged into something like the neck and shoulders of a wide-mouthed bottle, as shown in fig. 37.

The off wheel is fixed to the axle, which comes right through and has fixed to it just inside the neck of the bottle a bevel-wheel; the other wheel runs loose on the end of the axle and has cast upon its hub another and similar bevel-wheel, whilst two coned wheels running on pins fixed to the circumference of the bottle (or case as it is properly termed) engage these two bevel-wheels, and the gear acts in the usual way. This was the first gear constructed in so small a compass, and as it is closed in most thoroughly, there is less noise from the teeth, whilst the adoption of two coned wheels does a great deal to prevent undue shakiness. This is an easy running and most satisfactory gear. There are many more good adaptations of the same principle, but a bad balance gear, bad in principle or badly fitted, will entirely spoil a machine. Once in a way the gear may require cleaning, and care should always be taken to keep it well oiled, whilst careful riders after each oiling spin one wheel with the other on the ground so as to ensure the spread of the lubricant.

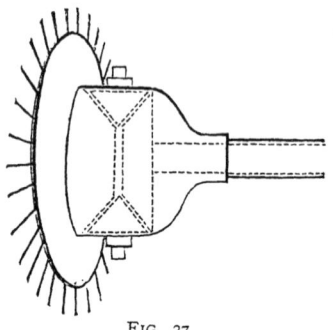

FIG. 37.

Throughout the foregoing remarks, we have, for the purposes of description, assumed that a balance gear only acts when power is communicated to it through the small coned wheel (or its equivalent). It will be obvious, however, that a balance gear equally acts when the machine is being pushed, or is running down hill, with the rider's feet on the rest. The reader will do well, therefore, clearly to grasp the general principles of all balance gears accurately constructed, viz. that they consist of a contrivance by which the two driving wheels are coupled together in such a way that either wheel can outstrip the other when the machine is deflected from a straight course by the steering; that when so running each wheel receives its due

CONSTRUCTION. 347

amount of force from the balance gear; that, when the machine is running straight, with an equal resistance opposed to the two driving wheels, each of the latter receives an equal share of the power; but with this further unavoidable drawback that, the driving wheels when opposed (as they usually are) by an unequal road resistance, are no longer in balance, and are therefore driven by the balance gear in unequal degrees, the effect being the same as if the machine were very slightly steered to right or left, although, under the circumstances supposed, the steering wheel prevents any actual deviation of the machine from a straight course.

GEARING LEVEL, UP AND DOWN.

One of the first points which a tricyclist requires to have explained to him is the gearing of his machine, for 'What are you geared to?' is a question which very often nonplusses the beginner. The gearing of a tricycle is dependent upon the relative size of the pulley wheels over which the chain or chains run, the difference in size increasing or decreasing the number of wheel revolutions as compared with the pedal revolutions.

Fig. 38 is merely a guide diagram to illustrate the positions of the pulley wheels in a balance-geared tricycle; the lower one B fixed firmly to the pedal crank, and the upper one A being part of the balance gear and carrying inside the pinion wheels of that gear (which is fully described elsewhere), and thus communicating the power to both the driving wheels; the relative sizes of A and B control the gearing of the machine, except when a two-speed gear intervenes, which will be fully explained further on.

FIG. 38.

There are three divisions into which gearing can be divided, viz. level gearing, gearing up, and gearing down.

LEVEL GEARING.

When a machine is level geared the pulley wheels are of exactly the same size, as in fig. 39; the chain C C passes over both, and as each pulley wheel necessarily carries the same number of teeth, and as the teeth are equidistant on each wheel, they naturally fall into the links of the chain in due proportion. For example, suppose each pulley wheel carries nine teeth, it is clear that if the bottom pulley B be rotated once, it will 'eat up' (to use a graphic and comprehensible expression) nine equidistant links of the chain, and in doing so will cause a corresponding number of links to be withdrawn from the upper wheel A, which will thus make a corresponding (complete) revolution. The pulley wheel A being directly in connexion with the main axle, it follows that for one complete turn of the pulley wheel B, which is rigidly keyed on to the pedal crank, the driving axle will also make one complete revolution; the machine in this case is said to be geared level to whatever may be the size of the driving wheels in the case of a tricycle, and to the driving wheel in the case of a dwarf bicycle, in which the same principle obtains without, however, the intervention of a balance gear. Supposing the tricycle thus geared to have 48-inch wheels, it would be conversationally described as 'geared level to 48.'

FIG. 39.

GEARING DOWN.

Gearing down may be defined as that arrangement of the pulley wheels which causes the pedals to revolve more frequently than the driving wheels. Fig. 40 shows such an arrangement. The lower pulley wheel, for easier comprehension, is supposed to be the same size as in the foregoing figure, and carries nine teeth, but the upper pulley wheel A is made

CONSTRUCTION.

larger and carries eighteen teeth (this merely to simplify the explanation, as in practical use such a combination would seldom be found). It is obvious that for one revolution of the bottom pulley wheel B (in effect, of course, one revolution of the pedal crank to which it is keyed), the bottom wheel B will as before take up nine links of the chain C C, but inasmuch as the upper wheel A has eighteen teeth upon its periphery, the nine teeth of the lower wheel only effect half a revolution of the upper wheel, and *two* complete revolutions of the wheel B (i.e. the pedals) are required to make A complete one revolution ; and as A is attached as heretofore to the main driving axle, when the pedals have made one revolution, the driving wheels will only have made half a revolution. Thus to arrive at the gearing of the machine it is necessary to take the result of a complete revolution of the pedals ; this, if applied to the former example, a 48-inch tricycle, would be half a revolution of a 48-inch wheel which equals 24-inch, and the machine would be said to be 'geared down to 24.'

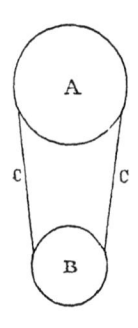

FIG. 40.

GEARING UP.

A machine is said to be geared up when the pedal revolutions are fewer than the revolutions of the driving wheel. Fig. 41 illustrates this point, using the proportions as before, and in this case they are not so unusual, for Mr. P. T. Letchford's racing Humber tricycle in the season of 1885 was fitted with 30-inch driving wheels geared up to 60, his top pulley having five and his bottom pulley ten teeth. In this figure the top pulley wheel A carries nine teeth and the bottom one B eighteen teeth. If the pedals (rigidly connected with B) are made to complete one revolution, the pulley wheel B will eat up eighteen links of the chain, but as wheel A only carries nine teeth, it must make *two* complete revolutions to satisfy the requirements of the wheel B. Wheel A being attached as before to the main axle, the driving wheels will have to make two complete revolutions for one turn of the pedals, and a 48-inch machine so arranged would be said to be 'geared up to 96.'

The mechanical advantages of gearing will be clear to the most superficial observer, even though such a one has but little knowledge of mechanics. For example, when a machine is geared down as in fig. 40, each pedal comes more frequently into action, and the crank leverage becomes of more value; thus supposing the geared-down machine to have a 6-inch crank, the rider is practically driving a 24-inch wheel with a 6-inch crank or lever. This provides an unnecessary amount of power, as 40- and 50-inch machines are easily driven by ordinary riders with 5-inch cranks, and although the immense power thus available at the low gearing may prove of service up steep hills, yet on the level the pace at which the feet would have to be rotated would tend to exhaust the rider. Conversely, of course, a geared-up machine requires more muscular exertion, but the pedals move more slowly. Supposing anyone foolish enough to have a machine geared up to 96-inch as in the last example, the rider would be driving a 96-inch wheel with a 6-inch crank, which would of course necessitate very hard labour indeed, and a moderate gear of about 56-inch will be found amply high enough for the strongest rider on the road. Light active riders without much muscular power will do better with a lower gearing, as they are able to pedal quicker with less exhaustion. For this reason a tolerably low gear is very advisable for ladies who ride tricycles, and 50-inch may be taken as a very fair average. Very heavy men with great muscular power are very soon exhausted by rapid pedalling, but they can be easily suited with a higher gearing, which simply requires more muscular exertion and less rapidity of motion. On the racing path, higher gears have proved successful. The machines used in races are exceedingly light, and the paths being level and easy, there is

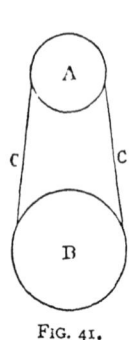

FIG. 41.

nothing to interfere with the running of the machine. Some riders have tried very high gears, up as high as 70 or even 80 inches, but the slow action was all against that quick spurting which is a *sine quâ non* in race riding, and moderate gears of about 60 to 64 are found most suitable. Mr. Percy Furnivall, the One Mile Amateur Tricycle Champion of 1885, won that race upon a Beeston Humber, with 40-inch wheels, which was geared thus : pulley wheel A (see foregoing figures) 10 teeth, pulley wheel B 15 teeth. In this case wheel A had to make three revolutions to two of wheel B's, or one turn of the pedals caused the driving wheels to turn one and a half times, the driving wheels being 40 inches in diameter, one and a half revolutions = 60 inches. Mr. Furnivall's machine would therefore be properly described as 'a 40-inch Humber geared to 60 inches.'

Gearing down is most advisable for weak riders and road men who primarily desire ease and comfort at the sacrifice of speed. A roadster tricycle with 50 inch wheels geared down to 44 inches or so, is in many cases a most suitable machine for the steady tourist. The large wheels are of especial value in mitigating the vibrations caused by the roughness of the road, the radial leverage being greater; and any rider of average weight who is desirous of securing comfort can soon satisfy himself as to the advantages which large wheels possess by practical experiment on rough or bumpy roads. Very diminutive riders and light weights can use a proportionately smaller wheel with comfort and ease, but for the average rider wheels not less than 46 inches in diameter are desirable, except in the case of a machine such as the Quadrant, in which all three wheels do their share of the weight-carrying, and special provision is made by fitting a large front wheel to prevent the discomforts so obvious in small-wheeled machines. For those who have the misfortune to be lame or weak in one leg, 'gearing down' affords a complete relief, for a machine geared down as low as in the foregoing example, i.e. to 24 inches, could be easily propelled with one leg, though, of course, at no very great pace. Messrs. Hillman, Herbert, & Cooper of Coventry have amongst their customers a gentleman with only one leg, the lost limb being replaced by a wooden one. He has one of their front-steering Premier tricycles, with a socket in place of a foot-rest for his artificial limb; the machine is geared down to about 30 inches, and although he lives in a hilly district, he is enabled to propel the machine at a pace which more than doubles his unaided rate of progression. This is a fair example of the especial value of low gearing. Beginners should always adopt a low gearing in the earlier stages of their novitiate, as they will not wish to attempt high speeds, and the easier work will enable the muscles to adapt themselves to the novel conditions without breaking down. After the first few months of riding different arrangements of gearing should be tried, until the one most suitable to the individual rider is discovered.

Gearing up, as pointed out above, offers especial advantages to strong, heavy, and muscular men, who, gifted by nature with plenty of physical energy, are capable of exerting the extra power required to propel the highly-geared machine. Such persons are easily exhausted by rapid movement, just as a heavy cart-horse, which would soon succumb if forced along at high speed, yet works satisfactorily at heavy but slow tasks. Many muscular and heavy men, somewhat past the heyday of youth, and not so active and lissome as they once were, have relinquished tricycling solely because their attempts to attain a good average pace upon a geared-down machine led to exhaustion and distress. Gifted with plenty of the power necessary for propelling a tricycle, they found themselves practically unable to apply it because of the rapid rotation of the pedals, the heavy and slow muscular frame suffering from the effort at rapidity. For such riders the change from a machine geared down to 45 inches to one geared up to 55 produces a complete revolution in their ideas as to the labour of riding. In place of the hasty plying of the feet and the breathless and exhausting attempts to accelerate their pace still more, the uncomfortable position, and the obvious waste of muscular power, the rider, mounted anew upon a high-geared, i.e. geared-up machine, will be seen sitting upright, in an easy attitude and driving his wheels with slow powerful strokes, finding a new and enhanced pleasure in the comfortable exercise of his muscular power and bodily weight. The experiences of the last few seasons will provide every cyclist with numerous instances of such a course proving in every way successful. Racing men as a body use high gearings; some, like Mr. Henry Sturmey of Coventry, a well-known writer on cycle construction, have tried gearing as high as 80 inches, but the gain in pace was not notable, whilst the difficulty of accelerating the speed—picking up the spurt—was a fatal drawback from a racing man's point of view. From 60 to 65 inches is the maximum for track gearing, where everything favours the easy running of the light and fragile racing machine.

The advantages of gearing up have been much increased by the reduction which has been effected in the weight of tricycles, a reduction for which every road rider owes to the racing men a debt of gratitude, inasmuch as the use of light machines upon the path has enabled and encouraged the makers to try and construct the road machine lighter too, so that at the present time machines are in constant use upon the road which a season or two back would have been considered light racers. The lightening of the roadster has enabled road men to use a much higher gearing than they could have done under the old system, and many of our best known men use a gearing of 60 inches and in some instances even more on the road. On the other hand, for very long road journeys a lower gear is sometimes adopted; thus Mr. T. R. Marriott, in his record ride in 1885 from Land's End to John o' Groat's, rode a Marriott & Cooper Humber tricycle geared only to 50 inches. High gearings can only be used upon the road with any real success by riders who, in addition to mere physical strength, are also practically accomplished in the art of pedalling, fully described elsewhere, which is a *sine quâ non* in the matter of racing and fast road work. When this has been thoroughly mastered, the rider can make the necessary experiments to ascertain which gear suits him best. It is customary with many cyclists who use tricycles or dwarf machines to alter their gearing for the winter. The lower bracket with the lower pulley wheel in the case of a tricycle (or the pulley wheels in the case of a safety bicycle) is changed for one with a wheel of smaller diameter and fewer teeth, and the chain shortened one link or so, thus making the machine easier to propel, but of course slower at the normal rate of pedalling. A good many racing men, on the other hand, ride all the winter through on high-geared machines, thus building up heavy muscle against the racing season, when plenty of path work and no road riding will again fine it down to racing shape; for hard work of any sort invariably slows the racing man, whilst path work will weaken him, so that he cannot ride well on the road for some time after he gives up racing and racing training.

TWO-SPEED GEARS.

The subject of two-speed, or 'speed and power' gearings, as they are more properly, but also more cumbrously termed, follows naturally upon a dissertation upon the effects of gearing up and down. Ere this the reader will have recognised the advantages which would obviously accrue to a rider if he were able to have a machine geared both up and down, so that whilst on the level he would be able to fly along with his wheels running at a high gearing, say, for example, over 60-inch, yet when he encountered a hill he would have the means of instantaneously changing his gear to 38 or 40 inches, and thus reap the known advantages of a low gear when facing a stiff ascent. The want of such a combination having declared itself to all practical observers very early in the history of the tricycle, many plans for effecting that object have been brought forward and practically tested.

Some of the earliest, used upon lever-driven machines, depended upon the various powers obtainable by shifting the attachment of the driving links along the pedal lever. This primitive plan had many disadvantages. The segment through which the pedal moved was notably enlarged when power was required, so that at the normal speed the rider had to ride with a very short reach, or else he would have to overreach himself at power; moreover, the lever action used was not at all suitable for cycling, and thus this earliest method of obtaining speed and power at will fell into disuse. Other plans depending upon the principle of the lever, and requiring a reciprocating movement of the same nature, were tried, and had the same result, and it became evident that two-speed gear to be successful must be combined with the widely popular rotary action. The earlier types were faulty; they threw cross and irregular strains upon various parts of their internal mechanism; they were mechanically vicious in construction, and only irregularly performed the work they were called upon to do, whilst some were in constant action except on the few occasions when hills presented themselves, thus setting up a continuous friction during the whole time the machine was being ridden with the normal speed on. This of course seriously diminished any advantages they might under other circumstances have possessed. Under some systems the internal friction rapidly wore out the gear, and caused it to fail in its functions after comparatively little use. Only two types possess any measure of practical value. The first type is that represented by the gear known as the crypto-dynamic, invented by Mr. W. T. Shaw, and manufactured commercially by the Crypto Cycle Company of Chiswell Street, with the various gears brought out approximating to it in general plan; and the other type is the two-chain system as successfully adopted by the Sparkbrook Company in their two-speed tricycle.

A practical and scientific cyclist writes as follows on this subject:—

We shall therefore limit ourselves to a general description of these two typical systems, under which all the others may be properly classed.

The Crypto-dynamic gear depends for its results on the action of an epicyclic train of wheels, hidden within a narrow box which bears on its outer circumference the pitch-teeth of an ordinary chain-pulley. The epicyclic train adopted in the Crypto is made up of three components, all working round a common centre; viz. a central pinion, a stud-disc carrying four small planet wheels in gear with central pinion, and also with an internally locked wheel which forms the third and outermost portion of the train. As is well known, the components of an epicyclic train, when set in motion, severally vary both as to velocity and direction, according as one or other is held fast or caused to act as the driver. Thus when the central pinion is fixed and the internally locked wheel driven, the stud-disc (or middle component) is by the small planet wheels carried round at a slower rate than the internal wheel (or driver). In other words, the internal wheel must pass round once, and a bit more, in order to procure a single complete revolution of the stud-disc; how much more depends upon the relative sizes of the internal wheel and the central pinion! Suppose this proportion to be such that the internal wheel has to make 1·5 revolution to one of the stud-disc (as is actually the case in the most popular form of the Crypto), the power is said to be 1·5, and this is the number by which the upper speed must be divided in order to ascertain the lower gearing. Suppose now that with these same proportions, and with the central pinion still fixed, the stud-disc bearing its planet wheels is driven round, the converse effect takes place; i.e. for each single revolution of the stud-disc the internal wheel makes 1·5 revolution. In this case the speeding-up is 1·5, and there is, of course, a loss of power corresponding to the gain of speed. This is the arrangement adopted by Mr. Britain, and formerly known under his name, though now merged in the crypto-dynamic gear. The one system gives an access of power; the other an access of speed. Deferring for the present any attempt at a technical description of the mechanism employed, we shall endeavour briefly to show how the principles of epicyclic gearing, as explained above, are made to produce the desired results.

In the power-gearing, as we said, 1·5 revolution of internal wheel (I.W.) produces 1 revolution of stud-disc (S.) Therefore 1 revolution of I.W. = $\frac{1}{1·5}$ or $\frac{2}{3}$ revolution of S. Now it is to the internal wheel that the power is *always* imparted by the crank-shaft either directly, if the Crypto is there fixed, or through the chain if, preferably, the Crypto is fitted to the main axle; whilst it is the stud-disc that *always* actuates the driving wheels of the tricycle. In the case of single-drivers, the stud-disc drives the wheel either directly or through the chain; in double-drivers, the balance gear is interposed between the stud-disc and the driving wheels.

The central pinion is always in unity with the clutch, and by means of the latter can, at will, be fixed immovably as in the cases supposed above, or it can be locked to the other components of the train, so that all three then revolve together, as one piece, in union with the chain-pulley, and the machine is then propelled at the higher of the two speeds, exactly as though the pulley on the upper axle were of the ordinary construction, and devoid of any internal mechanism. Suppose the pulleys to give a speed as of 60-inch wheels, then upon locking the centre pinion to the frame by putting the clutch over, the internal mechanism of the crypto begins to act, and the stud-disc reduces the speed to $\frac{2}{3}$ of 60-inch, i.e. 40-inch. In like manner 54-inch becomes 36-inch, and so on. Even the non-mechanical amongst our readers must see that the labour is necessarily lightened, and a sense of ease enjoyed, when the rider only performs two-thirds of the work previously demanded from him for each revolution of the pedal-shaft. In the most recent developments of the Crypto gear, the stud-disc is made to serve also as the driver of the balance gear, a combination which possesses many advantages as respects lightness, compactness, and general efficiency. The gearing-up principle, involving, as it does, the constant action of the epicyclic train except on the occasions when extra *power* is required, seems to have its chief utility as a substitute for pulleys and chains, over which it presents some considerable advantage in point of friction. For the benefit of those of our readers who desire to understand the mechanism of the Crypto gear, we here transcribe a description of that gear put forward by the makers.

Fig. 42 represents an outside view of the gearing, showing a portion of the chain and the lower part of the striking lever for changing speed.

In figs. 43 and 44, the internally-toothed wheel c, with its sleeve b, is shown removed from its position on the pedal-axle, in order that the connexion of this wheel c with the four pinions h, and of these with the central wheel e, may be clearly understood.

Fig. 45 shows the gearing in section, as applied to the pedal-shaft. a is the shaft or axle, keyed to which is the sleeve b forming the shaft of the internally-toothed wheel c. Revolving on the

358   CYCLING.

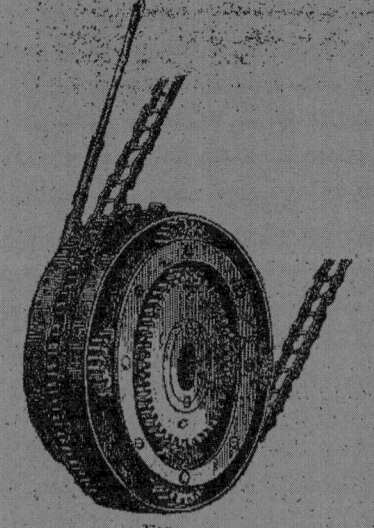

Fig. 42.

Fig. 43.   Fig. 44.

CONSTRUCTION.

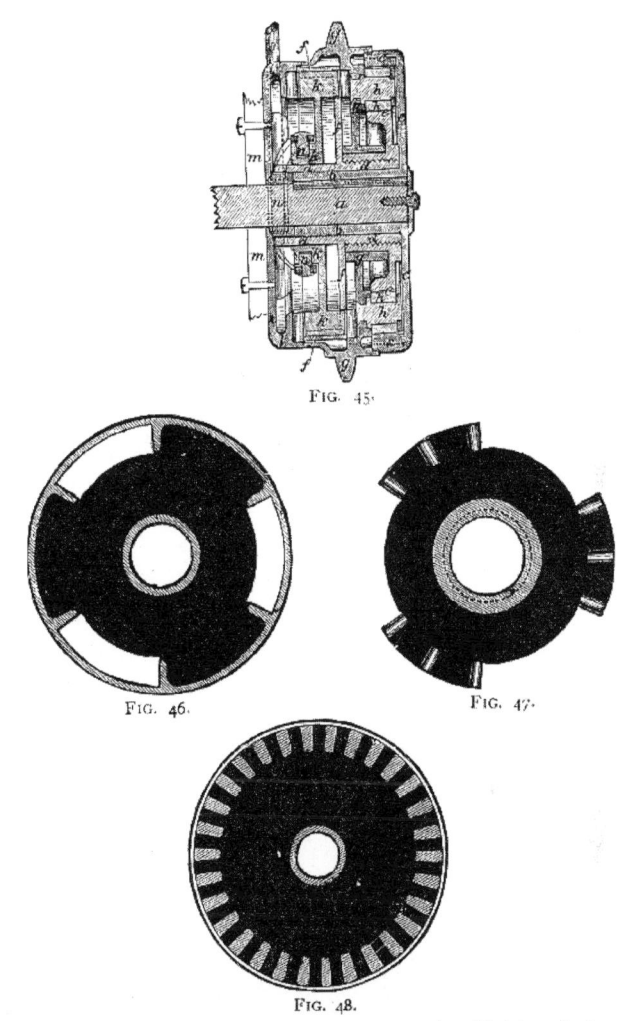

FIG. 45.

FIG. 46.

FIG. 47.

FIG. 48.

N.B.—The Crypto when constructed on the upper axle is modified thus: the ring of internal teeth is carried by the chain-pulley g, and the four pinions, with their spindles, are carried by the plate c, which latter imparts motion to the road-wheels.

sleeve b is another hollow shaft d, fixed upon which are the central wheel e and the flanged collar f. g is the chain-pulley with a hollow axle turning freely on shaft d. The pulley g on the side towards the internal wheel c carries four spindles and pinions h (two of which are here shown), gearing with the central wheel e, and the internal wheel c. The spindles on the side next the internal wheel are supported by a ring (seen in fig. 43) fastened to supports projecting from the side of the pulley at spots equidistant between the four spindles. Fig. 46 is a front view of the flanged collar f, with its three segmental slots, opposite which, on the face of the pulley g, is a circular row of sunken teeth, shown at fig. 48. A similar row of sunken teeth is cut in the face of the fixed disc l, which is attached to the frame of the machine m. Riding inside the flanged collar f, and in perpetual engagement with it, is the clutch k, shown in front view at fig. 47, which is a disc with three segmental pieces projecting from its periphery corresponding in size and shape with the segmental slots shown at fig. 46. The segmental projections (shown at fig. 47) are each of them armed on both sides with raised teeth shaped so as to fit the sunken teeth before referred to. The clutch k is terminated in the centre by a grooved ring, which takes a bearing on the sleeve d. By means of the lever o and fork connected with studs running in n the grooved ring, the clutch k may be slid along the sleeve d, so as to engage its teeth either with the sunken teeth on the pulley g, or with the sunken teeth on the fixed disc l; or it may be left in the central or free position, as shown in fig. 45. In the last-named position the gearing is free to rotate in itself, as in running down hill, and no work is done. If the clutch k is pushed along so as to engage with the sunken teeth on the chain-pulley g, the central wheel e, by means of the flanged collar f, is locked to the pulley, and being unable to rotate, the small pinions h and the internal wheel c are likewise bound to the pulley, and the whole of the gearing rotates as part and parcel of the chain-pulley. This is when speed is required. If, however, the clutch k is pushed along the other way so as to engage with the sunken teeth in the fixed disc l attached to the frame of the machine, the central wheel e is held fast and is unable to rotate, but the pulley g is left free, whereupon the pinions h upon being set in motion by the internal wheel c, run round the fixed central wheel e, and rotate the chain-pulley at a reduced speed relatively to that of the pedal-axle a and internal wheel c. It is by this means that the extra power is obtained. Its degree depends upon the relative sizes given to the central, planet and internal wheels composing the gearing.

It will be observed that all the parts have broad bearing-surfaces, not liable to cut, and that the sleeves move round each other in the same direction when the gearing is in operation, thus minimising friction.

The Crypto gear is a highly-finished and durable piece of mechanism; due provision has been made for adequate strength throughout; and the extra weight of the gearing, over and above that of an ordinary pulley, varies from $3\frac{1}{2}$ lbs. to 5 lbs. according to the nature of the machine. Its size is $5\frac{1}{8}$ inches × $2\frac{1}{2}$ inches.

In the two-speed arrangement, fitted by the Sparkbrook Company, two pairs of pulleys and two chains are employed, one set gearing up for speed, the other gearing down for power. The upper pulleys are fixed side by side, centrally on the main axle, and the chains are carried down to two pulleys running loose on the crank-spindle within the lower bracket. The clutch proper is fixed to the spindle, and is capable of engaging with either of the two pulleys, according as a little lever, pivotted to the central tube, is depressed by the left or right foot. Left in horizontal position, the lever withholds the clutch from contact with either pulley, and free pedals are the result. When the lever is pushed down by the foot (which is removed from the pedal for that purpose), the corresponding pulley is locked to the spindle and is capable of driving the machine forwards. Its adjacent pulley being free in the spindle, is then driven round by the chain, through which it is connected with the pulley on the upper axle.

The principal error into which the beginner in the use of a gear falls, is to attempt to keep up a high rate of speed when using the 'power.' As will have been gathered from the foregoing remarks upon gearing up and down, the pedals are the special point affected by the change. The machine running on at the same pace, when the change is made from a high gearing (speed) to a low gearing (power), the pedals will be notably accelerated as to the pace of their revolution. Now it is quite possible for a cyclist to mount one of the machines known as home-trainers—which consists mainly of a fly-wheel fitted with pedals, which the rider rotates as rapidly as possible for the purposes of practice—and without any check upon the fly-wheel, which revolves with very great ease, to utterly exhaust himself within three minutes, although when the fly-wheel has once been started very little muscular power is required to keep it moving. It is, in short, 'the pace that kills,' the extremely rapid motion of the legs, without any call upon the muscular powers for an effort, beyond that necessary to keep the legs moving, being quite sufficient to cause the exhaustion. In using a two-speed gear, the beginner rides at a fair pace with speed on until he arrives at a hill. Being naturally anxious to see how his new acquisition works, he puts on the power at once, and finding the pedals suddenly revolving with ease and rapidity, he almost unconsciously attempts to keep up the speed thus suddenly developed, with the inevitable result that in a very few minutes he is completely exhausted, not by the actual muscular effort, but by the rapidity of the action. 'To climb steep hills requires slow pace at first,' and this maxim is especially applicable to the use of speed and power gears. The user will therefore do well to bear in mind this strict injunction, 'Do not attempt to acquire speed when using the power gear.' When riding along the level with the speed gear in action, the rider should count the revolutions of the pedal and try and accustom himself to a regular rate of work, say, for example, 55 strokes per minute. On arriving at a hill the pace should be kept up with the speed gear until it is obviously slowed by the stiffness of the gradient; the rider, counting steadily and keeping the same rate of pedalling, should then shut in the power gear sharply, and, without accelerating the pedal revolutions at all, keep steadily at work. The relief will be instantly perceptible, but it is at first very difficult without great watchfulness to avoid undue rapidity in pedalling; the work suddenly becomes so much lighter, whilst the pedals seem almost to run away from the feet, that the novice is betrayed into hurrying; all the more so because at the same time the pace of the tricycle slows noticeably, and as most riders involuntarily gauge their rate of progression by the road or hedges they are passing, this is a sore temptation to spurt, which must, however, be resisted. By keeping up a regular and unaccelerated beat, the user of a gear will find that the ascent is easy, though the pace is relatively slow. At the same time it is sufficient to overtake all ordinary pedestrians, most carriages, and every tricyclist who walks his machine up-hill, and this, more especially when the tricycle is laden with luggage, is a material advantage, as the work of pushing the machine up-hill is both irksome and awkward. In those districts where long gradients or steep hills are frequent, an intelligently used two-speed gear will soon be regarded as a *sine quâ non*. If the gear is not intelligently used, if the rider indulges in scrambling and frantic attempts to attain a racing pace with a 36-in. gearing, he will find the gear worse than useless, and had better discard it. It will take the most careful and observant rider a couple of months to become properly *au fait* in the management of a gear, so that he shall know in a moment when, where and how to use it, and at what rate of speed he may safely attempt to progress. In many cases so much is expected from the gear that the user's first feeling is one of intense disappointment, which is only modified into doubt after some weeks of constant use. When the rider is in this state of mind, half doubting whether it is advisable to drag the extra weight of metal and fixings around with him, let him send his geared machine away, and use for a week—he won't want it longer—a machine geared to the middle power of his two-speeded tricycle; one day's, nay, one hour's riding on a give-and-take road will impress him more with the advantages and merits of the speed and power gear than any amount of theorising or dissertation. In no case would the assertion that we do not recognise a blessing until we have lost it be more appropriate, always supposing that the two-speed gear adopted is one of those which have been proved effectual by practice, and not one of the disintegrating contrivances which are occasionally palmed off upon the unwary as 'two-speed gears.' As might be naturally supposed, two-speed gears have proved of marked benefit to the users of tandems and sociables. When two persons are riding, it may often occur that one of the cyclists may become exhausted and weaker than his companion, especially, for example, when ladies ride, and then the other rider has to propel not only the machine, but an outside passenger in the person of his companion. In such cases the two-speed gear becomes a necessity, as every slight rise can be easily negotiated with its assistance. It is, for example, recorded in the cycling press that Mr. Hillier in the autumn of 1886 took a young cousin of his, weighing nearly nine stone, for a ride over some sixty miles of diversified, and in some places hilly country, and during the journey the young lady did not put her feet to the pedals for more than five miles altogether. With one exception all the hills were ridden, and as the high power of the gear fitted to the Humber tandem was 60 inches, such a trip would have been an absolute impossibility but for the lower power, which was about 38 inches, and this power enabled the rider to carry his passenger up several steep hills *en route*, and all could have been ridden had it been worth while to attempt the feat. Thus a two-speed gear on a tandem may be regarded as a partial guarantee against the failure of the weaker portion of 'the crew.' One of the most satisfactory fittings of a speed and power gear is that of the Crypto gear to the upper axle of a Humber tandem. As in the machine alluded to above, the strains are evenly distributed, the gear is comparatively out of the way of dust and grit; the striking rod being relatively short acts rapidly, and with complete rigidity, and is also very conveniently placed for the use of the rider. The upper axle, in fact, is without doubt the proper place for the gear to be placed, and in that position it is productive of the most satisfactory results.

In the use of two-speed gears certain points should be observed to secure the best results. When shifting the gear the pressure of the feet should be momentarily eased, and this with a very little practice will be found to be done automatically.

The shifting should be done sharply, but not too forcibly, as very little power is required to alter the clutch block if the pedal pressure is relieved as suggested. On the other hand, the shifting should not be done too lightly, or the clutch may not get home, and as a result will slip before the catch can drop into its place. This point can be studied with the machine at a standstill with advantage. There should never be any hurry in changing a gear, seeing that it can never be a matter of seconds, and the satisfactory working of the gear depends to a great extent upon its being properly used.

Lubrication should not be forgotten. The oil should be especially freely applied at first, so that all the parts of the gear may be fully supplied, and the superfluous oil which will ooze out should be carefully wiped off from time to time, so that it shall not get on the break-band; when it does, the latter should be taken off, and the surface of the leather cleaned with benzole, and roughed with a coarse file. When once one of the better class gears has got into running order by a few days' use, it will remain right in most cases for a very long time. This is especially so with the Crypto, in which special care has been taken to buttress all the parts one upon the other, and to guard screw heads and such like details, so that a check may be put upon any chance tendency to shake loose, and always supposing that the running is satisfactory after the first stiffness, which is inseparable from a new fitting, has worn off, it is highly impolitic to attempt to peer into the mystery box which contains the gearing.

The use of two-speed gears will assuredly extend, and many makers are now prepared to fit them to machines. Some few firms yet object to the extra trouble, but the buyer of a tricycle, single or double, who desires to ride easily and comfortably, should insist upon having one of these fittings adapted to his new mount. For racing, the two-speed gear is of no service; one rider did have a very high gear with a lower power in the American races in 1885, and the result was, that in shifting it at high speed it stuck at the free pedal, and he fell forward, causing the machine to come into violent collision with another competitor, a severe accident being the result.

The free pedal is of considerable service, and it is well that it is so, for it is obviously inseparable from the action of a two-speed gear. Its advantages are singularly apparent upon Humber pattern tricycles, as by putting the lever at the free point, the pedals become practically foot-rests, without interfering with that foot control over the steering which is of such moment in that type of machine. On tandems, too, especially when the break power is quite adequate, the free pedal is of peculiar advantage, as with a novice or a lady in front there is often a difficulty in regaining the pedals, after a run down hill, the rapidity of their rotation having to be checked ere it is safe for the novice to bring his or her foot within their range. Under these conditions the gentleman throws in the free pedal, and holding them horizontally they form a comfortable foot-rest on which the other rider's feet are kept. When the bottom of the hill is reached the speed gear is thrown in, after a word of warning, and no trouble is experienced in picking up the work.

SAFETY BICYCLES.

The production of the tricycle in its more practical and modern shape, which was of course a vast improvement upon its antitype, the 'velocipede,' induced a large number of persons, who from age, nervousness, or other causes were reluctant to trust themselves upon the giddy heights of an ordinary bicycle, to take to cycling in its safer form ; and although some of them soon learnt that a clever man could have as dangerous a fall as he desired out of a tricycle, yet the majority enlarged their experiences until nothing but the look of the thing prevented their attempting to ride the bicycle itself. Many of these recruits were, comparatively speaking, young men with plenty of energy, muscle, and activity ; as soon as they became sufficiently initiated into the mysteries of the sport, they began to recognise certain drawbacks which are inseparable from the use of the tricycle as compared with its more dangerous but less clumsy congener. The machine was heavy in contrast with the bicycle, and its bulk made it difficult to stable. In the meanwhile a number of ingenious ideas were being formulated in the direction of dwarf bicycles. The first in point of time was the 'Pony Bicycle,' constructed by the Coventry Machinist Company. This was a dwarf machine with a long swinging link on the end of the ordinary crank, at the bottom of which was placed the pedal, so that the rider had a straight leg with his foot very near the ground. This, however, was not very favourably received. The power of the rider was enormous, but the necessary rapidity of the pedalling was exhausting; the principle of gearing up had not been tested, and, if it had been, would have been inapplicable to the method of driving adopted; so the 'Pony,' after a brief run, fell into desuetude.

The first practical, and perhaps the most markedly successful, Safety was the invention of Mr. John Beal—'The Facile.' This little machine, which will be described further on, was brought out by Ellis & Co., of Farringdon Street. Being a lever machine, the action was shortened and made easier than the crank action of the 'Pony;' and although gearing up was as yet unapplied to it, still the very easy action enabled many riders to attain great pace upon it.

The successful use of the chain in tricycles opened the eyes of inventors to the possibilities which chain-driving possessed for Safety machines, and it occurred to one ingenious mechanician that a chain-driven bicycle geared up, with a small wheel, placing the rider very close to the ground, would not only rival the bicycle's rate of progression for ordinary road work, but also insure a certain amount of safety if the machine were constructed on proper lines. The small size of the front wheel was at the same time noted by every practical man as a disadvantage which would have to be encountered and provided for, the small radial leverage being liable to increase the relative effect of common road obstructions; and in the first Safety bicycle of this type placed upon the market this point was most fully recognised. Small wheels, as can be easily proved by practical experience, as well as by more scientific methods, jar terribly over bad roads, and the problem arose how these various disadvantages, inherent in wheels of small diameter and dependent on the same conditions, were to be overcome. In the course of numerous experiments it became evident that the rider could not with safety sit right over the front wheel, for not only would he find that there existed a strong tendency on the part of the hind wheel to tilt up, but the jar and vibration from the front wheel would be very great. It was therefore necessary to put the rider some way back, behind the front wheel centre, and also to carry the pedals back. A good deal of the rider's weight thus fell upon the rear wheel, and to make this also of small size simply transferred the source of the vibration from the front to the back wheel. It was found, therefore, that when the front wheel was diminished in size, the rear wheel had to be enlarged.

Fig. 49 may be taken to represent a Safety bicycle fitted with two equal sized wheels, the rider being seated at C between

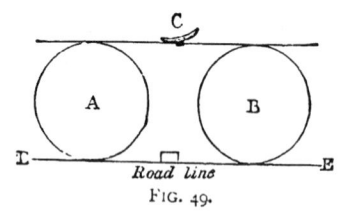

FIG. 49.

them. This vehicle in progressing, as in fig. 50, meets with an obstacle D. The wheel A rises over the obstacle, but the seat C does not rise nearly so high, and the rider's weight is thrown back towards B. A having surmounted the obstacle, the wheels resume momentarily the position of fig. 49, and

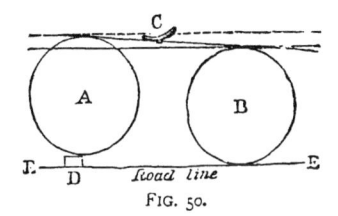

FIG. 50.

then B in its turn surmounts the obstacle (fig. 51). The radial leverage is of considerable importance, it being clear that a

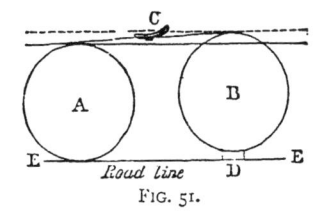

FIG. 51.

wheel three feet in diameter will surmount a six-inch obstacle with greater ease than an eighteen-inch wheel.

As pointed out above, the first satisfactory Safety was 'The Facile,' which was well named, the action being essentially easy; and it still retains its popularity as a sound and serviceable little roadster. This machine was followed in course of time by the Kangaroo type of Safety—a dwarf bicycle driven by chains on either side of the front wheel. These Safeties became very popular, but were in their turn superseded by the rear-driven Safety bicycle, of which type 'The Rover' was the pioneer.

An exhaustive account of the newest developments in single and tandem machines will be found in the second part of this chapter.

PART II.—MODERN CYCLES.

THE SAFETY BICYCLE.

Since the first edition of this work saw the light, the rear-driving Safety bicycle has rapidly made its way in public favour both upon the road and the path. It possesses certain qualities which must of necessity cause its votaries to increase in number, and eventually it will be the mount of the vast majority of cyclists. Its most conspicuous point of advantage is to be found in the fact that, as it is a geared machine, the actual leg-reach of the rider makes no difference at all in the pace, and, whether he be 4 feet or 6 feet in height, the cyclist can ride a machine geared as high as he pleases. The rear-driving Safety thus puts the shortest man on an equality with the tallest, and, as a result, with possibly one exception, no big man has ever shown to advantage on the path on a Safety. The Safety cracks are, almost without exception, men of, or under, the average height, stocky and muscular, and in very marked contrast to the best riders of the Ordinary on the racing-path, who have nearly all been tall men. Keith-Falconer, J. S. Whatton, W. L. Ainslie, Harry Osborne, H. L. Cortis, Herbert Synyer, Fred. J. Osmond, Richard Howell, R. H. English, and many more notable cyclists, stood six feet and over in their stockings.

Out of one thousand men chosen at random from the ranks of cycling, possibly not more than 10 per cent. would be tall enough or long enough in the leg to stand any chance in first-class Ordinary racing, and even then, when these riders were trained, but few would possess the special gifts which make a man a champion. On the other hand, *every one of the one thousand riders* can be a Safety champion, providing he has the powers, whatever his height and length of reach.

What applies to the path in this connection applies also to the road, and the safety of the rear-driver down hills, and in the dark, the smaller surface it presents to the wind, and the gearing possibilities, all make it additionally popular amongst the coming generation of riders. Not only does the 'young idea' adopt this type, but a number of steady and respectable *bonâ-fide* tricyclists have been induced to desert the three-tracker for the single-track machine. The actual difficulty of learning is very slight indeed, especially if the rider has a little preliminary practice on a tricycle, so as to accustom the feet to the rotary motion; and, when once this stage has been passed, the rider will never regret that he took the trouble to learn.

The particular advantages of the Safety, as compared with the tricycle, are set forth at some length in the chapter devoted to 'Cycling for Ladies,' and most of the remarks made therein will apply in the case under notice.

The development of the Safety has been very rapid. The original cross or T frame has been replaced by a 'diamond' or lozenge shaped frame, or by a five-sided frame, every effort being made to secure rigidity. The coned hinge heads have been replaced by the ball socket head, a decided improvement, the front part of the frame consisting of a tube through which the standard from the front forks passes, rotating upon two rows of balls placed at the top and bottom of the tube frame. This affords great ease of steering, great rigidity, and easy adjustment. The introduction of this improvement added still further to the rigidity of the already very stiff frames, and as the faster riders ignored springs, had for lightness sake very narrow rims and very inadequate tires, the average rider unquestionably found the machine by no means comfortable, owing to the increased vibration, unless he was wise enough to remedy these defects by insisting on bigger rims and rubbers and the fitting of an adequate spring and a comfortable saddle. It was not to be wondered that riders who habitually used narrow-rimmed wheels, with tires so small and hard as to be 'no better than bootlaces,' to quote one authority on such subjects, found in the inflated and hollow tires, by comparison, an amount of comfort which was not so apparent to the riders who had for years been careful to be supplied with big rubbers, effective springs, and comfortable saddles.

Unless some care is taken in the placing of the saddle and the adjustment of the handles on a Safety, the rider is pretty certain to acquire a very bad style, crouching forward, with the arms fully stretched, the saddle being placed far back. This is utterly wrong as regards the average road rider who does not wish to race. The position is borrowed from the racing-path, but it is only crudely copied. The racing man, it is true, lays over and sits back, but, if he is carefully watched, it will be seen that his chest is kept open, all his muscles are strung up, his lungs in full action, and that the whole effort only lasts for a rela-

FIG. 52.—BAD POSITION.

tively short time. He sits back because, on the path, skill is more effective than strength, and the best results from ankle action at high speeds are attained from a position behind the work.

For the road rider all this is different. He wants to work continuously for hours together; he is not strung up to a high pitch of excitement, and his lungs are not fully called upon; his position should be fairly upright, and his arm position easy when holding the handles; his saddle should not be placed too far back, as he can put in sufficiently effective ankle work on the flat, and in climbing hills the nearer approach to the vertical position will prove of assistance. The roadster machine should have a ⅞-inch rubber on the front wheel, and 1-inch on the back, or moderately-sized cushion tires may be used. The handles should never be put too low, a most frequent fault and most difficult to cure, when once the rider has got set to it. An effective break is a *sine quâ non*, and the front wheel spoon break will be found most generally useful and reliable, except in the case of inflated tires, when a hand break is best, the spoon tearing the tire up in a very awkward manner. A break should always be used—it is absurd to do hard work back pedalling down-hill— whilst to put the feet on the foot-rests and let the machine fly unchecked is a reckless and dangerous proceeding. With a properly fitted break long down-hill runs become purely restful; the feet, being put on the foot-rests, which should be within easy reach, assist in steadying the steering, whilst

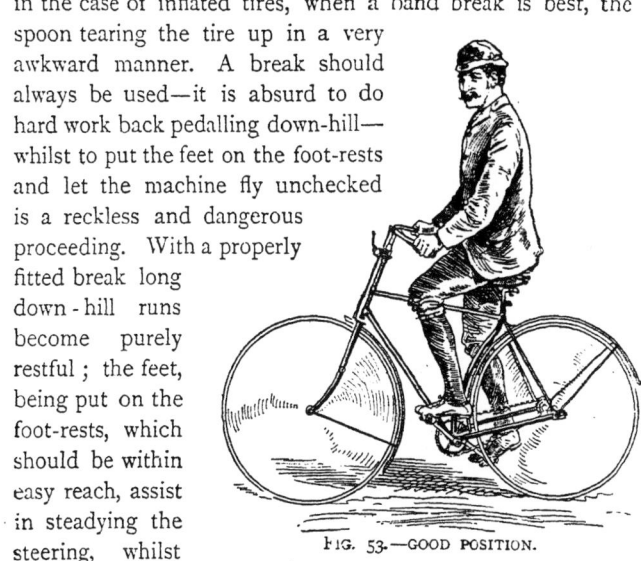

FIG. 53.—GOOD POSITION.

the break is ready to pull the machine up at short notice The tourist benefits of course by such rest.

The question of inflated and hollow tires is fully dealt with elsewhere. A Safety fitted with good sized soft rubbers, an adequate spring, and a comfortable saddle, will be found a sufficiently good mount for any person of average activity, weight, and vitality. The aged, the nervous, and the weak may need further protection, which may range from the spring-less rigid machine of the speediest road-rider to the rubber-tired Bath chair of the hopeless valetudinarian—not to mention that effective anti-vibrator, the ordinary 'stretcher.' For the rest, the general remarks on Safety bicycles and on construction will apply to this type of machine, which is unquestionably to be preferred for touring in hilly and strange districts, both by reason of its safety, handiness, and capacity of luggage carrying.

ORDINARY BICYCLES.

The Ordinary bicycle, as the full-sized machine of the first type is called, seems to be entering upon a new lease of popular favour—a development in the main due to the experience gained by the riders of rear-driven Safeties. The rider of the Ordinary bicycle in pre-Safety days considered it necessary to have his saddle very close to the head, so as to put him well over his work and to bring his handles close to him, these conditions being then considered essential to satisfactory riding. Naturally there were many falls, and the cyclist sought safety in a dwarf machine. He soon found, however, that in this type his handles were some way in front of him without interfering with his power; the same thing was true of his pedals. When fairly convinced of this, the rider reverted to the 'Ordinary' with the saddle placed relatively a long way back, and then found himself possessed of a large amount of added safety, whilst at the same time enjoying all the real pleasure which 'Ordinary' riding affords. But he also discovered that the vibration from a small and insufficiently tyred hind wheel was an immense drawback, and to meet that trouble a larger wheel was introduced. Of course the size was overdone at first; but a fairly large hind wheel, stoutly made, with a good-sized rubber, makes the new type of 'Ordinary' a singularly comfortable machine.

The general term applied to this new type is the 'Rational Ordinary'—one made by the Surrey Machinist Company; and the 'Farringdon,' manufactured by Messrs. Ellis & Co., may be quoted as typical of the style referred to. Fitted with ball heads, upright centres, and plenty of break power, the 'Rational Ordinary' will hold its own with any type of cycle, as is evidenced by the excellent performance of Godfrey White in the North Road Club's 100 mile race, he having covered that distance in 6 hrs. 48 min. 14 sec. on an Ordinary bicycle.

The Roadster and Racer bicycles of the Ordinary type may now be regarded as almost perfect. In Roadsters sound and adequate break fixings are a necessity. The Racer has been brought to a high pitch of perfection. One or two rear-driven full-sized bicycles are occasionally seen on our highways. One is the 'American Star,' a machine constructed in America and very popular in that country, as owing to its peculiar form it can be ridden with impunity over very large obstacles and rough ground. Mr. Stanley Heard, of Swansea, during visits to America, has ridden many miles on a 'Star' between the railway lines, bumping over the 'ties' or sleepers. As will be gathered from the illustration facing page 20, the machine is steered by means of the small wheel in front; it is driven by levers with a strap and pawl, the action on either side being independent. As might be supposed, it is heavy, and the steering is at first very unsteady. It possesses, however, unquestionable merits. Another bicycle steered in somewhat the same manner, but driven by a lever action, is constructed by the Claviger Cycle Company, and if perfected would doubtless possess all the merits of its American prototype.

Another type of full-sized bicycle will be found illustrated on page 160. The ''Xtraordinary' has long been popular with elderly riders who desire a certain measure of safety, and the same lines have been followed by the Claviger Company in their lever-driven 'Ordinary.' As was pointed out above, for road work and touring an ordinary bicycle on 'Rational' lines, with plenty of break power, can hardly be improved upon.

TRICYCLES AND TANDEMS.

In broad-guage machines a tremendous revolution has been effected since the first edition of this work was published. The types then popular have been superseded by others, and the machines generally are much better fitted and finished.

THE HUMBER TYPE TRICYCLES.[1]

When in 1880 an effort was made to improve the existing types of the broad-gauge machine, Mr. Thomas Humber turned his attention to a clumsy experimental machine with 60-in. driving wheels and a narrow handle-bar, which had been in the Beeston works for some time prior to 1879, and he soon effected such improvements that the remodelled machine was adopted by many prominent cyclists. The tricycle road championship and race of 1880 was won on a machine which was only colourably a tricycle. It was an ordinary bicycle, with two hind wheels a little distance apart. This, of course, gave the rider of the 'Rara Avis,' as the machine was called, a very great advantage; but the Humber tricycle, ridden by Mr. Hillier, though it failed to overhaul the winner, who had this somewhat unfair advantage, beat all the other tricycles in the race under somewhat unfavourable conditions. This machine, in its single form, has now quite disappeared; it has been superseded by the direct-steering or Cripper type tricycle, but these remarks do not apply to the still popular Humber tandem, which is shown in fig 54. The front saddle, handles, dropping bar, chain, and pedal cranks are all made removable, being held in place by a nut and two stays. The machine is steered by the rear rider, after the manner of an ordinary single Humber tricycle, which it in fact becomes when the front rider's seat and fittings are removed. As will be seen from the illustration, the riders are really seated on each side of the axle, and the heaviest must be placed behind or the machine will be liable to tip up, to meet which tendency the little safety wheel shown in front of the machine is fitted. The balance gear box is just hidden in the illustration by the left leg of the front rider. Both drivers drive it directly, and as a result the machine runs

[1] The illustration shows the President of the N.C.U., Lord Bury, mounted on a Humber Roadster. It is taken from a photograph by Hon. A. Keppel.

VISCOUNT BURY, K.C.M.G.
From a Photograph by the Hon. A. Keppel

CONSTRUCTION.

very straight and the weight is for the most part carried on the driving or, as it is much more reasonable to call them, carrying wheels, whilst the bite of the hind wheel upon the ground is rather more than just sufficient to enable the steersman to control the machine. The result in actual practice is that the machine runs marvellously fast, whilst the steering is particularly accurate and steady in the hands of a practised rider.

In purchasing a Humber tandem, the owner should con-

FIG. 54.—THE HUMBER TANDEM.

sider who is likely to occupy the front seat, as a light rider cannot satisfactorily fill the rear one if a heavy man is in front; but the disadvantages of light weight can be to a certain extent nullified by moving the saddle well back, which is usually very necessary with this type of tandem, for road work at least.

The rear seat should generally be arranged to suit the owner, as it is not adjustable, whilst the front seat is, and can be altered to suit each passenger. The handles should be low, so as to give a comfortable pull, without, however, overstretching the arms, as pointed out in earlier chapters, and should be brought rather back, so as to come more comfortably under control. The double-action Arab spring is especially advisable at the back. The rear rider will find that the presence of a person in front absolutely improves the steering, putting more weight on the carrying wheels, and taking some off the trailing wheel. The head (a ball head is an immense improvement) should be kept carefully adjusted, as a very slight looseness will soon wear beyond repair, owing to the immense strain which there is on that point, and care should also be taken to keep the hind wheel adjusted, as the accuracy of the steering depends to a great extent upon it. The machine will bear gearing up to 54-in. or over for ordinary riders. Comfortable foot rests are provided for the front rider, who should, however, be instructed to see that they are conveniently placed, as if not, they will cause him to reach forward, and thus disturb the balance, upon which everything depends. In descending very steep hills the front rider should sit well back. A two-speed gear is an excellent addition to this class of machine.

Taking a hint from the 'Rational' bicycle, quite a number of makers are now turning out this type of tandem fitted with a larger hind wheel than in previous patterns, and there is no doubt that the type in its tandem form will long remain popular with tourists and road riders generally. In its single form the Humber type, or 'double steerer,' has been almost entirely superseded by

THE CRIPPER TYPE TRICYCLE.

The name of this type is derived from the fact that the first machine of the pattern was ridden in open races by Mr. Cripps. It was designed and made at Beeston by Mr. Thos. Humber, and the first to appear in London was one sent to Mr. Lacy Hillier to be tested by him. Fig 55 is taken from a photo by Mr. H. St. J. Bashall of the Temple B.C., and shows the original form of the machine.

The steering is of the direct pattern, by means of a handle communicating directly with the front steering wheel, and the most convenient method of mounting and dismounting is by stepping on the axle from behind, most makers fitting for that purpose some sort of guard upon the left-hand side of the axle. In its details the original direct-steering tricycle pretty closely resembled the ordinary centrally-driven machine of its time, but it was not long before alterations and improvements were

FIG. 55.—MR. HUMBER'S 'CRIPPER' TRICYCLE.

made. The earlier machines were all automatic; that is to say, they were fitted with a cam and spring which brought the steering wheel back into position when the handles were released. After a time free steering was tried and pronounced successful, and automatic controllers are decidedly in the minority nowadays. Presently another alteration began to be noticeable. The wheel base grew longer and the front wheel began to increase in size, whilst simultaneously the rider was moved rather more forward, and the large-sized steering wheel became in part a carrying wheel as well. To merely give a list of the direct-steering or 'Cripper' type tricycles now offered to the public would fill a volume. Every maker constructs one or more machines of this pattern. The steering wheels are now made larger than the driving wheels, which have been reduced in size sometimes to an undue extent. All the successes of the past few years upon the racing path have been secured upon machines of this type.

The tandem of the Cripper or direct-steering type is, as might be expected, a very popular machine. The general lines are easily described : the front rider is placed rather further away from the axle, whilst his weight is balanced by the rear rider, who is placed behind the axle. The steering wheel is of large size, often as big as the carrying wheels, and as a matter of course the frame is strengthened and stayed so as to avoid any unsteadiness.

The methods by which the steering is effected are very various, there being a desire to place a lady rider in front, and at the same time to keep the control of the machine in the hands of the rear rider.

Messrs. Singer & Co., Coventry, and the Surrey Machinist Company both attain this desideratum in a very effective manner.

In other machines the steering is double, being linked from handle to handle or below the frame.

Amongst these machines, the Coventry Machinist Company's Club tandem ranks as one of the most successful.

Nearly every maker of note, however, constructs a direct-steering or Cripper type tandem. The type is deservedly popular, as it is steady and safe, especially down hill. The break power should be fully adequate, the wheel base well extended, and the riders not placed too near together. The front frame and steering wheel should be stout, as the strain thereon at high speeds and down hill is, of course, tremendous.

The weight of the riders should be carefully adjusted so as not to throw too much or too little weight upon the front wheel. The Cripper type tandem will undoubtedly hold its own for a long while, and it is difficult to see in what direction it can be surpassed for safety and comfort. The daily improvements in detail, however, make it quite impossible to give any lengthy description which would not soon be obsolete.

THE OLYMPIA TYPE.

This type of machine was introduced to the public in a practical form by Messrs. Marriott & Cooper. There had been tricycles of something the same pattern in the market before, but it was left to this firm to perfect the machine and put it prominently before the public.

The Olympia has a single driving wheel in the rear, without any of the complications of gear-boxes, and the rider is placed well back. The steering is effected by two smaller wheels placed upon a transverse axle. The machine in its single form has found much favour with the public. The tandem Olympia is also a success, some very remarkable performances having been accomplished on the road upon it. The steering is differential (i.e. the inner steering wheel strikes a smaller circle than the outer one on a curve), the weight is well placed, and the machine is very fast.

On the same lines, and claiming precedence in some material points, is the Corona tandem, made by the Crypto Cycle Company—an excellent machine in every way.

Imitation, says the proverb, is the sincerest flattery, and quite a number of Olympia type tricycles have been put on the market since the above-named firms popularised the machine.

THE QUADRANT TRICYCLE.

The advantages appertaining to wheels of large diameter have long been recognised by all practical riders, more especially by those who in the early days of tricycling were called upon to ride the front-steering tricycles, with very small steering wheels and very short wheel bases, which were at first adopted.

The jarring and jolting produced by these little wheels soon convinced the most unobservant riders of the advantages which larger steering wheels would possess; whilst others, again, recognised the value of a lengthened wheel base in easing the strain and jar of the road. The difficulty, however, was to mount satisfactorily so large a wheel as was required in a practical manner for steering purposes, and a good many methods were tried, which, however, did not prove satisfactory. At length the Quadrant Tricycle Company brought out the tricycle known by that name. The machine is central-geared, and very well constructed. Its especial features are to be found in the mounting of the large steering wheel. The front portion of the frame splits into a long fork, or U-shaped frame, carrying at its end two quadrant-shaped guides, in which the bearings carrying the steering wheel slide, the wheel being moved by the handles by means of connecting rods. As a result, the rider is put a trifle further forward, and the steering wheel becomes also in part a carrying wheel. By curving the quadrant-shaped slides fore and aft the steering wheel is thrown over slightly when turning; the chances of a loose tire are thus considerably reduced. The effect of this arrangement is in every way satisfactory. Vibration is reduced to a minimum, the steering is accurate, and the machine is extremely safe. Several different patterns are made, but the points of divergence are mostly in connection with the steering arrangements, some of the machines having the ordinary side steering, whilst others have bicycle-handle steering. The Quadrant tandem is a very sound type of front-steerer. Whilst this very simple and steady form of steering has also been practically applied to Safety bicycles of the Rover type, and as many of the eccentricities of that type of Safety arose from the unsteadiness of the heavy front wheel, it is more than probable that the Quadrant Safety will be as successful as is the Quadrant tricycle, and that is saying a good deal. The break and all incidental fittings are

PHOTOGRAPHY A-WHEEL

excellent, and if imitation be truly the sincerest flattery, the Quadrant Tricycle Company should indeed feel flattered, seeing how many firms are striving to satisfactorily mount a large steering wheel without infringing their patents.

THE COVENTRY ROTARY.

This is one of the oldest tricycles in the market. The machine was invented by James Starley, and manufactured by Messrs. Haynes & Jeffries under the title of the 'Coventry Tricycle.' As first made it was a lever tricycle, the driving wheel being rigidly fixed to a double-cranked axle, which was rotated by connecting rods. The adaptation of the rotary action with a chain worked a vast improvement in the machine, and in this form it passed into the hands of Messrs. Rudge & Co., and has become so far identified with them that it is officially styled the Rudge Rotary Tricycle. The Rotary differs very materially in design from almost every other tricycle in the market. On one side is placed the large driving wheel, which is rigidly fixed on a short axle which carries on its inner end the chain wheel; on the opposite side there is a long bar which carries on either end a small backbone head, and two Stanley-headed pairs of forks are fitted, carrying the steering wheels, which, of course, turn in opposite directions when the steering-handle is moved. It is clear, then, that if the machine were made very wide the single driving would cause a vast amount of 'screw' and consequent loss of power; but the Rotary is but 30 inches wide, and the side bar being of a good length, the small steering wheels, which are also carrying wheels, get a good grip of the ground and overcome to a very great extent the tendency to lateral motion. Once in a way, on very greasy stone sets, for example, the grip of the small wheels is found insufficient to overcome the lateral push of the driver, but for all practical purposes the grip is quite sufficient. The machine, which is a single-driver without many of a single-driver's drawbacks, can be built very light, and stay-rods judiciously disposed secure the necessary rigidity of the frame. The stay-rod from the rear end of the lateral bar to the driving-wheel end of the cross-bar forms a convenient luggage carrier if something more elaborate is not fitted, and the lateral bar is found most useful for many purposes. The photographer straps to it the legs of his camera, the 'sticks,' to use a professional term; a gun, an easel, a landing-net, or an umbrella will ride most comfortably when strapped along it, and, in brief, the Rotary tricycle may be said to be singulary well calculated to suit a vast number of riders who require stowage for a considerable quantity of luggage. The most important claim of the Rotary has, however, yet to be recorded. A large number of riders are much inconvenienced in the matter of stabling, and are compelled, if they ride ordinary tricycles, to pay heavily for standing room in some neighbouring coach-house. Riders thus circumstanced often give up cycling in disgust, but the Coventry Rotary is in many cases a satisfactory alternative; it can be wheeled through narrow doorways and passages with ease, and even if no outlet at the back of a house exists, it can stand in a room or a passage without occupying more lateral space than a perambulator. At first, especially after using other tricycles, the narrow wheel base seems dangerous and unstable, but after a few miles this feeling wears off. The sensitive steering is also an element of safety, and the marvellous performances which have been accomplished on the path and road on the Rotary are a standing testimony to its practical value. It must, however, be noted that heavy or largely-built riders feel cramped in the narrow space afforded by the machine. To riders unfortunate enough to lack the accommodation necessary for an ordinary tricycle the Rotary can be confidently recommended as in every way a reliable substitute.

SOCIABLE TRICYCLES.

The sociable trycycle, as the double one was most appropriately termed, took a great hold upon the public as soon as it was introduced; the 'Salvo' and 'Premier' sociables were amongst the first, and became immensely popular. Ladies as well as gentlemen patronised them; the two riders, seated side by side, could enjoy friendly converse as they progressed; and even now, when the tandem tricycle has completely overshadowed its predecessor, there is little doubt that for quiet and comfortable touring the sociable possesses many valuable points. As typical of its class we choose the sociable constructed by the Coventry Machinist Company, known as the 'Club Sociable,' which is adapted for a lady and a gentleman. The riders are placed side by side, the steering wheel is in front, and the break power is fully adequate; the machine is driven by one chain with a balance gear, and the pedals, on the side where the lady sits, are fitted with a Cheylesmore clutch action, so that they will remain still when the machine is running down hill, or when the roads are so good that the gentleman can relieve his passenger of unnecessary exertion. This free pedal contrivance is of the very greatest value, as the sociable is very safe down hill, and as a result the pace is often rather rapid, and it would be difficult or impossible for a beginner to pedal quickly enough, or to catch her pedals after a spin down hill under these conditions. Her companion simply instructs her to hold her feet still, and an easy and comfortable pose is the result, whilst the other rider can keep his feet at work or at rest as he chooses. When the lady is required to again assist in the propulsion of the machine, she simply revolves the pedals as fast as she conveniently can, and as soon as the clutch catches, she begins to perform her part of the work. That most dangerous accident, a blow behind the heel on the tendo Achilles, is also provided against. Many novices are lamed for a long while by incautiously bringing their heels within range of the flying pedals down hill, and this danger is provided against by the Cheylesmore clutch being fitted to the Club Sociable pedals on the lady's side.

SAFETY BICYCLES.

The pioneer type of Safety, the sturdy little Facile—now fitted with a most ingenious application of the Sun and Planet gear, which makes it possible to gear it up—is as much to the front as it was when the first issue of this volume was made, as on Saturday, November 10, 1888, Mr. Percy A. Nix, of the Brixton Ramblers, covered a distance of nearly 300 miles within 24 consecutive hours on one of these machines, and thus secured the coveted 'record.'

In the earliest machines of this make the trailing wheel was carried some distance away from the driving wheel, and the rider sat well back so as to put him just behind his work, the levers coming considerably behind the centre of the front wheel. Experience soon discovered many points which would admit of alteration, lightening, or strengthening. The wear in some parts, particularly at the point where the connecting-rod is affixed to the crank, was very severe. This has been obviated by the adoption of a very neat and effective ball-bearing. The pedal is an immovable bar of rubber, round which the foot rocks. Taken up with energy, the machine became very popular, and is in very general use; the front forks have a good rake backwards, which is conducive to safety, the hind wheel is not too small, nor is it tucked too closely under the driving-wheel, and the rider, unless he has a specially made machine, is placed very much between the two wheels, with his pedals exactly under him, thus being in the best position for the exertion of his strength. As the pedals carry to a great extent the weight of the rider, and are always well behind the centre of the driving wheel, and thus within the wheel base, the machine is obviously safer in that respect than any vehicle in which the foot may momentarily (necessarily at the moment of fullest work) pass out of the wheel base. The handles are conveniently placed low, thus giving the best position as regards the arms and shoulders for hill climbing and hard work generally, in which the little machine excels, the extra leverage and the nearly straight arm pull being especially valuable. The driving action of the Facile is quite different from the rotary action of ordinary cycles, the foot describing a segment of a circle backwards. If the weight be kept fully on the descending pedal when it has reached its lowest point, the retarding effect must be tremendous, and in practical use this is found to be so; the back-pedalling powers of a 'Facile' rider are always very noticeable.

To become a sound and good rider of the Facile entails a little care, without which no learner can succeed. He must first ascertain the exact stretch of his leg, and so adjust the pedal lever that he can throw out his leg without having to 'hold back' at the bottom of the stroke. When pedalling on good roads, and under favourable conditions, many good Facile riders let the pedal go momentarily at the bottom of the stroke, whilst others depend entirely upon a trick of the ankle to take the pressure off at the right moment, by dropping the heel very quickly at the lowest point. To thoroughly appreciate the Facile it is necessary to drop all rotary action riding for some time, and to ride only the little machine under notice; the novice may put the levers at a short reach, and ride thus for some time, studying the effect of over-pressure, and cultivating a quick little upward jerk of the toe to take off the power at the end of the stroke; the idea being to get as much pushing done as possible during the stroke, without retarding the machine by maintaining the pressure at the end of it.

Having satisfactorily mastered the action, the levers should be adjusted to gradually lengthen the stroke, until the leg is fairly extended at the lowest point. The heels should be kept well out, so that the joints act in a straight line; the position should be easy, and the rider should keep on altering the adjustment until he really sits upon the saddle, except when exerting the full force necessary for hard up-hill riding. The work of driving the machine, as compared with that necessary to propel an ordinary bicycle, is very light, as the leverage is great, and the wheel small. If pace is required, rapid action must be carefully practised. To secure this, the rider must make a marked difference between hard and light work, and should therefore try to cultivate the easy, light, rapid action, which, with but few exceptions, will carry him well through the longest day's journey. Of course hill practice should be taken, but nine out of ten men during the first season of their Facile riding are inclined to make too much of a job of it, the actual muscular force required being but slight, skill and easy rapidity of action being everything. The very simple motion of the legs through so limited a space and in one particular direction makes the Facile an especially favourable machine for heavy and elderly riders, whose stiffness of limb will not be productive of such fatiguing results on this favourite little Safety, whilst another very opposite class of riders, the young and weak, find the long leverage an adequate compensation for the extra rate of pedalling necessary to attain a reasonable degree of speed. This type of machine may be especially recommended to youths; it is very safe, vibration is carefully met and checked, and—a very important point—the reach is adjustable. The youthful cyclist will be able, as he grows, to alter the levers to meet his steadily lengthening stretch of limb, a valuable point in cases where the purse is not an over-deep one. The geared Facile is an excellent specimen of this class, and stands almost alone as one of the best examples of lever-driven Safety bicycles.

REAR DRIVING SAFETIES.

In this class the driving is effected by the rear wheel, and the steering by the front wheel; to quote the very lucid description of one observer, 'the big wheel is a little one, and the hind wheel is in front.' This type presents certain points of advantage, and others which do not tell in its favour. As the feet do not possess any direct control over the steering wheel, as they do in the ordinary bicycle, the steering itself becomes somewhat sensitive, and the hands cannot be removed from the handle-bar without danger.

This type of machine possesses the following advantages: *Safety*, *Easy Steering*, a *Narrow Tread*, a *Single Chain*, a *Good Luggage Carrier*, and lastly *Speed*.

As to its *safety*. Any observer will see at a glance that, from the position of the saddle with reference to the axle of the front wheel, headers are impossible. Mount the machine and ride it over bricks, large stones, &c., and a shaking is the only result to the rider; take it against any obstacle sufficient to stop the front wheel, and the machine will merely fall on its side, when all its rider has to do is to put his foot on the ground.

There is not much to be said as to the special attention necessary to attain a mastery of Safety machines. The rider must have constant practice to enable him to keep in good form for fast road work, and this exercise, when the gearing is high, should be graduated so as not to overstrain the muscles at first. In some cases the very long cranks fitted will be found irksome on long journeys, and the rider will do well to have the cranks proportionately shorter, and the gearing lowered to correspond. Thus if a six-inch crank, when the machine is geared to sixty inches, is found awkward and uncomfortable, the throw may very well be lessened to five and a half inches; and if the work is then found to be too heavy, the gearing may be reduced to fifty-five inches, or lower, with satisfactory results. This is a point to which makers and riders would do well to give more attention, as the varieties of machine are few as compared with the varieties of the men who ride them; and whereas one man may do well on a given machine, it may go far to break up another rider of equal physique, but different make and style of riding. The various bearings and working parts of a Safety should always be carefully looked after, as of course a very slight slip or alteration in the set of the pulley wheels may make a vast difference to the running of the machine; and the strain upon the bottom bearings on each side is considerable, as might be expected, seeing that a long crank on one side has nothing but the bearing to balance it on the other. Thus it often happens, especially with new machines, that the lower wheels do not run exactly parallel with the upper ones on the hub, and the result is that the chain rubs against the sides of the teeth, or, in very bad cases, mounts them, locking the wheel, breaking the forks or bearings, and in any case causing a severe fall. The rider on a new Safety should therefore frequently look at the pulley wheel or wheels, and run his eye along them to see that they are running true and straight. The chains require very careful adjustment, especially at first. If too tight they cause the bearings to bite, and tend to break the balls in them; whilst if they are too loose they may mount or slip off the teeth, and in any case are most uncomfortable in this condition. The rider should therefore be very careful to keep them at the right tension, which is best accomplished by slinging the machine and undoing the adjusting screws; put both chains dead tight by pulling down the sliding brackets or raising the wheel, as the case may be, then by equal and gradual stages loosening the chains until the wheel runs freely and the chains on either side appear equally loose. A very little looseness is sufficient, but it must be apparent. When the adjustment has been carefully made, the machine should be ridden for some little way to see that all is right, and then with the aid of a long-handled spanner the nuts should be finally tightened up. This may require to be done very frequently at first, especially with the less carefully constructed machines; but after due care the adjustment will remain practically rigid for a long time. The chains may be left dry, or oiled, but the best preparation to use with them is vaseline and plumbago.

Knee breeches and stockings are almost a *sine quâ non* for Safety riders, as the revolving cog-wheels and chains seize upon loose garments and cause severe falls. The vibration of all Safety machines is considerable for the reasons pointed out above, and the double-action Arab cradle-spring is a vast assistance in breaking the jar. In ordering a roadster plenty of rubber on the wheels should be stipulated for, as this is effective in the same direction.

TANDEM SAFETY BICYCLES.

A good many attempts have been made from time to time to construct a satisfactory tandem bicycle, but it was not until the rear-driving Safety bicycle had been perfected that the tandem became a practical development, and now it bids fair to prove a success. There are, of course, many points upon which inventors have yet to exercise their ingenuity, but the machines already before the public have demonstrated that the Tandem Safety Bicycle will in the future prove of value. The Premier, the Hero, and the Lightning tandems have as yet found most favour if ridden continuously by the same riders. There is little doubt that the machine is both safe and speedy. Moreover, a lady can in most cases occupy the front seat, and, strange to say, a person unable to ride a bicycle in the ordinary way can be put on in front of a skilful rider without interfering seriously with his comfort. Altogether the machine has a future before it, without question.

THE CHAIN.

The chain is a very important feature in tricycles and Safety bicycles, and as such deserves a word of notice. It is composed of steel links and pins, and is very carefully made, as so very much depends upon its wear and accuracy. Like certain other parts—rubber tires, springs, bearings, and the like—the chain used in the cycling trade is very largely supplied by one firm, the Abingdon Company, the chain in question being known by the same name, and being a speciality with the Company. The details of its construction are very numerous, just as the various operations to finish an ordinary pin are wonderfully multiplied. For the Abingdon chain immense care is taken with every small detail. The two sides of the link are stamped very accurately to gauge, having a raised and a depressed end to fit over and under the next link of the chain ; on the inside the hole prepared for the pin is circular but on the outside it is sexagonal, with a shallow drift cut round the circular orifice, all this being done in the substance of a thin link stamping. The pin with which the links are to be joined is of an exact gauge, the ends being carefully shouldered so as to bed up against the plates at the sides, and when put in position the pin-ends are riveted over, and in the process they spread out into the sexagonal drift on the outside of the link, and are thus prevented from revolving in the pin-holes. The whole design is most fully and carefully carried out, and the chain under the most critical inspection appears absolutely faultless, whilst the very close fitting does away with much of the 'stretch' so usually found in cheap chains. The Abingdon chain is now so widely adopted for all classes of chain-driven velocipedes, that it is hardly necessary to describe any other chain, the only points of divergence usually being found in the less careful and accurate finish of the others; though, of course, there are a number of other good chains in the market which do not enjoy the wide popularity and consequently the severe testing which this chain enjoys.

Another chain which has found much favour is Illston's self-lubricating chain. The idea is a very novel one. The middle link, usually a solid, is in this case made in two parts, and is hollow, and this hollow link is filled with a very thick grease. The slight motion of the double parts of the link and the pins, which pass through the viscid lubricant, cause it to work out in infinitesimal quantities; and thus the chain is kept lubricated without the necessity of oiling it—always a dirty job—for a practically unlimited time. This chain was used on the Cripper type tricycle upon which George P. Mills rode from Land's End to John o' Groat's, and he was much pleased with its working. Another of these chains has been in use for over eighteen months, and the amount of lubricant appears but slightly diminished. This chain only requires an occasional wiping to remove the dust, and has been proved by practical experience to be a very valuable innovation.

THE DICYCLE OR OTTO BICYCLE.

This type of machine, in which the rider balances himself above the axles of two wheels, found much favour with a few enthusiasts. For some seasons it has now, however, fallen into desuetude. Should it ever again become a popular mount, it will be in the shape of Welch's Patent Club Dicycle, made by the Coventry Machinist Company.

This very pretty little machine is a 'positive' steerer—that is to say, when the steering handle is turned to the right the machine at once turns to the right, whether the rider be driving or back-pedalling. It has been tested by some of the most experienced riders belonging to the Otto Cycling Club, and has been pronounced by them to be a decided advance upon all previous dicycles.

The merits of this peculiar class of machines are many: the balance is only maintained by the 'fixed points,' the pedals and saddle being always balanced one against the other, and in practice it is found that the weight of the rider is for the most part carried on the pedals. This must result in the perfection of propulsion, inasmuch as the bodily weight is inevitably employed at each descent of the pedal; moreover, the peculiar balance makes the machine progress very well against the wind, as on encountering a wind a rider can get so much more directly over his pedals. The machine makes but two tracks, and the running is peculiarly 'lively.'

MANUMOTIVE VELOCIPEDES.

Just as many a cyclist on entering a rowing boat for the first time longs to use his legs instead of his unaccustomed arms for its propulsion, so the rowing man, condemned through absence from the river to idleness as regards his favourite form of sport, desires to propel himself by the use of his arms upon a tricycle; and since the development of the lighter machines of the present day, the idea of a manumotive carriage, so familiar to our forefathers, has been frequently mooted. A large number of designs have from time to time been laid before the manufacturers and those practically acquainted with the resources of the trade, but very few have been sufficiently promising to warrant their being put practically upon the market. The best known and most widely used manumotive carriage, and the only one which has been pushed for any length of time, is the 'Velociman,' made by Messrs. Singer & Co. of Coventry. This vehicle was invented by the Rev. Mr. Charsley of Oxford, and has been carefully tested in practical use, and improved by its inventor since the day when, in a rather crude condition, it first saw the light. In its present improved form it has been widely adopted, and many cyclists would be surprised to learn the number of these machines which are yearly sent out from the Alma Street Works. As will be gathered from fig. 56, the machine is a balance geared rear-steering tricycle, but in place of the familiar rotary action and pedomotive gear there is a fixed crossbar which is practically the rider's stretcher. Mounting, the rider seats himself upon a comfortably upholstered seat, and finds on either side the horn handles of two vertical levers. These drive a cranked shaft which carries upon its right-hand end a toothed wheel, which in turn engages a short chain which runs over the gear box ; the action is a reach-out and pull-back, the seat does not shift, and the feet are placed firmly against the stretcher, though the machine is also fitted with a lever attachment in the form of a crossbar on which the feet can be placed when the work becomes very hard, and thus assist in driving the machine. The steering is perhaps the most original feature of the whole arrangement. A bar comes from the hind-wheel head to the back of the seat, where it is fitted with a half-circular cushioned back, against which the rider leans, and thus as long as he keeps his back unmoved steadies the steering, and makes the machine run straight ; a very slight twist of the hips will at once steer the carriage round any ordinary corner or curve, whilst for complete and short turns, which are never made at high speeds, the rider can reach round with one hand and steer the machine. Strange as it may seem, this method of steering, when mastered by practice, is accurate and remarkably steady.

The machine has an excellent record on the road, the Rev. Mr. Charsley himself, though no longer young, having ridden some very long distances thereon. Messrs. Singer hold testimonials from riders which at once demonstrate its use in special cases. A rural postman at Llandilo, who had the mis-

FIG. 56.

fortune to lose a leg in an accident, has not only been enabled to continue his work, covering over ten miles per day, by the aid of a velociman which was presented to him, but actually boasts of his pace, stating that he has covered six miles in 35 minutes. In another case, a machine was purchased by subscription for a gentleman who was only 3 ft. 6 in. in height and had little or no power in his lower limbs. His first essay was to ride twelve miles in three hours over hilly roads. Another rider, who had the misfortune to lose both legs, finds his velociman invaluable, and travels long distances upon it; and in many other such cases the machine has proved an invaluable boon. The following notes from the pen of one of the most experienced users of a velociman in the country convey all the necessary hints for its adequate management, whilst some details of the machine's performances are also added.

VELOCIMAN MANUMOTORS.

It may be advisable to give a few hints to beginners in riding the Velociman tricycle, but before doing so, it will be well to remark that when the peculiar action is acquired, there is no exercise more easy or more adapted to the natural motion of the body and limbs.

The Velociman is essentially a hand tricycle, and therefore the inventor has made the motion of the hands his first consideration. There is no doubt, however, that the additional foot power adds immensely to the ease of propulsion, especially when stiff hills have to be overcome.

Anyone who has had experience in rowing has felt the enormous power he gets when each scull meets an equal resistance from the water. There is no side strain, such as is felt when propelling a canoe by means of a paddle. For this reason the inventor of this machine so arranged the throw of the cranks that the lever should act simultaneously, giving as nearly as possible the sculling action when the cranks are below the centre; as they rise above the centre, the action of the arms becomes a pushing force, equally with both arms, thus retaining the equal tension of the muscles. Now there cannot be a pulling force without a stretcher, carefully adjusted, nor a pushing force without something to push from; hence one leg at least must always rest on the stretcher, while the back of the rider must feel the guiding pad during the entire forward stroke. This leads one to speak of the guiding pad. There is no part of the machine which needs a nicer adjustment than this. On it depends chiefly the ease of working. The writer has often met men riding this tricycle with apparent labour, because the adjustment of the levers to the pad was incomplete. He has altered it by shifting the ends of the levers, or reducing the throw of the cranks, and the consequent relief has been immediately visible. Let the rider bear this in mind. The machine must be so adjusted that, *when the arms are fully extended, the back must still just feel the pad.* This is necessary, too, for the guiding, and gives the rider perfect confidence. He feels the machine to be part of himself.

In turning a sharp corner, or completing the circle, since the movement of the back would be excessive, it is very easy to move one hand from its lever, and apply it immediately to the guiding pad.

The steering by means of the back is most perfect. The idea frightens many people, but the practice immediately dispels all fear. The movement of the back is so slight for any deviation required in ordinary riding that it is scarcely perceptible. The will of the rider seems to guide the machine without any thought of the why and the wherefore.

The inventor of the Velociman has ridden from London to Oxford, without a dismount at any of the hills. Those who know the road will recollect some formidable ones—for instance, Dashwood Hill, rising from the Wycombe Valley on to the Chilterns, through Stokenchurch—a hill always very loose and exceedingly steep, about three-quarters of a mile in length. He has also ridden from Oxford, through London, to within a few miles of Brighton, i.e. a hundred miles in a day. In fact, he was the first to show, on this machine, that a tricycle was capable of performing such long distances—a fact which has since been proved, in a much greater degree, by younger men than himself.

It will be seen from the engraving that the chain of this machine is very short, and at a considerable height from the ground. Hence it is not so subject to get clogged with road sand, and wants very little adjusting.

THE CARRIER CYCLE.

The issue of 'The Tricyclist' for August 10, 1883, contained a somewhat lengthy leader from the pen of its then editor, Mr. Lacy Hillier, upon 'The Practical Carrying Capacities of the Tricycle;' based upon a remark made by the Postmaster-General on August 1, in Parliament, to the effect that tricycles were not adapted for parcel carrying. The writer went at some length into the question, and pretty clearly demonstrated the fallacy of the remarks of the Postmaster-General. In subsequent issues of the same journal, many correspondents bore out the editorial remarks, one writer saying that he often carried 50 lbs. of goods upon his tricycle on a round of twenty-four miles. In the issue of September 7 of the same paper appeared another article headed 'A "Carrier Tricycle," A Suggestion Adopted,' announcing the fact that Messrs. G. Singer & Co. had taken the matter up.

The Coventry firm sent to the original inventor of the 'Carrier' an experimental machine—fitted with a seat for a passenger, in place of a basket, and though it was geared very low (42 inches), Mr. Hillier rode a mile on the Crystal Palace track with Mr. G. Pembroke Coleman (official handicapper and time-keeper to the N.C.U.), who weighed $11\frac{1}{2}$ stone, on the front seat, in 4 mins. $49\frac{1}{5}$ secs.

'The Evening Standard' was one of the first of the daily papers distributed by means of the 'Carrier,' and Messrs. Singer & Co. supplied the proprietors with some excellent machines, the weak points of which were soon discovered in practical work and corrected rapidly; whilst at the present time the 'Carrier' is found very stable, and wears well.

The next material advance made by this useful vehicle was its adoption by the Post Office authorities for use in connexion with the Parcels Post. Not only were single 'Carriers' adopted, but some excellent double ones were also put upon the road. The Parcels Post carriers are now fitted with a high round-topped holder, with separate compartments for heavy, light and lengthy articles. The appearance of the scarlet official tricycles in the streets of London, alongside the heavily laden newspaper tricycles, opened the eyes of business men to the capacities of the tricycle in this direction, and many of them soon began to adopt the tricycle for use in their own businesses. Singers have fitted up a carrier with a milk-can for the matutinal delivery of 'Simpson' in the London district; another with the ladders, paste-pot, and bills of a bill-poster in an extensive way of business,[1] whilst a thousand and one articles of daily consumption are distributed throughout the metropolis by means of the ubiquitous 'Carrier.'

THE COVENTRY CHAIR.

Yet another departure is to be found in the use of the tricycle as a passenger vehicle. The Coventry Chair, made by Messrs. Starley & Sutton, has been rather extensively tested, and it has been found that an active rider can carry an average person at a good rate for remarkable distances. On several occasions the regular use of Passenger Tricycles has been mooted, but up to date only spasmodic attempts have been made to put this scheme in working order. Possibly the day is not very far distant when the use of the Passenger Tricycle will equal in England the popularity of the Jinricksha of Japan.

THE COOLIE CYCLE.

The Coolie Cycle is a tricycle made by the Coventry Machinist Company, fitted with a seat and footboard in front for the 'sahib,' whilst a saddle and pedals behind accommodated the coolie, who, to use the phraseology of the early inventors of self-moving carriages, 'conducts' the machine. The company sent a number of these cycles to the East, where they doubtless afforded amusement for the passengers and exercise for the drivers.

Several other firms have from time to time made passenger-carrying vehicles, and doubtless in the future others will be put upon the market.

[1] See Introduction, page 55

ACCESSORIES.

Luggage bags offer a very wide selection to the rider, whether bicyclist or tricyclist; the former is somewhat curtailed in his choice by the exigencies of his mount, which does not find accommodation for any very extensive baggage. The well-known Multum-in-Parvo, and its descendant the Clytie, are excellent for the purposes of the bicyclist—always providing that they are put upon a properly fitted carrier, such as the folding backbone carrier, manufactured by Messrs. Lamplugh & Brown. Unless the bag is thus carried it is liable to slip, and, if it does so, may cause a very bad accident. In attaching any of these backbone bags care should be taken not to strap them to the saddle loops or to the loops of the spring, as in either case this course interferes with its elasticity and with the set of the saddle. On this same backbone carrier, a long bundle rolled in mackintosh, as suggested in the chapter on Touring, can be strapped, and if a stout piece of leather, some four inches wide, be made up in the parcel, it will form a convenient bottom for the package to rest upon on the transverse carriers. Some small bags are also made which can be carried on the head carriers, but this is not very convenient, except in the case of the Nagel carriers, and even then the mackintosh roll is to be preferred. The tricyclist is decidedly better off in the matter of luggage carrying, and here also the choice of the particular bag must be left to the rider; in a great majority of instances it will be found best to use those bags specially designed to fit the carrier of the individual machine. Thus there are some excellent bags designed to fit the carrier on Humber type double-steerers, and special bags are sold with the machine by many makers. Several large firms give great attention to this class of cycling necessaries, and the wheelman desiring a tourist's outfit in this line should apply to Messrs. Lamplugh & Brown, or Messrs. Brooks & Co. of Birmingham, who always hold large stocks of the best and newest designs in bags.

The wallet, or tool-bag, is generally supplied with the machine, and in the case of mere fancy appliances the choice rests with the rider, but it is always well for the buyer of a machine to inspect carefully the wallet supplied; in some cases the thing furnished is a cheap and ill-made piece of leather work. Stitching, however good, is by no means everlasting, and the jar will soon shake one or other of the small straps loose. The wallet falling to one side is almost certain to get nipped between the wheel and the backbone as it sways about; and a bad fall ensues. The best way to deal with this class of bag, if it cannot be replaced by something better, is to carefully cut the stitching and remove the two straps; then with a sharp knife or chisel cut two parallel slits on either side of the back of the bag. each slit being made just beyond the stitching. If the straps are then put through with the buckle in its proper place the attachments will be practically secure, and any accident which may be caused by their breaking away will be averted.

A rider should always have a wallet as large as may be convenient, and should carry in it:

1. The spanner supplied with the machine; 2, An adjustable spanner; 3, An oil can; 4, A piece of copper wire; 5, Some cotton waste. The spanners, &c., should be wrapped up in a piece of rag to prevent rattling. A warning of some importance may well be given here against the practice, in which so many riders indulge, of carrying bells, spanners, &c. in their pockets. Nothing can be more dangerous in the case of a fall than a bell, for example, in the breast pocket of a riding jacket. Serious bruising if not actual breaking of the ribs must ensue, and no rider can consider himself as absolutely safe from the chances of such an accident. Against these dangers a stout and properly fitted wallet is a complete protection.

BELLS AND GONGS.

Every cyclist of sense carries a bell or gong, for not only is this course required by the by-laws in most districts, but these appliances are also by far the most convenient for warning passengers and vehicles of the wheelman's approach. Certain qualities are required in these accessories. The bell or gong should sound loudly and with ease, and the ringing should be continuous under ordinary vibration ; it should be so made as to be silenced with ease, and it should wear well in all its parts. Nothing, for example, can be more annoying than the loss, perhaps miles from home on a dark night, of the clapper of the bell; and yet with some of these contrivances this is quite an ordinary occurrence.

It would be impossible within reasonable limits to give even the names of half the bells or gongs at present offered to the public. The well-known firm of Challis Brothers, of Homerton, have long been celebrated for the excellence of their wares in this line—some of their deep-toned bells and gongs being very good. J. Lucas, of Little King Street, Birmingham, has also a great reputation for this class of goods, his combination gong being decidedly one of the best things in this line. An internal clapper mounted on a spring keeps up a continuous ringing under almost a minimum of vibration, whilst by a very simple device it can be securely locked into silence ; an additional clapper with a convenient thumb-piece is also fitted, so that the rider can strike a single warning note at will. J. Harrison, of Birmingham, is another maker who caters cleverly for the gong-using public. Not only has he several excellent designs in bells and gongs, but he has one little invention peculiarly of service in this connexion in the shape of an adjustable gong attachment, simple in design, which enables the user to put a gong on to any machine with ease. This is a point of considerable importance, as many riders can testify who, having purchased elaborate gongs, found to their cost that they could not attach them to any convenient point of their machines.

An almost interminable variety of bells, gongs, and such like attachments are offered to the cycling public, and with the above-mentioned list of the cardinal points required, the rider will have little difficulty in finding some suitable and practical appliance for the purpose.

LAMPS.

A lamp for both bicycles and tricycles is a necessity. Some cyclists used to boast that they never used a lamp; but, like the gentleman who is proud to declare that he never wore a great-coat, the lampless cyclist places himself in a most uncomfortable position for no good reason. There was a time of course when the hub lamp was a serious source of danger, as it was ill-made, and the vibration to which it was exposed soon shook it to pieces, and it sometimes fell into the wheel, locking it and causing a nasty cropper. On one occasion a certain cyclist had an escape which was almost miraculous. He was flying a hill near Salisbury at top speed on a 60-inch Keen's Eclipse when a primitive hub lamp in the front wheel fell from its attachments, and was flung through the spokes and five or six yards down the road without causing an accident. The rider went on without stopping to pick up the dangerous fitting. Those days have now, however, passed, and the modern hub lamp is most solidly and soundly turned out by our best firms. There are, as might be expected, a very large number of patterns in the market, but the variations are generally to be found in the minor details of fixing, fitting, or attachment. A successful lamp for the use of cyclists should be of sound construction, all parts being rivetted and none soldered, of medium size and reasonable weight, with a good-sized reservoir, a fair width of wick (some of the wicks are unnecessarily large), giving a good light, and with an easily reached reflector. The tremendous vibration to which cycling lamps are exposed calls for some practical and trustworthy method of fixing and holding up the wick, and it may fairly be said that a thousand and one designs have been tried for effecting this and cognate objects. Salsbury, of Long Acre, has for many years been prominent as a practical and successful lamp-maker, and his goods are in every way serviceable. One of his latest lamps has a most simple contrivance for the effective management of the wick. A loop of stout wire is hinged at the back of the reservoir, and, passing forward on either side of the wick-holder, is bent over the front of the lamp. The result of this arrangement is that when the door of the lamp is shut it presses the forward end of the loop down and automatically locks the wick-holder, reservoir and wick-adjustment at one operation.

Lucas's King of the Road lamps also fully deserve the title. They are amongst the soundest, simplest, and safest lamps offered to cyclists, and every detail of the construction has been practically tested by thousands of users throughout the world. The fitting of prisms of coloured glass into the side-lights of lamps is a good idea, as it indicates to the drivers of any vehicle overtaking the cyclist the presence of the machine without the annoyance and danger which a tail-light always causes. In the matter of lamps the choice rests with the rider, but as a very great deal of his comfort, if not his safety, depends upon the quality and trustworthiness of his lamp, he will do well to patronise some old-established firm with a reputation for thoroughly sound work.

Every cyclist should carry a lamp, which will be found very conducive to his own comfort, as well as a means of keeping him out of the clutches of the law. Colza oil—into each quart of which a lump of camphor the size of a walnut has been put—will be found the best thing to burn; mixed oil will often smoke and fancy oils are not always obtainable. Colza is however to be purchased everywhere, and the rider is always sure of a supply in the most primitive village; olive oil burns well—if all the other oil be first emptied out. Reservoirs for carrying a supply of oil are sold, though few remain sound for any length of time in practical use; but tricyclists at any rate can always carry a stout flat bottle of oil, whilst a smaller one can be stowed in the wallet of the bicyclist. Riders who go in for long journeys at night should get a full-sized lamp with a large reservoir, and then have small wick tubes fitted, as a carefully trimmed $\frac{1}{2}$-inch wick will give a sufficient light, whilst the oil will not so soon be burnt out. As already suggested, the extra large wicks now fitted serve no good purpose. Nowadays, when side and back shutters are fitted to lamps, it does not often occur that much difficulty is found in lighting them even in a high wind. Some fixed flaming matches have been put in the market which are useful, though in a very high wind the lamp itself may be blown out; under such circumstances the flaming match may be laid across the wick and the lamp shut, when it will usually light up all right. Should the rider only have wax or ordinary matches, he may lay a couple across the wick and try to touch them off with another, and close the door in time to keep the wick alight—or if he has a vesuvian, he can strike it and put it alongside the matches and shut the door.

It very often happens that the comfort and safety of the rider depend entirely upon his getting his lamp alight in a heavy gale, and these hints collected by practical experience may under such circumstances be found of service.

LUGGAGE CARRIERS.

Luggage carriers are now almost invariably supplied by the makers of the machines on which they are used, with certain exceptions, and it will be usually found best to adopt the carrier usually fitted to the machine in the case of all classes of tricycles. The exceptions alluded to are the 'Nagel Carrier,' an ingenious wire contrivance fixed to the head of a bicycle, and so arranged that when the rider puts his legs over the handles going down hills, the carrier drops forward beneath them, being lifted back again, when the legs are removed, by a spring—the tension of which can be arranged with a strap. The idea is clever and fairly well carried out, though the top bracket is somewhat weak, and when it gives the break is put on by the pressure of the parcel. The other carrier is Lamplugh & Brown's handle-bar carrier, a very clever idea. Two short rubber-coated bars are clamped upon the handle-bar, and fitted with straps. They are pivoted on the clamp, and when a parcel is to be carried, they are put at right angles to the handle-bar and the package is strapped on; when no parcel is carried, the bars are folded back parallel with the handle bar, and they then form most convenient rests for the leg when going down hill with the legs over the handles. This fitting is very well finished stout and strong, and in practical use has proved one of the simplest and best of handle-bar luggage carriers.

THE SADDLE.

The saddle should always be most carefully selected. Many good riders are as loth to part with a saddle which suits them as a sportsman is to sell a gun, a dog, or anything else with which he has done well. A great many firms have made a speciality of cycling saddlery, and a number of excellent saddles have been offered for the consideration of the public. The saddles of Messrs. Lamplugh & Brown of Birmingham have always been found most practical; their well-known long-distance saddle being still in great favour, whilst the Record Saddle, an entirely novel contrivance, bids fair to prove a success in its way. A sound well-cut saddle should carry the rider's weight comfortably, without any tendency to ridginess, a very conspicuous failing in most cheap saddles. It will therefore be wiser for the beginner to buy a sound saddle of the ordinary type from a good maker, and, if once suited, to keep it until it is fairly worn out. Racing saddles should not be too small, but should afford a comparatively comfortable seat. The back may be turned up sharply, but the saddle, for reasons pointed out elsewhere, should never be 'pitched.' A suitable saddle is a necessity for the comfort of the cyclist.

COMBINED SADDLE-SPRINGS.

After a number of experiments, the combined saddle-spring has been perfected in England, and there are several on the market which are excellent for the purposes for which they are designed. Notable amongst them are those made by

Messrs. Brooks, and by Messrs. Lamplugh & Brown of Birmingham. The first, which is somewhat cumbrously called 'Brooks' B 70 International,' is an excellent saddle, possessing one great desideratum in an arrangement whereby the height at the back can be regulated at the will of the rider. This, though but a small point, is of the very greatest value to the user, as it enables him to secure for himself exactly the position he requires for comfort. This saddle is well constructed throughout, and is one of the best in the market. Very excellent, also, is the Anglo-American saddle made by Messrs. Lamplugh & Brown ; it is specially constructed so as not to become ridgy with wear, a fatal point with all the old American slung saddles, and it is an excellent fitting in every way. There are a number of other cleverly designed saddles in the market, and though in the ordinary bicycle close fitting is sometimes a desideratum, in Safeties and tricycles there is ample room for the fitting of anti-vibration contrivances, and nowadays no rider need suffer for want of them.

APPENDIX.

A RAPIDLY developing sport like cycling never stands still, its advance is constant; the records of to-day are but the average performances of to-morrow. Development follows development, existing standards are swept away, and others are erected in their places. New fields are sought by the active tourist, new courses for road records are discovered. The path records are simply so many ninepins, set up to be knocked over by the next comer.

Machines are being invented, developed, remodelled, day by day; the apparently perfect contrivance is but the crude germ of some startling development. Men and women are getting more expert as time goes on; the art of riding is becoming more commonly understood; obstacles are breaking down, prejudices passing away; the whole aspect of the sport is altering. These facts being so, any work which deals with the advancing tide must soon be overwhelmed.

General principles, general lines, may be laid down once for all, practical hints are current for all time and so on; but such a volume as this no sooner leaves the press than it falls behind in the matter of the ever-changing developments alluded to above.

The scope and purpose, therefore, of this appendix is to keep the cycling volume of the Badminton Library abreast of the times, to inform the reader of the latest and best performances, and the most notable feats accomplished on the cycle. The historical chapter brings the history of cycling down to a recent date, it traces the progress of the sport through what may be termed the Dark Ages of Cycling, and records, step by step, its advance to a period when its value to the community at large, its economic importance, its immense possibilities, were fairly guessed at, if not accurately gauged.

From this point forward, the particular steps in the concrete progress of the sport are not of special moment; all that is required for their full appreciation is to note the actual point reached, and to credit the men who have pioneered with all the merit of the task they have accomplished.

This is the scope and the object of this appendix, which will undergo careful and frequent revision.

Every effort has been made to secure absolute accuracy in the records, &c., herein set forth, but the authors will esteem it a favour if any reader detecting errors, or willing to afford additional information, will communicate with them.

All rights are reserved, and the tabular and other matter has been 'ear-marked,' and any unacknowledged excerpts will be dealt with accordingly.

THE CYCLISTS' CLUB HOUSE, LIMITED.

Early in 1890 Mr. W. J. Harvey, the energetic honorary secretary of the Kildare Bicycle and Tricycle Club, began to move in the matter of a central club for cyclists in London. The proposition had been mooted several times before, but without result. Securing the assistance of a number of gentlemen, Mr. Harvey pulled the thing through, and the Club House, No. 8 Queen Anne's Gate, was opened by an inaugural dinner in October, 1890. The premises are conveniently fitted up, and the club starts in a modest manner, and will, it is hoped, prove a progressive success. It already boasts a thoroughly representative membership, and several gentlemen with large experience in such matters have interested themselves in its future. The club is proprietary, being owned by 'The Cyclists' Club House Company, Limited.' Capital 2,000*l.*, in 1,000 shares of 2*l.* each. The club was burnt out on Christmas Eve, 1890, and has since been rebuilt, with several material improvements.

THE LEGAL ASPECTS OF CYCLING.

It would take more space than can well be spared to give anything approaching a satisfactory summary of cases of interest to cyclists. It will suffice to say that a cycle is a 'carriage' in the eye of the law, and to point out that our 'Universal By-laws'—phrase beloved of Bicycle Unionists—now obtain all over the country, and although in some benighted towns blue-coated authority does occasionally call upon the wheelman to light his lamp in accordance with the once obtaining local by-laws, the wheelman can now courteously inform his interlocutor that the law only requires him to light up one hour after sunset and to carry a bell. On all other points, if a cyclist finds himself in any trouble, and desires to study precedents and look into matters generally, he should communicate with the National Cyclists' Union, at 57 Basinghall Street, London, E.C., where a record is kept of all such cases. Here can be obtained much valuable information on all such points as may arise in such a matter, and, although in many ways the laws as applied to cycle users are somewhat vague and misty, there is never any harm done by looking up precedents and cases bearing upon the one at issue.

A MODEL RACE-MEETING PROGRAMME.

Clubs organising race meetings for the first time often ask, 'What races should the programme include?' Appended is an answer, but the proposed list must be modified to suit particular circumstances.

One Mile Open Handicap.

This is one of the stock pieces at a race meeting, and it may, if the entry is likely to be a very large one, be divided by the handicapper into first and second class handicaps, separate sets of prizes being offered in each race. The heats of the second-class race will be found very useful in arranging the time card so as to give the first-class riders a rest, a desideratum which has become difficult of attainment since all racing men adopted the one type of cycle.

A Scratch Race,

to be successful, must be supported by good and well-known riders, and a Challenge Cup of good value is the best prize, as it has the effect of bringing known men to compete for it year after year.

If further items are wanted, a short level race or handicap often produces a good race, and sport promoters will of course watch for any novelty or revival in cycle racing, such as Tandem Safety racing, Tricycle racing, and so on.

An interminable succession of heats should be avoided, and if an overwhelming number of entries is anticipated, it is much better to shorten the distance of the open handicaps, half-miles proving much less monotonous.

Careful management, with no waits, will under these conditions secure success, if success is to be secured.

RACING TRACK RULES.

The absence of rules always constitutes a distinct danger to men training on any path; but rules, however good, are useless unless they be enforced with a strong hand.

It is very seldom that a mere ground-man is found who will enforce the rules of a track with the proper degree of completeness. In most such cases the attendant, dependent to a great extent upon the generosity of the frequenters of the path, hesitates to check them when they do anything which is not exactly regular.

On the other hand, it is difficult to keep one in authority at the track at all times to enforce the rules, which, though theoretically accepted by everyone, are often broken by the very men who grumble most if they are infringed by others.

Under these conditions, if a ground-man is found who *does* enforce the rules, despite obloquy and abuse from the more thoughtless of the training-men, he should be supported by the authorities as a valuable and exceptional servant.

It is necessary that the rules should be short, brief, and to the point, and the following, drafted by Mr. G. Lacy Hillier, and to be found in 'The Art of Training for Cycle Racing,' a work published in 1888 in Berlin, in three languages, probably reduce the necessary regulations to a minimum :—

Rules to be Observed by Riders Training on this Track.

1. This path may only be ridden left (or right) hand inside.
2. Riders overtaking others must pass *on the outside only*, as in racing.
3. A rider, whether riding in a string or alone, should never slow suddenly, or cross the track, or swerve out, without giving notice of his intention by holding up his hand.

NOTE.—A cautious rider will *always* signal his intention to stop, whether he is alone or not. By *always* doing so, the chances of accident are much lessened.

4. A rider, before dismounting, should always give a signal (holding up his hand), and, if possible, should always ride off on the inside of the track, before getting off. If he must go to the outside, to a stool or similar convenience, he should be most careful to see that no one is behind him, or coming up at racing pace.
5. *No rider is permitted, under any consideration, to dismount on to the track.*

NOTE.—This last rule should be made absolute, as it is usually possible to ride right off, either inside or outside any path. Where all sorts of cycles train on the same path, this is a most salutary rule, as thoughtless tricyclists sometimes stop right in the middle of the path after a spurt.

If the above rules are consistently and carefully enforced by an attendant whose authority is steadily supported by the track authorities, the risks of accident will be most materially reduced.

AMATEUR CHAMPIONSHIPS.

THE AMATEUR BICYCLING CHAMPIONSHIP.

Run at Lillie Bridge, by the Amateur Athletic Club. Distance 4 miles.

		m.	s.
1871.	H. P. Whiting, A.A.C.	16	30
1872.	F. V. T. Honeywell, Surrey B.C.	17	25
1873.	H. P. Whiting, A.A.C.	14	37
1874.	H. P. Whiting, Velo. Sport de Paris	14	56
1875.	H. P. Whiting „ „	13	$30\frac{2}{8}$
1876.	The Hon. Ion Keith-Falconer, Camb. U.B.C.	13	6
1877.	Wadham Wyndham, London B.C.	13	$6\frac{1}{2}$
1878.	R. R. Mackinnon, Brighton A.C.[1]	14	$9\frac{3}{8}$
1879.	H. L. Cortis, Wanderers B.C.[1]	13	10

This competition was finally abandoned in favour of the Amateur Championships established by the then Bicycle Union, now the N.C.U. (See p. 416.)

THE 50 MILES ROAD RACE FOR THE TRICYCLING AMATEUR CHAMPIONSHIP.

(Sometimes called the Fifty Miles Road Ride.)

The first race was promoted by a tricycle agent in Kensington, and then a committee of the Tricycle Clubs took it up. It was dubbed a 'Ride' under the somewhat fatuous idea that this would disguise the fact that it was a race. The police interfered with the last contest for the title, run in 1883, and it was discontinued.

1879.—*Course—Kew Bridge to Blackwater and back.*

A. E. Derkinderin, 1st. S. Corbett, 2nd.
Time, 4 hrs. 55 mins.

1880.—*Course—Tally Ho Corner, Finchley, to St. Ibbs and back. Roads good, day fine.*

C. D. Vesey,[2] 1st. G. Lacy Hillier, 2nd.
Time, 4 hrs. 2 mins.

---

[1] Walk over.

[2] Vesey rode a machine called the 'Rara Avis,' which was simply a bicycle with two very light hind wheels placed close together. No special definition of a 'tricycle' existing, the Committee had no option but to give the medal to Vesey. Hillier, who started 13 minutes late, covered the course in 4 hrs. 10 mins., a record at the time.

1881.—*Course—10th milestone from Hyde Park, at Hounslow, viâ (just short of) Maidenhead, through Cookham, to a point 25 miles from the start, and back. Some parts very bad, loose shingle; very wet.*

G. Lacy Hillier, 1st.   P. G. Hebblethwaite, 2nd.
Time, 4 hrs. 53 mins.

1882.—*Course—From Barnet (Ganwick Corner), through Welwyn, to a point 25 miles out, and back. Roads good; day fine.*

M. J. Lowndes, 1st.   T. R. Marriott, 2nd.
Time, 3 hrs. 47 mins. 40 secs.

1883.—*Course—From Caterham Junction, viâ Oxted, Westerham, and Riverhead, to a point half a mile beyond Ightham, and back. Roads good; day fine.*

T. R. Marriott, 1st.   G. Smith, 2nd.

The police stopped the winner a mile short of the winning-post, and, in view of possible proceedings, no time was given.

10 MILES ROAD CHAMPIONSHIP OF SCOTLAND.

		m. s.			m. s.
1876.	D. McGregor	33 22	1881.	D. D. Bryson	31 29
1877.	R. S. Bryson	33 25	1882.	D. H. Huie	32 14
1878.	J. S. Purdie	32 58	1883.	,, ,,	37 50
1879.	D. D. Bryson	34 24	1884.	,, ,,	30
1880.	J. McGregor	33 30	1885.	J. Lamb	33 40

Distance altered to 50 miles (see 50 miles Road Championship of Scotland, below).

THE 50 MILES BICYCLE ROAD CHAMPIONSHIP OF SCOTLAND.

Originally the 10 Miles Road Championship of Scotland. (See above.)

Course—Coltbridge to the 26th milestone on Airdrie Road, and back.

		h. m. s.
1886, June 18.	J. H. A. Laing	3 19 30
1887, July 25.	D. Cleland	3 23 39
1888, June 18.	M. Bruce	3 14 54
1889, June 17.	P. F. C. Willcox	3 25 25
1890, June 16.	J. Steel	3 54 52⅗

WINNERS OF THE AMATEUR CHAMPIONSHIPS PROMOTED BY THE NATIONAL CYCLISTS' UNION.

	Name	Club	Time h. m. s.	Date	Place
1878—2 miles Bicycle..	Hon. Ion K. Falconer	C.U. Bi. C.	0 6 29	May 11	Stamford Bridge, Fulham, London.
,, 25 miles Bicycle..	A. A. Weir	O.U. Bi. C.	1 27 47 2·5	May 11	,, ,, ,,
1879—1 mile Bicycle ..	H. L. Cortis	Wanderers	0 2 59 1·5	June 12	,, ,, ,,
,, 5 miles Bicycle..	,,	,,	0 15 27 3·5	June 19	,, ,, ,,
,, 25 miles Bicycle..	,,	,,	1 24 4	June 26	,, ,, ,,
,, 50 miles Bicycle..	,,	,,	2 56 1 4·5	July 11	,, ,, ,,
1880—1 mile Bicycle ..	C. E. Liles	L.A.C.	0 2 55 1·5	June 24	,, ,, ,,
,, 5 miles Bicycle..	H. L. Cortis	Wanderers	0 15 10 3·5	June 24	,, ,, ,,
,, 25 miles Bicycle..	,,	,,	1 22 15 2·5	July 1	,, ,, ,,
,, 50 miles Bicycle..	,,	,,	2 56 11 2·5	July 8	,, ,, ,,
1881—1 mile Bicycle..	G. Lacy Hillier	Stanley	0 3 11 3·5	July 16	Belgrave Grounds, Leicester.
,, 5 miles Bicycle..	,,	,,	0 15 39 4·5	July 6	Recreation Grounds, Surbiton, Surrey.
,, 25 miles Bicycle..	,,	,,	1 27 43 3·5	July 16	Belgrave Grounds, Leicester.
,, 50 miles Bicycle..	,,	,,	2 50 50 2·5	July 27	Recreation Grounds, Surbiton, Surrey.
1882—1 mile Bicycle..	F. Moore	Warstone	0 2 47 2·5	July 8	Aston Lower Grounds, Birmingham
,, 5 miles Bicycle..	J. S. Whatton	C.U. Bi. C.	0 15 12 4·5	July 22	Crystal Palace, Sydenham, London.
,, 25 miles Bicycle..	F. Moore	Warstone	1 25 8 1·5	July 8	Aston Lower Grounds, Birmingham
,, 50 miles Bicycle..	Hon. Ion K. Falconer	C.U. Bi. C.	2 43 58 3·5	July 29	Crystal Palace, Sydenham, London.
,, 5 miles Tricycle	C. E. Liles	L.A.C.	0 19 39 2·5	Oct. 14	,, ,, ,,
1883—1 mile Bicycle ..	H. W. Gaskell	Ranelagh H.	0 2 55 2·5	July 14	Crystal Palace, Sydenham, London.
,, 5 miles Bicycle..	F. Sutton	Edgbaston H.	0 16 42 2·5	July 7	Aston Lower Grounds, Birmingham
,, 25 miles Bicycle..	C. E. Liles	L.A.C.	1 22 42 3·5	Aug. 4	Taunton Athletic Ground, Taunton.
,, 50 miles Bicycle..	H. F. Wilson	Surrey	2 46 26 3·5	July 21	Crystal Palace, Sydenham, London
,, 1 mile Tricycle..	C. E. Liles	L.A.C.	0 3 18 1·5	July 7	Aston Lower Grounds, Birmingham
,, 10 miles Tricycle	,,	,,	0 33 45	July 14	Crys.al Palace, Sydenham, London.

APPENDIX.

Year & Event	Rider	Opponent				Date	Venue
1884—1 mile Bicycle	H. A. Speechley	Ranelagh H.	0	3	30 4·5	June 21	Lillie Bridge Grnds., W. Brompton, Lond.
,, 5 miles Bicycle	R. Chambers	Speedwell	0	15	36 4·5	June 28	Sophia Gardens Track Cardiff.
,, 25 miles Bicycle	R. H. English	North Shields	1	22	20 4·5	July 26	N. Durham Track, Newcastle-on-Tyne.
,, 50 miles Bicycle	F. R. Fry	Clifton	2	51	16 3·5	July 19	Crystal Palace, Sydenham, London.
,, 1 mile Tricycle	C. E. Liles	L.A.C.	0	3	29 1·5	July 12	,, ,,
,, 5 miles Tricycle	,,	,,	0	17	30 1·5	July 12	,, ,,
,, 25 miles Tricycle	,,	,,	1	28	58	June 21	Lillie Bridge Grnds., W. Brompton, Lond.
1885—1 mile Bicycle	Sanders Sellers	Preston	0	2	47 1·5	June 13	Aston Lower Grounds, Birmingham.
,, 5 miles Bicycle	M. V. J. Webber	Vects	0	14	22 3·5	June 27	Jarrow Track, Newcastle-on-Tyne
,, 25 miles Bicycle	R. H. English	North Shields	1	20	13	July 25	Aylestone Road Grounds, Leicester.
,, 50 miles Bicycle	,,	,,	2	45	13 4·5	July 18	Crystal Palace, Sydenham, London.
,, 1 mile Tricycle	P. Furnivall	Berretta	0	3	5 2·5	July 11	,, ,,
,, 5 miles Tricycle	R. Cripps	Nottingham	0	16	53 1·5	June 13	Aston Lower Grounds, Birmingham.
,, 25 miles Tricycle	G. Gatehouse	C.U. Bi. C.	1	26	29 3·5	July 11	Crystal Palace, Sydenham, London.
1886—1 mile Bicycle	P. Furnivall	Berretta	0	2	46	June 26	Jarrow Track, Newcastle-upon-Tyne.
,, 5 miles Bicycle	,,	Gainsborough	0	14	44 1·5	July 24	Recreation Grounds, Long Eaton.
,, 25 miles Bicycle	J. E. Fenlon	,,	1	19	29 2·5	June 14	Recreation Grnds, Weston-super-Mare.
,, 50 miles Bicycle	,,	Berretta	2	47	21 1·5	Aug. 14	Lillie Bridge Grnds., W. Brompton, Lond.
,, 1 mile Tricycle	P. Furnivall	Cheylesmore	0	3	5 2·5	June 14	Recreation Grounds, Weston-super-Mare.
,, 5 miles Tricycle	F. W. Allard	Dublin U.C.C.	0	20	42 2·5	July 3	Hampden Park Track, Glasgow.
,, 25 miles Tricycle	R. J. Mecredy	,,	1	55	40 4·5	July 17	Alexandra Park Track, London.
1887—1 mile Bicycle	W. A. Illston	Speedwell	0	2	45 4·5	May 30	Aston Lower Grounds, Birmingham.
,, 5 miles Bicycle	,,	,,	0	16	49 1·5	July 30	,, ,,
,, 25 miles Bicycle	,,	Lewisham	1	19	2 3·5	Aug. 4	,, ,,
,, 50 miles Bicycle	J. H. Adams	Delft. Stud.	2	45	45	Aug. 1	,, ,,
,, 1 mile Tricycle	E. Kiderlen	Dublin U.C.C.	0	17	54 2·5	July 4	,, ,,
,, 5 miles Tricycle	R. J. Mecredy	Norwood S.	1	23	22 3·5	July 2	,, ,,
,, 25 miles Tricycle	F. J. Osmond	,,			21 1·5	May 30	,, ,,
1888—1 mile Bicycle	H. Synyer	Notts Boulevard	0	2	32 2·5	May 21	Coventry Cricket Grounds, Coventry.
,, 5 miles Bicycle	,,	,,	0	15	4 3·5	July 14	N. Shields Track, Newcastle-on-Tyne.
,, 25 miles Bicycle	J. H. Adams	Speedwel	1	22	34	Aug. 18	Worsley Track, Grimsby.
,, 50 miles Bicycle	F. P. Wood	Brixton	2	55	12 3·5	Sept. 1	Jarrow Track, Newcastle-on-Tyne.
,, 1 mile Tricycle	S. F. Edge	Anerley	0	3	14	June 30	Hanson Lane Grounds, Halifax.
,, 5 miles Tricycle	F. J. Osmond	Norwood S.	0	16	40 3·5	July 21	Paddington Recreation Ground, London.
,, 25 miles Tricycle	F. P. Wood	Brixton	1	19	17 3·5	May 21	Coventry Cricket Grounds, Coventry.

418   CYCLING.

Winners of the Amateur Championships promoted by the National Cyclists' Union—continued.

	Name	Club	Time h. m. s.	Date	Place
1889—1 mile Bicycle	August Lehr	Frankfort-am-M.	0 3 9 4·5	July 20	Paddington Recreation Ground, London.
,, 5 miles Bicycle	H Synyer	Notts Boulevard	0 18 24 1·5	July 27	,,
,, 25 miles Bicycle	F. J. Osmond	Brixton R.	1 18 27 2·5	July 20	,,
,, 50 miles Bicycle	J. H. Adams	Speedwell	2 42 14 4·5	Sept. 4	,,
,, 1 mile Safety	F. T. Fletcher	Ilkeston	0 3 16 3·5	Aug. 24	,,
,, 25 miles Safety	,,	,,	1 16 34 2·5	July 20	,,
,, 50 miles Safety	J. H. Adams	Speedwell	2 44 4 3·5	Aug. 28	,,
,, 1 mile Tricycle	H. H. Sansom	Nottingham	0 3 12	July 27	,,
,, 5 miles Tricycle	,,	,,	0 17 15 3·5	July 20	,,
,, 25 miles Tricycle	W. G. H. Bramson	Speedwell	1 20 27 1·5	July 27	,,
1890—1 mile Bicycle	F. J. Osmond	Brixton Ramblers	0 3 21 2·5	July 12	Paddington Recreation Ground London.
,, 5 miles Bicycle	,,	,,	0 14 34 4·5	July 19	,,
,, 25 miles Bicycle	,,	,,	1 14 47	July 26	,,
,, 50 miles Bicycle	,,	,,	2 44 12 3·5	July 30	,,
,, 1 mile Safety	R. J. Mecredy	Dublin U. Bi. C.	0 2 48 3·5	July 19	,,
,, 5 miles Safety	,,	,,	0 17 47	July 26	,,
,, 25 miles Safety	,,	,,	1 16 59 3·5	July 12	,,
,, 50 miles Safety	,,	,,	2 29 55 1·5	Aug. 13	,,
,, 1 mile Tricycle	K. N. Stadnicki	Irish Champion C.C.	0 3 52 3·5	July 26	,,
,, 5 miles Tricycle	H. H. Sansom	Nottingham	0 18 6 4·5	July 12	,,
,, 25 miles Tricycle	L. Stroud	Oxford U. Bi. C.	1 25 21 4·5	July 19	,,
1891—1 mile Bicycle	J. H. Adams	Speedwell	0 2 54 2·5	July 4	County Grounds, Bristol.
,, 5 miles Bicycle	U. L. Lambley	Armoury	0 15 13 3·5	June 14	,,
,, 25 miles Bicycle	J. H. Adams	Speedwell	1 16 24 3·5	July 18	Paddington Recreation Ground, London.
,, 50 miles Bicycle	,,	,,	2 28 14 4·5	July 22	,,
,, 1 mile Safety	{P. W. Scheltema-Beduin}	Trekvogels	0 3 0 1·5	June 14	County Grounds, Bri
,, 5 miles Safety	A. W. Harris	Leicester	0 18 24 4·5	July 18	,,
,, 25 miles Safety	F. J. Osmond	Speedwell	1 14 2	July 4	,,
,, 50 miles Safety	,,	,,	2 28 16 4·5	July 23	Paddington Recreation Ground, London.

APPENDIX. 419

,, 1 mile Tricycle	{P. W. Schellema-Beduin} W. G. H. Bramson	Trekvogels	0	3	20 2·5	July 18	County Grounds, Bristol.
,, 5 miles Tricycle	W. G. H. Bramson	London County	0	15	47 1·5	July 4	,, ,,
,, 25 miles Tricycle	Lewis Stroud	Speedwell	0	25	34 2·5	June 14	,, ,,
1892—1 mile Safety	A. A. Zimmerman	N.Y.A.C. and L.C.	0	3	57 4·5	June 25	Leeds.
,, 5 miles Safety	,,	,,	0	20	9 1·5	June 25	,,
,, 25 miles Safety	R. L. Ede	Stoke Newington	1	9	46 4·5	June 18	Herne Hill.
,, 50 miles Safety	A. A. Zimmerman	N.Y.A.C. and L.C.	2	37	23 3·5	July 7	Paddington Recreation Ground, London.
,, 1 mile Bicycle	J. H. Adams	Speedwell	0	2	57 3·5	June 18	Herne Hill.
,, 25 miles Bicycle	,,	,,	1	19	0 2·5	June 25	Leeds.
,, 50 miles Bicycle	W. Tischbein	Hallescher	2	44	53 1·5	July 20	Herne Hill.
,, 1 mile Tricycle	,,	,,	0	3	19	June 18	,,
,, 10 miles Tricycle	F. Bramson	London County	0	32	0 3·5	June 18	,,
1893—1 mile Safety	W. C. Sanger	{Telegram C.C. and L.C / Polytechnic and L.C.}	0	3	49 2·5	June 17	Herne Hill.
,, 5 miles Safety	A. J. Watson		0	13	2 3·5	June 17	,,
,, 25 miles Safety	J. W. Stocks	Hull Grosvenor	1	11	34 4·5	June 24	Newcastle.
,, 50 miles Safety	L. Stroud	Speedwell B.C.	2	35	8 1·5	July 12	Paddington.
,, 1 mile Tricycle	Fred Bramson	London County	0	2	54 2·5	June 17	Herne Hill.
,, 10 miles Tricycle	,,	,,	0	31	44 2·5	June 17	,,

CHALLENGE CUPS AND TROPHIES.

THE ANCHOR SHIELD.

Originally presented by the late Mrs. Dibble of Ripley to the Southern Cyclists' Camp in 1886; returned to the Misses Dibble in 1893, and presented by them to the London County Club as a Challenge Trophy for the 12 Hours Path Race at Herne Hill. To be won thre times. Put up for competition annually at the end of September. Value 30 guineas.

1893. C. G. Wridgway, 1st, 240 miles 690 yds. *Record.*
       A. W. Horton,   2nd, 238   „   620 „
       A. V. Linton,   3rd, 234   „ 1,420 „

THE ASHBURY CHALLENGE CUP.

Presented in 1875 by James Ashbury, Esq., to the Brighton Athletic Club. A Silver Cup, value 25 guineas, engraved with the B.A.C. Monogram, &c.

1875. B. J. Saunders.   1878. F. M. Cox.
1876. G. F. Duddridge.   1879. A. E. Saunders.
1877. R. R. Mackinnon.   1880. A. E. Saunders.
          1881. A. E. Saunders.

The Cup being won three times in succession, became the property of Mr. A. E. Saunders, of the Brighton Athletic Club.

THE CITY OF BRISTOL CHALLENGE VASE.
(Ordinaries.)

Value 50 guineas. Distance 5 miles.

1890, July 5. A. Milsom, J. Chamberlain, C. C. Bardsley   m. s.
                                                           14 55

THE BROOKES CUP.
(Safeties.)

Presented by Messrs. J. and H. Brookes, of Birmingham, and run for at the 'Sport and Play' Tournament, Aston Lower Grounds, Birmingham. Value 25 guineas. Distance 1 mile.

1890, Aug. 5. H. H. Sansom, W. C. Jones, H. Parsons . m. s.
                                                         2 $48\tfrac{2}{5}$

THE CAMBRIDGE UNIVERSITY ROAD CHALLENGE CUP.

Distance about 50 miles.

1878.	A. A. Honey, Sidney.	1884.	G. Gatehouse, Christ's.
1879.	H. S. Clarke, Trinity.	1885.	,, ,,
1880.	A. J. Crichton, Trinity.	1886.	G. F.C. Searle, St. Peter's.
1881.	E. H. Brown, St. John's.	1887.	G. Gatehouse, Christ's.
1882.	J. S. Whatton, Trinity.	1888.	W.L. Raynes, Pembroke.
1883.	,, ,,	1889.	B. W. Attlee, St. John's.

1890. S. E. Williams, Jesus.

THE CHELSEA CUP.

Presented by the Chelsea Bicycle Club. Value 50 guineas. Distance 5 miles. Usually run for at Stamford Bridge.

		m.	s.
1887, July 16.	E. M. Mayes, A. E. Langley, J. G. Paterson	14	59
1888, June 30.	E. M. Mayes, W. G. H. Bramson, E. W. Brewerton	15	$18\frac{1}{5}$
1889, July 13.	E. M. Mayes, F. P. Wood, W. G. H. Bramson	15	$4\frac{2}{5}$

E. M. Mayes having won the Cup three times, it became his property.

THE COWEN CHALLENGE CUP.

Presented in 1882 by Mr. Joseph Cowen, M.P. Competed for in August. Distance 2 miles. To be won three times.

		m.	s.
1882, Aug. 26.	T. D. Oliver, G. H. Illston	6	$57\frac{1}{5}$
1883, Aug. 25.	G. H. Illston, T. D. Oliver	6	$22\frac{2}{5}$
1884, Aug. 23.	D. H. Huie, R. H. English	5	$47\frac{2}{5}$
1885, Aug. 22.	C. E. Harling, T. D. Oliver	7	$41\frac{1}{5}$
1886, Aug. 7.	W. A. Illston, W. McAllister	6	$59\frac{2}{5}$
1887, Aug. 6.	W. A. Illston, T. H. English	6	$4\frac{1}{5}$
1888, July 16.	Herbert Synyer, J. J. Carruthers	5	$42\frac{2}{5}$
1889, Aug. 5.	W. A. Illston, W. C. Thompson	6	$6\frac{3}{5}$

The Cup became the property of W. A. Illston, and the competition lapsed.

THE 'CROSS' CUP.

Presented by W. Cross, Esq., of the Newcastle C.C. Run on the road—Gosforth Waggonway, Newcastle, to Alnwick. Distance about 60 miles.

		m. s.			m. s.
1882.	P. Thompson	6 22	1886.	R. Milthorpe	4 29½
1883.	H. Rowell	5 2	1887.	,,	4 49½
1884.	A. O. Challoner	5 15	1888.	,,	4 49½
1885.	H. Rowell	5 59½			

Milthorpe retained the Cup.

THE CRYSTAL PALACE CHALLENGE CUP.

10 miles. Run twice as a club team race, first two in to win.

			m. s.
1880.	{ G. Lacy Hillier 1st / J. R. Hamilton 2nd }	Druids B.C.	42 14⅘
1881.	{ C. Crute 1st / F. Allport 4th }	Sutton B.C.	32 35⅖

Altered to a 15 miles scratch race.

1882, Aug. 17. C. D. Vesey, H. R. Reynolds, J. D. Butler 46 22⅗
1883, July 26. C. E. Liles, F. L. Adam, W. Brown . 45 47⅖
1884, Sept. 11. R. H. English, R. Cripps, H. F. Wilson . 44 29⅗
1885, Sept. 10. J. H. Adams, W. Terry, A. R. Macbeth . 46 32⅕
1886, July 17. J. H. Adams, F. J. Osmond, E. W. Brewerton 47 37⅕
1887 July 16. J. H. Adams, F. J. Osmond, J. E. Fenlon 45 35⅕

Joseph H. Adams having won the Cup three times, it became his property, and the competition lapsed.

THE 'CUCA COCOA' CHALLENGE CUP.

Presented to the London County C. and A.C., Ltd, by Messrs. Root & Co., to be competed for in the Club's Amateur 24 Hours Path Race at Herne Hill. To be won three times. Put up for competition once each year, at the end of July. Value 100 guineas

1892. Frank W. Shorland, 1st, 413 miles 1,615 yds. *Record.*
J. Melville James, 2nd, 407 ,, 285 ,,
J. F. Walsh, 3rd, 384 ,, 874 ,,

1893. Frank W. Shorland, 1st, 426 miles 440 yds. *Record.*
F. T. Bidlake, 2nd, 410 ,, 1,110 ,, *Tricycle record.*
H Hammond 3rd, 393 ,, 310 ,,

APPENDIX.

THE HARROGATE CHALLENGE CUP.

Value 50 guineas. Distance 5 miles. Run for at Harrogate in Yorkshire, in connection with the North of England Cyclists' Meet and Camp on the first Monday in August each year, on a grass course.

Contests at this distance were promoted from 1881, and the results are added to keep the record complete. The course having been altered and improved each year, no times are given.

1881.	Charles Crute.	Sutton B.C.
1882.	J. W. Greenwood.	Leeds Crescent.
1883.	J. W. Greenwood.	Leeds Crescent.
1884.	D. H. Huie.	Edinburgh.
1885.	P. Furnivall.	Berretta B.C.

A Cup offered.

1886.	F. Robinson.	Coventry.
1887.	W. Dobson.	Seacroft.
1888.	Sydney E. Williams.	West Kent B.C.
1889.	J. W. Stocks.	Hull Grosvenor B.C.
1890.	F. J. Osmond.	Brixton Ramblers B.C.
1891.	Sydney E. Williams.	London County.
1892.	Sydney E. Williams.	London County.

Sydney E. Williams having won the Cup three times, it became his property, and the race lapsed.

THE INTERNATIONAL CHALLENGE SHIELD.

Value 50 guineas. Distance 5 miles.

			m.	s.
1886, May 22.[1]	P. Furnivall	. . . . .	16	1⅖
1887. No competition.				
1888, Aug. 25.[2]	F. P. Wood	. . . . .	17	18⅘
1889, Aug. 17.[2]	F. P. Wood	. . . . .	16	31⅘
1890, May 26.[3]	F. P. Wood	. . .		No time taken

The Shield became the property of Frank Peters Wood.

THE KENT HOUSE CHALLENGE CUP.

Distance 3 miles. Usually run for on the North Durham Track, Gateshead-on-Tyne.

1886, June 29.	W. A. Illston.	1888, July 18.	J. J. Carruthers.
1887, Aug. 8.	W. A. Illston.	1889, July 22.	J. J. Carruthers.
	1890, July 14.	J. J. Carruthers.		

The Cup became the property of J. J. Carruthers

---

[1] Run for at Alexandra Palace. [2] Run for at Bath. [3] Run for at Kensal Rise.

THE KILDARE CUP.

Given by the Kildare Bicycle and Tricycle Club. Run for annually. To be won twice in succession, or three times in all. Distance 5 miles. Run for at Lillie Bridge until the path was closed; then at Stamford Bridge and Kensal Rise. Value 50 guineas.

		m.	s.
1880, Sept. 25.	H. L. Cortis, A. P. Shaw, C. E. Liles	15	58$\frac{2}{5}$
1881, Sept. 17.	C. E. Liles, J. D. Butler, W. J. Reilly	15	35$\frac{1}{5}$
1882, Sept. 16.	H. W. Gaskell, C. E. Liles, J. D. Butler	15	54$\frac{4}{5}$
1883, Sept. 22.	C. E. Liles, H. W. Gaskell, H. A. Speechley	16	4$\frac{1}{5}$
1884, Sept. 13.	R. H. English, H. A. Speechley, E. M. Mayes	14	51$\frac{2}{5}$
1885, Sept. 19.	W. F. Ball, A. R. Macbeth, W. Terry	15	37$\frac{2}{5}$
1886, Sept. 11.	P. Furnivall, E. Mayes, J. E. Fenlon	16	3$\frac{2}{5}$
1887, Sept. 17.	F. J. Osmond, P. Furnivall, W. A. Illston	15	26$\frac{3}{5}$
1888, Sept. 15.	F. J. Osmond, D. McRae, W. G. H. Bramson	14	45$\frac{1}{5}$

The first Cup thus became Osmond's property, and a second was offered by the Club.

| 1889, Sept. 7. | E. M. Mayes, D. McRae, F. P. Wood | 15 | 22$\frac{1}{5}$ |
| 1890, May 31. | F. J. Osmond, L. Stroud, G. R. Adcock | 16 | 55$\frac{1}{5}$ |

The Club dissolved and the contest lapsed.

LONG EATON CHALLENGE CUP.

Value 50 guineas. Offered by the proprietors of the Long Eaton Track, near Trent Bridge, Nottingham, to be run for on that path. Distance 5 miles.

NOTE.—The Cup having been won in 1887 and 1888 by Herbert Synyer, was not put up in 1889, and the date chosen in 1890 was that fixed for the N.C.U. 5 miles Championship, of which Herbert Synyer was the holder. He, however, stayed at Nottingham, and finally won the cup.

		m.	s.
1887, July 16.	Herbert Synyer	16	34
1888, June 2.	Herbert Synyer	15	14$\frac{4}{5}$
1889.	Not put up for competition.		
1890, July 19.	Herbert Synyer	16	50$\frac{1}{5}$

Herbert Synyer became absolute possessor of the trophy.

THE PLYMOUTH CUP.
Value 100 guineas.

1889. E. M. Mayes.   1890. Douglas McRae

THE QUEEN OF THE WEST CHALLENGE VASE.

Value 30 guineas. Distance 5 miles.

		m.	s.
1886, Aug. 21.	W. F. Ball	17	12
1887, Aug. 27.	W. F. Ball	18	37$\frac{3}{5}$
1888, Aug. 25.	W. F. Ball	17	25$\frac{2}{5}$

W. F. Ball became absolute possessor of the trophy.

'THE SINGER CUP.'

Value 50 guineas. Run for on the Paignton Track. Distance 5 miles.

		m.	s.
1888, Aug. 6.	G. R. Adcock, W. F. Ball	16	39
1889, June 10.	J. B. Trenchard, S. H. Pearce	17	49$\frac{4}{5}$
1889, Aug. 5.	E. M. Mayes, G. R. Adcock	15	7$\frac{3}{5}$
1890, Aug. 4.	A. Milsom, F. J. B. Archer	15	43$\frac{3}{5}$

'THE SPORTING LIFE' CHALLENGE CUP.

Sometimes called the Fifty Miles Championship. Value 50 guineas. Run for at Lillie Bridge.

		h.	m.	s.
1877, Oct. 27.	Harry Osborne	3	18	55
1878, Oct. 26.	A. E. Derkinderin	3	9	56
1879, Nov. 8.	Harry Osborne	3	4	6$\frac{2}{5}$
1880, Oct. 30.	C. E. Liles	3	11	47
1881, Oct. 22.	C. E. Liles was stopped at 43 miles, when riding alone in wretched weather.			
1882, Oct. 21.	C. D. Vesey	3	10	0
1883, Oct. 13.	F. Sutton	3	6	41

Since this date nothing has been heard either of the contest or the Cup.

THE SURREY CUP.

Presented by the Surrey Bicycle Club. [A Cup was first offered on September 6, 1879. The other returns are added to keep the record complete. The Club held sports first in 1876.] Distance 10 miles. To be won three times. Usually competed for twice each year, in April and September, on grass, at Kennington Oval. Value 50 guineas.

		m.	s.
1877, Sept. 29.	Harry Osborne, W. Wyndham, F. T. East	36	10
1878, April 27.	W. Wyndham, E. J. Hall [distance 5 miles]	18	43$\frac{1}{5}$
1878, Sept. 28.	F. T. East, A. E. Derkinderin, W. Wyndham	35	34$\frac{4}{5}$[1]
1879, April 26.	H. L. Cortis, A. E. Derkinderin	40	12[2]

---

[1] Grass records.   [2] Only two finished.

THE SURREY CUP—*continued.*
First Cup offered.

		m.	s.
1879, Sept. 6.	H. L. Cortis, W. Popplewell, A. S. Brown	34	$31\frac{1}{2}$ [1]
1880, April 24.	H. L. Cortis, W. T. Thorn, W. Popplewell	38	58
1880, Sept. 18.	H. L. Cortis, G. Lacy Hillier, C. E. Liles	39	28

The first Cup having been won by Herbert Liddell Cortis, a second Cup was offered.

		m.	s.
1881, April 30.	G. Lacy Hillier, J. F. Griffith, J. R. Hamilton	35	$33\frac{1}{5}$
1881, Sept. 10.	J. F. Griffith, C. E. Liles, E. Hassell	37	55
1882, April 22.	{ C. A. Palmer } dead heat ; M. J. R. { J. F. Griffith } Dundas	38	$52\frac{4}{5}$
1882, June 3.	Dead heat run off on Crystal Palace Track. C. A. Palmer, 1st ; J. F. Griffith, 2nd	31	$17\frac{3}{5}$
1882, Sept. 9.	H. W. Gaskell, W. Popplewell, C. D. Vesey	38	26
1883, April 28.	H. W. Gaskell, F. Prentice, E. Moore	42	$9\frac{1}{5}$
1883, Sept. 15.	C. E. Liles, W. Brown, H. W. Gaskell	33	$59\frac{3}{5}$
1884, April 26.	H. F. Wilson, F. Prentice, H. H. Smith	36	$37\frac{3}{5}$
1884, Sept. 20.	H. A. Speechley, H. F. Wilson, R. Cripps	34	$12\frac{2}{5}$
1885, April 25.	R. Cripps, F. Prentice, C. L. Wadey	37	$4\frac{1}{5}$
1885, Sept. 12.	H. A. Speechley, W. Terry, A. R. Macbeth	37	$39\frac{1}{5}$
1886, April 17.	H. A. Speechley, P. Furnivall, A. P. Engleheart	41	$44\frac{1}{5}$

The second Cup having been won by Herbert A. Speechley, a third Cup was offered.

		m.	s.
1886, Sept. 18.	P. Furnivall, W. F. Ball, J. H. Adams	33	$40\frac{2}{5}$
1887, May 14.	P. Furnivall, H. Synyer, F. J. Osmond	32	$42\frac{2}{5}$ [2]
1887, Sept. 10.	P. Furnivall, W. F. Ball, F. J. Osmond	32	$36\frac{4}{5}$ [1]

The third Cup having been won by Percy Furnivall, a fourth Cup was offered.

		m.	s.
1888, April 7.	F. P. Wood, H. Synyer, E. M. Mayes	41	$50\frac{1}{5}$
1888, Sept. 8.	F. J. Osmond, W. F. Ball, F. P. Wood	32	$35\frac{4}{5}$ [3]
1889, April 27.	F. P. Wood, F. J. Osmond, T. Thitchener	41	17
1889, Sept. 14.	J. H. Adams, F. P. Wood, E. M. Mayes	31	10 [1]
1890, April 19.	F. J. Osmond, F. P. Wood, H. J. Howard	36	38
1890, Sept. 13.	F. J. Osmond, F. P. Wood, L. Stroud	30	$39\frac{3}{5}$ [1]

The fourth Cup having been won by F. J. Osmond, a fifth Cup was offered.

		m.	s.
1891, April 18.	H. H. Sansom, A. du Cros, A. G. Fentiman	31	$9\frac{3}{5}$
1891, Sept 12.	H. J. Howard, A. E. Good, A. W. Harris	28	$9\frac{3}{5}$

---

[1] Grass Records. [2] Run for at Lillie Bridge. [3] Course short.

		m.	s.
1892, April 23.	U. L. Lambley, A. E. Good, A. du Cros .	29	41$\frac{3}{5}$
1892, Sept. 10.	A. W. Harris, A. E. Good, C. G. Thiselton	29	8$\frac{2}{5}$
1893, April 22.	A. W. Harris, M. B. Fowler, U. L. Lambley	29	3$\frac{2}{5}$
1893, Sept. 9.	A. W. Harris, T. W. Good, F. Pope .	27	23$\frac{1}{5}$

The fifth Cup having been won by A. W. Harris, a sixth Cup will be offered.

THE SYDNEY CHALLENGE TROPHY.

Presented by the Sydney B.C. of New South Wales, as a perpetual Challenge Trophy, to the Surrey B.C.; distance usually one mile. Usually run for at Kennington Oval in April and September

		m.	s.
1885, April 25.	R. Cripps, W. Brown, F. Prentice . .	3	39$\frac{2}{5}$
1885, Sept. 12.	H. A. Speechley, W. Terry, J. H. Adams .	3	17$\frac{4}{5}$
1886, April 17.	E. M. Mayes, H. F. Wilson [1] . .	3	48$\frac{2}{5}$
1886, Sept. 18.	P. Furnivall, H. A. Speechley, J. H. Adams	3	2
1887, May 14.	H. Synyer, F. J. Osmond, E. W. Brewerton	2	52$\frac{4}{5}$
	(Run at Lillie Bridge.)		
1887, Sept. 10.	W. F. Ball, H. A. Speechley, A. E. Langley	3	12$\frac{1}{5}$
1888, April 7.	E. M. Mayes, H. Synyer, F. Robinson .	3	34$\frac{2}{5}$
1888, Sept. 8.	F. J. Osmond, W. F. Ball, S. E. Williams	3	52$\frac{1}{5}$
	(Distance short.)		
1889, April 27.	F. P. Wood, F. J. Osmond	3	14$\frac{2}{5}$

Distance altered to $\frac{1}{4}$ mile.

		m.	s.
1889, Sept. 14.	E. M. Mayes, J. H. Adams, W. G. H. Bramson	0	39$\frac{2}{5}$

Distance half a mile.

		m.	s.
1890, April 19.	F. J. Osmond, L. Stroud	1	33$\frac{3}{5}$

Altered to a 5 miles Race.

		m.	s.
1890, Sept. 13.	W. C. Jones, R. A. Lloyd, C. Friswell .	15	5$\frac{4}{5}$

Altered to 1 mile.

		m.	s.
1891, April 18.	A. du Cros, J. E. L. Bates, R. L. Ede .	2	50$\frac{1}{5}$
1891, Sept. 12.	A. W. Harris, P. W. Scheltema, A. G. Fentiman	3	5
1892, April 23.	A. du Cros, U. L. Lambley, A. W. Harris .	2	51$\frac{1}{5}$
1892, Sept. 10.	A. W. Harris, A. E. Good, C. G. Thiselton .	3	1$\frac{3}{5}$
1893, April 22.	A. W. Harris, U. L. Lambley, F. G. Bradbury	3	4$\frac{3}{5}$
1893, Sept. 9.	F. Pope, W. G. Chilvers, P. W. Scheltema-Beduin	3	4$\frac{3}{5}$

[1] Only two rode.

THE TORQUAY CUPS.

An Ordinary and a Safety Cup. Each valued at 50 guineas. Run for on the Torquay Track.

Ordinary.			Safety.	
		m. s.		m. s.
1889, Aug. 27. A. Milsom	.	14 45⅘	F. T. Fletcher	14 58⅕
1890, Aug. 26. F. W. Weatherley		16 4	R. J. Mecredy	14 56

THE WALLER CUP.

1 *mile. To be run for on Waller's Ground, Byker, near Newcastle-on-Tyne. To be won three times in succession.*

1882, April. T. D. Oliver.
  „ May 29. { T. D. Oliver / E. J. Wilkinson } dead heat.
  „ May 30. { T. D. Oliver / E. J. Wilkinson } dead heat.
  „ July 17. T. D. Oliver at length won.
  „ Sept.   T. D. Oliver.

Oliver having won the Cup three times in succession, retained it.

THE NEW WALLER CUP.

1883, June 2.	T. D. Oliver.	1884, Aug. 30.	R. H. English.
„ Sept. 1.	F. Sutton.	1885, June 6.	R. H. English.
	1885. R. H. English.		

English retained possession of the new Cup. The Byker Grounds having been built over before this date, no more cups were offered, and the competition lapsed.

THE WEST LANCASHIRE CHALLENGE CUP.

Value 50 guineas. Distance 2 miles.

1876.	W. O. Milner.	1881.	C. A. Palmer.
1877.	R. Hassard.	1882.	C. A. Palmer.
1878	A. Spring.	1883	G H. Illston.
1879	F. T. East.	1884	Sanders Sellers.
1880	J. R. Hamilton.	1885	H. H. Smith.

CYCLING ON THE GOODWIN SANDS.

It was in the spring of 1883 that a cyclist first rode upon the Goodwin Sands, upon which several cricket matches have been played. This fact escaped the notice of Mr. George Byng Gattie, the author of 'Memorials of the Goodwin Sands.' To Mr. Palmer Dalton, of the London Bicycle Club, belongs the unique honour of being the *first* to perform this feat.

On August 31, 1887, Messrs. F. Wimbush and A. E. Walker, of the Finchley Tricycle Club, and C. W. Brown, North Road Club, took ship from Deal beach, and landed on the sands, something of a race to be first taking place. In riding it was found necessary to keep very close to the water, the sand there, owing probably to the pressure of the water, being hard, whilst twenty yards away it was quite soft. The trio returned in safety to Deal. So at present the record of the Goodwin Sands stands thus :—

1883.	Palmer Dalton, London B.C.	Ordinary bicycle.
1887.	F. Wimbush, Finchley T.C.	Safety ,,
1887.	C. W. Brown, North Road Club	Ordinary ,,
1887.	A. E. Walker, Finchley T.C.	Safety ,,

HILL-CLIMBING TRIALS.

On September 4, 1880, the Surrey Bicycle Club promoted a hill-climbing competition, up Reigate Hill. The gradient averages 4½ in every 100, and the steepest part is 12 in 100. Total length from 'The Grapes' Hotel, Reigate, to the Suspension Bridge, 2,640 yds. Total rise, 420 ft. Forty-one riders in all got up, G. H. Coleman, of Leytonstone, being credited with the fastest time, 4 mins. 40 secs., but the clocking was questioned. H. L. Cortis rode the hill with one arm in a sling.

On August 20, 1881, the Hornsey and Canonbury Bicycle Clubs combined to promote a hill-climbing competition up Muswell Hill. Distance from starting-point, Victoria Hotel, to finish at Drinking Fountain, 800 yds. Average gradient, 1 in 12·78; 1,170 ft. from start gradient suddenly rises to 1 in 9·7 for 280 ft.;

650 ft. from the finish it rises to 1 in 8·7 for 310 ft., when it becomes 1 in 22·5 to finish.

NOTE.—Owing to certain alterations made at Muswell Hill, the stiffest portions of the rise have been markedly eased since the above data were taken.

Nineteen riders got up. No times were taken.

1886, Sept. 11. Finsbury Park C.C. Muswell Hill.

	m.	s.
P. L. Breysig	2	45
H. B. Saunders	3	9
D. Marks	3	12

1887, May 21. Weatheroak. Promoted by 'Sport and Play.' Gradients, 1 in 12, 1 in 10, 1 in 8, 1 in 6½, 1 in 7, 1 in 8, 1 in 10. Length, 1,060 feet. Surface bad.

	m.	s.
Frank Moore, Tricycle	1	$27\frac{3}{5}$
A. J. Wilson, Tricycle	1	$30\frac{2}{5}$
J. Moore, Safety	1	$36\frac{4}{5}$

1887, June 8. Wizard Hill, Alderley Edge. Promoted by the 'Athletic News.'

	m.	s.
A. M. Dutton, Safety	5	$1\frac{1}{2}$
T. W. Grace	5	3
H. R. Goodwin	5	$48\frac{1}{2}$

1887, August 20. Westerham Hill, Kent. Promoted by the Catford C.C.

	m.	s.
S. F. Edge, Safety	6	24
T. Simmonds, Safety	6	27
W. Travers, Safety	6	50
R. L. Philpot, first Ordinary	7	46
J. Moore, first Tricycle	7	50

1887, August 25. Promoted. Mowacre, Leicester. Length, 416 yds.; rise, 89, or 1 in 13; steepest, 1 in 8.

	m.	s.
J. Finney, Safety	1	26
W. Biddles, Ordinary	1	58
W. H. Cooper, Tricycle	1	$38\frac{3}{5}$

1888, August 18. Westerham Hill, Kent. Promoted by the Catford C.C.

	m.	s.
W. Chater Lea, Safety	6	46$\frac{3}{5}$
T. Simmonds, Safety	7	9$\frac{4}{5}$
C. M. Linley, Safety	7	44$\frac{3}{5}$

1888, October 20. Lucan Hill. Promoted by the Phœnix B.C., Ireland. Length, 350 yds. Steepest gradient, 1 in 9. No times taken.

A. Du Cros, 1st. W. Keating, 2nd. E. Bailey, 3rd.

1889, May 16. Alvington Shute, Carisbrooke, Isle of Wight Length, 1,100 yds. Stiffest rise, about 1 in 9.

	m.	s.
J. C. Millgate, Safety	4	17
J. H. Hale, Safety	4	22
J. R. Dear	4	22

1889, August 16. Titsey Hill, Kent. Promoted by the Catford C.C. Total rise, 370 ft. in 1,460 yds. Average gradient, 1 in 11·8. Steepest parts, 176 yds., 1 in 8·34, followed by 120 yds., 1 in 7·27.

	m.	s.
W. Chater Lea, Safety	6	10
M. S. Napier, Safety	6	43
C. M. Linley, Safety	7	1
Bertram Blount, first Tricycle	8	7
A. V. Puckle, first Ordinary	8	12

1890, June 28. Toys Hill, between Four Elms and Brasted, near Westerham, Kent. Promoted by the Catford C.C.

	m.	s.
Felix Greville, Safety	8	40
Chater Lea, Safety	8	51
C. Sangster, Safety	9	50

INTER-UNIVERSITY RACES.

1874, June 18. On the road, Oxford to Cambridge.

Eighty-five miles. First two in to win.

E. St. John Mildmay, C.U.Bi.C., 8 hrs. 5 mins.
Hon. J. W. Plunkett, C.U.Bi.C.
C. Penrose, D.B.B.C. (Dark Blue B.C., now O.U.Bi.C.)
C. F. Reed, D.B.B.C.
Cambridge won.

1875, May 10. St. Albans to Headington.

Fifty-two miles. First man in to win the race for his Club.

1. Hon. Ion Keith-Falconer, Cambridge, 4 hrs. 9 mins. 24 secs.
2. F. L. Dodds, Cambridge. | 3. W. d'A. Crofton, Oxford.
Cambridge won.

1876, June 28. Alexandra Palace Track.

Fifty miles. First man in to win the race for his Club.

1. W. d'A. Crofton, Oxford, 3 hrs. 22 mins. 54 secs.
2. J. H. W. Lee, Oxford. | 3. G. M. Parker, Cambridge.
Oxford won.

1877, June 11. Oxford Path.

The first man in scores the race for his Club.

Two Miles.

1. Hon. Ion Keith-Falconer, Cambridge, 6 mins. 1 sec.[1]
2. W. d'A. Crofton, Oxford.
Cambridge won.

Ten Miles.

1. Hon. Ion Keith-Falconer, Cambridge, 32 mins. 27 secs.[1]
2. W. d'A. Crofton, Oxford.
Cambridge won.

Twenty-five Miles.

1. J. C. Thorp, Oxford, 1 hr. 30 mins. 24 secs.
2. J. E. Julian, Oxford.
Oxford won.

Result of the three races, Cambridge won.

---

[1] Best on record at that date.

APPENDIX.

1878, May 18. Cambridge Track.

Two Miles.

1. W. d'A. Crofton, Oxford, 6 mins. 10 secs.
2. A. A. E. Weir, Oxford.
   Oxford won.

Ten Miles.

1. W. d'A. Crofton, Oxford, 33 mins. 28 secs.
2. C. H. F. Christie, Oxford.
   Oxford won.

Twenty-five Miles.

1. A. A. E. Weir, Oxford, 1 hr. 24 mins. 36 secs.[1]
2. R. W. Macleod, Cambridge.
   Oxford won.
   Result of the three races, Oxford won.

1879, May 10. Oxford Path.

Two Miles.

1. H. R. Reynolds, Oxford, 6 mins. 1 sec.
2. F. G. Mayor, Cambridge.
   Oxford won.

Ten Miles.

1. A. A. E. Weir, Oxford, 31 mins. 54 secs.[1]
2. F. F. Tower, Cambridge
   Oxford won.

Twenty-five Miles.

1. W. L. Ainslie, Oxford, 1 hr. 19 mins. 23 secs.[1]
2. C. H. F. Christie, Oxford.
   Oxford won.
   Result of the three races, Oxford won.

1880, May 26. Cambridge Track.

Two Miles.

1. C. A. E. Pollock, Cambridge, 5 mins. 56 secs.
2. { W. L. Ainslie, Oxford } Dead heat.
   { G. D. Day, Cambridge }
   Cambridge won.

---

[1] Best on record at that date.

Ten Miles.

1. W. L. Ainslie, Oxford, 31 mins. 42? secs.
2. F. F. Tower, Cambridge.

Oxford won.

Twenty-five Miles.

1. G. D. Day, Cambridge, 1 hr. 22 mins. 20⅖ secs.
2. D. J. S. Bailey, Cambridge.

Cambridge won.

Result of the three races, Cambridge won.

1881, May 8. Oxford Track.

Two Miles.

1. G. D. Day, Cambridge, 5 mins. 52 secs.
2. H. Oeschger, Oxford.

Cambridge won.

Ten Miles.

1. D. J. S. Bailey, Cambridge, 30 mins. 48⅖ secs.
2. H. Oeschger, Oxford.

Cambridge won.

Twenty-five Miles.

1. G. D. Day, Cambridge, 1 hr. 21 mins. 40 secs.
2. H. Muir, Cambridge.

Cambridge won.

Result of the three matches, Cambridge won.

1882, May 6. Cambridge Track.

Two Miles.

1. W. F. M. Buckley, Oxford, 5 mins. 52⅔ secs.
2. G. D. Day, Cambridge.

Oxford won.

Ten Miles.

1. J. S. Whatton, Cambridge, 31 mins. 38 secs.
2. W. F. M. Buckley, Oxford.

Cambridge won.

Twenty-five Miles.

1. G. D. Day, Cambridge, 1 hr. 20 mins. 8 secs.
2. { W. A. G. Walter, Oxford } Dead heat.
   { H. Muir, Cambridge }

Cambridge won.

Result of the three races, Cambridge won by 2 points to 1.

APPENDIX. 435

1883, June 5. Oxford Track.

Two Miles.
1. W. F. M. Buckley, Oxford, 6 mins. 37 secs.
2. J. S. Whatton, Cambridge.
    Oxford won.

Ten Miles.
1. W. F. M. Buckley, Oxford, 32 mins.
2. J. S. Whatton, Cambridge.
    Oxford won.

Twenty-five Miles.
1. W. K. Adam, Oxford, 1 hr. 27 mins. 12 secs.
2. W. A. G. Walter, Oxford.
    Oxford won.

Result of the three races, Oxford won by 3 points to 0

1884, July 2. Lillie Bridge.

Two Miles.
1. J. S. Whatton, Cambridge. 6 mins. $6\frac{3}{5}$ secs.
2. H. L. Paterson, Cambridge.
    Cambridge won.

Ten Miles.
1. J. S. Whatton, Cambridge, 33 mins. $3\frac{4}{5}$ secs.
2. A. B. W. Whatton, Cambridge.
    Cambridge won.

Twenty-five Miles.
1. S. Swann, Cambridge, 1 hr. 23 mins. 6 secs.
2. A. W. Rumney, Cambridge.
    Cambridge won.

Result of the three races, Cambridge won by 3 points to 0.

1885. No Inter-University match took place this year.

1886, June 23. At Oxford.

Ten Miles.
George Gatehouse, Cambridge, 32 mins. 36 secs.
W. J. Turrell, Oxford.
J. W. Fearnsides, Oxford.
Lewis Stroud, Oxford.
    Oxford won.

1887, June 11. At Cambridge.

One Mile.

George Gatehouse, Cambridge, *beat* W. J. Turrell, Oxford; 2 mins. $58\frac{3}{5}$ secs.

Lewis Stroud, Oxford, *beat* B. W. Crump, Cambridge; 3 mins. $3\frac{1}{5}$ secs.

W. A. C. Freemantle, Oxford, *beat* J. R. Darling, Cambridge; 2 mins. $50\frac{3}{5}$ secs.

Oxford won.

Four Miles.

George Gatehouse, Cambridge, 12 mins. $29\frac{1}{5}$ secs.
Lewis Stroud, Oxford.
W. A. C. Freemantle, Oxford.
B. W. Crump, Cambridge.
F. R. Armitage, Cambridge.

Cambridge won.

Fifteen Miles.

W. J. Turrell, Oxford, 48 mins. $7\frac{1}{5}$ secs.
J. W. Fearnsides, Oxford.
E. T. A. Wigram, Cambridge.
J. R. Darling, Cambridge.
G. F. C. Searle, Cambridge.

Oxford won.

Oxford won the match.

1888, July 21. Paddington Track.

One Mile.

W. J. Turrell, Oxford, *beat* W. McF. Orr, Cambridge; 3 mins. $36\frac{1}{5}$ secs.

B. W. Crump, Cambridge, w.o.

Butler-Harris, Oxford, *beat* W. L. Raynes, Cambridge; 3 mins. $2\frac{2}{5}$ secs.

Oxford won.

Four Miles.

W. J. Turrell, Oxford (no time taken).
W. L. Raynes, Cambridge.
Butler-Harris, Oxford.
W. McF. Orr, Cambridge.
B. W. Crump, Cambridge.

Oxford won.

APPENDIX.

Ten Miles.

W. J. Turrell, Oxford, 36 mins. 28$\frac{4}{5}$ secs.
W. L Raynes, Cambridge.
Butler-Harris, Oxford.
W. McF. Orr, Cambridge.
John Attleè, Cambridge.

Oxford won.
Oxford won the match.

1889, July 18. Paddington Track.

One Mile.

B. W. Crump, Cambridge, w.o.
S. E. Williams, Cambridge, *beat* Butler-Harris, Oxford; 2 mins. 55$\frac{4}{5}$ secs.
W. L. Raynes, Cambridge, *beat* G. A. Ellaby, Oxford; 3 mins. 10$\frac{3}{5}$ secs.

Cambridge won.

Four Miles.

S. E. Williams, Cambridge.
B. W. Crump, Cambridge.
Butler-Harris, Oxford.
John Attlee, Cambridge.
G. A. Ellaby, Oxford.
J. White, Oxford.

Cambridge won.

Ten Miles.

Lewis Stroud, Oxford.
W. L. Raynes, Cambridge.
B. W. Attlee, Cambridge.
G. A. Ellaby, Oxford.
W. J. Butterfield, Oxford.
G. E. C. Searle, Cambridge.

Oxford won.
Cambridge won the match.

1890, June 17.

One Mile.

Lewis Stroud, O.U.Bi.C., *beat* S. E. Williams, C.U.Bi.C.; 3 mins. 40$\frac{2}{5}$ secs.
C. C. B. Bardsley, O.U.Bi.C., *beat* the Hon. G. H. Scott, C.U.Bi.C.; 3 mins. 12$\frac{3}{5}$ secs.
B. W. Attlee, C.U.Bi.C., *beat* W. J. A. Butterfield, O.U.Bi.C.; 3 mins. 32$\frac{1}{5}$ secs.

Oxford won.

Four Miles

Lewis Stroud, Oxford, 13 mins. 32½ secs
S. E. Williams, Cambridge.
C. C. B. Bardsley, Oxford.
B. W. Attlee, Cambridge.
The Hon. G. H. Scott, Cambridge.
W. J. A. Butterfield, Oxford.

Oxford won.

Ten Miles.

Lewis Stroud, Oxford, 34 mins. 25 secs.
B. W. Attlee, Cambridge.
C. C. B. Bardsley, Oxford.
The Hon. G. H. Scott, Cambridge
W. E. Lloyd, Oxford.
S. E. Williams, Cambridge, fell.

Oxford won.
Oxford won the match.

LONDON BICYCLE CLUB v. CAMBRIDGE U.B.C.

1878, Oct. 26. Cambridge Track.

One Mile.

A. P. Trotter, Cambridge, *beat* Wadham Wyndham, L.B.C.; 3 mins. 0⅜ sec.
M. D. Rucker, L.B.C., *beat* O. G. M. Leeds, Cambridge; 3 mins. 7¾ secs.
W. T. Thorn, L.B.C., *beat* J. Scott, Cambridge; 3 mins. 2⅘ secs.

London won.

Four Miles.

A. P. Trotter, C.U.Bi.C., 13 mins. 13⅞ secs.
Wadham Wyndham, L.B.C.
J. F. Darrell, C.U.Bi.C.
M. D. Rucker, L.B.C.

Cambridge won.

Fifteen Miles.

W. T. Thorn, L.B.C., 52 mins. 40$\frac{2}{5}$ secs.
R. G. Trollope, L.B.C.
C. P. Wilson, C.U.Bi.C.

London won.
London won the match.

1879, June 10. Stamford Bridge Grounds.

One Mile.

Wadham Wyndham L.B.C., *beat* O. P. Fisher, C.U.Bi.C.; 3 mins. 0$\frac{4}{5}$ sec.
W. T. Thorn, L.B.C., *beat* H. S. Clarke, C.U.Bi.C.; 3 mins. 4 secs.
M. D. Rucker, L.B.C., *beat* J. W. Willink, C.U.Bi.C.; 3 mins. 6 secs.

London won.

Four Miles.

W. Wyndham, L.B.C., 12 mins. 37$\frac{1}{5}$ secs.
O. P. Fisher, C.U.Bi.C.
F. S. Colman, L.B.C.

London won.

Fifteen Miles.

W. T. Thorn, L.B.C., 50 mins. 34$\frac{4}{5}$ secs.
F. G. Mayor, C.U.Bi.C.
H. Nichols, C.U.Bi.C.

London won.
London won the match.

1880, May 29. Cambridge Track.

One Mile.

W. Wyndham, L.B.C., *beat* C. A. E. Pollock, C.U.Bi.C.; 2 mins. 59$\frac{3}{5}$ secs.
G. D. Day, C.U.Bi.C., *beat* Arthur Herbert, L.B.C.; 3 mins. 7$\frac{4}{5}$ secs.
O. P. Fisher, C.U.Bi.C., *beat* J. Scott, L.B.C.; 3 mins. 4 secs.

Cambridge won.

Four Miles.

W. T. Thorn, L.B.C., 12 mins. 32 secs.
C. A. E. Pollock, C.U.Bi.C.
F. G. Mayor, C.U.Bi.C.
A. Herbert, L.B.C.
O. P. Fisher, C.U.Bi.C.
O. Thorn, L.B.C.

A new scoring system was introduced in the Four and Fifteen Miles races, the first man scoring 6, the next 5, and so on. Thus in this race London scored 6, 3, 1 = 10, and Cambridge 5, 4, 2 = 11.

Cambridge won.

Fifteen Miles.

D. J. S. Bailey, C.U.Bi.C., 46 mins. 34½ secs.[1]
G. D. Day, C.U.Bi.C. } Dead heat.
W. T. Thorn, L.B.C.
W. Wyndham, L.B.C.
F. F. Tower, C.U.Bi.C.
A. D. Butler, L.B.C.

Cambridge won.
Cambridge won the match.

1881, May 21. Cambridge Track.

One Mile.

G. D. Day, C.U.Bi.C., *beat* W. Wyndham, L.B.C.; 3 mins. 6⅔ secs.
Harold Smith, L.B.C., *beat* C. A. E. Pollock, C.U.Bi.C.; 3 mins. 6¾ secs.
O. P. Fisher, C.U.Bi.C., *beat* O. G. M. Leeds, L.B.C.; 3 mins. 0⅕ sec.

Cambridge won.

Four Miles.

Harold Smith, L.B.C., 12 mins. 39⅘ secs.
G. D. Day, C.U.Bi.C.
W. Wyndham, L.B.C.
O. Thorn, L.B.C.
O. P. Fisher, C.U.Bi.C.
C. A. E. Pollock, C.U.Bi.C.

London won.

---
[1] Best on record.

APPENDIX.

Fifteen Miles.

G. D. Day, C.U.Bi.C., 51 mins. 0⅕ sec.
O. Thorn, L.B.C.
F. B. Westcott, C.U.Bi.C.
O. G. M. Leeds, L.B.C.
A. J. Crichton, C.U.Bi.C
A. H. Koch, L.B.C.

> Cambridge won.
> Cambridge won the match.

1882, June 22. Surbiton Recreation Grounds.

One Mile.

J. S. Whatton, C.U.Bi.C., *beat* Harold Smith, L.B.C. ; 3 mins. 0⅘ sec.
G. D. Day, C.U.Bi.C., *beat* C. A. Brown, L.B.C.; 3 mins. 8 secs.
A. B. W. Whatton, C.U.Bi.C., *beat* F. L. Adam, L.B.C. ; 3 mins. 4 secs.

> Cambridge won.

Four Miles.

J. S. Whatton, C.U.Bi.C., 13 mins. 9 secs.
J. F. Griffith, L.B.C.
C. A. E. Pollock, C.U.Bi.C.
E. H. Brown, C.U.Bi.C.
H. Smith, L.B.C.
O. Thorn, L.B.C.

> Cambridge won.

Fifteen Miles.

G. D. Day, C.U.Bi.C., 49 mins. 27⅔ secs.
J. F. Griffith, L.B.C.
H. R. Reynolds, L.B.C.
F. B. Westcott, C.U.Bi.C.
H. Muir, C.U.Bi.C.
C. A. Brown, L.B.C.

> London won.
> Cambridge won the match.

1883, June 9. Cambridge Track.

One Mile.

F. L. Adam, L.B.C., *beat* G. D. Day, C.U.Bi.C.; 3 mins. 1 sec.

A. B. W. Whatton, C.U.Bi.C., *beat* J. D. Butler, L.B.C.; 3 mins. 4 secs.

W. Wyndham, L.B.C., *beat* C. A. E. Pollock, C.U.Bi.C.; 3 mins. $4\frac{4}{5}$ secs.

London won.

Four Miles.

G. F. Beck, L.B.C., 12 mins. $26\frac{3}{5}$ secs
C. A. E. Pollock, C.U.Bi.C
J. D. Butler, L.B.C.
A. B. W. Whatton, C.U.Bi.C.
F. B. Westcott, C.U.Bi.C.
F. L. Adam, L.B.C.

London won.

Fifteen Miles.

W. Wyndham, L.B.C., 47 mins. $18\frac{2}{5}$ secs.
G. D. Day, C.U.Bi.C.
H. R. Reynolds, L.B.C.
M. H. Jephson, L.B.C.
L. C. Carr, C.U.Bi.C.
E. J. P. Olive, C.U.Bi.C.

London won.
London won the match.

1884, June 26. Lillie Bridge Track.

One Mile.

Oliver Thorn, L.B.C., *beat* J. S. Whatton, C.U.Bi.C.; 3 mins. $0\frac{4}{5}$ sec.

F. L. Adam, L.B.C., *beat* A. B. W. Whatton, C.U.Bi.C.; 3 mins. $6\frac{4}{5}$ secs.

M. Crosse, C.U.Bi.C., *beat* J. D. Butler, L.B.C.; 3 mins. 14 secs.

London won.

APPENDIX.

Four Miles.

J. S. Whatton, C.U.Bi.C., 13 mins. 7 secs.
A. B. W. Whatton, C.U.Bi.C.
J. D. Butler, L.B.C.
H. R. Reynolds, L.B.C.
D. McRae, L.B.C.
M. Crosse, C.U.Bi.C.

Cambridge won.

Fifteen Miles.

F. L. Adam, L.B.C., 50 mins. 26 secs.
H. R. Reynolds, L.B.C.
S. Swann, C.U.Bi.C.
A. W. Rumney, C.U.Bi.C.
Oliver Thorn, L.B.C.
G. W. P. Pridham, C.U.Bi.C.

London won.
London won the match.

1885, June 6. Cambridge Track.

One Mile.

J. S. Whatton, L.B.C., *beat* George Gatehouse, C.U.Bi.C.; 2 mins. 49 secs.
M. Crosse, C.U.Bi.C., *beat* W. Wyndham, L.B.C.; 3 mins. $11\frac{4}{5}$ secs.
H. R. Reynolds, L.B.C., *beat* A. W. Rumney, C.U.Bi C; 3 mins. $4\frac{3}{5}$ secs.

London won.

Four Miles.

George Gatehouse, C.U.Bi.C, 12 mins. 13 secs.
H. R. Reynolds, L.B.C.
W. Wyndham, L.B.C.
G. F. C. Searle, C.U.Bi.C.
E. I. Carr, L.B.C.
M. Crosse, C.U.Bi.C.

London won.

Fifteen Miles.

George Gatehouse, C.U.Bi.C., 48 mins. 5 secs.
H. R. Reynolds, L.B.C.
A. W. Rumney, C.U.Bi.C.
C. W. Fagan, C.U.Bi.C.
W. Wyndham, L.B.C.
E. I. Carr, L.B.C.

Cambridge won.
Cambridge won the match.

1886, July 1.

One Mile.

M. D. Rucker, L.B.C., *beat* G. F. C. Searle, Cambridge; 3 mins. $7\frac{2}{5}$ secs.
H. R. Schmettau, L.B.C., *beat* B. W. Crump Cambridge; 3 mins. $6\frac{3}{5}$ secs.
George Gatehouse, Cambridge, *beat* Harold Smith, L.B.C.; 2 mins. $58\frac{3}{5}$ secs.

London won.

Four Miles.

George Gatehouse, Cambridge, 11 mins. $53\frac{3}{5}$ secs.
Douglas McRae, London B.C.

London won.

Fifteen Miles.

Harold Smith, L.B.C., 47 mins. $38\frac{3}{5}$ secs.
D. McRae, L.B.C.

London won.
The L.B.C. won the match.

1887, June 11. Cambridge Track.

One Mile.

George Gatehouse, C.U.Bi.C., *beat* H. R. Schmettau, L.B.C.; 2 mins. $49\frac{3}{5}$ secs.
J. R. Darling, C.U.Bi.C., *beat* W. J. Turrell, L.B.C.; 3 mins. $3\frac{1}{5}$ secs.
F. C. Thorn, L.B.C., *beat* B. W. Crump C.U.Bi.C.; 2 mins. $53\frac{2}{5}$ secs.

Cambridge won.

Four Miles.

George Gatehouse, C.U.Bi.C., 11 mins. $20\frac{1}{5}$ secs.[1]
Douglas McRae, L.B.C.
W. J. Turrell, L.B.C.
H. R. Schmettau, L.B.C.
F. R. Armitage, C.U.Bi.C.
G. F. C. Searle, C.U.Bi.C.

London won.

Fifteen Miles.

Douglas McRae, L.B.C., 46 mins. $59\frac{4}{5}$ secs.
F. C. Thorn, L.B.C.
J. R. Darling, C.U.Bi.C.
G. N. Stunt, L.B.C.
E. T. A. Wigram, C.U.Bi.C.
B. W. Crump, C.U.Bi.C.

London won.
London won the match.

1888. No inter-club contest took place.

1889, June 15.

One Mile.

Douglas McRae, London B.C., *beat* W. McF. Orr, Cambridge; time, 3 mins. $16\frac{1}{5}$ secs.
H. R. Schmettau, London B.C., dead-heated with S. E. Williams, Cambridge, in 3 mins. 4 secs.
H. D. Faith, London B.C., *beat* E. R. Sykes, Cambridge; 3 mins. $6\frac{1}{5}$ secs.

London won.

Four Miles.

Douglas McRae, L.B.C, 1st., 12 mins. $44\frac{4}{5}$ secs.
W. McF. Orr, Cambridge, 2nd.
H. R. Schmettau, L.B.C., 3rd.
S. E. Williams, Cambridge, 4th.

London won.

---

[1] Time questioned.

Fifteen Miles.

Douglas McRae, L.B.C., 50 mins. 32 secs., 1st.
H. R. Schmettau, L.B.C., 2nd.
B. W. Attlee, Cambridge, 3rd.
S. E. Williams, Cambridge, 4th.

London won.
London won the match.

1890, June 14. Cambridge Track.

One Mile.

Sydney E. Williams, C.U.Bi.C., *beat* D. McRae, L.B.C.; 3 mins. $0\frac{1}{5}$ sec.
The Hon. G. H. Scott, C.U.Bi.C., *beat* H. R. Schmettau, L.B.C.; 2 mins. $51\frac{4}{5}$ secs.
B. W. Attlee, C.U.Bi.C., *beat* E. E. Barron, L.B.C.; 2 mins. $53\frac{2}{5}$ secs.

Cambridge won.

Four Miles.

Douglas McRae, L.B.C., 12 mins. $34\frac{4}{5}$ secs.
The Hon. G. H. Scott, C.U.Bi.C.
B. W. Attlee, C.U.Bi.C.
H. R. Reynolds, L.B.C.
S. E. Williams, C.U.Bi.C.
H. R. Schmettau, L.B.C.

Cambridge won.

Fifteen Miles.

Douglas McRae, L.B.C., 50 mins. $51\frac{4}{5}$ secs.
S. E. Williams, C.U.Bi.C.
The Hon. G. H. Scott, C.U.Bi.C.
B. W. Attlee, C.U.Bi.C.
H. R. Reynolds, L.B.C.
H. R. Schmettau, L.B.C.

Cambridge won.
Cambridge won the match.

RECORDS ON THE PATH.

BICYCLE RECORDS.

Date	Miles	Time h. m. s.	Name	Place
June 25, 1892[1]	¼	32⅕	J. H. Adams	Herne Hill.
June 7, 1890[2]	¼	35⅘	F. J. B. Archer	Paddington Track.
July 11, 1891	½	1 12⅗	U. L. Lambley	Herne Hill.
July 15, 1890	¾	1 51⅘	F. J. Osmond	Paddington Track.
,, ,,	1	2 28⅘	,,	,, ,,
May 23, 1888	2	5 12⅕	W. A. Illston	Coventry Track.
Sept. 8, 1887	3	8 14⅖	F. J. Osmond	Crystal Palace Track.
Sept. 10, 1891	4	10 51⅕	U. L. Lambley	Herne Hill.
,, ,,	5	13 44⅕	,,	,,
Sept. 2, 1891	6	16 36	B. W. Atlee	,,
,, ,,	7	19 26⅘	,,	,,
,, ,,	8	22 14⅕	,,	,,
,, ,,	9	25 1⅘	,,	,,
,, ,,	10	27 55⅕	,,	,,
,, ,,	11	30 46⅖	,,	,,
,, ,,	12	33 36⅗	,,	,,
,, ,,	13	36 28⅖	,,	,,
,, ,,	14	39 20⅕	,,	,,
,, ,,	15	42 13⅘	,,	,,
,, ,,	16	45 5⅗	,,	,,
,, ,,	17	48 1⅖	,,	,,
,, ,,	18	50 58⅗	,,	,,
,, ,,	19	53 53	,,	,,
,, ,,	20	56 51	,,	,,
,, ,,	21	59 43⅘	,,	,,
,, ,,	22	1 2 52	,,	,,
,, ,,	23	1 6 5⅕	,,	,,
,, ,,	24	1 9 23⅗	,,	,,
,, ,,	25	1 12 48⅗	,,	,,
Sept. 8, 1891	26	1 16 26⅖	F. J. B. Archer	,,
,, ,,	27	1 19 41⅗	,,	,,
,, ,,	28	1 23 7⅖	,,	,,
,, ,,	29	1 26 39⅘	,,	,,
,, ,,	30	1 30 12⅕	,,	,,
,, ,,	31	1 33 49⅗	,,	,,
,, ,,	32	1 37 32⅖	,,	,,
July 25, 1889	33	1 41 55⅘	J.H. Adams	Coventry Track.
,, ,,	34	1 44 57⅖	,,	,, ,,
,, ,,	35	1 48 6⅘	,,	,, ,,
,, ,,	36	1 51 16⅘	,,	,, ,,

[1] Flying start. [2] Standing start.

BICYCLE RECORDS—*continued.*

Date.	Miles	Time	Name	Place
		h. m. s.		
July 25, 1889	37	1 54 19⅖	J. H. Adams	Coventry Track.
,, ,,	38	1 57 24	,,	,, ,,
,, ,,	39	2 0 24⅘	,,	,, ,,
,, ,,	40	2 3 21⅕	,,	,, ,,
,, ,,	41	2 6 21⅘	,,	,, ,,
,, ,,	42	2 9 21⅘	,,	,, ,,
,, ,,	43	2 12 23⅗	,,	,, ,,
,, ,,	44	2 15 24	,,	,, ,,
,, ,,	45	2 18 23⅗	,,	,, ,,
,, ,,	46	2 21 24⅗	,,	,, ,,
,, ,,	47	2 24 36	,,	,, ,
,, ,,	48	2 27 41	,,	,, ,,
,, ,,	49	2 30 45⅖	,,	,, ,,
,, ,,	50	2 33 57⅖	,,	,, ,,
Aug. 22, 1888	51	2 47 21⅗	,,	Crystal Palace Track.
,, ,,	55	3 2 33⅘	,,	,, ,,
July 27, 1883	56	3 14 30	F. R. Fry	,, ,,
,, ,,	60	3 28 30	,,	,, ,,
,, ,,	70	4 3 17	,,	,, ,,
,, ,,	80	4 38 32	,,	,, ,,
,, ,,	90	5 15 2	,,	,, ,,
,, ,,	100	5 50 5⅖	,,	,, ,,
Sept. 29, 1884	101	6 43 27	G. Lacy Hillier	,, ,,
,, ,,	110	7 28 30	,,	,, ,,
,, ,,	120	8 7 26	,,	,, ,,
,, ,,	130	8 49 28	,,	,, ,,
,, ,,	140	9 33 54	,,	,, ,,
,, ,,	146	9 59 34	,,	,, ,,

HOUR RECORDS.

Hours	Date	mi. yds.	Name	Place
1	Sept. 2, 1891	21 180	B. W. Attlee	Herne Hill Track.
2	July 25, 1889	38 1520	J. H. Adams	Coventry Track.
3	Aug. 22, 1888	54 578	,,	Crystal Palace Track.
4	July 27, 1883	69 90	F. R. Fry	,, ,,
5	,, ,,	85 1400	,,	,, ,,
10	Sept. 29, 1884	146 250	G. L. Hillier	,, ,,

SAFETY BICYCLE RECORDS.

Date	Miles	Time	Name	Place
		h. m. s.		
Sept. 22, 1893[1]	$\frac{1}{4}$	$27\frac{1}{5}$	A. W. Harris	Herne Hill Track.
Sept. 20, 1894[2]	$\frac{1}{4}$	$31\frac{1}{5}$	T. Osborn	,, ,,
Sept. 20, 1894	$\frac{1}{2}$	1 0	J. Platt-Betts	,, ,,
,, ,,	$\frac{3}{4}$	1 $29\frac{4}{5}$	,,	,, ,,
,, ,,	1	2 $1\frac{3}{5}$	,,	,, ,,
Oct. 3, 1894	2	4 $19\frac{3}{5}$	,,	,, ,,
Sept. 27, 1894	3	6 $37\frac{4}{5}$	J. A. Robertson	,, ,,
,, ,,	4	8 $44\frac{1}{5}$	,,	,, ,,
,, ,,	5	10 $57\frac{2}{5}$	,,	,, ,,
Aug. 29, 1894	6	13 $12\frac{4}{5}$	G. R. Martin	,, ,,
,, ,,	7	15 $30\frac{2}{5}$	,,	,, ,,
Sept. 27, 1894	8	17 40	J. A. Robertson	,, ,,
,, ,,	9	19 $59\frac{3}{5}$	,,	,, ,,
,, ,,	10	22 $10\frac{2}{5}$	W. Henie	,, ,,
Sept. 27, 1894	11	24 $25\frac{1}{5}$	J. A. Robertson	,, ,,
,, ,,	12	26 $36\frac{3}{5}$	,,	,, ,,
,, ,,	13	28 $53\frac{1}{5}$	,,	,, ,,
,, ,,	14	31 $14\frac{1}{5}$	,,	,, ,,
,, ,,	15	33 $26\frac{4}{5}$	,,	,, ,,
,, ,,	16	35 $42\frac{2}{5}$	,,	,, ,,
,, ,,	17	37 $50\frac{2}{5}$	,,	,, ,,
,, ,,	18	40 $7\frac{4}{5}$	,,	,, ,,
,, ,,	19	42 $20\frac{1}{5}$	,,	,, ,,
,, ,,	20	44 $36\frac{1}{5}$	,,	,, ,,
,, ,,	21	46 $51\frac{2}{5}$	,,	,, ,,
,, ,,	22	49 $3\frac{3}{5}$	,,	,, ,,
,, ,,	23	51 $21\frac{1}{5}$	,,	,, ,,
,, ,,	24	53 $36\frac{2}{5}$	,,	,, ,,
,, ,,	25	55 $49\frac{1}{5}$	,,	,, ,,
,, ,,	26	57 $57\frac{2}{5}$	,,	,, ,,
Sept. 15, 1894	27	1 2 $51\frac{1}{5}$	J. Green	,, ,,
,, ,,	28	1 5 $13\frac{4}{5}$	,,	,, ,,
,, ,,	29	1 7 $21\frac{4}{5}$	,,	,, ,,
,, ,,	30	1 9 $50\frac{4}{5}$	,,	,, ,,
,, ,,	31	1 12 $9\frac{4}{5}$	,,	,, ,,
,, ,,	32	1 14 $30\frac{1}{5}$	,,	,, ,,
,, ,,	33	1 16 49	,,	,, ,,
,, ,,	34	1 19 $7\frac{1}{5}$	,,	,, ,,
,, ,,	35	1 21 $20\frac{1}{5}$	,,	,, ,,
,, ,,	36	1 23 $43\frac{1}{3}$	,,	,, ,,
,, ,,	37	1 26 1	,,	,, ,,
,, ,,	38	1 28 $20\frac{2}{5}$	,,	,, ,,

[1] Flying start. [2] Standing start.

SAFETY BICYCLE RECORDS—*continued.*

Date.	Miles	Time	Name	Place
		h. m. s.		
Sept. 15, 1894	39	1 30 40	J. Green	Herne Hill Track.
,, ,,	40	1 33 2 4/5	,,	,, ,,
,, ,,	41	1 35 26 1/5	,,	,, ,,
,, ,,	42	1 37 49 4/5	,,	,, ,,
,, ,,	43	1 40 13 2/5	,,	,, ,,
,, ,,	44	1 42 36 2/5	,,	,, ,,
,, ,,	45	1 45 3	,,	,, ,,
,, ,,	46	1 47 25 1/5	,,	,, ,,
,, ,,	47	1 49 46 4/5	,,	,, ,,
,, ,,	48	1 52 7 3/5	,,	,, ,,
,, ,,	49	1 54 28 3/5	,,	,, ,,
,, ,,	50	1 56 45 1/5	,,	,, ,,
Sept. 22, 1894	51	2 5 50 2/5	A. A. Chase	,, ,,
,, ,,	60	2 28 27 2/5	,,	,, ,,
,, ,,	70	2 53 45 4/5	,,	,, ,,
,, ,,	80	3 20 32 2/5	,,	,, ,,
,, ,,	90	3 47 53	,,	,, ,,
,, ,,	100	4 15 29 4/5	,,	,, ,,
,, ,,	110	4 45 37 1/5	,,	,, ,,
,, ,,	120	5 15 30 2/5	,,	,, ,,
,, ,,	130	5 45 38 4/5	,,	,, ,,
Oct. 13, 1894	140	6 15 57 3/5	G. Hunt	Putney Track.
,, ,,	150	6 43 45 1/5	,,	,, ,,
,, ,,	200	9 8 4 3/5	,,	,, ,,
,, ,,	250	11 32 26 2/5	,,	,, ,,
July 26–7, 1894	300	14 48 3 2/5	F. W. Shorland	Herne Hill Track.
,, ,,	350	17 43 11 3/5	,,	,, ,,
,, ,,	400	20 42 55	,,	,, ,,
,, ,,	450	23 29 54 1/5	,,	,, ,,
,, ,,	460	23 58 14 1/5	,,	,, ,,

Hour Records.

Hours	Date	mi.	yds.	Name	Place
1	Sept. 27, 1894	26	1670	J. A. Robertson	Herne Hill Track.
2	Sept. 15, 1894	50	0	J. Green	,, ,,
3	Sept. 22, 1894	72	750	A. A. Chase	,, ,,
4	,, ,,	94	580	,,	,, ,,
5	,, ,,	114	900	,,	,, ,,
6	,, ,,	134	780	,,	,, ,,
7	Oct. 13, 1894	155	1600	G. Hunt	Putney Track.
8	,, ,,	176	80	,,	,, ,,
9	,, ,,	197	445	,,	,, ,,
10	,, ,,	217	1700	,,	,, ,,
11	,, ,,	238	1110	,,	,, ,,
12	,, ,,	260	175	,,	,, ,,
13	July 27–8, 1894	257	1700	F. W. Shorland	Herne Hill Track.
14	,, ,,	286	743	,,	,, ,,
15	,, ,,	303	675	,,	,, ,,
16	,, ,,	321	261	,,	,, ,,
17	,, ,,	338	560	,,	,, ,,
18	,, ,,	355	0	,,	,, ,,
19	,, ,,	370	1630	,,	,, ,,
20	,, ,,	388	20	,,	,, ,,
21	,, ,,	405	500	,,	,, ,,
22	,, ,,	423	1540	,,	,, ,,
23	,, ,,	440	666	,,	,, ,,
24	,, ,,	460	1296	,,	,, ,,

TANDEM SAFETY BICYCLE RECORDS.

Date	Miles	Time (h. m. s.)	Name	Place
Sept. 21, 1893[1]	$\frac{1}{4}$	26$\frac{4}{5}$	A. W. Harris, J. Aram	Herne Hill Track.
Sept. 12, 1893[2]	$\frac{1}{4}$	31$\frac{4}{5}$	G. E. Osmond, T. W Good	,, ,,
July 19, 1894	$\frac{1}{2}$	1 0$\frac{3}{5}$	A. J. Watson, C. G. Thiselton	,, ,,
July 5, 1894	$\frac{3}{4}$	1 31$\frac{3}{5}$	A. J. Watson, C. G. Thiselton	,, ,,
,, ,,	1	2 2	,,	,, ,,
July 27, 1894	2	4 22$\frac{1}{5}$	J. E. Ridout, W. J. Jones	,, ,,
July 18, 1894	3	6 42	,,	,, ,,
,, ,,	4	8 54$\frac{2}{5}$	,,	,, ,,
,, ,,	5	11 9$\frac{1}{5}$	,,	,, ,,
,, ,,	6	13 18$\frac{3}{5}$	,,	,, ,,
,, ,,	7	15 34$\frac{1}{5}$	,,	,, ,,
,, ,,	8	17 51$\frac{1}{5}$	,,	,, ,,
,, ,,	9	19 59$\frac{4}{5}$	,,	,, ,,
,, ,,	10	22 10$\frac{1}{5}$	,,	,, ,,
Sept. 27, 1894	12	27 21$\frac{1}{5}$	E. Scott, G. McNish	,, ,,
,, ,,	15	34 0$\frac{4}{5}$	,,	,, ,,
,, ,,	20	45 16$\frac{1}{5}$	,,	,, ,,
,, ,,	25	56 25$\frac{2}{5}$	,,	,, ,,
,, ,,	30	1 7 37$\frac{3}{5}$	,,	,, ,,
,, ,,	35	1 19 0	,,	,, ,,
,, ,,	40	1 31 1$\frac{1}{5}$	,,	,, ,,
,, ,,	45	1 42 33$\frac{1}{5}$	,,	,, ,,
,, ,,	50	1 53 20$\frac{3}{5}$	,,	,, ,,

[1] Flying start. [2] Standing start.

HOUR RECORDS.

Hours	Date	mi. yds	Name	Place
1	Sept. 27, 1894	26 1,025	E. Scott, G. McNish	Herne Hill Track.

TRICYCLE RECORDS

Date	Miles	Time			Name	Place
		h	m.	s.		
Sept. 23, 1893	$\frac{1}{4}$			$33\frac{4}{5}$	L. Stroud	Herne Hill Track.
Sept. 13, 1894	$\frac{1}{2}$		1	$10\frac{3}{5}$	W. Ellis	,, ,,
,, ,,	$\frac{3}{4}$		1	$45\frac{3}{5}$	,,	,, ,,
,, ,,	1		2	$21\frac{1}{5}$	,,	,, ,,
Oct. 18, 1894	2		4	$56\frac{3}{5}$	,,	,, ,,
,, ,,	3		7	$28\frac{2}{5}$	,,	,, ,,
,, ,,	4		10	$3\frac{2}{5}$	,,	,, ,,
,, ,,	5		12	$35\frac{3}{5}$	,,	,, ,,
,, ,,	6		15	$6\frac{3}{5}$	,,	,, ,,
,, ,,	7		17	$39\frac{1}{5}$	,,	,, ,,
,, ,,	8		20	$12\frac{1}{5}$	,,	,, ,,
,, ,,	9		22	$44\frac{4}{5}$	,,	,, ,,
,, ,,	10		25	$16\frac{1}{5}$	,,	,, ,,
,, ,,	11		27	$44\frac{1}{5}$	,,	,, ,,
,, ,,	12		30	$21\frac{3}{5}$	,,	,, ,,
,, ,,	13		32	$54\frac{3}{8}$	,,	,, ,,
,, ,,	14		35	$31\frac{1}{5}$	,,	,, ,,
,, ,,	15		38	$3\frac{1}{5}$	,,	,, ,,
,, ,,	16		40	$34\frac{3}{5}$	,,	,, ,,
,, ,,	17		43	$14\frac{4}{5}$	,,	,, ,,
,, ,,	18		45	$53\frac{2}{5}$	,,	,, ,,
,, ,,	19		48	$29\frac{1}{5}$	,,	,, ,,
,, ,,	20		51	$4\frac{2}{5}$	,,	,, ,,
,, ,,	21		53	$37\frac{3}{5}$	,,	,, ,,
,, ,,	22		56	$11\frac{3}{5}$	,,	,, ,,
,, ,,	23		58	$42\frac{3}{5}$	,,	,, ,,
,, ,,	24	1	1	$17\frac{2}{5}$	,,	,, ,,
,, ,,	25	1	3	$46\frac{4}{5}$	,,	,, ,,
Oct. 1, 1894	30	1	20	$38\frac{4}{5}$	,,	,, ,,
,, ,,	35	1	33	$40\frac{4}{5}$	,,	,, ,,
,, ,,	40	1	47	$25\frac{3}{5}$	,,	,, ,,
,, ,,	45	2	1	$0\frac{3}{5}$	,,	,, ,,
,, ,,	50	2	14	29	,,	,, ,,
,, ,,	100	4	38	$58\frac{1}{5}$	,,	,, ,,
Sept. 20, 1894	150	7	53	41	E. Steel	Putney Track.
,, ,,	200	10	42	$42\frac{3}{5}$	,,	,, ,,
July 21–2, 1893	300	17	13	44	F. T. Bidlake	Herne Hill Track
,, ,,	400	23	27	$28\frac{3}{4}$	,,	,, ,,
,, ,,	410	23	58	$19\frac{1}{5}$	,,	,, ,,

TANDEM TRICYCLE RECORDS.

Date	Miles	Time	Name	Place
		h. m. s.		
Sept. 13, 1894	1/4	37 2/5	H. B. Hock, H. Smyth	Herne Hill Track.
,, ,,	1/2	1 20 2/5	,,	,, ,,
,, ,,	3/4	1 45 2/5	,,	,, ,,
,, ,,	1	2 21	,,	,, ,,
May 2, 1894	2	5 12 4/5	L. Stroud, J. E. L. Bates	,, ,,
,, ,,	3	7 42 1/5	,,	,, ,,
,, ,,	4	10 15 2/5	,,	,, ,,
,, ,,	5	12 55	,,	,, ,,
,, ,,	6	15 31 3/5	,,	,, ,,
,, ,,	7	18 5 3/5	,,	,, ,,
,, ,,	8	20 41 2/5	,,	,, ,,
,, ,,	9	23 20 2/5	,,	,, ,,
,, ,,	10	26 2	,,	,, ,,
,, ,,	11	28 42 2/5	,,	,, ,,
,, ,,	12	31 25 1/5	,,	,, ,,
,, ,,	13	33 59	,,	,, ,,
,, ,,	14	36 32 3/5	,,	,, ,,
,, ,,	15	39 5	,,	,, ,,
,, ,,	16	41 41 3/5	,,	,, ,,
,, ,,	17	44 14	,,	,, ,,
,, ,,	18	46 50 4/5	,,	,, ,,
,, ,,	19	49 26 2/5	,,	,, ,,
,, ,,	20	51 58 4/5	,,	,, ,,
,, ,,	21	54 31 3/5	,,	,, ,,
,, ,,	22	57 3 4/5	,,	,, ,,
,, ,,	23	59 36	,,	,, ,,
,, ,,	24	1 4 38	,,	,, ,,
,, ,,	25	1 7 26 1/5	,,	,, ,,
,, ,,	26	1 10 21 2/5	,,	,, ,,
,, ,,	27	1 13 13 2/5	,,	,, ,,
,, ,,	28	1 16 3 4/5	,,	,, ,,
,, ,,	29	1 18 46 1/5	,,	,, ,,
,, ,,	30	1 21 47 2/5	,,	,, ,,
Oct. 1, 1894	40	1 57 15 3/5	J. A. Poole, A. Hoffman	,, ,,
,, ,,	50	2 28 43 3/5	,,	,, ,,

One hour. 23 miles 310 yds. L. Stroud and J. E. L. Bates, Herne Hill.

Two hours. 40 miles 1510 yds. J. A. Poole and A. Hoffman, Herne Hill.

Hour Records.

Hours	Date	mi. yds.	Name	Place
1	Oct. 18, 1894	23 920	W. Ellis	Herne Hill Track.
2	Oct. 1, 1894	44 1100	,,	,, ,,
3	,, ,,	66 480	,,	,, ,,
4	,, ,,	86 1370	,,	,, ,,
5	Sept. 20, 1894	100 850	E. Steel	Putney Track.
6	,, ,,	116 1680	,,	,, ,,
7	,, ,,	133 65	,,	,, ,,
8	,, ,,	151 1690	,,	,, ,,
9	,, ,,	170 180	,,	,, ,,
10	,, ,,	187 170	,,	,, ,,
11	,, ,,	205 840	,,	,, ,,
12	,, ,,	223 1085	,,	,, ,,
13	July 22, 1893	233 320	F. T. Bidlake	Herne Hill Track.
14	,, ,,	250 0	,,	,, ,,
15	,, ,,	265 1550	,,	,, ,,
16	,, ,,	280 0	,,	,, ,,
17	,, ,,	296 500	,,	,, ,,
18	,, ,,	312 1135	,,	,, ,,
19	,, ,,	327 340	,,	,, ,,
20	,, ,,	343 380	,,	,, ,,
21	,, ,,	357 1680	,,	,, ,,
22	,, ,,	375 316	,,	,, ,,
23	,, ,,	392 20	,,	,, ,,
24	,, ,,	410 1110	,,	,, ,,

RECORDS ON THE ROAD.

LAND'S END TO JOHN O' GROATS.

The route, which has not always been closely adhered to, is as follows :—

Land's End Hotel.	Garstang, 395 miles.
Penzance.	Kendal, 430 miles.
Camborne.	Shap, 445 miles.
Redruth.	Penrith.
Bodmin, 60 miles.	Carlisle, 480 miles.
Launceston, 82 miles.	Ecclefechan.
Okehampton, 100 miles.	Lockerbie, 500 miles.
Exeter, 121 miles.	Beattock Bridge.
Collumpton.	Biggar, 545 miles.
Wellington.	Carlops.
Taunton, 154 miles.	Edinburgh.
Bridgwater, 163 miles.	Granton Ferry, 580 miles.
Cross, 179 miles.	Perth, 607 miles.
Bristol, 195 miles.	Pitlochrie.
Gloucester, 230 miles.	Blair Athole, 642 miles.
Tewkesbury.	Kingussie, 680 miles.
Worcester, 254 miles.	Carrbridge, 701 miles.
Kidderminster.	Inverness.
Bridgenorth, 282 miles.	Kessock Ferry.
Wellington (Salop).	Dingwall, 733 miles.
Hodnet.	Tain.
Market Drayton.	Meikle Ferry.
Nantwich.	Golspie, 785 miles.
Northwich.	Helmsdale, 800 miles.
Warrington, 353 miles.	Wick, 842 miles.
Wigan.	John o' Groat's House, 861 miles.
Preston, 382 miles.	

In 1880 Messrs. H. Blackwell, jun., and C. A. Harman, of the Canonbury B.C., made a run from 'end to end' on bicycles. Their estimate of the distance was nearly 900 miles, and they covered it in 13 days. The Hon. Ion Keith-Falconer created a great sensation in 1882 by riding over the same route in 12 days 23 hrs. 15 secs. James Lennox, A. Nixon, E. Oxborrow, T. R. Marriott, J. H. Adams, and many more have held the record, which at present stands to the credit of G. P. Mills, who went over the route on a tricycle in 3 days 16 hrs. 47 mins., finishing on June 8, 1893. Strange to say, the bicycle record is considerably behind the tricycle time, L. Fletcher's journey on a Safety bicycle having occupied 3 days 23 hrs. 55 mins.

LIVERPOOL TO EDINBURGH.

Route—Ormskirk (13 miles), Preston (32), Garstang (43), Lancaster (54), Burton (66), Kendal (76), Shap (92), Penrith (102), Plumpton (108), Carlisle (120), Ecclefechan (138), Lockerbie (145), Dinwoodie (153), Beattock Bridge (160), Crawford Inn (176), Biggar (192), Carlops (207), Edinburgh, Bank of Scotland (220).

This record route has not been much patronised, as the roads are, on the whole, very bad. It stood for some time to the credit of C. Lucas, who rode the distance in 21 hrs. 35 mins., and this time was cut by the present holder, as below.

1892, R. H. Carlisle, 15 hrs. 54 mins.

THE LONDON BICYCLE CLUB'S 100 MILES ROAD RACE.

In 1877 the L.B.C. instituted a Road Race from Bath to within nearly 6 miles of London, for members only. The race is kept very quiet, but always excites interest. It has resulted as follows:—

		h.	m.	s.
1877.	C. Walmesley; E. Tegetmier; A. D. Butler	8	23	30
1878.	F. E. Appleyard; W. T. Thorn; G. P. Coleman	7	18	55[1]
1879.	A. H. Koch; A. Herbert; P. Dalton	8	57	55
1880.	A. D. Butler only finished, owing to a violent N.E. gale	12	10	0
1881.	L. B. Reynolds; A. W. Barrett; H. R. Reynolds	7	55	0
1882.	H. R. Reynolds; G. F Beck; C. Newman and A. Barker dead heat for third place	7	26	0
1883.	H. R. Reynolds; L. B. Reynolds; H. Smith	7	28	0

[1] Best on record. This record stood unbeaten in the books until 1884. (See 100 Miles Road Record.)

458   CYCLING.

		h.	m.	s.
1884.	G. F. Beck; H. Smith; G. N. Stunt.	8	26	40
1885.	P. H. Watson; H. Smith; A. R. Ricardo.	7	33	43⅘

[In 1886 the route was altered for the first time, the riders leaving the London road near Slough, and riding N.E., *via* Stoke Pogis and Fulmer, into the Oxford-Wickham road, and thence by Denham to Rickmansworth— decidedly a slower route than the old one.]

		h.	m.	s.
1886.	Douglas McRae; A. C. Potter; L. Hartridge.	7	18	53

[In 1887 the route was again changed, starting from St. Albans *via* Hatfield, Welwyn, Biggleswade, Buckden, Alconbury Hill, Norman Cross, Wisbeach, to King's Lynn.]

		h.	m.	s.
1887.	Douglas McRae; F. H. Williams [only two finished].	8	38	38
1888.	F. H. Williams; F. C. Thorn; E. E. Barron	7	6	18
1889.	O. V. Cooke; A. W. Rumney; S. S. Legg	7	52	0
1890.	H. R. Reynolds; E. E. Barron; O. V. Cooke	6	40	45

LONDON TO BATH AND BACK.

Route—Hyde Park Corner, Hounslow, Maidenhead, Theale Newbury, Marlborough, Calne, Bath; 106 miles and back. The record was originally created by some of the pioneer riders of bone-shakers, who thought London to Bath a big enough feat. Walter Britten's record over the distance stood for six years, when C. A. Smith made a new record of 20 hrs. 55 mins. This he beat on September 9, 1889, when he rode the 212 miles in 17 hrs. 53 mins. 3 secs. Smith varied the usual procedure by starting from Hounslow, riding to Hyde Park Corner, and thence to Bath, finishing at Hounslow. This gave him a distinct advantage, as he rode the worst of the roads at the start; the 9¾ miles over lumpy roads and through traffic at the end of his long task would have taken more time to cover. After being several times essayed, this record now stands to the credit of C. G. Wridgway, as under.

Safety.

1893, Aug. 2   C. G. Wridgway, 14 hrs. 22 mins. 57 secs

APPENDIX.

LONDON TO BRIGHTON AND BACK. 'THE COACH RECORD.'

THE BRIGHTON COACH.

In July 1888 the late James Selby drove the Brighton Coach from the 'White Horse Cellars,' Piccadilly, *via* Croydon, Merstham,

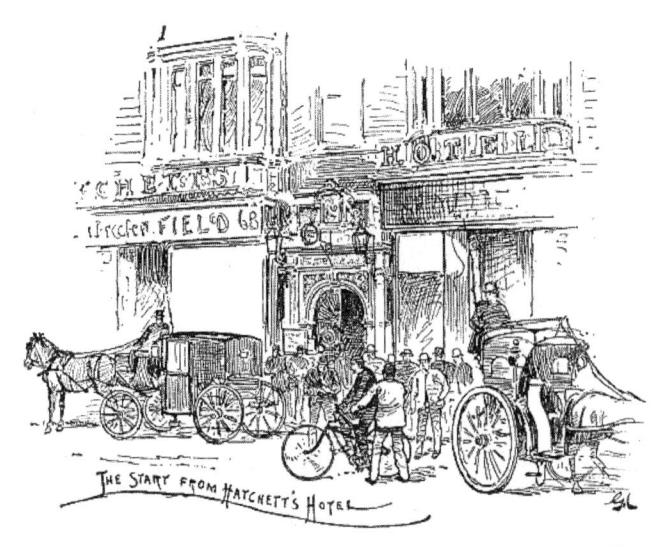

THE START FROM HATCHETT'S HOTEL.

Red Hill, Horley, Crawley, Hand Cross, Cuckfield, and Clayton, to Brighton and back. He had sixteen changes of horses. The distance is about 108 miles, and his times were—London to Brighton, 3 hrs. 36 mins ; London to Brighton and back, 7 hrs. 50 mins.

The performance attracted a good deal of attention, especially amongst cyclists, and it was confidently anticipated that the time accomplished would be beaten, but it remained longer 'on record' than was expected. The time was first beaten by a quartette of riders, using the same machine, and dividing the journey, Willis, Morris, Schafer, and Walker doing the journey in 7 hrs. 36 mins. 19⅗ secs. P. C. Wilson made an unsuccessful single-handed onslaught, as also did M. A. Holbein later on ;

CRAWLEY.—GOING DOWN.

and then another quartette, Shute, Girling, R. Wilson, and A. E. Griffin, did 7 hrs. 32 mins. ; their record being shortly afterwards reduced to 7 hrs. 25 mins. 15 secs. by E. and W. Scantlebury, Blair, and Arnott. P. C. Wilson again essayed the task, and failed ; and then F. Shorland, a stripling, covered the 'Coach Course' in 7 hrs. 19 mins., his outward journey occupying 3 hrs. 45 mins., his mount being a Facile inflated-tired safety bicycle. Shorland's performance created much enthusiasm, and it was regarded by many as almost an unbeatable record, whilst the advocates of the tire he used sought to secure for it all the credit of the performance.

On July 23, 1890, S. F. Edge, upon a Marriott & Cooper Safety, fitted with the firm's new cushion tires, not only for the

TURNING-POINT AT BRIGHTON.

first time beat the coach time for the outward journey, doing 3 hrs. 18 mins. 25 secs., but beat Shorland's time by 16 mins. 10 secs.,

CLAYTON HILL.—GOING HOME.

his full time being 7 hrs. 2 mins. 50 secs. But for a bad attack of cramp, which made it necessary for Edge to walk up Hand

Cross Hill on the return journey, his time would have been inside 7 hours.

On Sept. 3, 1890, C. A. Smith, mounted upon an inflated-tired Cumber Safety, succeeded in beating S. F. Edge's record. The down journey occupied 3 hrs. 26 mins. 3 secs., and the rider was delayed 10 mins. 30 secs. whilst procuring food. He reached

THE 'BLACK SWAN.' GOING HOME.—'PACEMAKER COMING ON.'

London again in 6 hrs. 52 mins. 10 secs. from the start, thus beating Edge's time by over 10 minutes.

Numerous fresh records have been made over this route, and at present the figures stand as under :—

Safety.
1893, Sept. 22. S. F. Edge, 5 hrs. 52 mins. 30 secs.

Tricycle.
1893, Oct. 4. W. W. Robertson, 7 hrs. 24 mins. 5 secs.

LONDON TO EDINBURGH.

Edinburgh Post Office to the G.P.O., London, or vice versâ. Distance nearly 400 miles.

Route—London, Barnet, Hatfield, Biggleswade, Buckden, Alconbury, Norman Cross (76 miles), Grantham (110), Retford (145), Wetherby (194), Leeming (222), Catterick (228), Durham (259),

Newcastle (274), Belford (322), Berwick (338), Dunbar (367) Haddington (379), Edinburgh (395¼).

This route was popularised by some of the earlier road record-makers, Alfred Bird, Alfred Nixon, and W. F. Sutton creating records between the two cities on tricycles. A number of well-known men have held this record, which at present stands thus :—

1892. R. H. Carlisle, 32 hrs. 55 mins.

LONDON TO LIVERPOOL.

G.P.O., London, to G.P.O., Liverpool.

1892. C. Lucas, 13 hrs. 4 mins.

LONDON TO YORK—'DICK TURPIN'S RIDE.'

Route—G.P.O., York, Selby (15 miles), Doncaster (35), Retford (52), Newark (73), Grantham (87), Stamford (108), Buckden (137), Biggleswade (152), Hitchin (163), Hatfield (177), Barnet (186), London, G.P.O. (197).

The route followed by Bonny Black Bess has always been attractive to cyclists, and many good men and true have essayed the record. Thorpe, Thorn, Reynolds, and others, have made records from London to York, or *vice versâ*, and the honours may, at present, be divided between the riders named below.

Safety Bicycle.

1892. F. W. Shorland, 12 hrs. 10 mins.

Tricycle.

1892. F. T. Bidlake, 13 hrs. 19 mins.

THE 12 HOURS ORDINARY ROAD RECORD.

This record at present stands as below :—

1891. J. F. Walsh, 175½ miles

THE 24 HOURS ORDINARY ROAD RECORD.

'All day' rides have of late years become much more systemised than they were at first, and the vast assistance obtainable by securing the services of pacemakers has now been fully exploited. Still, the pioneers who rode long distances without such aids should not be forgotten. H. S. Thorp, a long way back in the Seventies, rode 195½ miles in 22½ hours, from London to York. In 1876 Frank Smythe and W. E. N. Coston rode 205 miles in 22 hours. T. H. Wilkinson rode 200 miles, on a picked bit of road between Horley and Crawley, in 23 hrs. 19 mins., and G. T. Clough covered the same distance in 18 hours riding-time in 1877. Frank Smythe had another try on a picked bit of road, covering 218 miles; and then W. T. ('Billy') Thorn rode 162 miles in 17 hrs. 10 mins. before his machine broke down in a spin from London to York. Arthur Gilliatt, H. R. Reynolds, W. F. Sutton, and G. P. Mills all in turn held the 24 hours Bicycle Record. The honour at present rests with J. F. Walsh, who, on August 22, 1891, rode 312 miles inside 24 hours upon an Ordinary bicycle.

THE 50 MILES ORDINARY ROAD RECORD.

This has been held by many men, but has not been attempted so much of late owing to the popularity of the Safety for road work. R. J. Ilsley and J. F. Walsh both reduced the figures in 1890, but their records were in turn wiped out by the following:—

		h.	m.	s.
1891.	S. C. Houghton	2	45	55

THE 100 MILES ORDINARY ROAD RECORD.

This is an ancient and honourable record, which was held for a long while by Mr. F. E. Appleyard, who accomplished his grand time of 7 hrs. 18 mins. 55 secs., *unaided by pacemakers*, in the London B.C. race (which see). This time stood for a long while, but was eventually beaten by several riders, including Douglas McRae, F. H. Williams, and Theo. Godlee, who have all done better time on Ordinaries in the same race, though not over the same course, upon which Appleyard's time is as yet unbeaten on an Ordinary. G. R. White, J. F. Walsh, and others have held the record, which now stands to the credit of J. F. Walsh, as below:—

		h.	m.	s.
1891.	J. F. Walsh	6	22	15

THE 12 HOURS SAFETY ROAD RECORD.

This record has also been much sought after, and has been notably improved year by year. It at present stands to the credit of F. W. Shorland, as below :—

1893, Aug. 26. F. W. Shorland 195 miles.

THE 24 HOURS SAFETY ROAD RECORD.

The long-distance road record is one which it has always been the ambition of real stayers over a road course to hold, and it has been held by many a good man and true. The first regular Safety rides for twenty-four hours straight away were promoted by the makers of the 'Facile' bicycle, and it is with these contests that the first important Safety records at the distance are identified. W. Snook, J. H. Adams, E. Oxborrow, and many more, have held the record. After 300 miles had been compassed by M. A. Holbein the record rapidly improved, and was beaten both in 1892 and 1893, and now stands as under :—

1893, Aug. 26. F. W. Shorland, 370 miles.

THE 50 MILES ROAD SAFETY RECORD.

This record has been essayed and held by a vast number of men, amongst them being R. L. Ede and C. W. Schafer, who dead-heated by consent in 2 hrs. 38 mins. 3 secs., beating Holbein's record made on August 18, 1890. P. C. Wilson, and after him a ong list of other well-known men, beat the record in various contests on the North Road, and in paced trials. The record now stands as under :—

	h. m. s.
1893. A. Pellant	2 21 46

THE 100 MILES SAFETY ROAD RECORD.

The 100 miles Safety road record, like the others, was earliest made in races promoted by makers to boom certain types of machines, and E. Hale covered 100 miles in 6 hrs. 39 mins. 5 secs. in 1885. This record was beaten in 1888 by Holbein, who again beat his own time in 1890 by doing 5 hrs. 54 mins. 2 secs. in a North Road race on a cushion-tired machine. This record was, in due course, beaten by a user of an inflated tire, who had the additional good fortune to have a wind behind him throughout the whole of his straightaway run, in which he accompanied Edge and Bates when they made the 100 miles tandem tricycle road record (which see). The record at present stands thus :—

		h.	m.	s.
1893. E. Hale	. . . .	5	12	2

THE TANDEM TRICYCLE ROAD RECORDS.

These records are less often attempted than others on single machines, owing to the difficulty of getting two men who suit one another, and, as it is, the couples who have accomplished records have in many cases done but little work together, comparatively speaking; in fact, the tandem tricycle records have, for the most part of late, only served to introduce new machines to notice, and there is no doubt that if any two riders of average merit were to go thoroughly into the matter, and train and ride together for some time, better performances could be accomplished. The 100 miles tandem record was made when T. A. Edge accomplished his 100 mile Safety record (which see), and the riders had the assistance of a very strong wind from start to finish.

THE 12 HOURS TANDEM TRICYCLE ROAD RECORD.

1893. M. A. Holbein and F. T. Bidlake, 180½ miles.

THE 24 HOURS TANDEM TRICYCLE ROAD RECORD.

1893. M. A. Holbein and F. T. Bidlake, 333 miles.

THE 50 MILES TANDEM TRICYCLE ROAD RECORD.

		h.	m.	s.
1892. S. D. Begbie and H. Arnold	. . . .	2	19	9

THE 100 MILES TANDEM TRICYCLE ROAD RECORD.

		h.	m.	s.
1890, Oct. 18. S. F. Edge and J. E. L. Bates	. .	5	30	31

THE 12 HOURS TRICYCLE ROAD RECORD.

This record is held as under:—

1892. M. A. Holbein, 183½ miles.

THE 24 HOURS TRICYCLE ROAD RECORD.

Thomas R. Marriott, of the well-known firm of Marriott & Cooper, was one of the earliest exploiters of the possibilities of the tricycle, as, early in 1882, he rode 180 miles inside 24 hours on the Derby-Holyhead road. C. H. R. Gosset (the first man to ride 200 miles in 24 hours), W. F. Sutton, J. H. Adams, A. H. Fletcher, George P. Mills, and W. C. Goulding have all, at one time or another, held the record, which at present stands to the credit of M. A. Holbein, who, on June 14, 1892, rode 337 miles on the roads around Peterborough, Wisbeach, Buckden, Bedford, and Biggleswade.

THE 50 MILES TRICYCLE ROAD RECORD.

This record is held as under:—

		h.	m.	s.
1891.	S. D. Begbie	2	35	17

THE 100 MILES TRICYCLE ROAD RECORD.

This record has been held by many good men.

		h.	m.	s.
1892.	M. A. Holbein	5	54	44

HOME TRAINERS.

These are contrivances, more or less ingenious, upon which a cyclist can take exercise at home. Sometimes they are so designed that the rider can fix his machine upon them and pedal away against a graduated resistance; others are simple standards or pillars, carrying a saddle and a flywheel, with cranks and pedals, upon which riders can exercise in the same way.

In the winter home-trainer races are promoted by many clubs, the competitors pedalling away at top speed, whilst the excited spectators watch the progress of certain hands round the face of a dial—a contrivance put upon the market by Messrs. Hutchins and Hamilton, of Queen Victoria Street. There are home-trainer champions and home-trainer records.

The use of these contrivances in gymnasia is not altogether to be commended, as in such places other exercises might well be followed by cyclists, and the actual value of the home trainer from a racing point of view is practically *nil*. None of the men who have shone on these machines have done any real good upon the racing path.

In any case the trainer should never be used quite 'free'; some amount of check should be put upon the wheels, so as to make the task of driving them somewhat hard. This will to some extent develop the muscles, which mere pedalling fast against no resistance at all will never do; in fact, such a process only fines them down and weakens them.

It is possible that a rational use of the home trainer might to some extent assist a racing man who could not afford all the time necessary to get into condition; but even this is very doubtful, whilst for average cyclists, during the winter months, there are many exercises which would prove of much greater service physically. A little boxing, dumb-bell exercise, Indian clubs, or simple 'extension movements,' are all calculated to do more practical good than home-trainer work, during the dead season.

As our knowledge increases, exercises may be devised which will assist in the development of muscle suitable for cycling. Skipping is an excellent thing for the ankles, and strengthens them vastly, whilst the swing of the rope throws the chest open and exercises to some extent the upper part of the body. Of course, for working out the *rationale* of ankle action, the home trainer is of the greatest service at first, care being taken to have some resistance to work against.

Possibly the home trainer of the future may prove successful, but at present it can be safely said, with the above reservations, that there is nothing in it from a racing or road-riding man's point of view.

PNEUMATIC TYRES.

At the end of 1889 the pneumatic tire was brought prominently before the cycling world.

As early as 1845 a pneumatic tire for wheels had been patented by a Mr. Thompson; but it lacked the modern cycle to bring it to the practical test, and little more was heard of it.

The pneumatic tire when first introduced was in a rather crude state; it punctured, burst, and slipped, and the immense number of tire patents which have been taken out during the last three or four years are almost entirely designed to deal practically with one or other of the original drawbacks. Either they aim at preventing punctures or bursts, or at remedying the side slip so apparent in the earlier tires, whilst others, again, are designed to admit of easy and rapid access to the inner tube for patching purposes in case of injury.

The advantages obtained by the use of the air tire are most remarkable, and it is difficult to estimate the addition it has made to the average pace of the cycle, whilst it has not only thus made the task of propulsion at a given pace so much the easier, but has also materially reduced the vibration—a point which specially appeals to the elderly and more nervous rider. The younger cyclists, at the time of the tire's introduction, were apparently not conscious, in the majority of cases, of the vibration, judging from the wide-spread use amongst the faster riders of small tires and springless saddles; but without doubt they would be fully aware of it to-day if they changed from their air-tired machines to the solid-tired cycles of 1888.

The extraordinary financial success secured by the small company formed in Ireland to handle the Dunlop patents is now a matter of history—dividends ranging up to 175 per cent., substantial bonuses in the shape of new share issues to shareholders and profits estimated at 300,000*l*. on a nominal capital of 50,000*l*.

soon set inventive brains to work, and pneumatic tires of all degrees of merit were patented and put upon the market.

The tire of 1889 of course had the first run, and is still widely popular, despite a material change of design in 1892 and further modifications in 1893, whilst there are almost hundreds of other tires—many of great merit—some of which are being actively put upon the market.

One of the soundest and most reliable roadster pneumatic tires now before the public is the 1894 Clincher—tires, like wines, are known by the year of their birth. This tire represents one of the earliest air tires, and its radical principle—the *clinching* of the edges of the outer cover against the in-turned edges of the metal rim—has never been varied. There is no sounder or more reliable air tire on the market, and the projecting ridges on the surface of the cover reduce very materially the chances of side slip, and make it a tire peculiarly suitable for use on ladies' cycles.

The most conspicuous success of the past season on the racing path, however, has been attained by the Palmer tire, the invention of an American, who brought a few samples to England early in June, and persuaded several well-known racing men to try them, with such remarkable results that, though but a few pairs of tires were in use for a few weeks, the Palmer tire is now second to none in popular estimation. The tire is a tube tire, but in place of the one or more layers of canvas which are used to strengthen ordinary tube tires, the inventor winds spirally around the inner tube a continuous thread, keeping the turns just clear of each other. This layer of thread is then buried in a rubber coating, and another spiral is wound across the first the reverse way; again the threads are buried in rubber, and a thickened 'tread' affixed to come in contact with the ground. The absence of inter-thread friction and the directness of the pull in the line of strain are said to be the reasons of the undoubted pace of the tire, repairs of which are effected by the introduction of rubber plugs, as in other tube tires. The Palmer tire is now being manufactured in England, and will unquestionably be a success, if it does not actually prove to be *the* tire of the future.

The Boothroyd tire—the original tube tire—is also a success, the difficulties encountered in the earlier stages of its manufacture having now been overcome, whilst the method of repair has also been perfected, and the tire has been adopted by one of the largest makers in America for general use.

The various contrivances for affording rapid access to the inner tubes of composite tires vary from the intricate to the extremely simple.

In some cases the reliability of the tire depends upon extremely accurate fitting, and then the removal and replacing of the outer cover is a serious task for the ordinary cyclist; so much so, that in many cases the average user will rather seek the train than face the difficulties involved.

This drawback is met in a large class of tires in which the cover is mechanically fixed in various ways, perhaps the most practical of all being the wire 'cables' of the 1894 Preston-Davies. The edges of the outer cover contain several small wires twisted together into a cable; one end, finished with a knot or stop, is drawn into a slot, and the other, passing through a short tube which projects through the rim, is drawn tight by a nut, which screws down upon it. When this nut is removed the wire cable is loose, and the arch, or cover, can be lifted easily from the wheel. There is no need for extreme accuracy, no tight fitting, no expertness required, and the inner tube can be got at at any point instantly and repaired.

Apart from the tube tires mentioned above, the purchaser should be careful to choose a tire which is easily accessible, and should, by practical experience or inquiry from expert friends, ascertain that he can himself mount and dismount the tyre from the rim. An expert workman, daily handling hundreds of tires with strong fingers, can whip tires on and off with charming ease; but—apart from the possibility of the tires experimented with having been specially prepared with that end in view—it is often found quite impossible for an ordinary person to accomplish the apparently simple feat, and it is for this reason that a tire like the Preston-Davies, which can be lifted off with the finger and thumb when once the 'cable' is released, is to be particularly recommended.

The repair of pneumatic tires was at first a very serious operation for the uninitiated wheelman; but experience has simplified the task both as regards the composite and the simple tube tires. In the first class the outer arch is removed, the inner tube carefully examined, the hole discovered—if necessary, by inflating the tube and immersing it in water—and a small patch of rubber stuck over it with rubber solution. The neighbourhood of the hole should be well scraped with a knife or glass-paper, and the solution well spread over it. The small patch should be similarly treated, and a short time permitted to elapse before bringing them together, when the two surfaces will adhere firmly. A little French chalk is rubbed over the repair to prevent it sticking to the outer cover. The latter is replaced, and the tire re-inflated.

In the case of tube tires rubber cord of varying sizes is passed through the puncture in a perfectly simple manner, with the aid of a specially made needle. Such repairs, as regards small holes, are permanent. Larger holes are best cut with a special tool to a symmetrical circle, and repaired with nail-headed plugs of rubber, specially made for the purpose. These, when properly inserted, also make a sound repair. It often happens that if, after a repair of a tube tire, the surface in the neighbourhood of the plug be soaped, many minute leaks will be discovered. This is due to the air reaching the canvas, passing along or through the fibres, and finding its way out at any minute holes it might encounter. To remedy this, half a teacupful of water should be injected into the tire with the aid of the pump, the wheel spun a few times, and the seat of the leaks put upon the ground, the tire being fully inflated: the water will pick up any dusty matters in the tire, and, being forced into the canvas, will effectually stop the leaks from that point for a practically indefinite period.

Tube tires can be temporarily repaired in many ways: thorns will often remain in the tire, effectually plugging the hole they have made, whilst a common medicine-bottle cork, firmly fixed by tape, not only carried a heavy man over nine miles of hilly road, but held the air, without appreciable leakage, for several days after. The tube tire user should never despair of patching his tire up sufficiently to enable him to reach home.

INDEX

ABI

Abingdon ball-bearing, 320; chain, 391
Accelerators, 57
Accidents, 15; advice respecting, 164-167
Alexandra Park camp, 102
Allepodes, 57
Amateur championships: Amateur bicycling championship, 414; fifty miles road amateur tricycling championship, 414; ten miles road championship of Scotland, 415; fifty miles bicycle road championship of Scotland, 415; amateur championships promoted by the N.C.U., 416-419
Amateur, definition of an, 270
Amateurs, makers', 43, 107
American riders, 105
Anderson, Lieut., 113
Anti-vibration handles, 323
Arab cradle-spring, 7, 156, 161, 193, 323-325, 378, 390
Automatic steerers, 379

Backbone, the, 312
Bags, 'Saturday to Monday,' 20; 'Multum in Parvo,' 20, 400; Clytie, 197, 400
Balance gears, 340-347

CAP

Balfour, Lieut. E. A. J., 113, 114
Beachcroft, Mr. Melville, 120, 262
Bearings, 66, 200, 318-321
Bells, 401
Bicycle tandems, 12, 391; safety records, 452
Bicycle Touring Club; see under Cyclists' Touring Club
Bicycle Union; see under National Cyclists' Union
Birmingham branch of N.C.U., 38
Bivectors, 57
Boat-cycle, eight-oared, 69
Bone-shakers, 124, 321
Books as teachers, 23
Booth, Mr. Sclater, 271
Bown's ball-bearings, 66; rubber pedals, 317; Æolus bearings, 320
Braid, in dress, 222
Breaks, 165, 200, 255, 311
Brunswick black, 333
Bury, Lord, 98, 277, 376

Cabin John Bridge, 17
Cabs, tricycle, 7
Cairo, cycling at, 90
Cambridge U. Bi. C. v. London B.C., 438-446
Caps, 199, 212, 233

CAR

Carrier tricycles, 7, 55, 193, 398
Carriers, 400
Célérifère, the, 54
Chains, 390, 391
Challenge Cups and Trophies: the Anchor Shield, 420; Ashbury Challenge Cup, 420; Brookes Cup, 420; Cambridge University Road Challenge Cup, 421; Chelsea Cup, 421; City of Bristol Challenge Vase, 420; the Cowen Challenge Cup, 421; the 'Cross' Cup, 422; the Crystal Palace Challenge Cup, 422; the 'Cuca Cocoa' Challenge Cup, 422; Harrogate Challenge Cup, 423; the International Challenge Shield, 423; Kent House Challenge Cup, 423; Kildare Cup, 424; Long Eaton Challenge Cup, 424; Plymouth Cup, 424; Queen of the West Challenge Vase, 425; the 'Singer Cup,' 425; the 'Sporting Life' Challenge Cup, 425; Surrey Cup, 425; Sydney Challenge Trophy, 427; the Torquay Cups, 428; Waller Cup, 428; the New Waller Cup, 428; West Lancashire Challenge Cup, 428
Championship winners, record of, 414-419
Cheylesmore clutch gear, 338, 385
Choice of a machine, 11
Christopher, Major-Gen., 51, 278
Churchill, Lord Randolph, 119
Cinder tracks, 40, 41; see Tracks
Clerks of the course, 185, 289

CLU

Clothing, 189, 220, 390; see Dress
Club life, 50
Clubs: Amateur Athletic, 71, 75, 76, 85, 105, 107, 265, 273, 281, 284, 414; Anerley, 417; Anfield B., 68, 109; Armoury, 418; Berretta, 417, 423; Bicycle Touring (see under C.T.C.); Bicycle Union (see under National Cyclists' Union); Bradford B., 86, 292; Brighton A., 414, 420; Brixton B., 112, 120, 121; Brixton Ramblers B., 96, 120, 386, 417, 418, 423; Cambridge University, 6, 41, 267, 271, 414, 416, 417, 421, 432-446; Canonbury, 68, 81, 86, 234, 429, 456; Catford C., 119, 120, 430, 431; Cesky Velociped, Prague, 103; Chelsea B., 421; Cheylesmore, 417; Clarence B., 78; Clifton, 417; Connaught Rangers B., 86; Coventry, 423; Crichton B., 98; C.T.C. (see under); Delft Stud, 417; Druids B., 81, 422; Dublin U.C.C., 417, 418; Edgbaston, 416; Edinburgh, 423; Finchley T., 89, 277, 429; Finsbury Park, 430; Frankfort-am-M, 418; Gainsboro', 417; Hallescher, 419; Hornsey B., 429; Hounslow B., 120; Hull Grosvenor B., 419, 423; Ilkeston, 418; Irish Champion, 120, 418; Kildare B. and T., 120, 410, 424; League of American Wheelmen, 107; Leeds Crescent, 423; Leicester, 418; Lewisham B., 120, 417; London Athletic, 84, 260, 416, 417;

CLU

London B., 73, 75, 78, 93, 120, 121, 266, 267, 272, 279, 414, 429, 438-446, 457; London County, 419, 420, 423; London Scottish, 93, 97, 121; Middlesex B., 67; National Cyclists' Union (see under); Newcastle, 422; North Road, 10, 109, 110, 375, 429; North Shields, 41, 80, 417; Northern Counties Athletic Association, 270; Norwood S., 417; Nottingham, 417, 418; Notts Boulevard B., 120, 417, 418; Notts Castle C., 119; N.Y.A.C., 419; Otto Cycling, 393; Oxford University A., 260; Oxford University B., 119, 267, 271, 279, 280, 418, 432-438; Phœnix, 431; Pickwick B., 266, 267; Polytechnic C., 120, 419; Preston, 417; Ranelagh H., 416, 417; Ripley R. C., 121; Seacroft, 423; Society of Cyclists, 108; South London, T., 249; Speedwell B., 120, 417-419; Stanley, 120, 121, 273, 279, 416; Stoke Newington, 419; Surrey B., 68, 76, 80, 81, 85, 120, 267, 414, 416, 425, 427, 429; Sutton B., 96, 422, 423; Sydney (N.S.W.) B., 427; Telegram B., 419; Temple B., 266, 267, 270; Trekvogels, 418, 419; Tricycle Association, 90; Tricycle Union, 19; Vectis, 417; Velo de Paris, 414; Wanderers B., 75, 92, 94, 111, 266, 267, 270, 272, 414, 416; Warstone, 416; West Kent B., 74, 81, 92, 269, 423

CON

Clutch gear, 335, 337-340, 385
Clytie bag, the, 197, 400
'Coach Record,' 459
Coasting, 137
Cobb, Mr. G. F., M.A., 79
Colchester, visit of Society of Cyclists to, 108
Colony race meeting, 104
Colza oil, 404
Combination woollen garments, 194, 244
Combined saddle-springs, 406
Committees of race-meetings, 290
Connolly, Lieut., 113
Construction of cycles, 299; general mechanism, 299; head, 301; cone head, 302; Trigwell's ball-bearing head, 303; socket head, 304; Abingdon ball head, 304; Ariel head, 305; American head, 306; adjustment of head, 307; handle-bars, 308; handles, 310; break fittings, 311; backbone, 312; forks, 313, 315; hubs, 314, 331; cranks, 316; pedals, 317; bearings, 318; spring, 321; Arab cradle-spring 323; Harrington's tilt-rod, 324; Lamplugh & Brown's suspension saddle, 324; wheels, 327; the new Rapid tangent wheel, 330; tricycles, 333, 375; single and double drivers, 335; Cheylesmore clutch gear, 338, 385; single-chain balance gear, 340; James Starley's driving gear, 341; Sparkbrook balance gear, 345; gearing level, 348; gearing down, 348; gearing up, 349;

CON

two-speed gears, 354; Crypto-dynamic gear, 355; Safety bicycles, 366, 385; the Facile, 367, 369; the Kangaroo, 369; modern cycles, 370; the Safety, 370; Ordinary bicycles, 374; tandems, 375, 377, 380, 391; Humber type tricycles, 376; Cripper type, 378; Olympia type, 381; Quadrant tricycles, 381; Coventry Rotary, 383; sociable tricycles, 384; Safety bicycles, 386; rear-driving Safeties, 388; tandem Safeties, 391; the chain, 391; Dicycle, or Otto bicycle, 393; manumotive velocipedes, 393; velociman manumotors, 396; carrier cycles, 398; accessories, 400; bells and gongs, 401; lamps, 403; luggage carriers, 405; the saddle, 406; combined saddle-springs, 406; pneumatic tires, 469-472

Consuls, 34

Coolie tricycle, 399

Costume, 101; see Dress

Cotton goods in cycling, avoidance of, 223

Cotton wool, 216

Coventry, workmen of, 7; the metropolis of the cycle trade, 61; police on cycles, 85; see Machines and Makers

Coventry chair cycles, 8, 9, 399

Cramp, 145, 236

Cranks, 316

Croppers, 14, 165

Crypto-dynamic gear, 355-361, 364, 365

Cushion tires, 373

CYC

Cycling, progress of, reviewed, 1; numbers of cyclists, 3; relative speed and advantages of bicycles and tricycles, 4, 13, 14; for business purposes, 7; for invalids, 8; for pleasure, 9; adopted by royalty, 10; one advantage of the tricycle over the bicycle, 11; unsuitability of the bicycle for ladies, 11; choice of a machine, 11; precursors of modern cycles, 13; falls from cycles, 14-16; Kauffman's and McAnney's feats, 18; lightness of modern machines, 20; introduction of the suspension wheel, 21; the rider's novitiate, 23; books as teachers, 23; obstacles to be overcome, 25; dwarf or Safety bicycles, 28; clubs, 29, 49, 50; public dislike of, 29; the St. Albans coach, 30, 72; establishment of the National Cyclists' Union and the Cyclists' Touring Club, 30; road repair and surveying, 37; Birmingham meeting on road reform, 38; the 'Roads Improvement Association,' 39; pleas for racing, 40; the Twenty-five Miles Championship, 41; 'rings,' 42; the makers' amateur question, 43, 107; professionals, 44; electricity applied to cycles, 44-48; the press, 48; photography, 51; economics of, 54; early velocipedes, 57; self-moving carriages, 58; introduction of the bicycle from France, 59; Coventry as the metropolis

CYC

of cycle-manufacture, 61; James Starley in the field of invention, 64; manufacturing progress, 64; the first long-distance record, London to John o' Groat's house, 67; sports at the Crystal Palace, 69; medical opinion on healthfulness, 70, 101; establishment of Four Miles Amateur Championship by Amateur Athletic Club, 71; increasing popularity, 71; the Bath to London contest, 73; first meet at Harrogate, 74; attitude of the athletic associations, 75; the meet at Hampton Court, 75; the 'Sporting Life' Challenge Cup, 76; taken up by the clergy, 76; advent of the modern tricycle, 77; the 'Times' on the bicycle, 78; the Over Turnpike case, 82; relative merits of professional and amateur riders, 83; memorial against highway by-laws, 84; Stanley Show at Holborn Town Hall, 85; formation of the Amateur Athletic Association, 85; police on the wheel, 85; Harrogate camp, 86, 92, 94; opening of the Crystal Palace track, 89; the Tricycle Association, 90; a novel 'amateur' definition, 90; establishment of 'The Cyclist,' 90; a steam tricycle, 90; Prince Yeo of Siam as a cyclist, 91; movable championships, 91; bicycle ride on the Goodwin Sands, 96; the last Fifty Miles

CYC

road race, 99; discussion by ladies in camera on suitable costume, 101; Major Knox Holmes' match with Mr. Lacy Hillier, 104; marvellous American records, 105; visit of Society of Cyclists to Colchester, 108; George P. Mills' rides from Land's End to John o' Groat's, 109, 110; the Jubilee demonstration: presentation of 'The Cyclist' lifeboat to West Hartlepool, 111; military cycling, 112; establishment of a corps of volunteer cyclists, 113; increase of touring, 114; the N.C.U. 'universal by-laws,' 115; developments on the racing path, 115; danger of mixed races, 115; separation of Ordinaries and Safeties, 116; Ordinary racing, 116; Safety racing, 117; tricycle racing, 118; visit of the Prince and Princess of Wales to Paddington grounds, 119; inflated tires, 121; advance of cycling in public favour, 122; the road-racing abuse, 122: the whole art of riding (see Riding), 124-167; racing (see Racing), 168-186; touring (see Touring), 187-201; training (see Training), 202-219; dress (see Dress), 220-246; tricycle exercise medically prescribed for children with weak joints, 235; cost of a cycling outfit, 245; lady pioneers and their difficulties, 247; the fair sex on tandems, 248; the ladies' tricycle, 249,

CYC

250; the rear-driving Safety as a ladies' cycle, 251; racing paths (see Tracks), 258-264; the National Cyclists' Union and its work (see under), 265-291; Cyclists' Touring Club and its work (see under), 292-298; construction of machines, 299-369; modern cycles, 370-407; legal aspects of cycling, 411

Cyclists' Club House, Limited, 410

Cyclist's pocket dressing-case, 195

Cyclists' Touring Club, 3; formation and scope of, 30; working staff, 33, 34; arrangements with hotel proprietors, 35, 297; subscription and numbers, 37, 298; co-operates with the N.C.U. in road reform, 39; change of name from Bicycle Touring Club to C.T.C., 96, 292; meeting of lady members on the subject of dress, 101, 238, 297; resignation of Mr. N. F. Duncan, 107; spread of touring under its protection, 114; advantages of membership to tourists, 188, 296; the Handbook, 188; suitability of material of costume for touring, 220; prices of outfit, 245; Mr. Stanley J. A. Cotterell as secretary, 292; Mr. Walter D. Welford as secretary, 292; Mr. E. R. Shipton as secretary, 293; prospectus, 293; uniform, 297; road-book, 298; danger-boards, 298

DRE

DALZELL, Gavin, maker of a bicycle in 1836, 59

Dandy horse, the 13, 54, 59, 74

Danger-boards, 278, 298

Dickens, Charles, as a cyclist, 55, 85

Dicycles, 393

Doctors, 70

Donington Trust Road, the, 39

Draisnene, the, 13, 54, 122

Dress, 198, 212; C.T.C. costume, 220; usefulness and healthfulness to be considered first of all, 221; outer garments, 221; use of braid, 222; flannel and woollen material only to be used, 223; illnesses arising through the use of cotton or linen linings, 223; the jacket, 225, 227; Norfolk jacket, 227; webbing jackets, 227; the 'Weather Defiance' of the Sanitary Woollen Company, 228; the waistcoat, 228; knickerbockers or kneebreeches, 228, 229; gaiters, 228; knitted or webbing breeches, 230; pockets, 231; stockings, 231; garters, 233; head-gear, 233; C.T.C. helmet, 234; Canonbury Cycling Club helmet, 234; Stanley helmet, 234; shoes, 235; ladies' costume in detail, 238-243; under garments, 243; sweaters, 243; combinations, 244; cashmere neckerchiefs, 244; prices of cyclist's outfit, 245; maxims on, 245, 246

Dressing-case, pocket, 195

Dressing-room clerk at race-meetings, 184

DRU

Drury, Lieut.-Colonel E. D., 113
Dwarf bicycles, 115, 367

EDYE, Major, 113, 114
Electric Power and Storage Co., 46
Electric tricycles, 44-48
Elliman's embrocation, 151, 167, 218
Entry forms, N.C.U., 285
Events, on the track and on the road:—Amateur Athletic championship, 271; the Anchor Shield, 420; Ashbury Challenge Cup, 420; Brookes Cup, 420; Cambridge University Road Challenge Cup, 421; Caterham to Merton, 97; Chelsea Cup, 421; City of Bristol Challenge Vase, 420; Cowen Challenge Cup, 421; the 'Cross' Cup, 422; Crystal Palace Challenge Cup, 80, 103, 422; the 'Cuca Cocoa' Challenge Cup, 422; fifty miles championships (bicycle and tricycle, various), 76, 89, 91, 93, 99, 103, 106, 110, 414-419; five miles championships (bicycle and tricycle, various), 83, 93, 103, 106, 109, 110, 281, 416-419; four miles amateur championship, 414; Hamburg to Bönningstedt, 103; Harrogate Challenge Cup, 423; hundred miles road race, 110; International Challenge Shield, 423; Inter-University races, 432-438; Keen and Cortis's match at Moly-

EVE

neux Grounds, Wolverhampton, 83; Kent House Challenge Cup, 423; Kew Bridge to Blackwater, 82; Kildare Challenge Cup, 104, 424; Land's End to John o' Groat's, 68, 86, 92, 97, 109, 110, 353, 392, 456; Liverpool to Edinburgh, 457; London B. C. v. Cambridge U. Bi. C., 438-446; London B.C. 100 miles, 77, 457; London to Bath, 73, 77, 78, 458; London to Brighton, 68, 459; London to Edinburgh, 462; London to John o' Groat's, 67, 81; London to Liverpool, 463; London to York, 72, 78, 92, 463; Long Eaton Challenge Cup, 424; North Road Club 100 miles, 375; one mile championships (bicycle and tricycle, various), 74, 83, 92, 93, 98, 106, 108, 109, 281, 351, 416 419; Plymouth Cup, 424; Queen of the West Challenge Vase, 424; the 'Singer Cup,' 425; 'Sporting Life' Challenge Cup, 425; Surrey Cup, 100, 108, 425; Sydney Challenge Trophy, 425; ten miles championships (bicycle and tricycle, various), 98, 103, 415, 416, 419; Torquay Cups, 428; tricycle road championship, 1880, 376; twenty miles championship, 83; twenty-five miles championships (bicycle and tricycle, various), 41, 92, 93, 99, 103, 106, 108, 110, 271, 280-282, 416-419; two miles championships, 271, 280, 416; Two Miles Invitation, 81;

FAL

University Ten Miles Invitation, 80; Waller Cups, 428; West Lancashire Challenge Vase, 426

FALLS, 14
Foot-rests, 373
Forks, 313, 315
Fox, Major, 113
Friction, 26

GAITERS, 228
Garters, 233
Gearing, 28, 157, 338-366, 386
Gloves, 165
Gongs, 401
Goodwin Sands, riding on, 96, 429
Guide-books, 188

HAMPTON Court, the meet at, 75, 86, 91, 96, 102, 108
Handbook of the C.T.C., 188
Handicappers, 85, 116, 272, 287
Handicapping, 117, 182
Handle-bars, 87, 136, 138-143, 215, 255, 308, 323
Hand-rubbing after cycling exercise, 217
Harrogate camp meet, 74, 86, 92, 94, 99, 106
Harrogate, cycling at, 8
Harvey, W. J., 410
Head-dress, 199
Heads, 161, 301; see Construction
Helmets, 234
Hernia, 172, 173
Highway rates, 39, 40; by-laws, 84; Act, 271

JOU

Hill-climbing trials, 427-429
Hobby-horse, 13, 54·56, 62, 122
Home-trainers, 144, 145, 361, 468
Hostility to cyclists, 2
Hotels, 35, 297
Hubs, 314, 331
Hutchens, Mr. (N.C.U.), 271
Huxley, Professor, quoted, 1

ILLSTON'S self-lubricating chain, 392
Imperial crowners, 14, 16
Inflated tires, 121
International Tournament, 108
Inter-University races, 432-438
Inventors; see Makers

JACKSON, Sir Henry, 271
Jones, Mr. Warner, his treatise on cycling, 24, 28
Journals and literature referred to:— Athletic News, 430; Athletic Review, 207; Bicycling News, 16; C.T.C. Gazette, 190; Cyclist, 52, 62, 87, 90, 195; Cyclists' and Wheel-world Annual, 188; Daily Telegraph, 74, 88; Daily News, 72, 85; Evening Standard, 398; Indispensable Handbook both for the Bicycle and Tricycle, 52; Ixion, 59; Mechanics' Magazine, Museum, Register, Journal, and Gazette, 57; Nineteenth Century, 279; Paterson's Roads, 188; Phillips' Cyclists' Pocket Road Guides, 188; Pittsburg Dispatch, 17; Punch, 62; Sport and Play,

JUB

430; Sporting Life, 76, 425; Sturmey's Handbook, 344; Times, 78, 101; Tricyclist, 398; West Sussex Gazette, 74

Jubilee demonstration: presentation of 'The Cyclist' lifeboat to West Hartlepool, 111

Judges at race meetings, 183, 286-290

KANGAROO hunts, 107
Khedive of Egypt, 10
King of the Road lamp, 404
Knee-breeches, 228, 390
Knox Holmes, Major T., 104, 121

LABELS for parcels, 197
Ladies, riding costume, 101, 238; cycling for, 247
Lamps, 201, 403
Lap-scorers, 185, 289
Laying of tracks, 263
Legal aspects of cycling, 411
Leipsic, racing at, 106
Lifeboat, 'The Cyclist,' presented to West Hartlepool, 111
Linen in cycling, avoidance of, 223
London B.C. v. Cambridge U.Bi.C., 438-446
Luggage-bags, 400
Luggage-carriers, 400, 405

MCADAM, quoted on road repairing, 37
Macdonald's self-moving carriage, 58

MAC

Machines:—American Star, 16, 375; Beeston Cripper, 110; Beeston Humber, 65, 69, 109, 351; Carrier, 398; Challenge tricycle, 334; Cheylesmore rear-steerer, 338; Club dicycle, 393; Club sociable, 385; Club tandem, 380; Coolie cycle, 399; Corona tandem, 381; Coventry Rotary, 7, 334, 382, 383; Coventry Machinist bicycle, 15; Cripper tandem, 380; Cripper tricycle, 334, 378, 392; Devon, 337; Eclipse bicycle, 83, 403; Excelsior, 315; Facile, 328, 367, 369, 386-388; Farringdon bicycle, 374; Gentleman's bicycle, 16, 305, 321; Hero tandem, 391; Humber tandem, 109, 364, 376-378; Humber tricycle, 132, 171, 310, 314, 334, 345, 349, 366, 376-378, 379; Invincible, 314, 330; Invincible sociable, 101; Invincible tandem, 104, 109; Ivel Safety, 110; Kangaroo Safety, 369, 388; Lightning tandem, 391; Marlborough tricycle, 109; Marriott & Cooper's Humber, 108, 110, 353; Merlin, 338; New Patent Coventry tricycle, 77; New Rapid, 330; Olympia, 335, 381; Olympia tandem, 381; Omnicycle, 338; Otto, 393; Pony bicycle, 367; Premier, 315, 316, 352; Premier racer, 110; Premier Safety, 109; Premier sociable, 385; Premier tandem, 391; Quadrant Safety, 382; Quadrant tan-

MAK

dem, 382; Quadrant tricycle, 310, 334, 351, 381, 382; Ranelagh Club, 310; Rara Avis, 376, 414; Rational Ordinary, 374, 378; Rover, 28, 369; Rudge's Rotary tricycle, 383; the Safety, 251, 370-374; Salvo, 7; Salvo sociable, 385; Sparkbrook two-speed tricycle, 355; Stanley bicycle, 301; Star bicycle, 16; Velociman, 396; 'Xtraordinary bicycle, 160, 375

Makers and inventors, &c. :—
Abingdon Co., 391; Beal, John, 367; Boothroyd, 470; Bown & Co., 7, 320, 321; Brooks & Co., 400, 407; Carver, James, 316; Challis Brothers, 402; Charsley, Rev., 394, 395; Claviger Cycle Company, 375; Coventry Machinist Company, 64, 315, 321, 334, 367, 380, 385, 399; Crypto Cycle Co., 355, 381; Ellis and Co., 338, 367, 374; Harrington & Co., 7, 323, 324; Harrison, J., 402; Haynes & Jeffries, 77, 383; Hillman, William, 65; Hillman, Herbert & Cooper, 82, 164, 334, 351, 388; Humber, Thos., 169, 301, 376; Humber & Co., 301, 320; Hutchins & Hamilton, 468; Jones, F. Warner, 337; Lamplugh & Brown, 7, 324, 400, 405, 406, 407; Lucas, J., 402, 404; McDonald, D., 58; Marriott & Cooper, 108, 353, 381, 461; Mehew, Messrs., 58; Michaux & Co., 59; Palmer, 470; Preston-

NAT

Davies, 471; Quadrant Tricycle Co., 382, 383; Rudge & Co., 383; Salsbury, 403; Shaw, W. T., 355; Singer & Co., 64, 160, 320, 334, 380, 394, 395, 398; Smith, Milbrowe, 144; T. Smith & Sons, 7, 66, 301; Sparkbrook Co., 355, 361; Starley Brothers, 334; Starley, James, 7, 61, 64, 77, 340, 341, 383; Starley & Sutton, 399; Surrey Machinist Co., 317, 328, 331, 374; Thompson, 469; Trigwell, Watson & Co., 314

Makers' amateurs, 43, 107
Manivelociters, 57
Manumotive velocipedes, 393
Maps, 188
Matches, 405
Mayall, John, photographer, 60
Military cycling, 112
Model race-meeting programme, 411
Modern cycles, 370-407
Molyneux, Hon. R. G., 112
Multum-in-parvos, 20, 400
Myopy, 173

NAGEL carrier, the, 196, 400, 405
Napier, Sir Charles, quoted, 20
National Cyclists' Union, meeting convoked by the Birmingham branch on road reform, 38; co-operation with C.T.C. in improvement of highways, 39; absorption of the Tricycle Association, 90; publication of executive reports, 90; action on movable championships, 91; questions bona

NAT

fides of certain road performances, 105; disputes with Amateur Athletic Association, 105; meeting at Fleet Street and prospectus issued, 85, 267; objects and proposed constitution of the Union, 30, 268; definition of an amateur, 44, 270; universal by-laws for the regulation of cycle traffic, 115; establishment of championships, 271, 272; action on the Highways Act, 271; contest between amateurs and professionals, 271; aid from the Universities, 272; internal reform, 272; appointment of Mr. M. D. Rucker as handicapper, 85, 272; dissension with Bicycle Touring Club, 272; Mr. Lacy Hillier's scheme for the establishment of local centres, 273; rules relating to local centres, 273-276; working of the centres, 276; election of Lord Bury as President, 277; alteration of the Union's name, 278; institution of danger-boards, 278; the reserve fund, 278; assault cases taken up, 279; road repair, 101. 107, 279; action against eight road surveyors at the Halesowen court, 279; Mr. H. R. Reynolds' article on road-making in the 'Nineteenth Century,' 279; the control of cycle racing, 280; annual amateur championships, 280; tricycling championships, 281; war and peace with the A.A.A., 284; regulations for the government

POS

of race meetings, 182, 285; entries, 285; prizes, 285; attendants, 286; protests, 286; starting, 286; the enclosure, 287; general rules, 287; the officials, 288; definitions of machines, 290; definition of a novice, 291; record of championship winners, 416-419; other references, 4, 10, 31, 44, 71, 73, 85, 105, 107, 123, 411, 414

Norfolk jackets, 227, 240
North of England meet, Harrogate, 86, 294
Novice, definition of a, 291

OIL, 365, 404
Olive oil, 404

PARAFFIN, 200
Parkyns, Sir Thomas, his steam tricycle, 90
Partridge, Dr. G. B., on the treatment of wounds, 167
Passenger tricycles, 399
Pedalling, 132, 146, 148, 149
Pedals, 153, 163, 164, 255, 317, 361, 366
Phillips, Capt. R. E., 113, 114
Photography, 19, 51, 384
Pneumatic tires, 469; the 1889 tire, 470; the 1894 Clincher, 470; the Palmer, 470; the Boothroyd, 470; the Preston-Davies, 471; repair of, 471, 472
Police, on the wheel, 85; prohibition of road racing, 100; at race meetings, 185
Post Office, use of carrier-tricycle by, 398

PRE

Precursors of modern cycles, 13
Press, the cycling, 48; at race-meetings, 185, 287; see under Journals
Prices of cycling outfits, 245
Prince and Princess of Wales' visit to Paddington Recreation Grounds, 119
Prince Imperial, the, 74
Prizes, 186, 285
Professional riders, 44

RACE meetings, management, rules, and officials of, 182-186, 285-291; see N.C.U.
Races, pleas for, 40
Racing, its service to the cause of cycling, 168; clamour for light machines, 169; comparison of Lacy Hillier's 1880 60-inch Humber tricycle with G. Gatehouse's 44-inch Humber racer, 171; medical opinion on competitor's suitability, 171; physical drawbacks, 173; preliminary work on the road, 174; choice of a machine, 174; machine to be built for the rider, 176; the short throw and sprinting, 177; position of the handles, 177, 181; the saddle, 177, 181, 406; weight of machine, 179; editorial experience on lightness 179; size of cycle, 181; management of race meetings, 182-186, 285-291; styles of various riders, 209
Racing paths, 40; way round, 105; special requisites for, 258; composition of tracks, 259, 264; see Tracks

RID

Racing track rules, 413
Rat-trap pedals, 163, 164, 317
Recommended houses, 35
Record saddle, the, 406
Records on the path :—Bicycle records, 447; Safety records, 449; tandem Safety bicycle records, 452; tricycle records, 453; tandem tricycle records, 454
Records on the road :—Land's End to John o' Groats, 456; Liverpool to Edinburgh, 457; the London Bicycle Club's 100 mile road race, 457; London to Bath and back, 458; London to Brighton and back (the 'Coach record'), 459; London to Edinburgh, 462; London to Liverpool, 463; London to York, 463; Ordinary road records, 463-464; Safety road records, 465; tandem tricycle road records, 466; tricycle road records, 467
Resin, 200
Reynolds, H. R., on roads, 279
Riders :—
  Adam, F. L., 180, 422, 441-443
  Adam, W. K., 93, 435
  Adams, J. H., 110, 120, 417, 418, 419, 422, 426, 427, 447, 448, 457, 465, 467
  Adcock, G. R., 424, 425
  Ainslie, W. L., 370, 433, 434
  Allard, F. W., 109, 417
  Allen, Mrs., 106
  Allport, F., 422
  Appleyard, F. E., 77, 457, 464
  Aram, J., 452

Riders (*cont.*):—
  Archer, F. J. B., 120, 425, 447
  Armitage, F. R., 436, 445
  Arnold, H., 466
  Arnott, 460
  Attlee, B. W., 421, 437, 438, 446, 447, 448
  Attlee, J., 437
  Auster, A. C., 97
  Bailey, D. J. S., 434, 440
  Bailey, E., 431
  Baker, R. C., 90
  Ball, W. F., 110, 424-427
  Bardsley, C. C. B., 420, 437, 438
  Bardsley, W. H., 120
  Barker, A., 457
  Barrett, A. W., 457
  Barron, E. E., 446, 458
  Bates, J. E. L., 120, 427, 454, 466
  Battensby, T., 210
  Beck, G. F., 280, 442, 457, 458
  Begbie, S. D. 466, 467
  Beningfield, J. W., 266, 267
  Biddles, W., 430
  Bidlake, F. T., 422, 453, 455, 463, 466
  Bird, Alfred, 99, 463
  Blackwell, H., jun., 68, 81, 86, 456
  Blair, J., 460
  Blount, B., 431
  Bourdon, W., 100
  Bradbury, F. G., 427
  Bramson, F., 419
  Bramson, W. G. H., 418, 419, 421, 424, 427
  Brewerton, E. W., 421, 422, 427
  Breysig, P. L., 430
  Britten, W., 78, 458

Riders (*cont.*):—
  Brown, A. S., 82, 426
  Brown, C. A., 441
  Brown, C. W., 429
  Brown, E. H., 421
  Brown, J. W. M., 99
  Brown, W., 100, 103, 104, 422, 426, 427
  Bruce, M., 415
  Bryson, D. D., 415
  Bryson, R. S., 415
  Buckley, W. F. M., 434, 435
  Burston, G. W., 114
  Butler, A. D., 450, 457
  Butler, J. D., 422, 424, 442, 443
  Butler-Harris, 436, 437
  Butterfield, W. J., 437, 438
  Carlisle, R. H., 457, 463
  Carr, E. I., 443, 444
  Carr, L. C., 442
  Carruthers, J. J., 421, 423
  Challoner, A. O., 422
  Chamberlain, J., 420
  Chambers, R., 102, 106, 417
  Chase, A. A., 450, 451
  Chilvers, W. G., 427
  Choice, Miss J., 101
  Christie, C. H. F., 433
  Clarke, H. S., 412, 439
  Cleland, D., 415
  Clough, G. T., 464
  Cobb, G. F., M.A., 79, 267
  Coleman, G. H., 429
  Coleman, G. P., 77, 121, 39 457
  Colman, F. S., 439
  Cooke, O. V., 458
  Cooper, Edward, 21
  Cooper, F., 70, 74, 80, 92, 168, 260
  Cooper, W. H., 430

Riders (cont.):—
  Corbett, S., 334, 414
  Cornell, Walter, 266
  Cortis, H. L., 70, 75, 79-90, 92-95, 104, 107, 112, 260, 272, 370, 414, 416, 424-426, 429
  Coston, W. E. N., 72, 78, 464
  Cousens, 282
  Cowie, J. M., 210
  Cox, F. M., 420
  Crichton, A. J., 421, 441
  Cripps, Robert, 106, 282, 283, 378, 417, 422, 426, 427
  Crofton, W. d'A., 432, 433
  Crosse, M., 442, 443
  Crump, B. W., 119, 436, 437, 444, 445
  Crute, C., 92, 93, 422, 423
  Dalton, P., 429, 457
  Darling, J. R., 436, 444, 445
  Darrell, J. F., 438
  Davenport, Horace, 207
  Day, G. D., 433, 434, 439-442
  Dean, J. S., 86
  Dear, J. R., 431
  Derkinderin, A. E., 82, 334, 414, 425
  Dervil, E., 119
  Dobson, W., 423
  Dodds, F. L., 432
  Du Cros, A., 120, 426, 427, 431
  Du Cros, H., 121
  Duddridge, G. F., 420
  Duncan, O. G., 109
  Dundas, M. J. R., 426
  Dutton, A. M., 430
  East, Fred T., 80, 177, 318, 425, 428
  Ede, R. L., 419, 427, 46

Riders (cont.):—
  Edge, S. F., 68, 417, 430, 461, 462, 466
  Edge, T. A., 466
  Ellaby, G. A., 437
  Ellis, W., 453, 455
  Engleheart, A. P., 426
  English, R. H., 41, 80, 103, 104, 106, 117, 209, 210, 282-284, 370, 417, 421, 422, 424, 428
  English, T. H., 421
  Fagan, C. W., 444
  Faith, H. D., 445
  Fearnsides, J. W., 435, 436
  Fenlon, J. E., 89, 108, 110, 417, 422, 424
  Fentiman, A. G., 426, 427
  Finney, J., 430
  Fisher, O. P., 439, 440
  Fletcher, A. H., 110, 467
  Fletcher, F. T., 418, 428
  Fletcher, L., 68, 457
  Ford, Murray, 266
  Fowler, M. B., 427
  Freemantle, W. A. C., 436
  Friswell, C., 427
  Fry, F. R., 93, 99, 103, 417, 448
  Furnivall, Percy, 106, 108, 109, 110, 281, 351, 417, 423, 424, 426, 427
  Gaskell, H. W., 95, 98, 100, 102, 209, 210, 416, 424, 426
  Gatehouse, G., 41, 42, 106, 108, 110, 171, 282-284, 417, 421, 435, 436, 443-445
  Gilliatt, A., 464
  Girling, 460
  Godbolt, G. D., 90
  Godlee, T., 464
  Good, A. E., 426, 427
  Good, T. W., 427, 452

Riders (*cont.*):—
  Goodwin, H. R., 430
  Gosset, C. H. R., 96, 97, 98, 106, 467
  Goulding, W. C., 467
  Grace, T. W., 430
  Green, J., 449-451
  Greenwood, J. W., 423
  Greville, F., 431
  Griffin, A. E., 460
  Griffith, J. F., 88, 92, 426, 441
  Griffith, T., 97
  Hale, E., 109, 110, 465, 466
  Hale, J. H., 431
  Hall, E. J., 425
  Hamilton, J. R., 89, 179, 422, 426, 428
  Hammond, H., 422
  Harling, C. E., 421
  Harman, C. A., 68, 86, 456
  Harris, A. W., 418, 426, 427, 449, 452
  Hartridge, L., 458
  Hassard, R., 428
  Hassell, E., 426
  Heard, Stanley, 375
  Hebblethwaite, P. G., 91, 282, 415
  Henie, W., 449
  Herbert, A., 439, 440, 457
  Hillier, G. Lacy, 81, 87 92, 100, 102, 104, 105, 106, 112, 113, 120, 171, 273, 364, 376, 378, 398, 413-416, 422, 426, 448
  Hock, H. B., 454
  Hoffman, A., 454
  Holbein, M. A., 460, 465, 466, 467
  Honey, A. A., 421
  Honeywell, F. T. V., 267, 414
  Horton, A. W., 420
  Houghton, S. C., 464

Riders (*cont.*):—
  Howard, H. J., 426
  Howell, R., 370
  Huie, D. H., 99, 103, 415, 421, 423
  Hunt, G., 450, 451
  Ilsley, R. J., 464
  Illston, G. H., 97, 421, 428
  Illston, W. A., 81, 106, 108, 109, 110, 417, 421, 423, 424, 447
  James, J. M., 422
  Jephson, M. H., 442
  Jolly, F., 266, 267
  Jones, W. C., 119, 121, 420, 427
  Jones, W. J., 452
  Julian, J. E., 432
  Kauffman, 17, 18
  Keating, W., 431
  Keen, John, 70, 73, 74, 80, 83, 84, 97, 154, 178, 260, 272, 313
  Keith-Falconer, Hon. Ion, 68, 70, 80, 92, 93, 94, 96, 104, 180, 260, 267, 272, 370, 414, 416, 432, 457
  Kemp, Sidney, 88
  Keppel, Hon. Arnold, 15, 19
  Kiderlin, E., 108, 417
  Knox Holmes, Major T., 104, 105
  Koch, A. H., 441, 457
  Kohout, Josef, 103
  Laing, J. H. A., 415
  Laing, D. W., 99, 106
  Lamb, J., 415
  Lambley, U. L., 418, 427, 447
  Langley, A. E., 108, 421, 427
  Laurie, H. E., 119
  Lea, W. C., 431
  Lee, J., 109, 282
  Lee, J. H. W., 432

Riders (*cont.*) :—
  Lee, Sidney, 102, 103, 110, 281, 282
  Leeds, O. G. M., 438, 440, 441
  Lees, F., 210
  Legg, S. S., 458
  Lehr, August, 418
  Leitch, E., 120
  Lennox, James, 68, 97, 99, 457
  Letchford, P. T., 106, 108, 281, 282, 349
  Liles, C. E., 87, 88, 91, 92, 95, 97, 98, 99, 100, 102, 103, 109, 120, 153, 281, 282, 318, 416, 417, 422, 424-426
  Linley, C. M., 431
  Linton, A. V., 420
  Lloyd, R. A., 427
  Lloyd, W. E., 438
  Lowndes, M. J., 93, 95, 97, 98, 415
  Lucas, C., 457, 463
  McAllister, W., 421
  McAnney, 17, 18
  Macbeth, A. R., 422, 424, 426
  McGregor, D., 415
  McGregor, J., 415
  McKinlay, Peter, 93, 94
  Mackinnon, R. R., 414, 420
  Macleod, R. W., 433
  McNish, G., 452
  McRae, Douglas, 120, 424, 443-446, 458, 464
  McWilliam, W., 267
  Marks, D., 430
  Marriott, T. R., 68, 97, 98, 100, 353, 415, 457, 467
  Martin, G. R., 449
  Mayall, J., jun., 68
  Mayes, E. M., 108, 421, 424, 425, 426, 427
  Mayor, F. G., 433, 439, 440

Riders (*cont.*) :—
  Mecredy, R. J., 110, 417, 418, 428
  Mildmay, E. St. J., 432
  Millgate, J. C., 431
  Mills, G. P., 5, 68, 109, 110, 392, 457, 464, 467
  Milner, W. O., 91, 428
  Milsom, A., 420, 425, 428
  Milthorpe, R., 422
  Moore, E., 426
  Moore, Frank, 93, 416, 430
  Moore, J., 430
  Morris, G. L., 120, 460
  Muir, H., 434, 441
  Napier, M. S., 431
  Newman, C., 457
  Nichols, H., 439
  Nicolas, F. J., 103, 106
  Nixon, Alfred, 68, 97, 98, 101, 457, 463
  Nixon, John, 267
  Oeschger, H., 434
  Olive, E. J. P., 442
  Oliver, T. D., 421, 428
  Orr, W. McF., 436, 437, 445
  Osborn, T., 449
  Osborne, H., 76, 153, 370, 425
  Osmond, F. J., 109, 110, 112, 120, 122, 370, 417, 418, 422, 423, 424, 426, 427, 447
  Osmond, G. E., 452
  Oxborrow, E., 457, 465
  Palmer, C. A., 91, 260, 426, 428
  Parker, G. M., 432
  Parker, W. B., 91
  Parsons, H., 420
  Paterson, J. G., 421
  Paterson, H. L., 435
  Pearce, S. H., 120, 425
  Pellant, A., 465

RID

Riders (*cont.*):—
  Penrose, C., 432
  Percival, A. P. C., 75
  Philpot, R. L., 430
  Platt-Betts, J., 449
  Plunkett, Hon. J. W., 432
  Pollock, C. A. E., 433, 439, 440-442
  Poole, J. A., 454
  Pope, F., 427
  Popplewell, W., 81, 426
  Potter, A. C., 458
  Prentice, F., 426, 427
  Price, W., 120
  Pridham, G. W. P., 443
  Puckle, A. V., 121, 431
  Purdie, J. S., 415
  Ratcliffe, W., 108
  Raynes, W. L., 421, 436, 437
  Redwood, Boverton, 277
  Reed, C. F., 432
  Reilly, W. J., 424
  Reynolds, H. R., 92, 279, 280, 422, 433, 441-444, 446, 457, 458, 463, 464
  Reynolds, L. B., 457
  Ricardo, A. R., 458
  Richardson, Stephen, 266
  Ridout, J. E., 452
  Robertson, J. A., 449, 451
  Robertson, W. W., 462
  Robinson, F., 103, 423, 427
  Rogers, E. F., 90
  Rowell, H., 422
  Rucker, M. D., 12, 83, 85, 120, 266, 267, 272, 438, 439, 444
  Rumney, A. W., 435, 443, 444, 458
  Sanger, W. C., 419
  Sangster, C., 431
  Sansom, H. H., 119, 418, 420, 426

RID

Riders (*cont.*):
  Saunders, A. E., 420
  Saunders, H. B., 430
  Saunders, B. J., 420
  Scantlebury, E., 460
  Scantlebury, W., 460
  Schafer, C. W., 120, 460, 465
  Scheltema-Beduin, P. W., 119, 418, 419, 427
  Schmettau, H. R., 444-446
  Scott, E., 452
  Scott, Hon. G. H., 437, 438, 446
  Scott, J., 438, 439
  Scrutton, T. E., 95
  Searle, G. F. C., 421, 436, 437, 443-445
  Sellers, Sanders, 106, 417, 428
  Shaw, A. P., 424
  Shorland, F. W., 422, 450, 451, 460, 461, 463, 465
  Shute, L., 460
  Simmonds, T., 430, 431
  Sinclair, M., 99, 100
  Smith, C. A., 458, 462
  Smith, George, 100, 281, 415
  Smith, H., 440, 441, 444, 457, 458
  Smith, H. H., 426, 428
  Smith, J. S., 101, 104
  Smith, Mrs. J. S., 101
  Smyth, H., 454
  Smythe, Frank, 72, 78, 464
  Snook, W., 465
  Speechley, H. A., 102, 103, 104, 108, 109, 417, 424, 426, 427
  Spring, A., 428
  Stadnicki, K. N., 418
  Steel, E., 453, 455
  Steel, J., 415
  Stocks, J. W., 419, 423
  Stokes, H. R., 114

K K

Riders (*cont.*) :—
  Stroud, Lewis, 119, 418, 419, 424, 426, 427, 435-437, 453, 454
  Stunt, G. N., 445, 458
  Sturmey, Henry, 87, 113, 344
  Sutton, F., 97, 98, 416, 425, 428
  Sutton, W. F., 70, 93, 101, 463, 464, 467
  Swann, S., 435, 443
  Swindley, Harry J., 121
  Sykes, E. R., 445
  Synyer, Herbert, 120, 370, 417, 418, 421, 424, 426, 427
  Tanner, W. B., 81, 95, 261
  Tegetmeier, E., 457
  Terry, W., 106, 422, 424, 426, 427
  Thiselton, C. G., 427, 452
  Thitchener, T., 426
  Thompson, Alfred, 93, 96, 98, 102
  Thompson, P., 422
  Thompson, W. C., 421
  Thorn, F. C., 444, 445, 458
  Thorn, O., 440-443
  Thorn, W. T., 77, 78, 93, 280, 426, 438-440, 457, 463, 464
  Thorp, H. S., 72, 463, 464
  Thorp, J. C., 432
  Tischbein, W., 419
  Todd, Robert, 96, 120, 279
  Tomes, W., 74, 122
  Tough, J., 103
  Tower, F. F., 433, 434, 442
  Travers, W., 430
  Trenchard, J. B., 425
  Trollope, R. G., 439
  Trotter, A. P., 438
  Tubbs, A. H., 119
  Turner, E. B., 110, 117, 119, 120

Riders (*cont.*) :—
  Turner, Mr., of Paris, 60, 64, 84
  Turner, Rowley, 64
  Turrell, W. J., 435-437, 444, 445
  Venables, H. A., 91
  Vesey, C. D., 89, 90, 93, 97, 98, 414, 422, 425, 426
  Wadey, C. L., 426
  Walker, A. E., 429, 460
  Walmesley, C., 457
  Walsh, J. F., 422, 463, 464
  Walter, W. A. G., 434, 435
  Ward, W., 119
  Watson, A. J., 119, 419, 452
  Watson, P. H., 458
  Weatherley, F., 120
  Weatherley, F. W., 428
  Webb, H. J., 102, 103, 104, 281, 282
  Webber, M. V. J. A., 81, 106, 110, 417
  Weir, A. A., 271, 280, 416, 433
  Westcot, F. B., 441, 442
  Weston, Frank W., 86
  Whatton, A. B. W., 435, 441-443
  Whatton, J. S., 6, 93, 102, 309, 310, 370, 416, 421, 434, 435, 441-443
  Whish, M., 93
  White, Godfrey, 375
  White, G. R., 464
  White, J., 437
  Whiting, H. P., 414
  Wigram, E. T. A., 436, 445
  Wilkinson, E. J., 428
  Wilkinson, T. H., 464
  Willcox, P. F. C., 415
  Williams, F. H., 458, 464

RID

Riders (*cont.*) :—
  Williams, S. E., 109, 421, 423, 427, 437, 438, 445, 446
  Willink, J. W., 439
  Willis, E. J., 460
  Wilson, A. J., 5, 10, 109, 430
  Wilson, C., 282
  Wilson, C. P., 439
  Wilson, H. F., 98, 211, 416, 422, 426, 427
  Wilson, P. C., 460, 465
  Wilson, R., 460
  Wimbush, F., 429
  Wood, Frederic, 82
  Wood, F. P., 120, 417, 421, 423, 424, 426, 427
  Woolnough, 'Bobby,' 82, 93
  Wridgway, C. G., 420, 458
  Wyndham, Wadham, 75, 280, 414, 425, 438-440, 442-444
  York, E., 29, 280
  Zimmerman, A. A., 419
Riding, early practice on boneshakers, 124 ; unsuitability of 'Safeties' for instruction, 126 ; engagement of properly qualified teachers, 127 ; use of the horizontal bar, 128 ; assistance of a friend, 129 ; steering, 130 ; pedalling, 132 ; dismounting, 133 ; mounting, 133-136 ; style, 136 ; pose of the body, 138 ; position of the handles, 138 ; short and long reach, 139 ; grip of the handles, 140-142 ; 'grasshopper' fashion, 141 ; steering with feet, 142 ; ankle-work, 143-154 ; the grindstone action, 143 ; use of the home trainer, 144 ; diagrams illustrating proper

SEC

pedalling, 146, 148, 149 ; treatment for early muscular fatigue, 151 ; training with left and right leg alternately, 152 ; the downward thrust and the quick clawing recovery, 153 ; leg-reach, 154 ; measuring for size of wheel, 155 ; gearing, 157 ; adjustment of saddle, 157-160 ; looking after springs, 160 ; loose heads, 161 ; attention to wheels, their bearings, 163 ; choice of pedals, 163; position of step, 164 ; accidents, 164-167 ; how to minimise a fall, 165 ; treatment of wounds, 166
Rings, 42
Ripley, 73, 95, 97
Road performances questioned, 105
Road surveyors, 27, 38, 39, 279
Roads, 37 ; improvement of, 101, 279
Roads Improvement Association, the, 39
Running, 2, note

SADDLES, 129, 157-160, 181, 200, 255, 406 ; combined saddle-springs, 406
Safeties, 12, 28, 115, 117, 126, 142, 156, 251-256, 320, 366-374, 386-391; records, 449-452, 465
St. Albans coach, incident of the, 30, 72
Sanitary Woollen Co., 194, 228, 243
Savile, Col. A. R., 112, 113, 114
Secretaries of race-meetings, 183, 290

SEL

Self-moving carriages, 58
Sherbrooke, Lord, 74
Shipton, Mr. E. R., 113, 293
Shirts, 198, 244
Shoes, 143, 145, 212, 215, 235, 236, 255
Singer & Co.'s works, description of, 64
Sociables, 12, 384
Society of Cyclists, 95
Socks, 212
Sore throat, 223
Southern Camp, the, 94; at Tunbridge Wells, 106
Spencer, Charles, introduction of the bicycle in his gymnasium, 60; his claim to have taught Charles Dickens the bicycle, 84, 85
Springs, 126, 156, 160, 161, 321–326, 406
Stanley Show, 85, 90, 96
Stapley, Lieut. H., 113
Starters, 184, 287, 289, 290
Steam tricycle, a, 90
Step, the, 164
Stockingnette, 199
Stockings, 232, 390
Stones, 26, 37
Stop-watch, 213
Sturmey, Mr. Henry, 111, 113, 353; his handbooks, 344
Sun and Planet gear, 386
Suspension wheels, 21
Sweaters, 243

Tandem Safety bicycles, 391; records, 452
Tandems, 4, 5, 12, 256, 310, 364, 366, 375, 377, 380, 381, 382, 452, 454, 455
Tangent wheels, 330

TRA

Teachers of cycling, 127
Telegraph-board steward at race meetings, 184
Thilum, 218
Thirst, 205
Tilt angle-rod, Harrington's, 324
Tires, inflated, 121; pneumatic, 469
Timekeepers, 183, 289
Tool-bags, 401
Touring, 187; the Cyclists' Touring Club, 188; planning out a tour, 188; an average day's journey, 189; selection of inns, 189; desirability of companionship, 190; large parties not satisfactory, 190; training in preparation, 190; necessaries, 192; luggage carriers, 193; combination woollen garments, 194; details of the kit for a bicyclist, 195; the cyclist's pocket dressing-case, 195; the tricyclist's outfit, 196; forwarding changes by parcels post, 197; luxuries, 198; machine to be overhauled before starting, 199; tools to be carried, 200; the lamp, 201; suitability of C.T.C. dress, 220
Tracks:—Agricultural Hall, 69; Alexandra Palace, 81, 82, 108, 110, 261, 417, 425, 432; Aston Lower Grounds, Birmingham, 106, 416, 417, 420; Aylestone Road Grounds, Leicester, 106, 417; Bath, 423; Belgrave Road Grounds, Leicester, 92, 416; Birmingham, (new track at Aston), 263; Brighton, 263; Bristol, 263, 418, 419; Cambridge, 79,

81, 259, 433, 434, 436, 438–440, 442-444, 446; Cardiff, 417; Coventry, 102, 263, 417, 447, 448; Crystal Palace, 41, 69, 74, 81, 89, 92, 93, 95, 96, 99, 103, 104, 106, 112, 210, 259, 261, 282, 398, 416, 417, 422, 447, 448; Glasgow, 109, 417; Halifax, 417; Harrogate, 423; Herne Hill, 419, 420, 422, 447-455; Jarrow, 106, 109, 417; Kennington Oval, 425, 427; Kensal Rise, 262, 423, 424; Leeds, 419; Lillie Bridge, 81, 102, 104, 110, 258, 261, 281, 414, 417, 424, 425, 426, 427, 435, 442; Lincoln, 89; London County Grounds, 262; Long Eaton, 110, 263, 417, 424; North Durham, Newcastle-on-Tyne, 103, 417, 419, 423; North Shields, 263, 417; Oxford, 260, 432–435; Paddington, 119-121, 262, 264, 417, 418, 419, 436, 437, 447; Paignton, 263, 425; Putney, 447, 455; Stamford Bridge, 83, 84, 259, 260, 271, 272, 280, 416, 421, 424, 439; Surbiton, 79, 80, 86, 87, 91, 92, 93, 260, 310, 416, 441; Taunton, 416; Torquay, 263, 428; Waller's Ground, Byker, 428; Wallsend, 103; Weston-super-Mare, 108, 263, 417; Worsley, 417

Training, 202; the professional athlete of yore, 202; his drastic treatment, 204; the old treatment applied to modern athletes, 204; the new style, 205; dangers of hurry, 206; concurrent development of physical and mental powers, 208; employment of a competent trainer, 208; varying temperaments of riders to be studied, 209; sprints and sharp finishes, 210; long-distance preparation, 210; over-competition, 211; dress, 212; the object to be aimed at, 212; weight and work, 212; gauging progress in pace, 213; in the dressing-room, 213, 217; use of the pacemaker, 214; the look-out, 214; sitting straight and pedalling evenly, 214; crooked feet and wobbling shoulders, 215; at the handles and on the saddle, 215; body and head to be kept still, 215, 216; the evening's work, 216; hand rubbing after exercise, 217; early discouragements, their explanations and remedies, 218

Tricycle Association, the, 277
Tricycle Conference, 95, 99
Tricycle Records, 453
Trigwell's ball-bearing head, 303
Trivectors, 57
Turnpike Trust Continuance Acts, 39
Two-speed gears, 354

UMPIRES, 185, 289, 290
University bicycling clubs, competitions between, 432-438

VARICOSE veins, 173
Velociman manumotors, 394, 396
Velocipedes, 57, 333, 393

Volunteer cyclist corps, establishment of, 113

WALKING, 2, note
Wallets, 401
Ward's woollen garments, 194
Waterproof, 197, 244
Welch's patent Club dicycle, 393

West Kent B.C. meeting, 102
Whatton's handle-bars, 309
Wheels, 21, 27, 101, 155, 163, 327, 332, 333
Woollens, 194, 195
Wounds, treatment of, 166

YEO, Prince of Siam, 91
York coach, the, 72

Printed in Great Britain by
Amazon.co.uk, Ltd.,
Marston Gate.